# PRESUMPTIONS AND BURDENS OF PROOF

# PRESUMPTIONS AND BURDENS OF PROOF

## AN ANTHOLOGY OF ARGUMENTATION AND THE LAW

EDITED BY HANS V. HANSEN, FRED J. KAUFFELD, JAMES B. FREEMAN, AND LILIAN BERMEJO-LUQUE

The University of Alabama Press
*Tuscaloosa*

The University of Alabama Press
Tuscaloosa, Alabama 35487-0380
uapress.ua.edu

Typeface: Garamond and Avenir

Cover design: Sarah Scarr

Library of Congress Cataloging-in-Publication Data

Names: Hansen, Hans V., editor.
Title: Presumptions and burdens of proof : an anthology of argumentation
and the law / edited by Hans V. Hansen, Fred J. Kauffeld, James B. Freeman,
and Lilian Bermejo-Luque.
Description: Tuscaloosa : University of Alabama Press, 2019. | Series: Rhetoric,
law, and the humanities | Includes bibliographical references and index.
Identifiers: LCCN 2018049289| ISBN 9780817320171 (cloth) |
ISBN 9780817392260 (ebook)
Subjects: LCSH: Reasoning. | Presumptions (Law) | Burden of proof.
Classification: LCC BC177 .P7357 2019 | DDC 160—dc23
LC record available at https://lccn.loc.gov/2018049289

# Contents

# Preface

This volume was originally conceived by Fred Kauffeld and myself in 2003. Due to various factors (some personal, some professional), we were unable to finish the undertaking as planned. The project was revived in 2015 at the prompting of James B. Freeman and Lilian Bermejo-Luque, who gave it new life by adding their labor to what had already been done. It is due to their contributions and encouragement that the project was finally completed. I very much regret that some of the contributors who wrote essays especially for this collection had to wait a long time to see their fine essays published.

Sadly, Fred Kauffeld passed away in April 2017. His detailed and insightful work on presumptions and burdens of proof (or, as he preferred, "probative burdens") influenced and inspired us all. We, the remaining editors, wish to dedicate the final product to him as acknowledgment of both his scholarship and his friendship. We will sorely miss them both. We offer the book, too, to Christine Beatty, Fred's wife, so that she may be reminded of how much Fred meant to us and to the larger community of argumentation scholars.

~

As this publication goes to press, we would like to thank Professor Max Nelson of the Department of Greek and Roman Studies at the University of Windsor, who generously assisted us with several of the translations from the Latin and Greek. We are also especially grateful to Ms. Sulma Portillo and the care she took in standardizing the notes and references for each of the chapters, and to Ms. Sheila Flavel for her fine work in compiling the index. At the University of Alabama Press, we want to thank all the staff who facilitated the production of this book. We were especially fortunate to have Ms. Irina du Quenoy as our copyeditor. Finally, we thank Mr. Dan Waterman, acquisitions editor at the University of Alabama Press, for his confidence in our project, and his patience.

Hans V. Hansen
Windsor
October 2018

# PRESUMPTIONS AND BURDENS OF PROOF

# Introduction

This collection of essays brings together important historical sources about the notions of presumption and burden of proof with a series of contemporary essays that develop these concepts further, showing their application in academic fields as diverse as law, epistemology, rhetoric, linguistics, and communication theory. The concepts of presumption and burden of proof have been part of jurisprudential literature since early formulations of Roman law, and although all the contemporary contributors to this volume appreciate this fact, their own chapters extend the original legal insights to new, broader, extralegal areas of research. The role of presumptions in communication has been widely recognized in the philosophy of language since the 1960s, and the community of argumentation theorists that came to self-awareness at the end of the last century likewise agrees that the distribution of presumptions and burdens plays a crucial role in the regulation of disagreements. However, scholars, teachers, and students have not had convenient access to a ready collection of both classical and contemporary sources that would introduce them to the traditional literature on presumptions and burdens of proof while giving them insights into current research initiatives. The present collection aims to remedy this lacuna.

Both parts 1 and 2 have their own introductions giving a detailed and integrated overview of the essays we have brought together; hence, in this general introduction it is only necessary to make a very brief mention of the themes of each of the chapters we have included.

Part 1 of this anthology consists of the historical sources we deem most important for contemporary scholars to be aware of. It begins with a selection from Aristotle's *Topics* on the role of received opinions (*endoxa*) in argumentation: these may be viewed as presumption-like propositions that are to be tested through argumentation. Aristotle's seminal text is followed by Hanns Hohmann's survey essay outlining significant developments in the notion of burden of proof in medieval law. Both presumption and burden of proof take on sharper dimensions in the excerpts that follow. Namely, Jeremy Bentham distinguishes *technical* (legal) and *natural* (extralegal) procedures of justice and notes that they allocate the burden of proof by different standards, thereby recognizing that presumption and burden of proof have application outside the law. It is Richard Whately, however, who, in the nineteenth century, is credited with importing the notions of presumption and burden of proof from legal theory to argumentation theory generally. In his view, presumptions favor the status quo while the burden of proof falls on those who oppose it. Alfred Sidgwick openly criticized Whately's position, denying that a theory of presumptions could serve the end of rational inquiry, because a burden of proof attaches to all claims. The excerpt from James B. Thayer introduces what has since become a firmly established distinction between two kinds of burdens of proof: the *burden of proving* (in which the main proposition at issue falls on the prosecutor) and the *burden of giving evidence* concerning points of contention (which may fall on either party during the course of a trial). Part 1 concludes with C. P. Ilbert's essay on evidence, which provides a concise formulation of the legal ideas about presumption and probative burdens that influenced nineteenth- and twentieth-century thinking about the topic.

The second part of the anthology consists of contemporary analyses and research initiatives relating to the study of presumptions and burdens of proof. Ten of the twelve essays were written especially for this collection. They may be grouped under three themes. The first group consists of essays that take up and extend traditional rhetorical and dialectical aspects of presumptions and burdens introduced in the readings in part 1. The second group has a common interest in developing the contributions that presumptions and burdens of proof theory can make to epistemology and informal logic. The last group of essays falls within the philosophy of language and is especially concerned with connecting presumptions and burdens with speech-act theory. This is a coarse classification of the essays in part 2; the reader will find that most of the essays touch on all the themes mentioned here.

More specifically, the following contributions to this volume continue the traditional work on presumptions and burdens of proof: In the excerpt from *Decision by Debate* by Douglas Ehninger and Wayne Brockriede, we find a development of Whately's ideas of presumption and burden of proof laid out for the modern student. This essay, which was written for a textbook, will be accessible to all and makes a suitable first reading for the study of presumptions and burdens of proof. This is followed by Frans H. van Eemeren and Peter Houtlosser's essay, which views burden of proof through the pragma-dialectical lens. It both shows the influence of Aristotle in locating the use of burdens of proof in dialectical contexts and echoes Sidgwick's insistence that the burden always falls on the assertor. In his essay about the judicial roots of presumption and burden of proof, legal scholar Richard Gaskins gives a modern account of the legal aspects of presumption and burden first introduced in the essays by Hohmann, Bentham, and Thayer. James Crosswhite elaborates the nature of presumptions and burdens in the spirit of Chaïm Perelman and Lucie Olbrechts-Tyteca's *The New Rhetoric*, thereby furthering the rhetorical perspective that can be traced back to Whately. The last essay in this group is by G. Thomas Goodnight. It is a wide-ranging study of how the interplay of presumptions underlies public political argumentation, identifying not only the different presumptions of liberals and conservatives but also those that motivate the argumentation of counterpublics.

All the essays above are concerned with showing how presumptions and burden of proof have a role in regulating interpersonal argumentation. The next group of essays acknowledges this dynamic aspect of presumptions and burden of proof but changes the emphasis to elaborating how these concepts work in the service of epistemology and informal logic. Nicholas Rescher's views, presented in his *Dialectics: A Controversy-Oriented Approach to the Theory of Knowledge*, begin from the medieval model of disputation and work toward a contemporary model of epistemic justification. It is worthy of study from both the rhetorical and the epistemic perspectives and, accordingly, Fred J. Kauffeld and James B. Freeman have combined their efforts to write an essay summarizing and clarifying Rescher's influential contribution. In a separate chapter, James B. Freeman, who has been influenced by Rescher's views, focuses on a fundamental problem in informal logic, which is that argumentation must have some starting points, including acceptable premises. Here Freeman argues that premise acceptability can be satisfactorily analyzed in terms of the concept of presumption. David Godden's essay considers various ways in which presumptive truth could be considered as a unique modality in comparison to assertions and assumptions in practical reasoning.

The last group of essays considers presumptions and burdens in light of speech act and communication theory. Douglas Walton's essay provides a fitting transition from the epistemological and logical perspectives to the focus on speech acts. He analyzes the speech act of presumption in terms of the framework of conversational dialogues. This model allows him to clearly distinguish the distinct roles of assertions, assumptions, presumptions, and presuppositions. Edna Ullmann-Margalit approaches the speech act of presumption in a different way. She finds a strong connection between presumptions and H. P. Grice's cooperative principle of communication as introduced in his "Logic and Conversation." The four maxims put forth by Grice (quality, quantity, relation, and manner) give us four different presumptions underlying successful communication. Some even call them presumptions of communication. Lilian Bermejo-Luque turns her attention to distinguishing presumptive claims from presumptive inferences through a close analysis of the speech act of presuming. In her view, the correctness condition of argumentation involving presumptions either as premises or as warrants is based not on dialogical rules of procedure but on the correctness conditions of the speech act of presuming. The final paper in this collection is by Fred J. Kauffeld. His essay takes insights from normative pragmatics as a basis for giving an account of speech acts, a perspective that he illustrates with an analysis of advising and proposing. The obligations associated with speech acts such as these arise in connection with the pragmatic consequences of performing them, not from an epistemic or dialectical framework.

The last pages of the volume contain a short bibliography of work on presumptions and burden of proof that will be useful to both students and researchers.

Hans V. Hansen

# PART 1
# HISTORICAL SELECTIONS

The Early History of Presumptions and Burdens of Proof

This introduction is a survey of the concepts of presumption and burden of proof as they are found in some of the key writings on that subject, from Aristotle to the early twentieth century. Even though most of the authors we consider here were working within the legal framework, they also had an appreciation for how these concepts could function in extralegal argumentation.

Although the earliest mentions of presumptions and burden of proof are found in Roman law, kindred notions can be found earlier in Greek philosophy. Aristotle (384–322 BC) identified a kind of syllogistic argument that takes generally accepted views or reputable opinions or common beliefs (*endoxa*) as premises. Such arguments he called dialectical, contrasting them on the one hand with demonstrative arguments that take first principles as premises and, on the other hand, with contentious arguments that only appear to take reputable opinions or first principles as their starting points.[1] This characterization of a dialectical premise turns out to be similar to that of a presumption in several ways, as we can see from Aristotle's rather complicated definition.[2] A dialectical proposition is one that is:

(1) accepted by (a) everyone, or (b) most people; or
(2) accepted by (a) the wise, or (b) the majority of the wise, or (c) the most notable or reputable of the wise; or is a proposition that is
(3) like a proposition identified in (1) or (2); or is
(4) the contradictory of a contrary of a proposition satisfying (1) or (2); or is
(5) in accordance with one of the recognized arts, and is
(6) not paradoxical, and is
(7) actually held by someone.

Conditions (1) and (2) and (5) to (7) give us criteria for identifying existing reputable opinions; conditions (3) and (4) provide us with ways to extend the class. One of Aristotle's examples of a dialectical proposition is that "one should do good to one's friends."[3] Aristotle's students would have known that it was a proposition attributed to Simonides and therefore had the status of a reputable opinion under condition (2).[4] Because both "good" and "enemies" are contrary terms, this proposition has two contraries,

One should do evil to one's friends, and
One should do good to one's enemies,

and, respectively these have the contradictories,

One should *not* do evil to one's friends, and
One should *not* do good to one's enemies,

which by condition (4) makes these last two reputable opinions as well.

What is most notable is that dialectical propositions gain their status by having the relational property of being believed to be true by everyone, or nearly everyone, or some person who is taken to be a kind of authority or expert. This is also a mark of epistemic presumptions, but not of legal presumptions (unless we think of the law as "someone"). Dialectical premises contrast with demonstrative premises, which one comes to know through induction (*epagōgē*) and which do not owe their status to anything outside themselves.[5] Moreover, demonstrative premises are *a priori* and must be true, whereas dialectical premises are *a posteriori* and could be false. Like presumptions in general, they are defeasible. We see also that dialectical propositions, like presumptions, can be the basis of further reasoning, as is shown by the use of contraries above.

Dialectical propositions, like presumptive propositions, have a degree of credibility that makes them acceptable starting points for argumentation. Aristotle typically reviews the extant endoxa in the various fields he investigates, such as the soul, nature, ethics, etc. In one of the models of dialectical argumentation we can extract from the *Topics* and the *Sophistical Refutations*, we can picture the answerer as having adopted an endoxa as his thesis and having to defend it against the pressing questions of an interlocutor, but being allowed to answer only either "yes" or "no."[6] In hindsight we might describe this form of dialogue as one in which the answerer is maintaining a proposition with presumptive backing while the interlocutor has assumed a burden of proof in his attempt to unseat the answerer's thesis.

In summary, for Aristotle, reputable opinions are propositions that are specified by falling under one of the seven conditions outlined. They owe their initial credibility to the fact that someone speaks for them, that their source should be taken seriously. Some of them appear to be culturally dependent propositions, especially the ethical ones—and others are more metaphysical or scientific in character, for example, "contradiction is impossible," "all things are in motion," and "being is one."[7] Endoxa are to be taken as starting points in argumentation, although they may eventually turn out to be unacceptable. In this way, they resemble what we have later come to think of as presumptions.

From Hanns Hohmann's essay "Presumptions in Legal Argumentation: From Antiquity to the Middle Ages," we gain insights into the early life of the concepts of presumption and burden of proof as they developed in the Roman and medieval periods. He first gives us examples from the sixth century *Digest* of the *Corpus Iuris* illustrating "the subtle interplay of empirical and normative considerations." From the earliest days of Roman law, observes Hohmann, presumptions have fallen into two categories. Some of the examples found in the *Digest* are empirical in nature and are in this respect similar to probability arguments. One example is that of a son who is missing in war; he will be presumed to be dead. Other presumptions have a definite normative aspect: for example, if a woman has received a certain gift, and the giver is not known, early Roman law held that it should be presumed—even without evidence—that the gift came from her husband because that would be more decent.

The rule stated at the outset of the *Digest* is that "proof lies on him who asserts, not on him who denies," a rule based on considerations of fairness rather than empirical considerations. However, since it has exceptions, it is only a general rule: in some cases, the burden lies on the one who is in the better position to provide the proof, regardless of whether he is the assertor. Other examples of presumptions mentioned in the *Digest* are that if a mother and one-year-old child both die in a shipwreck, it is to be presumed that the child died first (for the reason that a greater part of the wife's fortune dedicated to the welfare of the child is no longer needed and should therefore remain with her family); another is that if a will can be interpreted in such a way that it favors the freeing of a slave, it should be interpreted that way. Still another presumption is that if a couple originally suspected of adultery eventually marries, this is taken as an admission of their adultery. From his discussion of these examples, Hohmann concludes that many of the legal presumptions in early Roman law served to resolve uncertainties in favor of polices rather than empirical likelihoods.

The second part of Hohmann's discussion of presumptions focuses on the medieval period and is based on Pilius's *Libellus Pylei Disputatorius*, a compilation of laws from the latter part of the twelfth century. Pilius's conception of presumption is that it "is a kind of argument whose distinguishing characteristic is that it takes as its starting point an extrinsic sign for a matter which cannot be established more directly, particularly by means of witnesses." Pilius took this conception of presumption as applying in particular to the topics of the person and the act which lead to considerations of, for example, the kind of action it was, the habits of the agent, his associates, and the rumors about him.[8] Such topics had their home in rhetorical practice but Pilius attempts to place them within the law by finding legal precedents for them. In a very general way, we can see a connection between the endoxa of Aristotle and the codification of presumptions Pilius tries to bring about.

Jeremy Bentham (1748–1832) is best known as the founder of British utilitarianism, but in fact his education and predominant interest were in jurisprudence and the reform of legal systems. His earliest publication (*A Fragment on Government*, 1776) was a criticism of Blackstone's codification of British law (*Commentaries on the Laws of England*, 1765). For this collection we have taken a short passage—"Of the Burthen of Proof: On Whom Shall It Lie?," from Bentham's 1843 *Introductory View of the Rationale of Evidence for the Use of Non-Lawyers as Well as Lawyers*—that reveals his views on the difficulties attending the allocation of the burden of proof as well as his critical attitude toward the law and the legal profession.

Bentham distinguishes natural and technical approaches to the question of burden of proof. By "the technical approach" he means the requirements of the judicial system; by "the natural approach" he means questions of justice outside the legal system. For questions of natural justice, he holds that the burden should be assigned to the party for whom it would be least difficult to provide proof. This is a utilitarian position: that procedure which causes least pain or inconvenience for all parties affected is preferable. To Bentham's dismay, the British legal system upheld a different criterion, namely, that the burden of proof should fall on the person who makes the allegations. In Bentham's view, this standard for the burden of proof plays havoc with the "collateral ends of justice," causing delays and unnecessary expense; moreover, it may be that the defendant is in a much better position to give evidence than the accuser. Nevertheless, Bentham seems to admit the rationality of making the providing of proof incumbent on the accuser: the defendant can win without presenting proof if the accuser presents no proof at all; but the accuser can win only if he provides a proof.

Bentham accused the legal system of his time of developing procedures that did not serve the public well. Instead of the simple rule that Bentham supported, the existing law books complicated procedure. They proposed, for example, that the burden should lie with the affirmative claim rather than with the negative. But Bentham observed that, by a twist of language, affirmatives can be made negatives and vice versa. Furthermore, he intimated that the standard of proof was not always clear and that this caused needless prolongation of trials; and, as the proceedings were extended, the cost to the litigants and the profit to the lawyers increased. Bentham went so far as to say that many of the cases being dragged out in courts because of the technical requirements of the law would not even be recognized as cases under natural justice, in which the burden would lie "in each individual case upon that one of the parties on whom it will sit lightest."

Bentham's place in this collection is important because he clearly differentiates the burden of proof under the judicial system from that under the system of natural justice; moreover, he points to the fact that the assignment of burdens may be used to frustrate the ends of justice as much as presumptions may be used to ease its course.

Richard Whately (1787–1863) is credited with stimulating interest in the concepts of presumption and burden of proof among argumentation scholars. He began to insert paragraphs about presumptions and burden of proof in his *Elements of Rhetoric* beginning with the third edition in 1830.[9] He saw that in a disagreement it was an advantage to have the presumption and that one might well weaken one's position by giving it up. In Whately's account presumptions and burdens are correlative, but presumption is the more basic practical concept in that it is more readily identified and therefore allocates the burden of proof indirectly. It is in fact often easy, according to Whately, to see on which side the presumption lies; indeed, he gives a list of examples (which I have re-ordered). Namely, there is a presumption, claims Whately,

(1) in favor of every man's innocence until he is proven guilty;
(2) in favor of ownership of that of which a person or corporation is in actual possession;
(3) in favor of the harmlessness of any given book;
(4) in favor of existing institutions;
(5) against every change;
(6) in favor of the opinions of people who have authority; and
(7) against paradoxical claims (or in favor of received opinions).[10]

The first of these is a familiar presumption of law. The second and third also appear to be legal presumptions since they deal with matters that would normally be settled through courts and have their source in policy rather than in experience. Presumptions (4) and (5) have political and ideological overtones more so than legal ones in that they embody the view that the status quo should be maintained unless there is good reason to make changes. Finally, presumptions (6) and (7) appear to be wholly of an epistemic nature in that they are concerned with what is reasonable to believe. These are illustrative examples of what Whately means by "presumption"; it is by no means an exhaustive inventory. Whately thought it was a rule of argumentation that the side with the presumption should not put itself at risk by offering arguments as long as the other side is saddled with the burden of proof.

On the question of shifting the burden of proof it was Whately's view that some presumptions have more weight than others. Thus, a burden of proof could be shifted by invoking a counterpresumption that had more weight than the first presumption considered; for example, the presumption against a change might be considered to be weightier than the presumption that restrictions are an evil. In an earlier work, *Elements of Logic*, Whately volunteered another idea, namely that the use of an ad hominem argument can sometimes be used legitimately to shift the burden of proof by making an advocate realize that his position is, or appears to be, inconsistent. It is not clear from Whately's account, however, whether he thought *ad hominems* really shift the burden of proof or whether they just create a burden of rejoinder and only appear to shift the burden of proof.[11]

Historically important as Whately's contribution has been, it has been equally the source of puzzlement, calling forth numerous interpretive studies; among the foremost are those by Bruce Gronbeck and Michael Sproule. Gronbeck, working under the supervision of Douglas Ehninger (the editor of the reissued edition of Whately's *Rhetoric* in 1963), wrote a highly regarded master's thesis[12] titled "Archbishop Richard Whately's Doctrine of 'Presumption' and 'Burden of Proof': An Historical-Critical Analysis." In this work, Gronbeck found that Whately developed three distinct "legal interpretations of the concepts."[13] The first is presumptions as preoccupation of the figurative ground. This aspect takes existing institutions and established beliefs to have a presumption that should not be given up unless someone gives good reasons for doing so. Being under an obligation to provide such good reasons is having the burden of proof. (This preoccupation model is developed further in Ehninger and Brockriede's 1963 textbook, *Decision by Debate*, an excerpt from which is included in part 2 of this collection.) In contrast to the preoccupation interpretation, Whately also came to realize that the predispositions of audiences have a role in allocating presumptions: audiences by some "whimsical and unaccountable feelings" defer to certain authorities, thereby granting them the presumption in argument. The third interpretation of presumption and burden of proof found in Whately's *Rhetoric*, according to Gronbeck, is that presumptions are either inferences or give rise to inferences. In his interpretation[14] these inferential presumptions come to light through Whately's explanation of shifting the burden of proof by means of counterpresumptions. One rebuts a presumption by using a counterpresumption (a general proposition) as a premise to infer a proposition alternative to the original presumption. In this way presumptions are connected to inferences. Gronbeck allows that Whately's view of presumptions-as-inferences is underdeveloped; however, he notes that it was the dominant approach in the law books at the time.[15] Interestingly, these three different facets or dimensions of presumption—preoccupation, deference, and inference—continue to weave themselves in and out of the discussions on presumption and burden of proof.

In an influential 2009 article titled "The Psychological Burden of Proof: On the Evolutionary Development of Richard Whately's Theory of Presumption,"[16] Michael Sproule maintains that Whately's views about presumptions and burdens of proof changed over the several editions that the *Elements of Rhetoric* underwent during his lifetime, from the time they were first introduced in the third edition (1830) to the final, seventh edition of 1846. Whately began with a model that imitated the legal determination of presumption and burden of proof, Sproule argues, and gradually moved to a more psychological model that reached its fullest articulation in the seventh edition.

The gist of the legal model with which Whately began in the third edition of the *Rhetoric* has it that the burden should fall on the party who wants to bring changes to existing institutions or beliefs. (G. Thomas Goodnight calls this the conservative presumption.) Things should be left as they are unless there is sufficient reason to change them: the presumption of innocence is an instance of this general tenet. On this legal model the allocation of presumption and burden is objective and is made independently of the inclinations of a jury, or more generally, an audience. However, Sproule's view is that later editions of the *Rhetoric* promote the idea that presumptions and burdens are really assigned according to social and psychological factors, that is, audiences assign presumptions and burdens to speakers based on the former's attitudes toward ideas and sources of information. This psychological interpretation of Whately emerges from the latter's insertion of paragraphs on deference in the later editions of his work, in which he defined deference as "an *habitual* Presumption in favour of [someone's] decisions or opinions."[17] But as deference is connected to authority, so authority is connected to presumption. Hence, the ideas and sources that audiences consider authoritative are the ones to which they defer, and hence the ones to which they award the presumption. This approach to the allocation of presumptions and burdens is not only sociological—in that the agencies assigning obligations are actual audiences—but is also psychological, even on Whately's terms. This is because in his view deference, unlike admiration and respect, is rooted in the faculty of feeling rather than the faculty of understanding; the analysis of feelings, of course, falls within the field of psychology. This means that deference operates in accord with psychological principles, not principles of rationality, that is, of logic or epistemology. It is Sproule's view that, for Whately, the psychological interpretation of presumption and burden of proof ultimately supersedes and encompasses his earlier and simpler legalistic model.

Sproule's analysis is of interest in another respect, because he explores the possibility that Whately's ideas about presumption, although plainly making a connection with the legal tradition in England, were also influenced by the concept of presumption appearing in religious tracts in the years immediately preceding the publication of the *Elements of Rhetoric*. For example, Edward Hawkins (1789–1882) had proposed that presumption should be accorded to traditional teachings and practices and recognized as a valid claim.[18] If this is so it implies that legal thought was not the only influence on the development of Whately's doctrine of presumption and burden of proof. Interestingly, these concepts are still at work in more recent discussion of religious belief as witnessed by the exchange of ideas provoked by Antony Flew's article "The Presumption of Atheism."[19]

Whately's importance lies in the fact that he took a set of concepts—"presumption" and "burden of proof"—that had been explicitly nourished within the dialectical settings of legal traditions and extended them to a broader rhetorical model of argumentation. With few exceptions, every one of the subsequent articles in this collection refers to Whately's account of presumptions and burdens of proof. This is a fair measure of his influence and the importance of his work.

Not everyone, however, has been an enthusiastic supporter of Whately's views. Alfred Sidgwick (1850–1943), another Englishman and prolific author of essays and books about logic, found fault with them on at least two counts. Our selection, the chapter "The Burden of Proof," is taken from his 1884 book, *Fallacies, A View of Logic from the Practical Side*.

For Sidgwick, the theory that if there is a "fair presumption" in favor of a belief, or if the belief accords with the prevailing opinion, the assertor is excused from the burden of proof and it is placed instead on the doubter, is not workable outside of a legal framework, as Whately had assumed. The reason Sidgwick gives is that in many instances it is impossible to say whether a given proposition has presumptive status. What will count as a presumption in a society will not only vary over time but will also not be fully determinable at any time. Hence, outside the law, disagreements cannot be truly tried by basing them on presumptions. The correct view, according to Sidgwick, is to adopt the general rule that *s/he who asserts must prove* whether what is asserted is a positive or a negative proposition, whether it is an affirmation or a denial. (Hohmann found this rule as early as the sixth-century *Corpus Iuris*.) This makes the basis of the burden of proof a required speech act rather than a legal or epistemic condition or the psychological propensities of an audience. For Sidgwick, then, not only does one rule allocating the burden replace a number of diverse sources identifying presumptions, but the concept of presumption does no work at all, and the correlativity thesis is empty.

Sidgwick is more sensitive to the various uses of language than Whately. The contrast between them can be highlighted if we imagine a proselytizing missionary at work in the New World, attempting to convert the indigenous people to Christianity. When faced with a skeptical inhabitant, Whately's view would give the presumption to the missionary because Christianity is an established institution; by correlativity, the burden will then fall on the puzzled native to give reasons why she should not accept Christianity. Sidgwick's approach is different: he would assign the burden to the missionary because the missionary is the one doing the asserting, saying that his religion is the true one; in contrast, having only expressed a doubt or puzzlement, the native will have no burden of proof. In Sidgwick's view, Whately failed to differentiate expressing a doubt from asserting a denial.

Interestingly, Sidgwick distinguishes the *need for proof* from the *burden of proof*. The need for proof is psychological and is decided by the audience if it needs a proof to be convinced; in this case it is incumbent on the arguer to give a proof. The audience, however, does not allocate the burden of proof: the assertor has the burden whether or not s/he is asked to discharge it by those in need. So, what the audience has influence over is whether the obligation the assertor has ought to be activated; not whether he or she has a burden. It may be that Sproule's insight about the role of audiences with respect to burdens of proof fits better with Sidgwick's than with Whately's view, especially if the psychological thesis is weakened to be a claim about the need for proof rather than the obligation to prove, the latter being associated with an epistemic standard.

Sidgwick's criticism of Whately came some fifty years after the early editions of the *Elements of Rhetoric*. Whereas Whately tried to extend both the legal concepts of presumption and burden of proof to the larger arena of argumentation in general, Sidgwick insisted that only the *burden of proof* could do any useful work outside legal frameworks. He scorned the idea that presumptions could serve a useful purpose in natural argumentation and that they could function to allocate probative burdens in argumentation.

James Bradley Thayer (1831–1902) was an American jurist who was trained at Harvard University and later taught there. He was a member of the famous Metaphysical Club that met in Boston in the early 1870s and whose membership included Charles Peirce, William James, and Oliver Wendell Holmes Jr. As the excerpts from the late nineteenth-century article we have included by him show, he had a special interest in the historical development of law.

The main focus of Thayer's article is to untangle what he considers to be a serious confusion involving the meaning of "burden of proof." He distinguishes two senses of "burden of proof": the one burden is that of *establishing a proposition against all counterargument or evidence*, while the other burden is *to bring forward argument or evidence* in support of a proposition, an obligation that may fall upon either side at different points throughout legal proceedings. The plaintiff has the obligation to establish her proposition against all counterargument and evidence and therefore also has a burden of bringing evidence; the defendant does not have a burden to establish a proposition but if she should at any time throughout the trial make a claim then she would incur a burden of bringing forward argument or evidence. Thayer was the first to mark this distinction, which was later taken as a commonplace by other writers on the subject. Rescher, for example, indicates the distinction as a difference between an initiating burden and an evidential burden.[20] Others mark the distinction with the terms *global* and *local burdens of proof.*

Thayer's essay is a rich resource of nineteenth-century legal scholarship on the notions of burden of proof. It contains several long quotations giving different accounts of the role of the burden of proof in legal argumentation. For instance, quoted from W. M. Best's *Principles of Evidence*, we find that burdens of proof can be shifted either "by those presumptions of law which are rebuttable; by presumptions of fact of the stronger kind; and by every species of evidence strong enough to establish a *prima facie* case against a party." Another passage from Best answers the question of where the evidential burden lies at any point during the trial: it rests on the side against whom the case would be decided if no further evidence was produced.

In Thayer's view, it is important to do away with the ambiguous use of "burden of proof," although he concedes that the phrase itself cannot be done away with. The question then is whether we can reform our usage so that it attaches in the future to only one of the two meanings. In favor of attaching the meaning of "burden of proof" to that of "going forward with proof," Thayer finds that it agrees largely with common usage both within and outside the law and also that it is the more comprehensive of the two meanings, including the duty of meeting a prima facie case, or a presumption, as well as that of going forward with evidence at the beginning of the trial. Favoring the other meaning of "burden of proof"—that of establishing a given proposition—Thayer finds that that is the sense the expression originally had in Roman law, and that it is the one that has been preferred by some members of the United States legal system; however, the modern legal systems are very different from the ancient Roman system, and the recommended usage by the superior courts has not caught on. Hence, Thayer recommends that the phrase "burden of proof" should have the restricted meaning of "burden of 'making out a prima facie case,'" and that the other traditional sense of "burden of proof"—that is, that of making out a given proposition, might be renamed the "burden of establishing."

The final selection we have made for the historical part of this anthology is from an essay titled "Evidence," found in the eleventh edition of the *Encyclopædia Britannica*. In this text, Sir Courtenay Peregrine Ilbert (1841–1924) distinguishes ordinary and legal presumptions. He writes, "A presumption in the ordinary sense is an inference [. . .] The subject of presumptions, so far as they are mere inferences or arguments, belongs not to the law of evidence, or to law at all, but to rules of reasoning."[21] Ordinary presumptions are inferences or arguments to the effect that "what has happened in some cases will probably happen in others of the like nature." In his characterization, presumptions of fact are inductive arguments: based on experience, we think the same kind of thing will probably happen again. Accordingly, the study of ordinary, or factual, presumptions belongs to the rules of reasoning. Presumptions of law, however, do not have an empirical basis: they say that a court must draw such-and-such an inference given particular facts or evidence. Such legal presumptions are created by courts or legislatures and are based on public policy or demands of convenience.

Presumptions of law may be divided into those that are conclusive and those that are not. Conclusive presumptions are exceptionless (e.g., that a child under seven years cannot commit a felony) and hence are not defeasible as are all other presumptions, like the one directing the court to presume that a person is dead if he has not been heard from for seven years by those who would be expected to hear from him. The latter presumption can be cancelled or overridden by some kinds of evidence.

Ilbert readily identifies a connection between presumptions and burdens of proof, noting that the effect of a presumption is to impose a duty on those who disagree with it of "bringing forward evidence to meet it." Ilbert in fact endorses the correlativity thesis for presumptions and burdens of proof, writing that legal rules may be expressed either in terms of presumption or in terms of burden of proof. (The correlativity would not apply to conclusive presumptions.) Like Thayer, Ilbert recognizes two senses of "burden of proof": the burden of proving the proposition on which the case depends and the burden of producing evidence. The latter may switch from side to side as a trial proceeds and is in general governed by the rule that he who alleges a fact must prove it; however, there are exceptions to the general rule, for example, that the burden of proving absence of fraudulent intent belongs to the accused party. All in all, Ilbert's view is the one that comes closest to that of many contemporary argumentation theorists who are studying the concepts of presumption and burden of proof.

↽

A number of distinct ways of identifying the burden of proof have been proposed: (1) the burden belongs to the assertor; (2) it belongs to whoever holds the affirmative thesis; (3) it belongs to the party for whom it would be easiest to provide evidence; (4) it belongs to the party opposing the presumptive view; (5) it belongs to the party who would lose the case if the outcome had to be decided at this point; (6) it belongs where the law says it belongs. The distinction between the burden of proving a proposition and the burden of bringing evidence is a later development clarifying an ambiguity present in earlier statements of "burden of proof." The distinction between legal and nonlegal (natural) presumptions begins to develop with Bentham and is recognized by all the subsequent writers on the topic. Legal presumptions have a normative bent in accord with policy objectives of legal systems, but some of them are also adopted on grounds of convenience. Natural presumptions too have a normative dimension but are rooted in epistemological concerns based on experiential considerations and reflect people's sense of caution (e.g., the presumption against paradoxical views, the reliance on authority). Our study of the notions of presumption and burden of proof confirms the thesis that argumentation discourse essentially involves an intermingling of factual and normative considerations. New research in the area, as exemplified in part 2 of this volume, reflects the belief that further analyses of these concepts and their relation to each other will give us a deeper understanding of what reasonableness in argumentation is, and that this in turn will be a beneficial influence on our discursive practices.

Hans V. Hansen

## Notes

1. Aristotle, *Topics*, trans. J. L. Ackrill, in vol. 1 of *The Complete Works of Aristotle*, ed. J. Barnes (Princeton, NJ: Princeton University Press, 1984), bk. 1, pt. 1.
2. Aristotle, *Topics*, bk. 1, pt. 10.
3. Aristotle, *Topics*, bk. 1, pt. 10.
4. See Polemarchus's attempt to defend the proposition that "justice is to benefit one's friends and harm one's enemies," in Plato, *The Republic*, 2nd ed., trans. Desmond Lee (London: Penguin, 1987), 332d.
5. Aristotle, *Posterior Analytics*, trans. J. Barnes, in vol. 1 of *The Complete Works of Aristotle*, ed. J. Barnes, bk 2, pt. 19.
6. In *On Sophistical Refutations* (at 165b) Aristotle recognizes several different kinds of dialogue, the second of which is dialectical dialogues. The model is further clarified in *Topics* (Book 1), and the ways in which this model of dialogue can be abused by the use of fallacies is the object of study in *On Sophistical Refutations* (passim).
7. Aristotle, *Topics*, bk. 1, pt. 11.
8. See, for example, Aristotle: "In rhetorical argument proofs from signs are founded on consequences; for, when men wish to prove that a man is an adulterer, they seize upon the consequence of that character, namely that the man dresses himself elaborately or is seen wandering about at night—facts that are true of many people, while the accusation is not true." In *On Sophistical Refutations*, trans. E. S.

Forster (Cambridge, MA: Harvard University Press, Loeb Classical Library, 1958), 167b8–167b12.

9. For the history of the development of Whately's *Elments of Rhetoric*, we rely on J. Michael Sproule, "The Psychological Burden of Proof: On the Evolutionary Development of Richard Whately's Theory of Presumption," *Communication Monographs* 43, no. 2 (1976): 115–29. Sproule does not mention that Whately had employed these concepts in his *Elements of Logic*.

10. This list is compiled from Richard Whately, *Elements of Rhetoric: Comprising an Analysis of the Laws of Moral Evidence and of Persuasion, with Rules for Argumentative Composition and Elocution*, 7th ed., rev. (London: John W. Parker, 1846; repr., Carbondale, IL: Southern Illinois University Press, 1963), 110–15. See this volume, ch. 4.

11. For further discussion, see Douglas N. Walton, *Arguer's Position* (Westport, CT: Greenwood Press, 1985); and Douglas N. Walton, *The Place of Emotion in Argument* (University Park: Penn State University Press, 1992).

12. Bruce E. Gronbeck, "Archbishop Richard Whately's Doctrine of 'Presumption' and 'Burden of Proof': An Historical-Critical Analysis" (master's thesis, University of Iowa, 1966).

13. Gronbeck, "Whately's Doctrine," 78.

14. Gronbeck, "Whately's Doctrine," 93.

15. Gronbeck, "Whately's Doctrine," 94.

16. Sproule, "Psychological Burden," 115–29.

17. Whately, *Elements of Rhetoric*, 118. See this volume, ch. 4, para. 20.

18. Sproule, "Psychological Burden," 129.

19. Antony Flew, "The Presumption of Atheism," *Canadian Journal of Philosophy* 2, no. 1 (1972): 29–46.

20. Nicholas Rescher, *Dialectics: A Controversy-Oriented Approach to the Theory of Knowledge* (Albany: State University of New York Press, 1977), 27.

21. Courtenay Peregrine Ilbert, "Evidence," in *Encyclopædia Britannica*, 11th ed. (New York: Encyclopædia Britannica, 1910), 10:15.

# 1

# Dialectical Propositions (from *Topics*)

## ARISTOTLE

## 1

[100a18] Our treatise proposes to find a method whereby we shall be able to reason from opinions that are generally accepted[1] about every problem propounded to us, and also shall ourselves, when standing up to an argument, avoid saying anything that will obstruct us. First, then, we must say what reasoning is, and what its varieties are, in order to grasp *dialectical reasoning*: for this is the object of our search in the treatise before us.

Now reasoning is an argument in which, certain things being laid down, something other than these necessarily comes about through them. (a) It is a "demonstration," when the premises from which the reasoning starts are true and primary, or are such that our knowledge of them has originally come through premises which are primary and true: (b) reasoning on the other hand, is "dialectical," if it reasons from opinions that are generally accepted. Things are "true" and "primary" which are believed on the strength not of anything else but of themselves: for in regard to the first principles of science it is improper to ask any further for the why and wherefore of them; each of the first principles should command belief in and by itself. On the other hand, those opinions are "generally accepted" which are accepted by everyone or by the majority or by the philosophers—i.e., by all, or by the majority, or by the most notable and illustrious of them. Again (c), reasoning is "contentious" if it starts from opinions that seem to be generally accepted, but are not really such, or again if it merely seems to reason from opinions that are or seem to be generally accepted. For not every opinion that seems to be generally accepted actually is generally accepted. For in none of the opinions which we call generally accepted is the illusion entirely on the surface, as happens in the case of the principles of contentious arguments; for the nature of the fallacy in these is obvious immediately, and as a rule even to persons with little power of comprehension. So then, of the contentious reasonings mentioned, the former really deserves to be called "reasoning" as well, but the other should be called "contentious reasoning," but not "reasoning," since it appears to reason, but does not really do so.

Further (d), besides all the reasonings we have mentioned there are the misreasonings that start from the premisses peculiar to the special sciences, as happens (for example) in the case of geometry and her sister sciences. For this form of reasoning appears to differ from the reasonings mentioned above; the man who draws a false figure reasons from things that are neither true and primary, nor yet generally accepted. For he does not fall within the definition; he does not assume opinions that are received either by every one or by the majority or by philosophers—that is to say, by all, or by most, or by the most illustrious of them—but he conducts his reasoning upon assumptions which, though appropriate to the science in question, are not true; for he effects his mis-reasoning either by describing the semicircles wrongly or by drawing certain lines in a way in which they could not be drawn.

The foregoing must stand for an outline survey of the species of reasoning. In general, in regard both to all that we have already discussed and to those which we shall discuss later, we may remark that that amount of distinction between them may serve, because it is not our purpose to give the exact definition of any of them; we merely want to describe them in outline; we consider it quite enough from the point of view of the line of inquiry before us to be able to recognize each of them in some sort of way.

## 2

[101a25] Next in order after the foregoing, we must say for how many and for what purposes the treatise is useful. They are three—intellectual training, casual encounters, and the philosophical sciences. That it is useful as a training is obvious on the face of it. The possession of a plan of inquiry will enable us more easily to argue about the subject proposed. For purposes of casual encounters, it is useful because when we have counted up the opinions held by most people, we shall meet them on the ground not of other people's convictions but of their own, while we shift the ground of any argument that they appear to us to state unsoundly. For the study of the philosophical sciences it is useful, because the ability to raise searching difficulties on both sides of a subject will make us detect more easily the truth and error about the several points that arise. It has a further use in relation to the ultimate bases of the principles used in the several sciences. For it is impossible to discuss them at all from the principles proper to the particular science in hand, seeing that the principles are the prius of everything else: it is through the opinions generally held on the particular points that these have to be discussed, and this task be-

longs properly, or most appropriately, to dialectic: for dialectic is a process of criticism wherein lies the path to the principles of all inquiries.

## 3

[101b5] We shall be in perfect possession of the way to proceed when we are in a position like that which we occupy in regard to rhetoric and medicine and faculties of that kind: this means the doing of that which we choose with the materials that are available. For it is not every method that the rhetorician will employ to persuade, or the doctor to heal; still, if he omits none of the available means, we shall say that his grasp of the science is adequate.

## 4

[101b11] First, then, we must see of what parts our inquiry consists. Now if we were to grasp (a) with reference to how many, and what kind of, things arguments take place, and with what materials they start, and (b) how we are to become well supplied with these, we should have sufficiently won our goal. Now the materials with which arguments start are equal in number, and are identical, with the subjects on which reasonings take place. For arguments start with "propositions," while the subjects on which reasonings take place are "problems." Now every proposition and every problem indicates either a genus or a peculiarity or an accident—for the differentia too, applying as it does to a class (or genus), should be ranked together with the genus. Since, however, of what is peculiar to anything part signifies its essence, while part does not, let us divide the "peculiar" into both the aforesaid parts and call that part which indicates the essence a "definition," while of the remainder let us adopt the terminology which is generally current about these things and speak of it as a "property." What we have said, then, makes it clear that according to our present division, the elements turn out to be four, all told, namely either property, or definition, or genus, or accident. Do not let anyone suppose us to mean that each of these enunciated by itself constitutes a proposition or problem, but only that it is from these that both problems and propositions are formed. The difference between a problem and a proposition is a difference in the turn of the phrase. For if it be put in this way, "'An animal that walks on two feet' is the definition of man, is it not?" or "'Animal' is the genus of man, is it not?" the result is a proposition: but if thus, "Is 'an animal that walks on two feet' a definition of man or no?" [or "Is 'animal' his genus or no?"]² the result is a problem. Similarly, too, in other cases. Naturally, then, problems and propositions are equal in number: for out of every proposition you will make a problem if you change the turn of the phrase. [. . .]

10

[104a1] First, then, a definition must be given of a "dialectical proposition" and a "dialectical problem." For it is not every proposition nor yet every problem that is to be set down as dialectical: for no one in his senses would make a proposition of what no one holds, nor yet make a problem of what is obvious to everybody or to most people: for the latter admits of no doubt, while to the former no one would assent. Now a dialectical proposition consists in asking something that is held by all men or by most men or by the philosophers, i.e., either by all, or by most, or by the most notable of these, provided it be not contrary to the general opinion; for a man would probably assent to the view of the philosophers, if it be not contrary to the opinions of most men. Dialectical propositions also include views which are like those generally accepted; also propositions which contradict the contraries of opinions that are taken to be generally accepted, and also all opinions that are in accordance with the recognized arts. Thus, supposing it to be a general opinion that the knowledge of contraries is the same, it might probably pass for a general opinion also that the perception of contraries is the same: also, supposing it to be a general opinion that there is but one single science of grammar, it might pass for a general opinion that there is but one science of flute-playing as well, whereas, if it be a general opinion that there is more than one science of grammar, it might pass for a general opinion that there is more than one science of flute-playing as well: for all these seem to be alike and akin. Likewise, also, propositions contradicting the contraries of general opinions will pass as general opinions: for if it be a general opinion that one ought to do good to one's friends, it will also be a general opinion that one ought not to do them harm. Here, that one ought to do harm to one's friends is contrary to the general view, and that one ought not to do them harm is the contradictory of that contrary. Likewise, also, if one ought to do good to one's friends, one ought not to do good to one's enemies: this too is the contradictory of the view contrary to the general view; the contrary being that one ought to do good to one's enemies. Likewise, also, in other cases. Also, on comparison, it will look like a general opinion that the contrary predicate belongs to the contrary subject: e.g, if one ought to do good to one's friends, one ought also to do evil to one's enemies. It might appear also as if doing good to one's friends were a contrary to doing evil to one's enemies: but whether this is or is not so in reality as well will be stated in the course of the discussion upon contraries. Clearly also, all opinions that are in accordance with the arts are dialectical propositions; for people are likely to assent to the views held by those who have made a study of these things, e.g., on a question of medicine they will agree with the doctor, and on a question of geometry with the geometrician; and likewise also in other cases.

# Notes

This is an excerpt from Aristotle's *Topics*, book 1, and dates from approximately 350 BC. The translation is by W. A. Pickard-Cambridge, taken from volume 1 of *The Works of Aristotle Translated into English* (London: Oxford University Press, 1928). The accompanying technical notes are here omitted. The material in square brackets, including the Bekker pagination, is inserted by the editors of this volume. The orthography of the original has been largely preserved.—Eds.

1. [Here "generally accepted" is a translation of the Greek word *endoxa*; it has also been translated as "common belief" and "reputable opinion."]
2. [These square brackets are in the text.]

# 2

# Presumptions in Legal Argumentation

## From Antiquity to the Middle Ages

### HANNS HOHMANN

Presumptions help us make decisions under conditions of uncertainty. Such decisions are also the business of rhetoric, and so one might expect to find a discussion of presumptions in the ancient handbooks of that discipline; as a matter of fact, however, the term *praesumptio* there appears only to refer to the anticipation of counterarguments and is thus used as an equivalent to *prolepsis*.[1] Instead, we find the concept of presumption as related to decisions about doubtful facts and the distribution of burdens of proof emerging in the context of Roman law. In this chapter I will sketch in broad outline the transition of the concept of presumption from a relatively subordinate part of the Roman law to a central feature of legal disputations in the revival of Roman law in the Middle Ages. I will first discuss features of presumptions in the codification of Roman law that was undertaken at the behest of the emperor Justinian in the sixth century AD and later became known as the *Corpus Iuris*. In my discussion here, I will focus primarily on the *Digest*, a vast collection of juristic pronouncements by leading Roman jurists, collected from a literature spanning six centuries.[2] Then I will focus on the treatment of presumptions in the second edition of Pilius's *Libellus Disputatorius*, written by Pilius of Medicina in the second half of the twelfth century. In conclusion, I will briefly point to elements of these developments that may be useful in considering the renewed contemporary discussion about the role of presumptions in argumentation, a discussion that has been stimulated particularly by Richard Gaskins's *Burdens of Proof in Modern Discourse*, which highlights the paradigmatic significance of the rhetorical manipulation of burdens of proof in legal reasoning.[3]

⮑

Even before the term *praesumptio* was used to denote the concept, the Roman jurist Quintus Mucius Scaevola introduced, at the turn from the second to the first century BC, a presumption into legal controversies about the source of property that had passed to a woman. He argued that "when it is not clear where the property has come from, it is more correct and decent to hold that she got it from her husband or someone in his power." The later jurist Pomponius (second century AD), who transmitted this pronouncement to us, added the comment that "Quintus Mucius appears to have taken this view in order to avoid any disgraceful inquiry involving a wife."[4] This early use of presumption in legal argumentation already shows the subtle interplay of empirical and normative considerations that characterizes the treatment of presumptions in the Roman law of the *Corpus Iuris* as a whole.

Legal presumptions take as their starting point an established fact (in the example: a married woman holds property of uncertain origin) and then draw from this a conclusion about an uncertain matter (here: the origin of the property, which is presumed to have come from the husband). The structure of presumptions thus resembles that of arguments from probability, and in the Roman law we find several references to presumptions that people make as a matter of empirical fact. For instance, a father presumes his son missing in war to be dead;[5] people assume that slaves of some nationalities are better than slaves of other nationalities;[6] or they assume that a more recently enslaved person will be easier to deal with than a slave of long standing;[7] or a father assumes that his wife will ultimately deliver to the children whatever part of his property she has taken.[8] In such cases, people form factual expectations on the basis of what they perceive to be likely. Legal presumptions may also be based on such perceptions of empirical probability, but they need not be. Once they are established, legal presumptions create an *entitlement* to the conclusion toward which they point (barring the possibility and permissibility of proof to the contrary).

The most fundamental legal presumption, that in favor of defendants, is a case in point. It is stated at the outset of the *Digest* chapter titled "On Proof and Presumption" that "proof lies on him who asserts, not on him who denies."[9] This rule is not based on the observation that plaintiffs are generally *less likely* to make believable assertions than defendants, but rather on the perception that it is *fairer* to impose the burden of proof on the plaintiff. This is even clearer when we look at the burden of proof in criminal cases, where in fact it is more likely than not that the defendant is guilty, since more defendants are convicted than acquitted. And that the underlying judgment about the presumption of innocence is normative rather than empirical is made quite clear in what the jurist Ulpian reports to us[10] about a rescript of the emperor Trajan, who held that in criminal cases nobody should be condemned on suspicion because "it was preferable that the crime of a guilty man should go unpunished rather than that an innocent man be condemned."[11] The emphasis is here not so much on which presumption is more likely to be correct but on which is less likely to lead to less acceptable consequences.

While generally it may be regarded as fairer to impose the burden of proof on the plaintiff, the law of presumptions also establishes modifications of this principle. Even before the general rule is stated,[12] the very first excerpt under the *Digest* title "Proof and Presumptions" establishes the exception that "if the issue is whether someone has a clan or a *gens*, he must prove it."[13] Here the burden of proof is imposed on the party who is in a better position to provide the required evidence, regardless of whether that party is the plaintiff or the defendant.

One of the reasons why it is fair to shift the burden to the defendant may of course be that it appears more likely that the plaintiff's assertion is correct. Thus for instance a defendant who has initially denied receiving a payment must prove that it was owed once it is later shown that he did in fact receive it, while generally the plaintiff who claims to have paid unowed money must prove that it was not owed.[14] Even without the legal presumption, an observer would be suspicious of a defendant who chooses to deny receiving money rather than admitting receipt and asserting that the money was owed, an assertion that would have the greater likelihood on its side and that the plaintiff would then have to disprove. But the legal presumption does more than point to this shifted probability; it concludes that in such cases the likelihood of the defendant's liability is great enough to justify shifting the burden of proof, even though this will mean that some defendants will have to return money in fact owed to them, simply because they cannot prove that it was owed.[15]

This presumption also gives to the fact of denial of receipt of payment more weight than to all other potential credibility factors, such as the parties' reputations for veracity: the fact that the plaintiff may be a notorious liar or desperately short of cash, and the defendant a person of well-known probity or immense wealth, does not lead to a similar shift of the burden of proof in such cases; even though these facts, too, can have a definite bearing on who is likely to be telling the truth in such cases and may in some instances arguably even have a greater bearing than the denial, which may sometimes be due to carelessness or forgetfulness rather than deceptive intent. Thus, even where presumptions rely on and reinforce pre-existing empirical probabilities, they entail normative judgments as to which probabilities deserve such special reinforcement; and this reinforcement goes beyond merely highlighting the empirical force of certain probabilities by giving them the effect of shifting the burden of proof, while disregarding the potential countervailing probability implications of other circumstances.

Moreover, in several cases legal presumptions are clearly not, or at least not clearly based on, empirical probabilities. This is the case especially in situations where the sequence of deaths is at issue and where no clear proof is available. Thus in a case where a mother and her one-year-old child die in a shipwreck and her husband will receive her entire dowry if the child survived the mother and only part of the dowry if the child died before the mother, it is to be presumed that the infant died earlier, so that the husband receives only part of the dowry.[16] In this passage it is claimed that this decision was made because "it was more likely (*verisimilius*) that the infant died before its mother," but there is really no clear empirical evidence for the contention that children die before adults in disasters.[17] And in another passage where a woman died in a shipwreck along with her son who had attained puberty, the reason given for the presumption that the son died *after* the mother is not that this is more likely, but that it is *humanius*,[18] which may be translated as "more generous." The question is of course for whom this is more generous, and the answer is that this assumption allows for the son to inherit from the mother and thus for more of her estate to remain in her husband's family upon the son's death, which would be regarded as an appropriate outcome in the normal course of events. In contrast, in the other case the wife's family receives the benefit of the doubt because the apparent purpose of the arrangement passing on her entire dowry to the husband was to provide for her child, a purpose that can no longer be served once the child is dead.

That presumptions are often a vehicle for promoting a desirable policy rather more than aiming at decisions based on factually accurate findings becomes especially apparent in cases involving the freeing of slaves, where doubts are not infrequently resolved by the law in favor of liberty. In one passage in the *Digest*, the burden of proving that the testator did not intend to free a slave is imposed on the heirs in cases when there is "a presumption that liberty appears to have been conferred" because the words of the will can be interpreted that way, even if other interpretations are possible as well.[19] This legislative intent to favor liberty by means of presumptions is even clearer when it is established that in cases where a female slave is to be freed if her firstborn child is male, and she then bears twins one of whom is male, and it cannot be established whether the boy was born first, it is to be presumed that he was, because "the more humane view should be adopted whereby the slave obtains her freedom and her daughter the status of being freeborn on the presumption that the male child was the firstborn."[20]

The intent to promote appropriate policy rather than accurate fact-finding by means of presumptions is most apparent in cases where presumptions are irrebuttable, that is, where proof contrary to what is presumed is not allowed. It is doubtful to what extent the Roman law of the *Corpus Iuris* established such irrebuttable presumptions.[21] In one passage in the *Code*, the fact that a man and woman who were suspected of adultery later start living together or marry is treated as tantamount to a confession of adultery, leading to their punishment for that crime; the possibility of a contrary proof in their defense is not mentioned, but this could be due to the great unlikelihood that such a proof of the negative could ever be offered, rather than to the fact that such a proof is legally foreclosed.[22]

But I think that the legal provision with which this brief discussion of presumptions in the Roman law began should also be considered in this context. When Scaevola gives a married woman who has property of uncertain origin the benefit of the doubt by holding that "when it is not clear where the property has come from, it is more correct and decent (*verius et honestius*) to hold that she got it from her husband or someone in his power," and Pomponius explains this by saying that "Quintus Mucius appears to have taken this view in order to avoid any disgraceful inquiry involving a wife,"[23] it appears that in the absence of clear proof already in the possession of the plaintiff who claims that the property did not come from the husband, further investigations are not to be permitted in order to prevent "disgraceful inquiry" (*turpis quaestus*), even if this might after all prove the plaintiff's claim. It appears that in the absence of readily available proof to the contrary, the wife's claim to her reputation is valued more highly than the plaintiff's financial interests, regardless of what the facts might prove to be upon closer inspection: what is more decent (*honestius*) is more important than what is more correct (*verius*).

At this point we can conclude our brief survey of the use of presumptions in the Roman law by highlighting two points. First, while presumptions typically are introduced in cases of factual uncertainties, these uncertainties are often used to achieve outcomes promoting certain policies rather more than to resolve each situation in favor of the empirically more probable assumption; normative appropriateness is thus often elevated over empirical correctness. Second, even where the argument for the normative appropriateness of the favored outcome is not explicitly made, it is important that the person who must decide the case be persuaded that this normative evaluation of the outcome is right, or at least not completely unacceptable, since the presumption can often easily be undercut by denying that the uncertainty that gives rise to the presumption actually exists. To take the example just discussed, the judge can accept a weak proof of the claim that the property did not come from the husband, and thus avoid the presumption in favor of the wife. Another possibility would be that the judge could interpret the rule to apply only to a woman of completely unblemished reputation, and then accept proof of some blemish making the presumption inapplicable. The procedural shift of the burden of proof to one party in such cases is thus not always completely effective in avoiding that an at least implicit substantive evaluation of the claim of the other party favored by the presumption may have an influence on the outcome. The distinction between rhetorical and legal presumptions is thus not as clear-cut as it might initially seem.

⌒

While the rhetorical vicissitudes of presumptions remain at least partially submerged in the Roman law of Antiquity, its revival in the Middle Ages, beginning at the turn from the eleventh to the twelfth century, brightly highlights their multifarious argumentative uses. As a particularly clear example of this explicit rhetoricization of presumptions, I will briefly discuss the second edition of Pilius's *Libellus Disputatorius*, written by Pilius[24] of Medicina, probably in the final decade of the twelfth century.[25] The starting point for Pilius's discussion of presumptions in the first book of this work[26] is the realization that in legal scholastic disputations, as well as in the trials for which these largely serve as a preparation, it is often necessary to deal with doubts about uncertain matters.[27] In such situations, presumptions serve as a kind of incomplete proof; they provide, by means of extrinsic signs, credence or confirmation for a doubtful matter.[28] This characterization of presumptions is close to Cicero's definition of the concept of "argument," much relied upon throughout the Middle Ages, in his *Topica*: per Cicero, an argument is a course of reasoning that provides confirmation for a doubtful matter.[29] According to this conception, a presumption is a kind of argument whose distinguishing characteristic it is that it takes as its starting point an extrinsic sign for a matter that cannot be established more directly, particularly by means of witnesses. Once such more direct proof becomes available, the presumption is destroyed, unless the law excludes such contrary proof; this corresponds to the modern legal distinction between rebuttable and irrebuttable presumptions.[30] But Pilius's conception is broader than the modern legal notion of presumption, since it opens for his discussion the entire range of inartistic proofs, not merely of facts but also of the legal characterization of actions as permissible or impermissible, justifiable or unjustifiable, excusable or inexcusable. This broadening is made possible by Pilius's linkage of proof (*probatio*) with argumentation (*argumentum*) by way of the definitions just cited. What nevertheless keeps presumptions in this sense linked with the modern conception is the fact that they have *normative* force: presumptions are not merely assumptions that people hold *de facto* but premises on which one is entitled to rely *de jure*.

In accordance with the broad scope of his conception of presumptions, Pilius chooses for his treatment a conceptual scheme clearly rooted in the rhetorical theory of the *status rationales*; this scheme, which he probably derived from a work on canon law that had been published a few years earlier, the *Summa* of Sicard of Cremona,[31] uses two basic distinctions. The first is that between extrinsic and intrinsic facts, in which extrinsic facts extend from observable actions to questions of intentionality and negligence;[32] the category of intrinsic facts includes, in Pilius's view, matters such as a person's specific intentions or consent, or the interpretation of the law or of a written document.[33] After this first basic distinction, the second leads us directly to the status rationales, by differentiating between doubts about the substance[34] and the quality of a fact; the former concerns the question whether something was done or not, the latter the question whether it is good or bad.[35] These are precisely the questions that characterize, respectively, the rhetorical status of *conjectura* (matters of fact) and *qualitas* (matters of quality); the status of *definitio* (matters of definition) is no longer part of the scheme, since its presence was based on a distinction between the legal and the extralegal characterization of actions, which has no place in a fully developed and professionalized legal system where *all* aspects of the judicial evaluation of an act are seen as subject to *law*, which incorporates *both* specific written legal rules and general principles of law and equity.[36]

Within the issue of the *substance* of extrinsic facts, equivalent to the rhetorical issue of *conjectura*, the scheme used by Pilius further distinguishes several topics.[37] Where his predecessors use the term *locus*, familiar from the tradition of rhetoric and dialectic, Pilius uses the term *modus*, which was generally applied to types of arguments in the work of the glossators. These places or modes of presuming are readily recognizable as in large part derived from the rhetorical topics of the person and the act. Thus we find here references to the person of the agent and the person with whom the agent interacts; to time, place, and mode of action; to the habits, associates, age, and necessities of the agent; to subsequent actions, indications, and rumors concerning the act. To these Pilius adds a number of general considerations affecting the evaluation of an act rather more than the question whether it did in fact occur;[38] this, too, has a precedent in the topics of the consequences of the act in rhetorical theory.[39]

The rhetorical topics of the person and the act are also the main source for the classification of modes of arguing about the *quality* of extrinsic facts in Pilius's scheme.[40] The applicability of these topics to the issue of quality as well as to the issue of conjecture is implied by the fact that in classical rhetorical theory they had been introduced as components of *all* proof; but their presence in the evaluation as well as in the ascertainment of facts is actually brought out more clearly here in Pilius's work than in rhetorical handbooks such as Cicero's *De inventione*, which was one of the main texts used for rhetorical instruction during that period. Again Pilius adds to the scheme of his canon law predecessors some further modes he has found emphasized in his Roman law sources.[41] And he greatly expands the category *ex causa* (from the case), under which he includes a large number of special circumstances and case types;[42] here we also find some modes of presuming related to Cicero's more dialectically oriented topics *adiuncta negotio*,[43] such as genus and species,[44] the greater and the lesser,[45] and part and whole.[46]

What distinguishes Pilius's treatment of these topics from that found in the rhetorical handbooks—apart from additions to and adaptations of modes of presuming derived from a much-expanded body of technical law—is the source from which the probabilities invoked derive their probative force. In the classical tradition of rhetoric, it was the common sense of the community, a view of how the world worked and should work, premises posited by the orator as shared between him and the deciding audience, that undergirded the artistic arguments of the rhetor. But now, in a more technically complex and increasingly professionalized legal system, the lawyer's argumentative art focuses on the law as the primary foundation of forensic arguments. To establish that the legal advocate is entitled to rely on certain presumptions, Pilius supports every topic he introduces with often copious references to his legal sources, citing primarily the *Corpus Iuris*.

Pilius's audience consists of professional jurists, who are expected to find the modes of presuming persuasive because they are authoritatively supported, not because they recognize in the advocates' assumptions their own. But that contrast should not be overstated: on the one hand, the juristic sources themselves are to a considerable extent a codification of common sense; and on the other, as Pilius's treatment of these arguments shows very clearly, the authorities cited do not completely determine either the advocate's argument or the judge's decision. And what links the ancient rhetor and the medieval jurist is the search, among the premises endorsed as persuasive or even recognized as binding by the audience, for arguments that can support both sides in a controversial case.

Pilius provides a systematic presentation of authoritative sources for arguments supporting as well as opposing contentions, such as: that a certain act has been or will be committed or not committed; that the act was permissible or impermissible; that intent or negligence were or were not present; that the agent did or did not have certain intentions, did or did not know certain things; that such knowledge or ignorance does or does not have legal significance; that consent was or was not given; that laws or declarations should be interpreted broadly or narrowly; that an act should or should not be regarded as aggravated or excused or mitigated by circumstances; that someone should or should not be punished for the actions of another, etc. The opposition between the principles invoked for and against such contentions is not treated primarily as posing a theoretical problem that calls for a resolution but as an opportunity for finding arguments for and against the propositions in question. Which of these arguments to use is, in effect, left to the judgment of the advocate; which to accept to the discretion of the judge.

We can now end this brief look at an example of the medieval legal uses of presumptions by again noting two points: First, for Pilius, legal presumptions are not monolithic rules that unequivocally determine in advance in every case which side in a dispute has a unitary presumption in its favor. Second, his discussion emphasizes that in controversial cases a variety of presumptions tend to be available to both sides, and that the outcome depends on which of the arguments presented persuade the judging audience.

~

In conclusion, I will sketch two ways in which this highly compressed historical survey of the development of legal presumptions impinges on contemporary discussions of the function of presumptions in argumentation.

First, I would like to suggest that the treatment of presumptions in Pilius's *Libellus Disputatorius* shows that the supposedly "legal" conception that traditional textbook treatments of presumptions have associated with Whately is not only questionably attributed to that author:[47] it is not even an adequate representation of the way presumptions operate in the law. Legal presumptions do not constitute (1) "a unitary advantage that is objectively assigned by rules [. . .] to the side that upholds the status quo," and they do not require (2) "that all affirmative argument be encumbered by a corollary burden of proof such that the affirmative must amass a preponderance of evidence [. . .] on all crucial issues."[48] Legal presumptions as discussed by Pilius rather approximate the psychological notion of presumption ascribed to Whately by Michael Sproule, a conception constructing presumption "as consisting of (1) a potentially great number of argumentative advantages, which (2) may be simultaneously conferred on both sides of dispute"; and even if they do not result, as do such psychological preferences, from "audience preferences for particular arguments or sources of information"[49] but rather from authoritative legal pronouncements, such preferences will still have an important influence on the interpretation and acceptance of presumptions by the judging audience. Admittedly Pilius is more forthright than many more recent writers on legal presumptions in highlighting the rhetorical openness inherent in legal argumentation, but this is increasingly being acknowledged in contemporary literature on the subject as well.[50]

At the same time, I think that this proximity of the "psychological" burden of proof to legal presumptions should also encourage us to look more closely for the normative as well as empirical elements entering into audiences' constructions of their presumptions, as well as into speakers' constructions of these same audience presumptions.

Finally, our look at the role of presumptions in the Roman law of the *Corpus Iuris* suggests that Gaskins's discussion of the rhetorical uses of burdens of proof in modern discourse points to argumentative procedures that can already be found in ancient law. But this comparison also suggests that the masking of substantive considerations behind the procedural shift of the burden of proof[51] can perhaps not be quite as rhetorically effective as Gaskins appears to assume; the substance behind the procedure must still be persuasive if the shift of the burden of proof is to be effective.

A good example of this is actually provided by the school desegregation cases that Gaskins discusses extensively.[52] After *Brown v. Board of Education*,[53] which avoided a formal overruling of the "separate but equal" doctrine[54] by purporting to find that segregated schools simply could not be both separate and equal, some courts in the South took this apparent shift in the burden of proof at face value and heard and accepted factual evidence that schools could in fact be equal though segregated.[55] Defenders of the United States Supreme Court's decision shifted from matters of *factual* proof to an emphasis on the *moral* unacceptability of segregation,[56] and the court itself finally made the openly *legal* pronouncement that it is "no longer open to question that a State may not constitutionally require segregation of public facilities."[57] What this may suggest is that in every case in which a reliance on the burden of proof is central to the openly declared argument, the audience of the court must still be able to recognize and willing to be persuaded by an underlying substantive argument, based on the consequences achieved and the values served by this shift, if this rhetorical strategy is to work.

# Notes

This is an original essay written specifically for this volume.—Eds.

1. Quintilian, *Institutio Oratoria*, trans. H. E. Butler (New York: G. P. Putnam's Sons; London: William Heinemann, 1922), bk. 9, ch. 2, lines 16–18.

2. On the creation of the (later so-called) *Corpus Iuris* in the sixth century AD, see Wolfgang Kunkel, *An Introduction to Roman Legal and Constitutional History*, 2nd ed., trans. J. M. Kelly (Oxford: Clarendon Press, 1973), 163ff. Besides the *Digest*, the other parts of the *Corpus Iuris* are the *Institutes*, a brief basic introduction to the law for students; the *Code*, a collection of imperial legal pronouncements of the emperors before Justinian; and the *Novellae*, legal provisions created by Justinian himself.

3. Richard H. Gaskins, *Burdens of Proof in Modern Discourse* (New Haven, CT: Yale University Press, 1992).

4. *Corpus Iuris Civilis. Volumen Primum. Institutiones, Digesta*, 12th ed., ed. T. Mommsen and Paul Krüger (Berlin: Weidmann, 1911), 24.1.51.

5. *Corpus Iuris Civilis*, 12.6.3.

6. *Corpus Iuris Civilis*, 21.1.31.21.

7. *Corpus Iuris Civilis*, 21.1.37.

8. *Corpus Iuris Civilis*, 31.67.10.

9. *Corpus Iuris Civilis*, 22.3.2.

10. *Corpus Iuris Civilis*, 48.19.6.

11. Compare to a similar thought already expressed in Antiphon's *On the Murder of Herodes*, in *Antiphon. Andocides*, ed. and trans. K. J. Maidment, vol. 1 of *Minor Attic Orators* (Cambridge, MA: Harvard University Press, 1982), 91. Here, the defendant urges the jury to give him the benefit of the doubt: "If, then, you must make any mistake, it would be less of an outrage to acquit me undeservedly than to condemn me without just cause; for the former is only a mistake, while the latter is also an eternal disgrace." Such passages show that the idea of the presumption of innocence is not a creation of the Common Law.

12. *Digest*, 22.3.2.

13. *Digest*, 22.3.1.

14. *Digest*, 22.25 pr.

15. This could occur for instance if a cash payment is witnessed, but the transfer of goods for which the cash constitutes the payment was not witnessed.

16. *Digest*, 23.4.26 pr.

17. The same presumption is expressed more generally also in *Digest*, 34.5.23.

18. *Digest*, 34.5.22.

19. *Digest*, 40.5.24.8.

20. *Digest*, 34.5.10.1.

21. Rudolf Motzenbäcker, *Die Rechtsvermutung im Kanonischen Recht* (Munich: Kommissionsverlag Karl Zink, 1958), 26ff.

22. Motzenbäcker, *Die Rechtsvermutung*, 28–29.

23. *Digest*, 24.1.51.

24. In the sources, the name is also spelled Pillius, Pylius, Pyleus, Pileus, etc.; the spelling Pilius appears in one document in his own hand. See Aldo Adversi, *Appunti biobibliografici sul giureconsulto Pillio da Medicina* (Florence: Sansoni, 1960), 8; and this spelling is also preferred in a major handbook on the legal literature of the period. See Peter Weimar, "Die legistische Literatur der Glossatorenzeit," in *Handbuch der Quellen und Literatur der neueren europäischen Privatrechtsgeschichte: Mittelalter (1100–1500)*, ed. Helmut Coing (Munich: Beck, 1973), 238–39.

25. The work is not yet available in a printed edition; the most reliable text is given by a manuscript from the fourteenth century, located in the Austrian National Library in Vienna (cod. Vindob. 2157 fol. 36r–87v); the first book has been edited from that text, with consultation of another manuscript in the Chapter Library at Olmouce (Czech Republic) in Jurgen Meyer-Nelthropp, *"Libellus Pylei Disputatorius Liber Primus"* (PhD diss., Universität Hamburg, 1959). I have worked with that edition and with a microfilm of the Vienna manuscript, which I have also been able to study in the Österreichische Nationalbibliothek. For discussions of the work, see Erich Genzmer, "Die Iustinianische Kodifikation und die Glossatoren," in *Atti del Congresso Internazionale di diritto romano (Bologna 1933)* (Pavia: Successori Fratelli Fusi, 1934), 1:426ff.; Stephan Kuttner, "Réflexions sur les brocards des glossateurs," in *Mélanges Joseph de Ghellinck* (Gembloux: Duculot, 1951), 2:772ff.; Motzenbäcker, *Die Rechtsvermutung*, 62ff.; Adversi, *Appunti biobibliografici*, 30–31; Giovani Santini, *Università e società nel XII secolo: Pillio da Medicina e lo Studio di Modena. Tradizione*

*e innovazione nella scuola dei glossatori* (Modena: S.T.E.M.-Mucchi, 1979), 261ff. On Pilius's life, see Adversi, *Appunti biobibliografici*, 7–18; J. A. Clarence-Smith, *Medieval Law Teachers and Writers, Civilian and Canonist* (Ottawa, ON: University of Ottawa Press, 1975), 30–31; Santini, *Università e società*, 161. The following discussion of Pilius's *Libellus Disputatorius* is adapted from a longer paper I have written published as "Rhetoric in Medieval Legal Education: *Libellus Pylei Disputatorius*," *Disputatio: An International Journal of the Late Middle Ages* 4 (1999): 59–73.

26. This book will hereinafter be referred to as *LPD*, and passages from it will be cited by folio number from the Vienna manuscript (cod. Vindob. 2157 fol. 36r–87v).

27. On the disputations in the medieval faculties of law, see Gérard Fransen, "Les Questions disputées dans les facultés de droit," in *Les Questions disputées et les questions quodlibétiques dans les facultés de théologie, de droit, et de médecine* (Turnhout: Brepols, 1985), 223ff.

28. *LPD*, 36. Presumpcio est rei de qua queritur semiplena probatio vel rei dubie aliquibus signis extrinsecis credulitas seu fides. (I have retained the orthography of the manuscript.) (Presumption is the partial [literally "half"; i.e., other evidence needs to be added to make the proof complete] proof of a matter which is in dispute, or the belief or faith in a doubtful matter based on some extrinsic signs.)

29. Cicero, *Topica*, 2.8. Itaque licet definire [...] argumentum [...] rationem quae rei dubiae faciat fidem. (Thus one may define [...] an argument [...] as a course of reasoning which provides confirmation for a doubtful matter.)

30. See, for example, Charles T. McCormick, *McCormick's Handbook of the Law of Evidence*, 2nd ed., ed. Edward W. Cleary (St. Paul, MN: West Publishing, 1972), 802ff.

31. Albert Lang thinks that Pilius may have encountered this work not directly but through an anonymous work on canon law now usually referred to as the *Tractatus de praesumptionibus* (Lang prefers the title *Perpendiculum*), which he feels apparently relied on and somewhat modified Sicard's treatment of presumptions ("Rhetorische Einflüsse auf die Behandlung des Prozesses in der Kanonistik des 12. Jahrhunderts," in *Festschrift für Eduard Eichmann zum 70. Geburtstag* [Paderborn: Schöningh, 1940], 122ff.). See also Albert Lang, "Zur Entstehungsgeschichte der Brocardasammlungen," *Zeitschrift der Savigny-Stiftung für Rechtsgeschichte, Kanonistische Abteilung* 62 (1942): 109ff. But Motzenbäcker argues that Sicard's is the later work (*Die Rechtsvermutung*, 93).

32. This becomes clear at *LPD*, 51r ff.

33. Lang overlooks that Pilius, in this respect not following Sicard or the *Perpendiculum*, here treats matters of interpretation as a subcategory of questions of intrinsic fact, rather than as a separate category; therefore, he has not announced a third category and then failed to address it, as Lang charges ("Zur Entstehungsgeschichte," 134). Pilius does treat the category of intrinsic facts (*LPD*, 55r ff.), although he does not mark the subdivisions of substance and quality here, whose usefulness in this context had already been doubted in the *Perpendiculum* ("Zur Entstehungsgeschichte," 133); but he does observe the subdivision into matters of intention or consent (55r ff.; including matters of knowledge and ignorance of fact or law [55v f.], the ques-

tion whether ignorance excuses [56r ff.], and issues of the significance of the knowledge and consent of others [57r f.] and of subsequent approval [58r f.]), and also addresses matters of broad and strict interpretation (especially 59r ff.), here focused on private declarations rather than laws. Questions of the strict or equitable interpretation of the law are addressed at 53v, and issues of ambiguity in written documents at 54r, thus *before* the section on intrinsic facts, which begins at 55r; so Lang is right insofar as he notes some structural inconsistency in Pilius's treatment of interpretation.

34. Or essence; Pilius uses these terms interchangeably.

35. *LPD*, 36v. Quibus modis presumatur. Variis modis contingit. Presumi siquidem incertitudo quandoque vertitur circa factum extrinsecum. Puta cum de voluntate vel consensu cuiusque queritur vel de Iuris seu alicuius scripture interpretacione. Item quandoque dubitatur de facti substantia. Sitne aliquid factum vel non. Quandoque essencia certa constituta de eius qualitate disputatur. Scilicet sitne bonum vel malum quod factum deprehenditur. ([Let's discuss] in which [different] ways presumption is to be used. It occurs in various circumstances. Presume if and whenever uncertainty arises about an extrinsic fact. Consider it [that is, presumption] when someone's intention or consent is at issue, or the interpretation of the Law or of the writing of another. The same [applies] whenever the substance of a fact is doubted, [that is] whether something was or was not done. [Also] when, the basic action having been securely established, its quality is [still] disputed. That is, when it is to be determined whether the act done is good or bad.)

36. That *qualitas* was the domain of the jurists is already recognized in Cicero's *De inventione* (1.11.14). He assigned to the *Iuris consulti*, within the *constitutio generalis* (his term here for the *status qualitatis*), the *constitutio negotialis*, which is concerned with "what the law is according to civic custom and equity"; his oratorical practice, for example in the *Pro Caecina* (65ff.), shows that they were also concerned with the interpretation of the written law and of legal documents; eventually they also addressed questions which Cicero assigns to the other part of the *constitutio generalis*, the *constitutio iuridicalis*, whose name already signals its link with matters of law.

37. *LPD*, 36v f.

38. *LPD*, 37r. These are not to be found in Sicardus's *Summa* and the *Perpendiculum*; see Lang, "Zur Entstehungsgeschichte," 128f.

39. For the *consecutio negotii*, see, for example, Cicero, *De inventione*, 1.28.43; for the topical theory of the attributes of the person or the act as the core of argumentative proof, see *De inventione*, 1.24.34ff. For a discussion of the development of that theory in Roman Antiquity, see Michael C. Leff, "The Topics of Argumentative Invention in Latin Rhetorical Theory from Cicero to Boethius," *Rhetorica* 1, no. 1 (1983): 23–44.

40. *LPD*, 37r ff.

41. *LPD*, 38v f.; Lang, "Zur Entstehungsgeschichte," 130.

42. *LPD*, 39r ff.

43. *LPD*, 40v ff.

44. *LPD*, 40v.

45. *LPD*, 43v.

46. *LPD*, 48v f. Compare Cicero, *De inventione*, 1.28.41f., on the *adiuncta negotio*; on the dialectical cast of these *topoi*, see Leff, "Topics," 30.

47. That is the central contention argued in J. Michael Sproule, "The Psychological Burden of Proof: On the Evolutionary Development of Richard Whately's Theory of Presumption," *Communication Monographs* 43, no. 2 (1976): 115–29.

48. These are characteristics of the "legal" conception of presumption in argumentation pointed out by Sproule, "Psychological Burden," 126.

49. These are elements of the interpretation of Whatelian presumption offered by Sproule, 115.

50. For an overview, see, for example Gaskins, *Burdens of Proof*, 15ff.

51. Gaskins, 47ff., 75.

52. Gaskins, 54ff.

53. 347 US 483 (1954).

54. Established in *Plessy v. Ferguson*, 163 US 537 (1896).

55. See, for example, *Stell v. Savannah-Chatham County Board of Education*, 220 F. Supp. 667 (S. D. Ga. 1963); reversed 318 F.2d. 425 (5th Cir. 1963).

56. See, for example, Edmond Cahn, "Jurisprudence," *New York University Law Review* 30, no. 1 (1955): 150–69.

57. *Johnson v. Virginia*, 373 US 61 (1964).

# 3

# Of the Burthen of Proof

## *On Whom Shall It Lie?*

JEREMY BENTHAM

(A question produced by undue exclusion of evidence.)

§1. Answer to the question, on the ground of Natural Procedure.

The obligation of adducing proof, on whom—i.e., on which of two contending parties—shall it on each occasion be imposed? In this may be seen a question, the answer to which is, under the *technical* system of procedure, encompassed with endless difficulties.

On the ground of natural justice, which is the only justice—under the reign of natural procedure, nothing can be more simple—nothing can be more easy.

On that one of the parties, says the answer, let the obligation be, in each individual instance, imposed, by whom, in that instance, if fulfilled, the fulfilment of it will be attended with least inconvenience;—inconvenience meaning always delay, vexation, and expense.

But how and when can it be known which that party is? *Answer*: Under technical procedure, never:—care, as hath been seen,—effectual care—has ever been taken that it shall not be.

Under natural procedure, along with so many other points that may require to be ascertained, it becomes ascertained—ascertained of course—at the initial meeting of the parties *coram judice*.[1]

Nay:—but by the party by whom the allegation is made, by him it is that the truth of it ought to be proved. Such is the aphorism which on this occasion commonly, and not unnaturally or unplausibly, presents itself.

But, besides that it is in the technical, rather than in the natural system, that it would be found to have its root, and that accordingly the collateral ends of justice, viz. avoidance of unnecessary delay, vexation, and expense, are altogether disregarded by it,—so it is, that as statutes have been drawn up, the application of it has been found embarrassed by knots more easily cut than untied.[2]

Under the *natural* system, *allegation* is itself proof:—at least, in so far as in relation to the *principal* matter of fact in question, or any matter of fact that is considered as evidentiary of it, the *party alleging* alleges himself to have been a *percipient* witness.

At the same time, generally speaking, it is not so good proof—proof to such a degree trustworthy—as an allegation to the same effect would be, if made by an extraneous witness.

Much less is it as good proof, as an allegation, made to the same effect, by the *adverse* party—by the party to whose interest it is adverse. In his mouth, if his evidence be to the same effect, no allegation respecting perception can be necessary;—declaration of persuasion—i.e., admission, in which declaration of persuasion is included—of persuasion, how slight soever, so it be on that side, is sufficient.

In this point of view, the opposite to the aphorism in question, has therefore more of truth in it than the aphorism itself. Supposing the matter in question to have fallen within the cognizance of the adverse party,—of the party adverse to him by whom the allegation is made—the mouth of such adverse party is the properest out of which proof of it can come:—the mouth out of which it will come in the most satisfactory shape:—the proof may in that case be considered conclusive.

In another point of view, true it is, that the author of the allegation is the party on whom it is *incumbent* that *proof* of it shall have been exhibited, or rather that *evidence* shall have been bestowed upon it. Incumbent?—upon that party, in what sense incumbent? In this sense, viz. that if such evidence fail to be bestowed, he it is by whom the evil consequences of such failure will be felt.

On this occasion, the *plaintiff's* side of the cause is the side which is naturally the first, if not the only one, that presents itself to view. Why? Because, on the plaintiff's side, if his be the side that prevails, there must, in every instance, have been something that has been regarded as having been proved:—whereas to the *defendant* it may happen, not only to contend, but to contend with success, when and although on *his* side nothing has been proved, or so much as been attempted to be proved:—nothing alleged but the opposite of some proposition that has been alleged on the plaintiff's side. For on the side of the *defendant*, such is the state of the case, where, on the side of the *plaintiff*, the *allegation*, together with whatsoever *other* proof, if any, it has found for its support, has failed to obtain credence.

## §2. Practice of the English Equity Courts in relation to this head.

Among the artifices of the technical system, has been the keeping the means of obtaining proof—the means of securing the forthcomingness, whether of persons or things, for the purpose of evidence, in a state of the most perfect imperfection possible. In this policy, two advantages have been sought for and obtained:—in the first place, the uncertainty whether the proof necessary to success will after all be found obtainable—that uncertainty, in which the worst cause need never despair to find more of less of encouragement and incitement to perseverance: in the next place, the plunder collectable and collected in the course of the slow and expensive steps made requisite to be taken for the obtainment of the proof, in a track, every inch of which is kept as open as possible to dispute.

In a court of equity, for example, the evidence which, under natural procedure, you might at the first meeting get from your adversary, without a farthing's worth of expense, in a couple of minutes,—you obtain, if fortune be in your favour, at the end of as many years, and at the expense of as many hundreds of pounds:—the noble, and learned, and pious, and indefatigable keeper of the king's conscience, with eyes lifted up to heaven, lips invoking that God to whom he is soon to render his account, right hand upon "the sacred tabernacle of truth his breast," self-chained all the while to the judgment seat, like the pillar-saint to his pillar, and denying himself his natural rest, to expedite you:—musing ever and anon, with a mixture of pity and astonishment, on the unhappy condition of those barbarian regions, which, not only on the continent of Europe, but even in this our island, it is said, are to be found, to which the blessings which it is the province of a *court of equity* to dispense, are unknown,—so completely unknown, that not so much as the name of it is to be found in their language.

Here there may be seen a scantling of that state of things, in and by virtue of which a question naturally of such subordinate importance, and so easily settled, as that concerning the *onus probandi*, has been converted into a question of cardinal importance, on which it may often happen, that the fate of the cause, and of the parties in respect of it, may have to hinge.

## §3. Practice of the English Common-Law Courts in relation to this head.

Thus much as to equity procedure: observe now how the matter stands, at the stage of jury-trial, at common law.

At the trial, sits the plaintiff in one part of the court, and the defendant in the same or another. In this supposition, there is nothing of extravagance—nothing but what is every now and then realized. For the purpose of Judge and Co., had it been necessary that, in the physical sense of the word exclusion, an exclusion should have been put upon the parties in that case, that in that or in any other sense, an exclusion would long ago have been put upon them, need not be doubted—an exclusion with the same right, and the same reason, and the same facility, as that with which, so far as concerns testimony, an exclusion in cases and on pretences such as have been seen, has been put upon extraneous witnesses. But so long as, figuratively speaking, he is in the presence of judge and jury, no suitor is suffered to come into or remain in court, without a gag in his mouth,—so long as, literally speaking, a suitor on one side is not only not compelled, but not permitted to give answer to so much as a single question put to him by a suitor on the other, the doors of the judicatory remain as yet unclosed against those to whom what is called *justice* is administered:— and while his ruin is decreeing (for, without exaggeration, the loss of any single trial, such is the expense of it, would to any one of a vast majority of the whole number of the people, be absolute ruin,) while this is passing, the man who has right on his side may, if so it be that his conception can comprehend the explanation given him of the jargon that passes in his hearing, have the satisfaction of hearing with his own ears the proximate cause of the ruin to which, with so deliberate a solemnity and regularity, he is doomed.

Be this as it may, within a yard or two of the plaintiff (to resume the case,) sits the defendant. At this stage at last, if by half a year, or a whole year, or more than a year, spent in doing nothing but fee-gathering, the rapacity of Judge and Co. could be satiated,—at this last, or almost last stage, if the plaintiff being allowed to put a question or two to the defendant, so it were that the defendant were on pain of loss of his cause obliged to answer him, that evidence, which at the very outset of the cause might have been, would now at last be, *extracted*, or, according to circumstances, at least indicated.

As it is, no such question being to be put, the consequence is,—that if so it be that it being determined that it is on the plaintiff the burthen of proof lies, no other than that which is thus refused to him being at the moment within his reach—a *nonsuit*, or according to circumstances, a *verdict* against him, is the consequence.

If it be the defendant who finds himself in the like disastrous situation, the defendant's not being the situation in which a nonsuit can be suffered, an adverse verdict is the least misfortune by which he can be affected.

If, having right on your side, you have a verdict against you,—a misfortune which, on the part of your law advisers, any suppressed breach of a rule, never declared or so much as made, may on the occasion of any suit or cause at any time bring down upon you,—then so it is, that for ultimate success your only chance depends upon a motion for a new trial; that is, a second trial is the worst mode imaginable, in order to know whether a third trial in the same less bad mode as the first shall take place.

If, instead of having a verdict against you, it be your good or ill fortune to receive the indulgence of a nonsuit, the consequence is—that on condition of retreading a certain number of useless and expensive steps, a quarter of a year, or half a year, or a whole year afterwards, according to the latitude of the scene of action—according as it is to the south or to the north—a second trial, though not in this case under the name of a new trial, is at your command.

In this statement may be seen the effect of the question, the curious and learned question concerning the *onus probandi*, and the use of it to those for whose profit the delay, vexation, and expense, have been manufactured:—of this question, as of questions in abundance of the like nice and curious frame, and amongst others, questions concerning evidence,—see many of the proceeding chapters and the succeeding one.

Such are the questions on which, after arguments addressed to the jury alone, the jury remaining in the state of puppets, so large a part of the time which ought to be employed, in arguments on which the jury, with assistance only from the judge, should decide, is consumed.

Of the immense heap of pestilential matter of which the chaos called jurisprudence is composed, no inconsiderable proportion is composed of cases which, under the primitive system of personal appearance, could not have had existence.

Such, for example, are those which belong to the question concerning the *onus probandi.*[3]

On this head, as on so many others here touched upon,—justice, genuine justice allows but of one general rule:—the burthen of proof, lay it in each individual case upon that one of the parties on whom it will sit lightest: a point which cannot be ascertained but by the explanation above mentioned.

Look to the books, and here, as elsewhere, instead of clear rules, such as the nature of things forbids to be established by anything but statute of law, you have darkness palpable and visible.

The affirmative is that which shall be proved:—plausible enough:—but affirmative or negative depends not merely on the nature of the fact but also on the structure of the language employed in the description of it. After, and not withstanding this rule, come exceptions: and who shall assign an end,—among lawyers, who would wish to assign an end,—to the string of exceptions?

In the onus probandi may be seen one of those innumerable gulphs into which many fortunes are destined to be thrown, but which no number of fortunes will fill up.

An offence is created, and in the creation of it, in relation to that offence in the character of causes of justification or exemption, a number of circumstances are established. On the part of the plaintiff, the existence of the act of delinquency is of course to be proved:—but of the several circumstances, any one of which suffices to exempt a man from the penalty,—to entitle the plaintiff to the service he demands at the hands of the judge, shall it be necessary for him to prove the non-existence respectively?—or shall the proof of the act in question suffice, unless on the part of the defendant the existence of one or more of them to be proved?

Having to his own satisfaction sufficient assurance, that on the part of him whom he is prosecuting, no one of all the appointed causes of justification or exemption has existence, so sure as the confrontation had place, being assured of finding in the answer, or even the silence of the defendant, sufficient proof,—he would exempt himself in the first instance, and ultimately the defendant, from the expense attendant on the proof, supposing it possible, of all those negatives. But the lawyers, with whose interest security on the part of suitors and clients is incompatible, have taken care that there shall not be any such assurance. In the darkness in which he is left to grope his way, the plaintiff, under the guidance of a professional adviser, whose profit increases with the burthen, under the impossibility of learning an opinion and a will which he to whom it belongs to form it has not yet formed, loads himself, if he be able, with the whole of the vexation and expense of which it is supposed that by any possibility it can happen to it to be pronounced necessary. If, sinking under the burthen, he fail in his conjecture concerning that which it has been rendered impossible for him to know, be the justice of his case ever so clear, he loses it.

It is the interest of the fraternity, that the traps thus laid on the plaintiff's side for catching plaintiffs should be multiplied to infinity, that, on the defendant's side, a man, be the badness of his cause ever so clear, may be encouraged to defend himself: accordingly, it was a maxim of Lord Chancellor Rosslyn,[4] that no cause ought ever to be given up as desperate.

But, men are thus discouraged from commencing a cause: and unless a cause be begun, how can it be continued? No such thing: if, setting aside the traps, the plaintiff's cause be good, he is assured that it is good:—but nothing is said of the traps—they do not come till afterwards.

A legislative draughtsman who understood his business, would, in penning the substantive part of a new law, make due provision for the solution of these difficulties in procedure:—but as the system is constituted, it is not the interest of any legislative draughtsman to understand the business:—and if he did understand the business, what he would understand still better is,—that so long as the reproach of incapacity can be avoided, it is his interest to multiply and not to diminish the number of all such difficulties. Nor, after all, does the nature of the mischief admit of anything like a co-extensive remedy, other than the restoration of that feature of primitive justice—confrontation of the parties at the outset *coram justice*—which a man at the head of the law, had he as many hands as Briareus,⁵ would cut them all off sooner than he would co-operate in, or even be a witness to the restoration of.

## Notes

From *An Introductory View of the Rationale of Evidence for the Use of Non-Lawyers as Well as Lawyers* (published in 1843; composed 1812), in *The Works of Jeremy Bentham*, ed. John Bowring (New York: Russell and Russell, 1962), vol. 6, chap. 28. The materials in square brackets are added by HVH. The orthography of the original has been preserved.—Eds.

1. [The Latin term "coram non judice" means, in a UK legal context, "before one who is not a judge."]
2. In the English books of practice, matter relative to the *onus probandi* is here and there to be found, but no chapter or section is to be found with any such title at the head of it. It is, however, a sort of matter which on one occasion or other is not unfrequently coming into view.
In Peake on Evidence [Thomas Peake, *A Compendium of the Law of Evidence* (London, 1801)], matter relative to this head is to be found in Part I Ch. I inituled, "*Of the General Rules of Evidence*," and in Part II. Ch. V inituled, "*Of the Evidence in Actions on Statutes.*"
3. See Peake, 272.
4. [Alexander Wedderburn, 1st Earl of Rosslyn (1733–1805); became Chief Justice of the court of Common Pleas in 1780.]
5. [Fifty-headed, hundred-handed figure of Greek mythology.]

# 4

# Presumptions and Burden of Proof

RICHARD WHATELY

## Presumption and Burden of proof.

[1] It is a point of great importance to decide in each case, at the outset, in your own mind, and clearly to point out to the hearer, as occasion may serve, on which side the *Presumption* lies, and to which belongs the [onus probandi] *Burden of Proof*. For though it may often be expedient to bring forward more proofs than can be fairly demanded of you, it is always desirable, when this is the case, that it should be *known*, and that the strength of the cause should be estimated accordingly.

[2] According to the most correct use of the term, a "Presumption" in favour of any supposition, means, not (as has been sometimes erroneously imagined) a preponderance of probability in its favour, but, such a *pre-occupation* of the ground, as implies that it must stand good till some sufficient reason is adduced against it; in short, that the *Burden of proof* lies on the side of him who would dispute it.

[3] Thus, it is a well-known principle of the Law, that every man (including a prisoner brought up for trial) is to be *presumed* innocent till his guilt is established. This does not, of course, mean that we are to *take for granted* he is innocent; for if that were the case, he would be entitled to immediate liberation: nor does it mean that it is antecedently *more likely than not* that he is innocent; or, that the majority of these brought to trial are so. It evidently means only that the "burden of proof" lies with the accusers;—that he is not to be called on to prove his innocence, or to be dealt with as a criminal till he has done so; but that they are to bring their charges against him, which if he can repel, he stands acquitted.

[4] Thus again, there is a "presumption" in favour of the right of any individuals or bodies-corporate to the property of which they are in *actual possession*. This does not mean that they are, or are not, *likely* to be the rightful owners: but merely, that no man is to be disturbed in his possessions till some claim

against him shall be established. He is not to be called on to prove his right; but the claimant, to disprove it; on whom consequently the "burden of proof" lies.

## Importance of deciding on which side lies the *onus probandi*.

[5] A moderate portion of common-sense will enable any one to perceive, and to show, on which side the Presumption lies, when once his attention is called to this question; though, for want of attention, it is often overlooked: and on the determination of this question the whole character of a discussion will often very much depend. A body of troops may be perfectly adequate to the defence of a fortress against any attack that may be made on it; and yet, if, ignorant of the advantage they possess, they sally forth into the open field to encounter the enemy, they may suffer a repulse. At any rate, even if strong enough to act on the offensive, they ought still to keep possession of their fortress. In like manner, if you have the "Presumption" on your side, and can but *refute* all the arguments brought against you, you have, for the present at least, gained a victory: but if you abandon this position, by suffering this Presumption to be forgotten, which is in fact *leaving out one of, perhaps, your strongest arguments*, you may appear to be making a feeble attack, instead of a triumphant defense.

[6] Such an obvious case as one of those just stated, will serve to illustrate this principle. Let any one imagine a perfectly unsupported accusation of some offence to be brought against himself; and then let him imagine himself—instead of replying (as of course he would do) by a simple denial, and a defiance of his accuser to prove the charge,—setting himself to establish a negative,—taking on himself the burden of proving his own innocence, by collecting all the circumstances indicative of it that he can muster: and the result would be, in many cases, that this evidence would fall far short of establishing a certainty, and might even have the effect of raising a suspicion against him;[1] he having in fact kept out of sight the important circumstance, that these probabilities in one scale, though of no great weight perhaps in themselves, are to be weighed against absolutely nothing in the other scale.

[7] The following are a few of the cases in which it is important, though very easy, to point out where the presumption lies.

## Presumption in favour of existing institutions.

[8] There is a Presumption in favour of every *existing* institution. Many of these (we will suppose, the majority) may be susceptible of alteration for the better; but still the "Burden of proof" lies with him who proposes an alteration; simply, on the ground that since a change is not a good in itself, he who demands a change should show cause for it. No one is *called on* (though he may find it advisable) to defend an existing institution, till some argument is ad-

duced against it; and that argument ought in fairness to prove, not merely an actual inconvenience, but the possibility of a change for the better.

## Presumption of innocence.

[9] Every book again, as well as person, ought to be presumed harmless (and consequently the copy-right protected by our courts) till something is proved against it. It is a hardship to require a man to prove, either of his book, or of his private life, that there is no ground for any accusation; or else to be denied the protection of his Country. The Burden of proof, in each case, lies fairly on the accuser. I cannot but consider therefore as utterly unreasonable the decisions (which some years ago excited so much attention) to refuse the interference of the Court of Chancery in cases of piracy, whenever there was even any *doubt* whether the book pirated *might* not contain something of an immoral tendency.

## Presumption against a Paradox.

[10] There is a "Presumption" against anything *paradoxical*, i.e., contrary to the prevailing opinion: it may be true; but the Burden of proof lies with him who maintains it; since men are not to be expected to abandon the prevailing belief till some reason is shown.

[11] Hence it is, probably, that many are accustomed to apply "Paradox" as if it were a term of reproach, and implied absurdity or falsity. But correct use is in favour of the etymological sense. If a Paradox is unsupported, it can claim no attention; but if false, it should be censured on *that* ground; but not for being *new*. If true, it is the more important, for being a truth not generally admitted. "Interdum vulgus rectum videt; est ubi peccat."[2] Yet one often hears a charge of "paradox and nonsense" brought forward, as if there were some close connexion between the two. And indeed, in one sense this is the case; for to those who are too dull, or too prejudiced, to admit any notion at variance with those they have been used to entertain (para doxan[3]), *that* may appear nonsense, which to others is sound sense. Thus "Christ crucified" was "to the Jews, a stumbling-block," (paradox,) "and to the Greeks, foolishness;" because the one "required a sign" of a different kind from any that appeared; and the others "sought after wisdom"[4] in their schools of philosophy.

## Christianity, presumptions against and for.

[12] Accordingly there was a Presumption against the Gospel in its first announcement. A Jewish peasant claimed to be the promised Deliverer, in whom all the nations of the Earth were to be blessed. The Burden of proof lay with

Him. No one could be farily called on to admit his pretensions till He showed cause for believing in Him. If He "had not done among them the *works* which none other man did, they had not had sin."⁵

[13] *Now*, the case is reversed. Christianity *exists*; and those who deny the divine origin attributed to it, are bound to show some reasons for assigning to it a human origin: not indeed to prove that it *did* originate in this or that way, without supernatural aid; but to point out some conceivable way in which it *might* have so arisen.

[14] It is indeed highly expedient to bring forward evidences to establish the divine origin of Christianity: but it ought to be more carefully kept in mind than is done by most writers, that all this is an argument "ex abundanti,"⁶ as the phrase is,—over and above what can fairly be called for, till some hypothesis should be framed, to account for the origin of Christianity by human means. The Burden of proof, *now*, lies plainly on him who rejects the Gospel: which, if it were not established by miracles, demands an explanation of the greater miracle,—its having been established, in defiance of all opposition, by human contrivance.

## The Reformation.

[15] The Burden of proof, again, lay on the authors of the Reformation:⁷ they were bound to show cause for every *change* they advocated; and they admitted the fairness of this requisition, and accepted the challenge. But they were *not* bound to show cause for *retaining* what they left unaltered. The Presumption was, in those points, on their side; and they had only to reply to objections. This important distinction is often lost sight of, by those who look at the "doctrines, &c. of the Church of England as constituted at the Reformation," in the mass, without distinguishing the altered from the unaltered parts. The framers of the Articles kept this in mind in their expression respecting infant-baptism, that it "ought by all means to be *retained*." They did not introduce the practice, but left it as they found it; considering the burden to lie on those who denied its existence in the primitive church, to show *when* it did arise.

[16] The case of Episcopacy is exactly parallel: but Hooker⁸ seems to have overlooked this advantage: he sets himself to *prove* the apostolic origin of the institution, as if his task had been to *introduce it*.⁹ Whatever force there may be in arguments so adduced, it is plain they must have far *more* force if the important Presumption be kept in view, that the institution had notoriously existed many ages, and that consequently, even if there had been no direct evidence for its being coeval with Christianity, it might fairly be at least supposed to be so, till some other period should be pointed out at which it had been introduced as an innovation.

## Tradition.

[17] In the case of any *doctrines* again, professing to be essential parts of the Gospel-revelation, the fair *presumption* is, that we shall find all such distinctly declared in Scripture. And again, in respect of commands or prohibitions as to any point, which our Lord or his Apostles did deliver, there is a presumption that Christians are bound to comply. If any one maintains, on the ground of Tradition, the necessity of some additional article of faith (as for instance that of Purgatory) or the propriety of a departure from the New Testament precepts (as for instance in the denial of the cup to the Laity in the Eucharist) the burden of proof lies with him. We are not called upon to prove that there is no tradition to the purpose;—much less, that no tradition can have any weight at all in *any case*. It is for *him* to prove, not merely generally, that there is such a thing as Tradition, and that it is entitled to respect, but that there is a tradition relative to each of the points which he thus maintains; and that such tradition is, in each point, sufficient to establish that point. For want of observing this rule, the most vague and interminable disputes have often been carried on respecting Tradition, generally.

[18] It should also be remarked under this head, that in any one question the Presumption will often be found to lie on different sides, in respect of different parties. *E.G.*, In the question between a member of the Church of England, and a Presbyterian, or a member of any other Church, on which side does the Presumption lie? Evidently, to each, in favour of the religious community to which he at present belongs. He is not to separate from the Church of which he is a member, without having some sufficient reason to allege.

[19] A Presumption evidently admits of various degrees of strength, from the very faintest, up to a complete and confident acquiescence.

## Deference.

[20] The person, Body, or book, in favour of whose decisions there is a certain Presumption, is said to have, so far, "Authority"; in the strict sense of the word.[10] And a recognition of this kind of Authority,—an *habitual* Presumption in favour of such a one's decision or opinions—is usually called "Deference."

[21] It will often happen that this deference is not recognized by either party. A man will perhaps disavow with scorn all deference for some person,—a son or daughter perhaps, or an humble companion,—whom he treats, in manner, with familiar superiority; and the other party will as readily and sincerely renounce all pretension to Authority; and yet there may be that "habitual Presumption" in the mind of the one, in favour of the opinions, suggestions, &c. of the other, which we have called Deference. These parties, however, are not

using the *words* in a different sense, but are unaware of the state of the *fact*. There is a Deference; but *unconscious*.

## Arrogance.

[22] Those who are habitually wanting in Deference towards such as we think entitled to it, are usually called "*arrogant*"; the word being used as distinguished from self-*conceited*, *proud*, *vain*, and other kindred words. Such persons may be described as having an habitual and exclusive "self-deference."

[23] Of course the persons and works which are looked up to as high authorities, or the contrary, will differ in each Age, Country, and Class of men. But most people are disposed,—measuring another by their own judgment,—to reckon *him* arrogant who disregards what *they* deem the best authorities. That man however may most fairly and strictly be so called who has no deference for those whom he *himself* thinks most highly of. And instances may be found of this character; *i.e.*, of a man who shall hold in high estimation the ability and knowledge of certain persons—rating them perhaps above himself—whose most deliberate judgments, even on matters they are most conversant with, he will nevertheless utterly set at naught, in *each particular case* that arises, if they happen not to coincide with the idea that first strikes his mind.

## Admiration and deference, distinct.

[24] For it is to be observed that *admiration, esteem*, and *concurrence in opinion*, are quite distinct from "Deference," and not necessarily accompanied by it. If any one makes what appears to us to be a very just remark, or if we acquiesce in what he proposes on the account of the reasons he alleges,—this is not Deference. And if this has happened many times, and we thence form a high opinion of his ability, this again neither implies, nor even necessarily produces Deference; though in reason, such *ought* to be the result. But one may often find a person conversant with two others, A, and B, and estimating A without hesitation as the superior man of the two; and yet, in any case whatever that may arise, where A and B differ in their judgment, taking for granted at once that B is in the right.

## Grounds of deference.

[25] Admiration, esteem, &c. are more the result of a judgment of the *understanding*; (though often of an erroneous one;) "Deference" is apt to depend on *feelings*;—often, on whimsical and unaccountable feelings. It is often yielded to a vigorous *claim*,—to an authoritative and overbearing demeanour. With

others, of an opposite character, a soothing, insinuating, flattering, and seemingly submissive demeanour will often gain great influence. They will yield to those who seem to yield to them; the others, to those who seem resolved to yield to no one. Those who seek to gain adherents to their School or Party by putting forth the claim of *antiquity* in favour of their tenets, are likely to be peculiarly successful among those of an arrogant disposition. A book or a Tradition of a thousand years old, appears to be rather a *thing* than a *person*; and will thence often be regarded with blind deference by those who are prone to treat their contemporaries with insolent contempt, but who "will not go to compare with an old man."[11] They will submit readily to the authority of men who flourished fifteen or sixteen centuries ago, and whom, if now living, they would not treat with decent respect.

[26] With some persons, again, Authority seems to act according to the law of Gravitation; inversely as the squares of the *distances*. They are inclined to be of the opinion of the person who is *nearest*. Personal *Affection*, again, in many minds, generates Deference. They form a habit of first, *wishing*, secondly, *hoping*, and thirdly, *believing* a person to be in the right, whom they would be *sorry* to think mistaken. In a state of morbid depression of spirits, the same cause leads to the opposite effect. To a person in that state, whatever he would be "sorry to think" appears probable; and consequently there is a Presumption in his mind *against* the opinions, measures, &c. of those he is most attached to. That the degree of Deference felt for any one's Authority ought to depend not on our feelings but on our judgment, it is almost superfluous to remark; but it is important to remember that there is a danger on *both* sides;—of an unreasonable Presumption either on the side of our wishes, or *against* them.

## Deference as to particular points.

[27] It is obvious that Deference ought to be, and usually is, felt in reference to particular points. One has a deference for his physician, in questions of medicine; and for his bailiff, in questions of farming; but not *vice versa*. And accordingly, Deference may be misplaced in respect of the *subject*, as well as of the person. It is conceivable that one may have a *due* degree of Deference, and an *excess* of it, and a *deficiency* of it, all towards the same person, but in respect of different points.

## Men often self-deceived as to their feelings of deference.

[28] It is worth remarking, as a curious fact, that men are liable to deceive themselves as to the degree of Deference they feel towards various persons. But the case is the same (as I shall have occasion hereafter to point out[12]) with

many other feelings also, such as pity, contempt, love, joy, &c.; in respect of which we are apt to mistake the *conviction* that such and such an object *deserves* pity, contempt, &c. for the *feeling* itself; which often does not accompany that conviction. And so also, a person will perhaps describe himself (with sincere good faith) as feeling great Deference towards someone, on the ground of his *believing* him to be *entitled* to it; and perhaps being really indignant against *any one else* who does not manifest it. Sometimes again, one will mistake for a feeling of deference his *concurrence* with another's views, and admiration of what is said or done by him. But this, as has been observed above, does not imply Deference, if the same approbation would have been bestowed on the same views, supposing them stated and maintained in an anonymous paper. The converse mistake is equally natural. A man may fancy that, in each case, he acquiesces in such a one's views or suggestions from the dictates of judgment, and for the reasons given; ("What she does seems wisest, virtuousest, discreetist, best";[13]) when yet perhaps the very same reasons, coming from another, would have been rejected.

## Statements of fact liable to be disregarded, when coming from those whose judgment is undervalued.

[29] It is worth observing also, that, though, as has been above remarked, (ch. ii. §4) questions of *fact*, and of *opinion*, ought to be decided on very different grounds, yet, with many persons, a statement of facts is very little attended to when coming from one for whose judgment (though they do not deliberately doubt his veracity) they have little or no Deference. For, by common minds, the above distinction, between matters of fact and opinion, is but imperfectly apprehended.[14] It is not therefore always superfluous to endeavour to raise a Presumption in favour of the judgment of one whom you wish to obtain credit, even in respect of matters in which judgment has, properly, little or no concern.

[30] It is usual, and not unreasonable, to pay more Deference—other points being equal—to the decisions of a *Council*, or *Assembly* of any kind, (embodied in a Manifesto, Act of Parliament, Speech from the Throne, Report, Set of Articles, &c.,) than to those of an individual, equal, or even superior to any member of such Assembly. But in one point,—and it is a very important one, though usually overlooked,—this rule is subject to something of an exception; which may be thus stated: in any composition of an individual who is deemed worthy of respect, we presume that whatever he says must have *some* meaning,—must tend toward *some* object which could not be equally accomplished by *erasing* the whole passage. He is expected never to lay down a rule, and then add exceptions, nearly, or altogether coextensive with it; nor in any way to have so modified and explained away some assertion, that each portion

of a passage shall be virtually neutralized by the other. Now if we interpret in this way any *joint*-production of several persons, we shall often be led into mistakes. For, those who have had experience as members of any deliberative Assembly, know by that experience (what indeed any one might conjecture) how much *compromise* will usually take place between conflicting opinions, and what will naturally thence result. One person, e.g., will urge the insertion of something, which another disapproves; and the result will usually be, after much debate, something of what is properly called "splitting the difference:" the insertion will be made, but accompanied with such limitations and modifications as nearly to nullify it. A fence will be erected in compliance with one party, and a *gap* will be left in it to gratify another. And again, there will often be, in some document of this class, a total *silence* on some point whereon, perhaps, most of the Assembly would have preferred giving a decision but could not agree *what* decision it should be.

[31] A like character will often be found also in the composition of a single individual, when his object is to *conciliate several parties* whose views are conflicting. He then *represents*, as it were, in his own mind, an Assembly composed of those parties.

[32] Any one therefore who should think himself bound in due deference for the collective wisdom of some august Assembly, to interpret any joint-composition of it, exactly as he would that of a respectable individual, and never to attribute to it anything of that partially-inconsistent and almost nugatory character which the writings of a sensible and upright man would be exempt from,—any one, I say, who should proceed (as many do) on such a principle, would be often greatly misled.[15]

[33] It may be added, that the Deference due to the decisions of an Assembly, is sometimes, erroneously, transferred to those of some individual member of it; that is, it is sometimes taken for granted, that what they have, jointly, put forth, is to be interpreted by what he, in his own writings, may have said on the same points. And yet it may sometimes be the fact, that the strong expression of his sentiments in his own writings, may have been omitted in the *joint*-production of the Assembly, precisely because *not* approved by the majority in that Assembly.

## Transferring the Burden of proof.

[34] It is to be observed, that a Presumption may be *rebutted* by an opposite Presumption, so as to shift the Burden of proof to the other side. *E.G.*, Suppose you had advised the removal of some *existing* restriction: you might be, in the first instance, called on to take the Burden of proof, and allege your reasons for the change, on the ground that there is a Presumption against every

Change. But you might fairly reply, "True, but there is another Presumption which rebuts the former; every *Restriction* is in itself an evil;[16] and therefore there is a Presumption in favour of its removal, unless it can be shown necessary for prevention of some greater evil: I am not bound to allege any *specific* inconvenience; if the restriction is *unnecessary*, *that* is reason enough for its abolition: its defenders therefore are fairly called on to prove its necessity."[17]

[35] Again, in reference to the prevailing opinion, that the "*Nathanael*" of John's Gospel was the same person as the Apostle "*Bartholomew*" mentioned in the others, an intelligent friend once remarked to me that *two names* afford a "prima facie" Presumption of two persons. But the name of *Bar*tholomew, being a "Patronymic," (like Simon Peter's designation *Bar*-Jona, and Joseph's Sirname of *Bar*sabas, mentioned in Acts;—he being probably the same with the Apostle "Joseph Barnabas," &c.,) affords a Counter-presumption that he must have had *another* name, to distinguish him from his own kindred. And thus we are left open to the arguments drawn from the omission, by the other Evangelists, of the name of Nathanael,—evidently a very eminent disciple,—the omission by John of the name of the Apostle Bartholomew,—and the recorded intimacy with the Apostle Philip.

## Presumption against Logic.

[36] In one of Lord Dudley's (lately published) letters to Bishop Copleston, of the date of 1814, he adduces a presumption against the Science of Logic, that it was sedulously cultivated during the dark periods when the intellectual powers of mankind seemed nearly paralysed,—when no discoveries were made, and when various errors were wide-spread and deep-rooted: and that when the mental activity of the world revived, and philosophical inquiry flourished, and bore its fruits, Logical studies fell into decay and contempt. To many minds this would appear a decisive argument. The author himself was too acute to see more in it than—what it certainly is—a fair Presumption. And he would probably have owned that it might be met by a counter-presumption.

## Counter-presumption.

[37] When any science or pursuit has been unduly and unwisely followed, to the neglect of others, and has even been intruded into their province, we may presume that a *re-action* will be likely to ensue, and an equally excessive contempt, or dread, or abhorrence, to succeed.[18] And the same kind of re-action occurs in every department of life. It is thus that the thraldom of gross superstition, and tyrannical priestcraft, have so often led to irreligion. It is thus that "several valuable medicines, which when first introduced, were proclaimed,

each as a panacea, infallible in the most opposite disorders, fell, consequently, in many instances, for a time, into total disuse; though afterwards they were established in their just estimation, and employed conformably to their real properties."[19]

[38] So, it might have been said, in the present case, the mistaken and absurd cultivation of Logic during ages of great intellectual darkness, might be expected to produce, in a subsequent age of comparative light, an association in men's minds, of Logic, with the idea of apathetic ignorance, prejudice, and adherence to error; so that the legitimate uses and just value of Logic, supposing it to have any, would be likely to be scornfully overlooked. Our ancestors, it might have been said, having neglected to raise fresh crops of corn, and contended themselves with vainly thrashing over and over again the same straw, and winnowing the same chaff, it might be expected that their descendants would, for a time, regard the very operations of thrashing and winnowing with contempt, and would attempt to grind corn, chaff, and straw, all together.

[39] Such might have been, at that time, a statement of the counter-presumption on this point.

## Presumption overthrown.

[40] Subsequently, the presumption in question has been completely done away. And it is a curious circumstance that the very person to whom that letter was addressed should have witnessed so great a change in public opinion, brought about (in great measure through *his* own instrumentality) within a small portion of the short interval between the writing of that letter and its publication, that the whole ground of Lord Dudley's argument is cut away. During that interval the Article on Logic in the "Encyclopaedia Metropolitana"[20] (great part of the matter of it having been furnished by Bishop Copleston) was drawn up; and attracted so much attention as to occasion its publication in a separate volume: and this has been repeatedly reprinted both at home and in the United States of America, (where it is used as a text-book in, I believe, every College throughout the Union,) with a continually increasing circulation, which all the various attempts made to decry the study, seem only to augment: while sundry abridgements, and other elementary treatises on the subject, have been appearing with continually-increased frequency.

[41] Certainly, Lord Dudley, were he *now* living, would not speak of the "general neglect and contempt" of Logic at present: though so many branches of Science, Philosophy, and Literature, have greatly flourished during the interval.

[42] The popularity indeed, or unpopularity, of any study, does not furnish, alone, a decisive proof of its value: but it is plain that a presumption—whether

strong or weak—which is based on the fact of general neglect and contempt, is destroyed, when these have ceased.

[43] It has been alleged, however, that "the Science of Mind" has not flourished during the last twenty years; and that consequently the present is to be accounted such a dark period as Lord Dudley alludes to.

[44] Supposing the statement to be well-founded, it is nothing to the purpose; since Lord Dudley was speaking, not, of any one science in particular, but of the absence or presence of intellectual cultivation, and of knowledge, generally:—the depressed or flourishing condition of Science, Arts, and Philosophy on the whole.

[45] But as for the state of the "science of mind" at any given period, *that* is altogether a matter of opinion. It was probably considered by the Schoolmen to be most flourishing in the ages which we call "dark." And it is not unlikely that the increased attention bestowed, of late years, on Logic, and the diminished popularity of those Metaphysicians who have written against it, may appear to the disciples of these last a proof of the low state (as it is, to Logical students, a sign of the improving state) of "the Science of Mind." That is, regarding the prevalence at present of logical studies as a sign that ours is "a dark age," this supposed darkness, again, furnishes in turn a sign that these studies flourish only in a dark age!

## Presumptions for and against the learned.

[46] Again, there is (according to the old maxim of "peritis credendum est in arte sua"[21]) a presumption, (and a fair one,) in respect of each question, in favour of the judgment of the most eminent men in the department it pertains to;—of eminent physicians, e.g., in respect of medical questions,—of theologians, in theological, &c. And by this presumption many of the Jews in our Lord's time seem to have been influenced, when they said, "have any of the Rulers, or of the Pharisees believed on Him?"

[47] But there is a counter-presumption, arising from the circumstance that men eminent in any department are likely to regard with jealousy any one who professes to bring to light something unknown to themselves; especially if it promise to *supersede*, if established, much of what they have been accustomed to learn, and teach, and practice. And moreover, in respect of the medical profession, there is an obvious danger of a man's being regarded as a dangerous experimentalist who adopts any novelty, and of his thus losing practice even among such as may regard him with admiration as a philosopher. In confirmation of this, it may be sufficient to advert to the cases of Harvey[22] and Jenner.[23] Harvey's discovery of the circulation of the blood is said to have lost him most of his practice, and to have been rejected by every physician in Europe above

the age of forty. And Jenner's discovery of vaccination had, in a minor degree, similar results.

[48] There is also this additional counter-presumption against the judgment of the proficients in any department; that they are prone to a bias in favour of everything that give the most palpable *superiority* to themselves over the uninitiated, [the Idiotae,²⁴] and affords the greatest scope for the employment and display of their own peculiar acquirements. Thus, e.g., if there be two possible interpretations of some Clause in an Act of Parliament, one of which appears obvious to every reader of plain good sense, and the other can be supported only by ingenious and far-fetched legal subtlety, a practical lawyer will be liable to a bias in favour of the latter, as setting forth the more prominently his own peculiar qualifications. And on this principle in great measure seems founded Bacon's valuable remark; "harum artium sæpe pravus fit usus, *ne sit nullus*."²⁵ Rather than let their knowledge and skill lie idle, they will be tempted to misapply them; like a schoolboy, who, when possessed of a knife, is for trying its edge on everything that comes in his way. On the whole, accordingly, I think that of these two opposite presumptions, the counter-presumption has often as much weight as the other, and sometimes more.

## No necessary advantage to the side on which the presumption lies.

[49] It might be hastily imagined, that there is necessarily an *advantage* in having the presumption on one's side, and the burden of proof on the adversary's. But it is often much the reverse. *E.G.*, "In no other instance perhaps," (says Dr. Hawkins, in his valuable "Essay on Tradition,") "besides that of Religion, do men commit the very illogical mistake, of first canvassing all the objections against any particular system whose pretensions to truth they would examine, before they consider the direct arguments in its favour."²⁶ But why, it may be asked, *do* they make such a mistake in *this* case? An answer which I think would apply to a large proportion of such persons, is this: because a man having been brought up in a Christian-Country, has lived perhaps among such as have been accustomed from their infancy to *take for granted* the truth of their religion, and even to regard an *uninquiring* assent as a mark of commendable *faith*; and hence he has probably never even thought of proposing to himself the question,—Why should I receive Christianity as a divine revelation? Christianity being nothing *new* to him, and the *presumption* being in favour of it, while the burden of proof lies on its opponents, he is not stimulated to seek reasons for believing it, till he finds it controverted. And when it *is* controverted,—when an opponent urges—How do you reconcile this, and that, and the other, with the idea of a divine revelation? These objections strike by their *novelty*—by their being opposed to what is generally received. He is thus ex-

cited to inquiry; which he sets about,—naturally enough, but very unwisely,—by seeking for answers to all these objections: and fancies that unless they can all be satisfactorily solved, he ought not to receive the religion.[27] "As if (says the author already cited) there could not be truth, and truth supported by irrefragable arguments, and yet at the same time obnoxious to objections, numerous, plausible, and by no means easy of solution." "There are objections (said Dr. Johnson[28]) against a *plenum* and objections against a *vacuum*; but one of them must be true." He adds that "sensible men really desirous of discovering the truth, will perceive that reason directs them to examine first the argument in favour of that side of the question, where the first presumption of truth appears. And the presumption is manifestly in favour of that religious creed already adopted by the country. . . . Their very earliest inquiry therefore must be into the direct arguments, for the authority of that book on which their country rests its religion."

[50] But reasonable as such procedure is, there is, as I have said, a strong temptation, and one which should be carefully guarded against, to adopt the opposite course;—to attend first to the objections which are brought against what is established, and which, for that very reason, rouse the mind from a state of apathy. Accordingly, I have not found that this "very logical mistake" is by any means peculiar to the case of religion.

[51] When Christianity was first preached, the state of things was reversed. The Presumption was against it, as being a novelty. "Seeing that these things *cannot be spoken against*, ye ought to be *quiet*," was a sentiment which favoured an indolent acquiescence in the old Pagan worship. The stimulus of novelty was all on the side of those who came to overthrow this, by a new religion. The first inquiry of any one who at all attended to the subject, must have been, not,— What are the objections to Christianity?—but on what grounds do these men call on me to receive them as divine messengers? And the same appears to be the case with those Polynesians among whom our Missionaries are labouring: they begin by inquiring—"Why should we receive this religion?" And those of them accordingly who *have* embraced it, appear to be Christians on a much more rational and deliberate conviction than many among *us*, even of those who, in general maturity of intellect and civilisation, are advanced considerably beyond those Islanders.

[52] I am not depreciating the inestimable advantages of a religious education; but, pointing out the *peculiar* temptations which accompany it. The Jews and Pagans had, in their early prejudices, greater difficulties to surmount than ours; but they were difficulties *of a different kind*.[29]

[53] Thus much may suffice to show the importance of taking this preliminary view of the state of each question to be discussed.

# Notes

From Richard Whately, *Elements of Rhetoric: Comprising an Analysis of the Laws of Moral Evidence and of Persuasion, with Rules for Argumentative Composition and Elocution*, 7th ed., rev. (London: John W. Parker, 1846; repr., Carbondale: Southern Illinois University Press, 1963). The paragraph numbering in square brackets at the beginning of paragraphs has been added for ease of reference. Endnotes in square brackets have been added by HVH. The orthography of the original has been preserved.—Eds.

1. Hence the French proverb, "Qui s'excuse, s'accuse."
2. ["Sometimes the masses see what is right and sometimes they are mistaken." Horace, *Epistles*, 2.1.63.]
3. [para doxon]
4. [1 Cor. 1:23]
5. [John 15:24]
6. ["out of abundance, overflowing"]
7. [Sixteenth-century changes to the Roman Catholic church.]
8. [Richard Hooker, sixteenth-century English theologian.]
9. On the ambiguous employment of the phrase "divine origin"—a great source of confusion among theologians—I have offered some remarks in Essay II. "On the Kingdom of Christ," §17. 4th edit. [Whately, *The Kingdom of Christ Delineated in Two Essays* (London: B. Fellowes, 1841).]
10. See article "Authority," in appendix to *Elements of Logic*. [In that article a primary sense of "authority" is identified as involving judgment, testimony, or example.]
11. Shakespeare, *Twelfth Night*. [Act 1, scene 3.]
12. Part II. ch 1, §2. [Whately, *Elements of Rhetoric*.]
13. Milton. [*Paradise Lost*, bk. 7.]
14. It is a curious characteristic of some of our older writers, that they are accustomed to cite authorities,—and that most profusely,—for matters of opinion, while for facts they often omit to cite any.
15. In studying the Scriptures we must be on our guard against the converse-mistake, of interpreting the Bible as if it were *one* Book, the joint-work of the Sacred Writers, instead of, what it is, several distinct books, written by individuals independently of each other.
16. See "Charges and other Tracts," p. 447. [Whately, *Charges and Other Tracts* (London: B. Fellowes, 1836).]
17. See Essay II. "On the Kingdom of Christ," §33.
18. I dwelt on this subject in a Charge to the Diocese of Dublin, 1843.
19. *Elements of Logic*, Pref. p. x.
20. [Whately is referring to the article that eventually became his *Elements of Logic*.]
21. ["One ought to believe the experts in their own areas of expertise."]

22. [William Harvey (1578–1657), Englishman who discovered the circulation of the blood.]

23. [Edward Jenner (1749–1823), English physician and pioneer of vaccination.]

24. [Latin for "less educated, inexperienced persons."]

25. ["Often improper use is made of these arts so there is no use for them at all."]

26. [Edward Hawkins (1789–1882), English academic and university officer. Whately is referring to Hawkins, *A Dissertation upon the Use and Importance of Unauthoritative Tradition* (Oxford: Baxter, 1819), 82.]

27. See the Lessons on Objections, in the "Easy Lessons on Christian Evidences" [(London: John W. Parker, 1838)].

28. [Samuel Johnson (1709–1784), English poet, quoted in *Life of Samuel Johnson, LL.D.*, by James Boswell (1791).]

29. [*Elements of*] *Logic*, Appendix.

# 5

# The Sportsman's Rejoinder

## RICHARD WHATELY

There are certain kinds of argument recounted and named by Logical writers, which we should by no means universally call Fallacies; but which *when un-fairly* used, and *so far as they are* fallacious, may very well be referred to the present head;[1] such as the "*argumentum ad hominem*," [or "personal argument,"] "*argumentum ad verecundiam*," "*argumentum ad populum*," &c., all of them regarded as contradistinguished from "*argumentum ad rem*;" or, according to others (meaning probably the very same thing) "*ad judicium*." These have all been described in the lax and popular language before alluded to, but not scientifically: the "*argumentum ad hominem*," they say, "is addressed to the peculiar circumstances, character, avowed opinions, or past conduct of the individual, and therefore has a reference to him only, and does not bear directly and absolutely on the real question, as the '*argumentum ad rem*' does:" in like manner, the "*argumentum ad verecundiam*" is described as an appeal to our reverence for some respected authority, some venerable institution, &c. and the "*argumentum ad populum*," as an appeal to the prejudices, passions, &c. of the multitude; and so of the rest. Along with these is usually enumerated "*argumentum ad ignorantiam*," which is here omitted as being evidently nothing more than the employment of *some* kind of Fallacy, in the widest sense of that word, toward such as are likely to be deceived by it.

It appears then (to speak rather more technically) that in the "*argumentum ad hominem*" the conclusion which actually is established, is not the *absolute* and *general* one in question, but *relative* and particular; viz. not that "such and such is the fact," but that "*this man* is bound to admit it, in conformity to his principles of Reasoning, or in consistency with his own conduct, situation," &c.[2] Such a conclusion it is often both allowable and necessary to establish, in order to silence those who will not yield to fair general argument; or to convince those whose weakness and prejudices would not allow them to assign to it its due weight. It is thus that our Lord on many occasions silences the cavils of the Jews; as in the vindication of healing on the Sabbath, which is parallelled by the authorized practice of drawing out a beast that has fallen into a pit. All this, as we have said, is perfectly fair, provided it be done plainly, and *avowedly*; but if you attempt to *substitute* this partial and relative Conclusion for a more general one—if you triumph as having established your proposition absolutely and universally, from having established it, in reality, only as far as it relates to your opponent, then you are guilty of a Fallacy of the kind which we are now treating of; your Conclusion is not in reality that which was, by your own account, proposed to be proved. The fallaciousness depends upon the *deceit*, or attempt to deceive. The same observations will *apply* to "*argumentum ad verecundiam*," and the rest.

## Notes

From Whately's *Elements of Logic*, 9th ed. (London: Longmans, Green, 1875), 142–43. In square brackets are notes by HVH. The orthography of the original has been preserved.—Eds.

1. [Fallacies of irrelevant conclusion, commonly called *ignoratio elenchi*. Whately, *Elements of Logic*, 139.]

2. The "*argumentum ad hominem*" will often have the effect of shifting the *burden of proof*, not unjustly to the adversary. (See *Rhet.* Part 1, Chap. III., §2. [Whately's *Elements of Rhetoric*. See this volume, ch. 4.]) A common instance is the defense, certainly the readiest and most concise, frequently urged by the Sportsman, when accused of barbarity in sacrificing unoffending hares or trout to this amusement: he replies, as he may safely do, to most of his assailants, "why do you feed on the flesh of the harmless sheep and ox?" and that this answer presses hard, is manifested by its being usually opposed by a *palpable falsehood*; viz. that the animals which are killed for food are sacrificed to our *necessities*; though not only men *can*, but a large proportion (probably a great majority) of the human race actually *do*, subsist in health and vigour without flesh-diet; and the earth would support a much greater human population were such a practice universal.

When shamed out of this argument they sometimes urge that the brute creation would overrun the earth, if we did not kill them for food; an argument, which if it were valid at all, would not justify their feeding on *fish*; though, if fairly followed up, it *would* justify Swift's proposal for keeping down the excessive population of Ireland. The true reason, viz. that they eat flesh for the gratification of the palate, and have a taste for the pleasures of the table, though not for the sports of the field, is one which they do not like to assign.

# 6

# The Burden of Proof

## Alfred Sidgwick

Supposing a Thesis sufficiently free from the taint of unreality,[1] two other main objections or opportunities for attack remain. And the first of these, as already said, is the objection that no proof has been attempted,—that the thesis is a *mere* assertion, standing entirely without support or evidence.

Evidence, it should be at once noticed, is not here used in the more restricted sense that would contrast it (e.g.) with "authority" or with "hearsay;" but as broadly as possible, so as to include the weakest kinds of evidence as well as the strongest. It is just as truly an argument, for example, however fragile, to claim that a given assertion is true because it occurs in a certain book, or was made by a certain person, as any other "reason given for belief" would be. The contrast between supported and unsupported assertions does not depend on the strength or weakness of the reasons, but on whether or not reasons of any kind are given. The full question as to the burden of Proof is sufficiently confusing in itself, without our introducing further entanglements prematurely.

Two cases are to be distinguished:—(1) Where an assertion is put forward simply as "self-evident," or free from all need of Proof; and (2) where the assertor supposes (or tries to lead his audience to suppose) that his sole concern as assertor is to frustrate, one by one, attempts at Disproof made by some one else.

The first case need not detain us long. For while fully admitting that without some "self-evident" truths, no Proof of any assertion would be possible, it can hardly be denied that what seems self-evident to one person may seem to another to stand much in need of external support. And since the whole meaning of the Need of Proof is need as felt by the audience, and not as the assertor happens to think the audience ought to feel it, they, and not he, must be the arbiters. If the assertion is not to them self-evident, they are under actual disability to believe it until external evidence is produced. I am speaking, of course, of genuine belief, intelligent and rational, and not of mere voluntary acceptance of a formula, as an act of obedience or otherwise. It may, indeed, often happen that the grounds are so numerous, or have been so long forgotten through disuse, that their production will be difficult or impossible. Deep-lying and complicated beliefs, especially when illumined by emotion, or when the more physical element in them is prominent, are very liable to this difficulty,—the beliefs (e.g.) on which our likes and dislikes of persons or of systems, or of courses of actions, are founded. But none the less unsatisfactory must such beliefs remain to an audience not already convinced, until the grounds can be openly brought forward and examined: and our concern is, of course, entirely with the point of view from which the assertion is still a *thesis*, and not with that from which it is a firmly established conclusion. Until the grounds can be examined no test is possible: the assertion may or may not be true, for all the audience can say. Against the honest objection, "This is not self-evident to *me*," there is clearly no appeal; and no remedy except through the production of real external evidence.

The second case, however, is far more complicated; sufficiently so, in fact, to have notoriously confused the mind of no less a logician than Archbishop Whately.[2] This is another of the numerous cases where statement is easy but application difficult, and where the whole practical value depends on the application. Stated shortly, the fundamental rule is that "He who asserts must prove;"[3] and so long as an assertion is undisputed, difficulty cannot arise. But the chief source of real perplexity lies in attempting to keep a clear line between denying a thesis, and merely reserving judgment,[4] or between disputing an argument and merely asking to have it expanded and made satisfactory. This, at least, is one of the points at which confusion is in the first place most apt to creep in. It is obvious that an unsupported assertion may or may not be true, and it should be carefully noted that the absence of produced evidence,—or even the absence of the possibility of producing evidence,—is a very different thing from Disproof. Where nothing *is* said either for or against a thesis, its truth simply remains an open question; and where nothing *can* be said, the doubt is only more permanent in character, not otherwise more triumphant. The objection, "This is bare assertion," does not attack directly the truth of the assertion in question, but attacks the supposition that such truth is as yet established. Hence assertions which are confessedly mere suggestions escape unscathed, since all the harm which the doctrine of the burden of proof can do to them is done already, and willingly, by their assertor himself. It is only where an assertion is definitely made that the grounds of belief can be demanded with any meaning.

The simple statement of the rule, that "he who asserts must prove," needs, however, certain explanations before it can be accepted in its entirety: and the best way to bring these forward seems to be by pushing the simple rule into its extreme cases. In the first place, then, if the burden of proving lies always on him who asserts, it is clear that whoever asserts that a thesis is false must accept a burden too: and also that he who asserts a reason as sufficient, or claims that it is certainly insufficient, is in exactly the same position. These three cases do not present much difficulty, and will, I think, be readily admitted by all.

Suppose, for example, I assert some article of popular faith,—such as that women ought not to enter the learned professions; my audience may either accept the assertion offhand, or deny it offhand, or be content to ask for reasons. In the first case the burden passes simply unnoticed. In the second case, the audience, as assertors accept a burden of their own. In the third case, the burden rests on me, just as it would if I proclaimed the most startling novelty. For the doubt may be suggested that though widely believed, the assertion is possibly without secure foundation. That is to say, two courses are now open to me—unless my audience are unusually feeble disputers—either to take my stand on the bare unsupported assertion, and so leave my questioner certainly unconvinced; or else to attempt to remove the burden by producing the best available reason. If I adopt the latter course, it is clear that any permanent removal of the burden depends on the strength of the evidence brought forward. But the difficulty is, that at every stage of an argument the line between interrogation and flat denial is often hard to preserve, and a sophist, when pushed by awkward questions, will always try to shift the burden upon his questioner. Thus, I may perhaps argue, in favour of women's restrictions, that "one needs to know that a given innovation is *not* dangerous, before proceeding to say confidently that the time has come when it may be made." Very true, but I am now shifting my own ground, and trying to fasten on my questioner a positive assertion which he has never made. I have quite ignored the third alternative that lies between "saying confidently that the time has come" and my own equally confident original assertion that such time has *not* yet arrived; namely, the alternative of holding my tongue, or at least of softening assertion into mere suggestion and asking modestly to hear the possible objections. If my opponent understands the doctrine of the burden of proof, he naturally proceeds to point out my mistake. We need not develop this particular argument any further, since enough has been shown to illustrate the point immediately before us. Whatever reasons I may produce, so long as difficulties in seeing their cogency are genuinely felt, it is clearly my concern to remove them if I can.

Secondly, it may seem undeniable that even the most cautious sceptic cannot escape a certain responsibility. The burden of proof must rest on him who asserts that an assertion is *doubtful*, just as much as on him who asserts it is true or untrue. But two very different meanings may be distinguished, in calling an assertion doubtful,—the one, that I (the objector) feel a doubt; the other, that you (the assertor) *ought* to feel one. If I merely intend the former of these two meanings, my responsibility (which may still be fully admitted) applies not at all to the point at issue, but to a matter of side-interest,—the question whether

I am, or am not, honest in making the demand. It is conceivable that I shall not take any pains at all to avoid the imputation of quibbling. The sceptic may in general be more easily content to leave the other side alone. We are seldom as anxious to prove our ignorance or obtuseness as to prove our knowledge or insight, and hence the sceptic may cheerfully neglect such burden as falls on him. And, in any case, the course he chooses to take in this matter does not affect the point at issue between the two parties.

Lastly, it follows that even he who asserts the most widely accepted doctrine cannot escape the "burden" of supporting it by reasons. The burden of proof rests, for example, on those who maintain the theory of gravitation or of the rotundity of the earth, just as truly as on anyone who should set up for his thesis the denial of either: the difference is that in asserting such truths as these the burden is apt to pass unnoticed, from the fact that the evidence is strong enough to shift it easily, while in denying them the burden might really be felt as a serious weight. And this leads us to speak of the chief practical difficulty in the matter,—the point where Practice demands that inquiry shall be stifled.

Whately's doctrine of the burden of proof[5] was brought forward, as his readers will remember, partly for the purpose of annihilating Infidelity by a short and easy method: but it is none the less worth considering in itself, since the confusion into which he fell is a very excusable one, though probably not often effective against the more modern kind of Infidel. "There is a Presumption," he writes, "in favour of every *existing* institution"[6] [. . .] "Christianity *exists*; and those who deny the divine origin attributed to it are bound to show some reason for assigning to it a human origin."[7] Of course, there is "a presumption in favour of every existing institution." Since it already exists, any one wishing to abolish or alter it must, of course, in the first place make an assertion to that effect, and also produce his reasons,—or else nothing will probably be done. But a presumption of this kind is a very different thing from a presumption that *an assertion made by an existing institution is true.* Various forms of paganism exist; are we therefore to believe without inquiry whatever their followers may choose to assert about them? No doubt this verbal ambiguity was complicated also with another confusion,—that between *denying* and *questioning* the divine origin of the institution: the Archbishop very naturally failed to put himself exactly in the position of a real unbeliever, and was considering only the case of one who should set out to prove *to a believer* that his belief was misplaced. In such a case certainly the burden would in the first place lie on the infidel, as being the person making the assertion. But it is surely not often that infidels are so generous. Or rather, to put it more fairly, they have not the same reason to be anxious to convert believers as the latter have (admittedly) to convert them,—since no infidel pretends to believe that a Christian will miss incalculable benefits on account of his Christianity. Hence it is the unbelievers who really take the unassertive position, not professing to have any valuable information on the points directly in question, which information they are eager to impress on the other side; but quietly willing to examine (with minds, at least professedly, open and candid) any assertion brought forward and supported. It is the believer whose mind—even on his own showing—is no longer open: he it is who claims to have already weighed all the arguments and arrived at a firm decision; who claims the possession of valuable information which he is burning to impart,—information so valuable that, except on the plea of extreme difficulty in producing unexploded[8] reasons, it seems almost cruelty on his part to be content with bare assertion. Certainly, any one who should set up, to a believer, the thesis "Christianity is of purely human origin" must bring forward his reasons for that thesis, or else expect the believer to remain unshaken: but on the other hand any one who sets up, to an unbeliever, the thesis "Christianity is of divine origin" is in exactly the same position. Professed ignorance, however often a mere pretence, and however often (when real) a sign of culpable indifference or of pitiable want of power, is also the natural and normal position of the anxious mind, until anxiety is removed by the production of evidence that at least seems sufficient.

And here it seems in place to notice that the real difficulty as to the burden of proof is somewhat deeper and more serious than might be supposed either from a bare statement of the fundamental rule, or from a rough description of the cautious attitude in one or two rather artificial controversies. In Logic altogether there is often a danger of treating words as more than counters, and so of giving an air of wordiness and trickery to the results attained; and in all this matter of the burden of proof the danger in question is perhaps especially active. It is not only in disputes and verbal arguments that the correct placing of the burden is important, but wherever we are called upon to judge whether all objections to an assertion have been properly taken into account; as where, for instance, we have to decide between accepted theory and awkward fact. The difficulty at last resolves itself into that of saying what shall constitute "practically conclusive" prejudice.

How far, for example, are we "bound to explain away" a so-called fact? If we already have an apparently well-established theory regarding, say, the impossibility of corpses reviving, or of "spirits" holding communication with the living, or even if our theory goes no further than to deem some given behaviour of mind or matter a physical impossibility, what is the rational attitude towards a claimed miracle, or ghost-story, or mere narration of marvellous fact for which no explanation is offered?

We need not now, of course, hesitate at any purely verbal obstacle. We may say, if we like, that the bare notion of a "miracle" involves a contradiction in terms; this merely means that if we were sufficiently wise there would be no room for wonder. But that the blind should receive their sight in an unexpected manner, or that a conjuror's performances should lie beyond our powers of explanation, involves no contradiction or impossibility, except on the assumption that we have already exhausted all there is to learn. When Mr. Venn[9] says that "few men of any really scientific turn would readily accept a miracle, even if it appeared to happen under their very eyes," what is meant is that, though surprised at first, they would either "soon come to discard it afterwards, or so explain it away (i.e., bring it under known laws) as to evacuate it of all that is meant by miraculous."

The rough and ready doctrine may be called that of the existence of "fair presumptions," whether left indefinite, as in common parlance,[10] or—as in law—defined to some extent by set rules. It amounts, in brief, to this, that where there exists a "fair presumption" in favour of a belief, or where a belief is in harmony with prevailing opinion, the assertor is not "bound" to produce evidence, but that whoever doubts the assertion is bound to show cause why it should *not* be believed. The value of this procedure, as a short cut or as a weapon against mere obstruction, must be apparent at once. A Law Court, for example, one of whose avoidable limitations seems to be the occasional necessity of sacrificing the individual to the average—i.e., of resting content with caring not at all about the *minima* of justice—may derive on the whole great advantage from such special rules, at any rate as regards speed in getting through its work. Thus, a person found in possession of stolen goods soon after the theft, is presumed to be a thief, and has to prove innocence although he is the accused party. If a married woman in this awkward situation proves that she stole the goods in the presence of her husband, but asserts that he compelled her to steal them, she escapes the burden of proving this latter assertion, since the Law considers it self-evident.[11] And every rule that dictates in general how given facts of admissions shall be construed, is an example of this procedure. Convenient, however, as such a plan may be where there is an authority competent to frame the rules, it is obvious that outside certain artificial institutions, existing for some special purposes, no such authority exists. Argument in general cannot undertake to be bound by what this man or the other, or any body of men may happen to consider a "fair presumption." Logic shrinks into mere cleverness under the bondage of Rules for Debate, and dogma cramps the reasoning powers. If, as Whately claimed, those who put forward assertions in harmony with "prevailing opinion"[12] were to be altogether exempt from giving a reason for the faith that is in them, or if those who bring forward facts in opposition to prevailing opinion were to be thereby ruled out of court at once, with whom would rest the right of deciding what assertions and facts really come within such privilege? Even an Archbishop, it must be acknowledged, might fail to catch the precise moment when a struggling truth really begins to "prevail":

and ordinary folk, who only desire to follow the safest leader, have often the greatest possible difficulty in deciding which party shall claim their allegiance and support. At least it might very well happen that any two people should fail to agree as to what *is* the prevailing opinion,—much more, as to what it ought to be. Perhaps then we must rely upon the submissiveness of our audience? Such a view comes near being an "Idol of the Cave."[13] Rather, it should perhaps be called an Idol of the Hothouse,—a tender plant, that can never thrive long in the open air.

Common-sense has, of course, a very justifiable liking for short cuts wherever practicable. Rough and ready rules for interpreting facts have a value certainly, even outside a Court of Justice. But there is all the difference between using these as our servants, and allowing them to become our masters. So long as they are employed confessedly as a mere apparatus for saving time at the cost of some exactness, no harm is done: for where the thesis is more than usually important we can take more than the usual care. But if we suppose that whenever a bold assertor takes refuge behind his two-thirds majority, the spirit of free inquiry ought at once to apologise tamely for having dared to put awkward questions or to bring forward awkward facts, we have only ourselves to blame for the loss we suffer. The assertor who shirks inquiry can always be shown to be shirking, by the simple process of putting the question clearly and letting others see that it remains unanswered.

Both the practice of relying on prevailing opinion then, and also readiness in accepting subversive facts as undeniable, have a double edge, and need a little care in using. If Science lays down a theory, or Guesswork a doctrine, conflicting facts or probing questions may both be awkward. But a question differs, after all, from an asserted "fact" in one very important particular,—it carries no burden itself. A "fact" stands in need of evidence, whether or no it conflicts with theory: and clearly, the firmer the theory the greater the caution required in accepting evidence for the conflicting fact. We find, no doubt, very often, that the case (or difficulty) with which a "fact" is accepted depends more on prejudice against (or for) a given theory than on the presence (or absence) of undeniable support for the fact itself: but even where the fact does rest on evidence of its own, we should not forget that in judging that evidence also there is involved a very large amount of rough and ready presumption; that in all observation there is involved a certain amount of inference. To say that the supporter of a theory is in any way "bound to explain away" a given supposed fact, may be just as high-handed a proceeding as for the theorist to condemn the fact unheard. It must be proved to be a fact before it has any bearing on the theory; otherwise, it is clearly a case of "so much the worse for the facts." There can thus be no law laid down which shall settle all disputed cases *a priori*: we can only come back, after all, to the one fundamental principle that wherever proof is demanded, we must either be prepared with sufficient evidence, or prepared to see the hopeful proselyte unconvinced.

Shortly, we may sum up the worst of the difficulties surrounding the question as to the burden of proof as due partly to the unfortunate ambiguity of the expression itself, and partly to an endless source of trouble,—the practical need of striking some balance between faith and hesitation. The mere ambiguity of the expression may be met by remembering that the "must" of the rule is only sanctioned by the assertor's eagerness to convince his audience; and that to "assert" must therefore be defined to exclude that milder type of assertion where we either state an opinion as a fact in our mental history, or tentatively and with a view to learning what the objections to it really are.

In Logic, then, when we speak of the burden of proof, we are not speaking of some artificial law,—some merely legal, or perhaps Parliamentary rule,—with artificial penalties attached to it. No doubt much that has been written, even in logical works, has been written with some such view. For centuries after Aristotle's time, argument appears to have been regarded as a kind of intellectual game, in which each player might try to obtain what advantage he could, so long only as he obeyed the rules laid down. The microscopic ingenuity with which the Schoolmen carried on the elaboration of these rules was well worthy of a better object. But here, at any rate, we are free from any such limitations. No penalty follows the misplacement of the burden of proof, in the strict sense in which we have here used the expression, except the natural consequences that the assertion remains untested, and the audience therefore (if inquiring) unconvinced. To lay the burden on another, therefore, is not to demand Proof at the point of the sword, but rather to request it as a favour. There is no "obligation" on any one to prove an assertion,—other than any wish he may feel to set an inquiring mind at rest, or to avoid the imputation of empty boasting. It is a natural law alone with which we are here concerned,—the law that an unsupported assertion may, for all that appears, be either true or false. And a corollary is that the more intelligent the audience the less easy will it be to pass off upon them a bare assertion under the pretense that they are in any way "bound" to disprove it or explain it away.

And, as regards the practical need of recognising fair presumptions, the best key seems to be to keep quite clear the fine distinction between two really different doctrines; one, the firm foundation of all the cogency that Proof can ever attain, and the other the tottering shelter for boastfulness that fears to be found out. The former may be described as the doctrine that before we can safely *accept* a given theory we are bound to discard all possible rival ones: the latter the doctrine that before we can presume to *decline to accept* a given theory, we are bound to provide an efficient substitute. Nakedly stated like this, perhaps, their difference is easy enough to see, but there are aspects (or uses to which they may be put) under which they become rather more difficult to keep distinct. Thus, for example, a theory occurs to us as satisfactory, and instead of actively trying to find out all that can be said against it, or what rival theories are possible, we entitle it a "provisional theory," or a "working hypothesis," and then proceed at once to dismiss all doubts from our mind. I am not, of course, saying that this provisional contentment is always to be avoided,—only that there is more of it in circulation than would, perhaps, be the case if our notions of the burden of proof were kept quite clear. The inclination to believe without inquiry has long ago become a confirmed habit of the human race; dating, no doubt, from the times when sheer necessity—poverty of knowledge—led us to invent our facts: while the use of provisional theories as such, i.e., with full recognition of their imperfections, seems to be an art which, with all our good intentions, we are only slowly learning.

Further, since where no Reason is given the Thesis may be either true of false, a second corollary is, as already noted, that the absence of a reason given is no conclusive condemnation of the assertion made. Whether it should even raise a presumption of weakness depends, of course, on circumstances. It would not do so, for example, where the assertor, without any motive for untruth, is merely relating unmistakably facts within his own experience,—as that he came down by the Midland Railway, or that he usually buys his books at a certain shop. As a broad rule, in fact, we might say that the need for proof depends on three classes of circumstances,—the likelihood of mistake, the likelihood of falsification, and the importance of the assertion made. Where all three of these are at a minimum, the need for proof is at a minimum too: where any one of them rises into prominence, the demand for proof begins. Thus the assertion (1) that I saw a ghost, or, (2) that defendant was elsewhere at the time the deed was committed, or, (3) that the earth will be baked to a cinder in 1897, would be generally felt to stand in need of evidence. Closely tied up with the need of Proof is, of course, the presumption of weakness which its continued absence is apt to raise. That is to say, where the need is strong the call is usually audible; and deafness is known to be often largely voluntary. But so far as appears, no general rule can be framed for judging of the strength of such presumption in a given case. Even distinct unwillingness to produce the grounds of belief is an ambiguous sign,—much more so is the mere absence of evidence, however strong the call for Proof. Unquestioning faith, for example,—the failure to see any necessity for examining the grounds—is often a cause of unsupported assertion. So is the simple desire to avoid trouble. So is distrust of our audience. So again, as already noticed, are the mere number and extent of the reasons, and our fear of failing to do them justice. Insecure faith—the fear of losing the belief if strict inquiry should be made—is only one cause among many: nor, even if it were the sole explanation of such unwillingness, would the sign be beyond dispute. For misplaced timidity in our beliefs is not altogether unknown.

Much the same applies to the case where the assertor does produce evidence, time after time—either old arguments or new ones—and yet every time such evidence is found, by the best tests obtainable, to be insufficient. The practical difficulty is that of saying *where* our rooted distrust shall begin. The failure of argument, however long continued, never indeed amounts to conclusive disproof; since either the real difficulty in producing the sufficient grounds, or the assertor's want of skill, may be to blame. But it can hardly be denied that the presumption does in certain cases become very strong indeed,—quite sufficiently so for many rough practical purposes. Since, however, there does not yet appear to be any means of generalizing the cases satisfactorily, it seems best only to notice this as a standing difficulty in the complete practical theory of Proof, at present beyond the reach of anything more definite than what may be called a kind of logical tact. It is, however, a side issue, and does not affect the "burden of proof" itself.

It is quite possible, therefore, to be over-pedantic or vexatiously unpractical, in demanding Proof, just as in demanding explanation of the meaning of a term. And in this case as in the former the question of whether a given demand is on the whole conducive to the interests of practice may indeed itself be raised and answered, but otherwise lies quite outside the scope of our inquiry. In strictness any assertion may have its grounds called for; and until they are produced and examined, the assertion remains *untested*. Whether practical convenience decides that in certain cases the assertion may safely be left in this state, is another matter. We are only concerned with those assertions which are already erected into theses; i.e., which have, in the opinion (mistaken or not) of the audience, sufficient importance and doubtfulness to make proof desirable and demanded.

## Notes

From Alfred Sidgwick, *Fallacies, A View of Logic from the Practical Side* (New York: D. Appleton, 1884), pt. 2, ch. 3. The endnotes in square brackets have been added by HVH. The orthography of the original has been preserved. —Eds.

1. [Sidgwick introduces the term "unreal proposition" to designate a class of propositions insusceptible of proof (*Fallacies*, 42). He means to include grammatical well-formed nonsense as well.]

2. [Richard Whately (1787–1863), author of *Elements of Rhetoric*. See this volume, ch. 4.]

3. Even in Law this maxim seems to be fundamental. *Cf.* Sir Jas. Stephen's *Digest of the Law of Evidence*, 3rd. ed. pp. 100 ff. "The burden of proof as to any particular fact lies on that person who wishes the Court to believe in its existence" (art. 96). See also articles 93 and 95. [Sidgwick is referring to James Fitzjames Stephen, *Digest of the Law of Evidence*, 3rd ed. (London: Macmillan, 1877).]

4. Hence De Morgan and others have preferred to treat displacement of the burden of proof as a case of *Ignoratio Elenchi*. See also the examples at p. 188 of this book. [Augustus De Morgan (1806–1871), British mathematician and logician. The reference is to his *Formal Logic; or, The Calculus of Inference, Necessary and Probable* (London: Taylor and Walton, 1847). De Morgan discusses *Ignoratio Elenchi* on 260–67.]

5. *Rhetoric*: Part i. chap. iii §2. [Whately, *Elements of Rhetoric*, this volume, ch. 4.]

6. [Whately, *Elements of Rhetoric*, this volume, ch. 4, para. 8.]

7. [Whately, *Elements of Rhetoric*, this volume, ch. 4, para. 12.]

8. [Sidgwick may have meant "unexplored."]

9. *Logic of Chance*, p. 450. [John Venn (1834–1923), British logician, author of *The Logic of Chance*.]

10. And perhaps in Science. Thus Professor Tyndall, in speaking (*Floating Matter of the Air*, p. 305) of the experiments to disprove Spontaneous Generation, claims that whereas life in the sealed test-tube may always be due to errors of manipulation, the absence of life "involves the presumption of correct experiment." The difference between scientific "presumption" and unscientific is, however, worth noting. By this claim it is not meant that a single failure to find life in certain conditions is sufficient at once to remove all doubt: the patience with which Professor Tyndall's own full investigation was conducted bears witness to the contrary. But it is merely claimed that where the instances for and against are equal in number, the evidence is "not equally balanced," and that "as regards the fruitful flasks [a careful inquirer] would . . . repeat the experiment with redoubled care and scrutiny, and not by one repetition only, but by many, assure himself that he had not fallen into error." [John Tyndall (1820–1893), British physicist and natural philosopher. The reference is to John Tyndall, *Essays on the Floating Matters of the Air* (New York: Appleton, 1884).]

11. Cf. Stephen. *Digest of the Law of Evidence*. Articles 95 and 96. Cf. also De Morgan *Formal Logic*, 261.

12. [Whatley, *Elements of Rhetoric*, this volume, ch. 4, para. 10 and para. 11.]

13. [The idol of the cave is one of Frances Bacon's four idols explained in *Novum Organon*, bk. 1, aphorisms 53–58. *Novum Organon* was originally published in 1620. Although we don't know which edition Sidgwick was looking at, a good recent edition is the one edited by Lisa Jardine and M. Silverthorne (Cambridge: Cambridge University Press, 2000). The idol of the cave tempts a person to see everything through the eyes of his own favorite discipline or subjective perspective.]

# 7

# The Burden of Proof

JAMES B. THAYER

If we conceive to ourselves a legal system in which the pleadings, if any there be, admit of only one defence, that of mere negation,—that is to say, where not merely the pleading is negative in form, but where no other than a purely negative defence is open under it, and all other defences, as if they were cross actions, require a separate trial; we can see that the phrase Burden of Proof (*Onus probandi, Boweislast, Fardeau de la preuve*) may have a very simple meaning. Under such a system the defendant has nothing to prove; it is the plaintiff, the *actor*, who has the duty of proving, while the defendant, the *reus*, has only the negative function of baffling the plaintiff.

If, on the other hand, we picture a system in which any defence whatever may be open upon a plea of general denial, in which a defendant who stands upon the record as merely denying, may, at the trial, turn himself into a plaintiff by setting up an affirmative defence, and the original plaintiff may become a defendant by merely denying this new case of his adversary; then we observe that so simple a conception of the proof and the duty of proving, is no longer possible. Either party may have it, and it may shift back and forth during the trial, because each party in turn may set up, in the course of the trial, an affirmative ground of fact, which, if he would win, he must, of course, make good by proof. We can no longer say when the pleading is over and before the trial begins, "the proof belongs here and cannot belong elsewhere; the *onus probandi* is on the plaintiff and it cannot shift."

If now we further conceive that under this last system the action of the tribunal passing upon questions of fact is subject to review, so that an appellate court may have to consider whether such a body as a jury has acted reasonably in weighing evidence and counter-evidence, and whether the judge who has presided over a trial by jury has rightly ordered the trial, and rightly instructed the jury as to comparing and weighing evidence, we may see that questions will be introduced into legal discussion as to the respective duties of the parties in producing evidence at different points of the trial, and in meeting evidence produced against them, which may be wholly absent from another system where there is no such judicial revision of the method of using and estimating the evidence. The conception is brought to light of producing evidence to meet the pressure of an adversary's case, a duty which may belong to either party, and to both parties in turn; and this conception now takes its place in legal discussion and requires its own terminology.

Let us further suppose that this new topic,—new in the sense of requiring now to be discriminated and discussed,—the mere duty of producing evidence, belonging thus to neither party exclusively, and to each by turns, gets also called the burden of proof; it becomes plain that, as regards the meaning of this term, we have advanced from a region of simple and clear ideas to one which is likely to be full of confusion. We have, in fact, proceeded from conceptions which we may roughly describe as those of the Roman law and of some later systems founded upon it, to those which fill and perplex the books of our common law to-day.

If now, furthermore, recognizing that there are these two wholly distinct notions of the burden of proof, both called by the same name, we then observe that, as regards one of them, the duty of establishing, it is often a very difficult thing to determine whether a given defence be an affirmative one or not, and so to decide which party has the burden of the proof in this sense, and that the common-law judges have fallen into the way of giving as the test,[1] as the regular professional "rule of thumb," for telling who has this burden of proof, a precept which selects a circumstance common to both meanings of the term, and, indeed, generally characteristic of the other one, namely, the duty of going forward with evidence,—we shall see how the confusion is likely to be heightened.

Finally, if we go on to remark the way in which this topic is mixed up with that of presumptions, as when it is said that "presumptions of law and strong presumptions of fact shift the burden of proof," we have a glimpse of another fruitful source of confusion; and in fact these two subjects of presumption and the burden of proof have intercommunicated their respective ambiguities and reflected them back and forth upon each other in a manner which it is well-nigh hopeless to follow out.[2]

If all this or the half of it be true, it will be admitted that he would do a great service to our law who should thoroughly discriminate, explore, and set forth the legal doctrine of the burden of proof. But that would be a large undertaking. [. . .]

At present I am concerned with no such task as this, but only with an attempt to help rid this phrase, the burden of proof, of some of the distressing ambiguity that attends it, (a) by pointing out the different conceptions for which it stands, and bringing to view some important discriminations; (b) by considering the possibility of a better terminology for the subject; and (c) by indicating its proper place in our law.

I. In legal discussion this phrase is used in two ways:—

(1) To indicate the duty of bringing forward argument or evidence in support of a proposition, whether at the beginning or later.

(2) To mark that of establishing a proposition as against all counter-argument or evidence.

It should be added that there is a third indiscriminate usage, far more common than either of the others, in which the term may mean both or either of the first two. The last is very common; the first or second, that is to say, any meaning which makes a clear discrimination, is much less usual.

II. It will be convenient at this point to illustrate the different uses of the term by some citations.

(1) The use of it in ordinary, untechnical speech, as indicating the effect of a natural probability or presumption, of the pressure of evidence or argument previously introduced, and of what is called a mere "preoccupation of the ground," may be seen in a passage from Bishop Whately's "Elements of Rhetoric:"[3] "It is a point of great importance [. . .] to point out [. . .] on which side the presumption lies, and to which belongs the *(onus probandi)* burden of proof. [. . .] According to the most correct use of the term, a 'presumption' in favor of any supposition means [. . .] in short that the burden of proof lies on the side of him who would dispute it."

Of the same use of it in our law books, the following are instances: (a) "The burden of proof is shifted by those presumptions of law which are rebuttable; by presumptions of fact of the stronger kind; and by every species of evidence strong enough to establish a *prima facie* case against a party." (Best, Evidence,[4] s. 273.) And again: "As [. . .] the question of the burden of proof may present itself at any moment during a trial, the test ought in strict accuracy to be expressed thus, viz.: 'Which party would be successful if no evidence at all, or no more evidence, as the case may be, were given.'" (b) A very clear expression of this sense of the term is found in Lord Justice Bowen's opinion in Abrath *v.* No. East. Ry. Co.[5] "In order to make my opinion clear, I should like to say shortly how I understand the term 'burden of proof.' In every lawsuit somebody must go on with it; the plaintiff is the first to begin, and if he does nothing he fails. If he makes a *prima facie* case, and nothing is done by the other side to answer it, the defendant fails. The test, therefore, as to burden of proof is simply to consider which party would be successful if no evidence at all was given, or if no more evidence was given than is given at this particular point of the case, because it is obvious that during the controversy in the litigation there are points at which the onus of proof shifts, and at which the tribunal must say, if the case stopped there, that it must be decided in a particular way. Such being the test, it is not a burden which rests forever on the person on whom it is first cast, but as soon as he, in his turn, finds evidence which, *prima facie*, rebuts the evidence against which he is contending, the burden shifts until again there is evidence which satisfies the demand. Now, that being so, the question as to onus of proof is only a rule for deciding on whom the obligation rests of going further, if he wishes to win." (c) From Mr. Justice Stephen's Digest of Evidence[6] we may gather that he understands this to be the established usage in England. And the like is laid down for Scotland.[7]

(2) As to the second sense of the term, expressing the duty of the actor to establish the grounds upon which he rests his demand that the court shall move in his behalf,—that is the sense to which, since the year 1832,[8] the Supreme Court of Massachusetts has sought to limit the expression. (a) In 1854[9] it was put thus: "The burden of proof and the weight of evidence are two very different things. The former remains on the party affirming a fact in support of his case, and does not change in any aspect of the cause; the latter shifts from side to side in the progress of a trial, according to the nature and strength of the proofs offered in support or denial of the main fact to be established. In the case at bar, the averment which the plaintiff was bound to maintain was that the defendant was legally liable for the payment of tolls. In answer to this the defendant did not aver any new and distinct fact, such as payment, accord and satisfaction, or release; but offered evidence to rebut this alleged legal liability. By so doing he did not assume the burden of proof, which still rested on the plaintiff; but only sought to rebut the *prima facie* case which the plaintiff had proved."

(b) In the following passage may be seen an instance of what is not uncommon now-a-days, a recognition of this as one sense of the term, and also of the other. In 1878,[10] Lord Justice Brett remarked, with valuable comments on the case of Watson *v.* Clark (1 Dow, 336), that "The burden of proof upon a plea of unseaworthiness to an action on a policy of marine insurance lies upon the defendant, and so far as the pleadings go it never shifts. [. . .] But when facts are given in evidence, it is often said that certain presumptions, which are really inferences of fact, arise and cause the burden of proof to shift; and so they do as a matter of reasoning, and as a matter of fact."[11] (c) In New York,[12] Church, C. J., for the court, expresses himself thus: "The burden of maintaining the affirmative of the issue, and properly speaking, the burden of proof remained upon the plaintiff throughout the trial; but the burden or necessity was cast upon the defendant, to relieve itself from the presumption of negligence raised by the plaintiff's evidence."

[. . .]

IV. As regards a proper terminology for the conceptions now indicated by the "burden of proof." It seems impossible to approve a continuation of the present state of things, under which ideas of great practical importance, and of very frequent application, are so imperfectly and dubiously intimated. What can be done? Of courses that are theoretically possible there are three; to abandon the use of this phrase and choose other terms, or to fix upon it one of the two meanings now in use, and find another phrase for the other. In favor of the first course, there are the obvious reasons of clearness and precision. But it would be a mere dream to imagine that the phrase could ever be wholly banished from legal usage. We might as reasonably expect to exclude it from the common speech of men. Use it we must.

It remains only to choose in what sense it shall be used. Or shall we say here also, that it is hopeless to make a change? No doubt it is difficult, but it cannot be hopeless. A change is simply necessary to accurate legal speech and sound legal reasoning; and we may justly expect that those who have exact thoughts, and wish to express them with precision, will avail themselves of some discrimination in terminology which will secure their end. Particular courts, or judges, or writers, may adopt the course of discarding this phrase altogether and substituting other terms; that is an intelligible plan. But if any one prefers to follow the course which seems certain to be taken by the current of legal usage, that of retaining the phrase in some sense or other, he will be driven, if he would speak accurately, to tie up the term to a single meaning. Which then shall it be, that of going forward with proof, or that of establishing a given proposition in the upshot?

(a) In favor of the former there seem to be these considerations: (1) It is the meaning that the term has in common speech. Whoever, men say, asserts a paradoxical proposition, has the burden of proof. But equally, they say, whoever supports his paradoxical proposition by sufficient evidence to make it probable, shifts the burden of proof, and now his adversary has it upon him.[13] (2) This is also a common legal usage. (3) It is a very comprehensive sense, for it includes not merely the duty of meeting a prima facie case against you, but also that of meeting a presumption, and that of going forward at the beginning. This last may be fixed upon the plaintiff by a mere rule of practice, as in Massachusetts,[14] irrespective of his true place in the procedure; or by the same considerations which determine whether a case is affirmative or negative; but, however fixed, the duty itself is in its nature merely the duty of going forward with the argument or the evidence, a duty wholly separable from that of finally establishing.

(b) In favor of the other meaning it may be said (1) that it is the one which is prominent in the Roman law and in countries which have the Roman system of pleading; and (2) that for this exclusive sense there is a certain body of legal authority, *e.g.*, that it has been formerly adopted as the only proper usage by one of our best courts, the Supreme Court of Massachusetts, and, in particular opinions, has been approved by other tribunals and judges.[15] But (1) as to its use in the Roman system, although it would be desirable to harmonize our use of the term *onus probandi* with theirs, that cannot well take place so long as our conceptions, our methods of legal procedure, and the questions which enter into our legal discussions are so unlike theirs.[16] It may be observed also that the immediate intuitus of the phrase, as used in that system, was rather to the duty, at the beginning, of going forward with evidence, than to the duty at the end, of holding the case made out; these two things, as I have said, are quite separable. According to the Roman conception he who had furnished evidence at the outset had furnished *probatio*. If counter evidence were offered, he must, indeed, keep up his *probatio*; but the notion of *probare* and *probatio* was answered by a prima facie case. (2) As regards the fact, that there is high authority for fixing upon the phrase the single meaning of a burden of establishing, it may be doubted whether experience favors a continuance of this experiment. Chief Justice Shaw began it in 1832,[17] and not, as I venture to think, with a sufficient recognition of the fact that the other use of the phrase was also perfectly well fixed in legal usage. During the following twenty-eight years of his most valuable judicial life, he was able to hold the terminology of his court with fair success to the new rule, and to establish it in that State. But the example of this strictness has not, I believe, been followed. The discrimination thus boldly marked has been recognised often in other courts, and this meaning allowed and even preferred, or suggested as the only proper one, in particular opinions; but, so far as I know, no other court has undertaken to distinctly and steadily reject the other meaning.

Let me illustrate the difficulties that have attended the Massachusetts experiment. In 1840[18] Chief Justice Shaw restates his view, and calls the other use of the word "a common misapprehension of the law on the subject." But in 1842[19] the opinion of the court distinctly lays down the other doctrine: "The [auditor's] report being made evidence by the statute, it necessarily shifted the burden of proof; for being *prima facie* evidence, it becomes conclusive where it is not contradicted or controlled." In 1844 (Taunton Iron Co. *v.* Richmond, 8 Met. 434) the reporter, afterwards Mr. Justice Metcalf, gives a decision of the court (Shaw, C. J.) that an auditor's report is prima facie evidence for the party in whose favor it is made, and adds in his head-note the expression, "and changes the burden of proof." In 1848[20] the court (Metcalf, J.) state that, in a suit by the payee of a promissory note against the maker, "the burden of proof is on the maker" to establish want of consideration. But two years later,[21] they say that the burden of proof is on the plaintiff, and remark (Fletcher, J.) of the previous case that "there is a sentence in this opinion which may be misunderstood; [. . .] [quoting it]. This must be understood to mean that the burden of proof is on the maker to rebut the *prima facie* case made by producing the note, otherwise the *prima facie* evidence will be conclusive." In this same year, 1850,[22] the court (Metcalf, J.), while distinguishing, in the case of an alteration in a writing, between "the burden of proof" and the "burden of explanation," define the burden of proof in terms borrowed from Baron Parke, but not understood by him or in English legal usage to be limited to the duty of establishing:[23] "The effect [. . .] would be that if no evidence is given by a party claiming under such an instrument, the issue must always be found against him; this being the meaning of the 'burden of proof.' I Curteis, 640." In 1858[24] the court (Dewey, J.) remark upon the fact that the Chief Justice of the lower court had used the phrase in another than "the more precisely accurate use of the term [. . .] as now held by the court," but they conclude that it did not mislead the jury. In 1859[25] the judge below ruled that "the burden of proof was upon the defendant to [. . .] control the auditor's report," and the court (Bigelow, J.) is obliged again to set forth the discrimination between "the technical sense" of the burden of proof and the other; and then follows what looks like a confession that their exclusive use of the word had not gained any firm hold in the seven and twenty years since Judge Shaw had begun it. "This mode of using the phrase, though somewhat loose and inaccurate, *is quite common*, and where not improperly applied to a case, so as to confuse or mislead the jury, cannot be held to be a misdirection."[26]

Considering, therefore, that the widest legal usage, both in England and here, applies the term "burden of proof" in a sense which is satisfied by making out a prima facie case; that this sense covers the greater variety of situations, viz., not merely the case of one who has a prima facie case, or a presumption against him, but also that of him upon whom rests the duty of going forward with evidence at the beginning; and that it corresponds with the use of the phrase in ordinary discourse,—it would seem wise to fix upon it this meaning only, and to employ for the duty of making out a given proposition, some term, like that, already widely used, of the burden of establishing; in other words, to adopt the meaning which is so carefully stated by the Lord Justice Bowen in Abrath *v.* North-Eastern Railway Co.[27]

V. Whereabout in the law shall we place the subject of the burden of proof? It is common in our system to treat of it, when treated at all, in books on evidence; and the result is that it is little discussed, for it does not belong there.[28] It belongs, as the law of evidence does, to the auxiliary, secondary, "adjective" part of the law; but it is by no means limited to the situation where parties are putting in "evidence"; it applies equally where the "evidence" is all in. It covers the topic of argument, of legal reasoning; and equally of reasoning about law and about fact; while the law of evidence relates merely to matter of fact offered to a judicial tribunal as the basis of inference to another matter of fact. To undertake to crowd within the limits proper to the law of evidence the considerations necessary for the determination of matters of a far wider scope, like those questions of logic and general experience and substantive law involved in the subjects of Presumption and Judicial Notice and that compound of considerations of the same character, coupled with others relating to the history and technicalities of pleading and mere forensic procedure, which lie at the bottom of what is called by this name of the "Burden of Proof,"—to attempt this is to burst the sides of the smaller subject and to bring obscurity over the whole of it. And, moreover, it is to condemn this topic, so important in the daily conduct of legal affairs, and so much needing a clear exposition, to a continuance of that neglect, and that slight and merely incidental treatment which it has so long suffered.

## Notes

From James B. Thayer, "The Burden of Proof," *Harvard Law Review* 4, no. 2 (1890): 45–70. Excerpts taken from pages 45–51 and 65–70. Notes in square brackets are by HVH. The orthography of the original has been preserved. —Eds.

1. "The proper test is, which party would be successful if no evidence at all were given." Alderson, B., in Amos *v.* Hughes, 1 Moo. & Rob. 464.
2. "Look to the books," says Bentham, in speaking of the burden of proof (Works, vi, 139) "and . . . instead of clear rules. such as the nature of things forbids to be established by anything but statute of law, you have darkness palpable and visible."
3. Part 1. c. 3, s. 2. [Richard Whately, *Elements of Rhetoric*, this volume, ch. 4.]
4. [William M. Best, *Treatise on the Principles of Evidence* (Philadelphia: T. & J. W. Johnson, 1849).]
5. 32 W. R. 50, 53. In the regular report (11 Q. B. D. 440, 455–56) the phraseology is slightly, but not materially, different.
6. Articles 95 and 96 and the illustrations. [James Fitzgerald Stephen, *A Digest of the Law of Evidence*, 4th ed. (London: Macmillan, 1887).]
7. Dickson, Evidence in Scotland 2 ed., ss. 12–16. [William Gillespie Dickson, *A Treatise on the Law of Evidence in Scotland*, 2nd ed. (Edinburgh: Bell and Bradfute, 1864).]
8. Powers *v.* Russell, 13 Pick. 69.
9. Central Bridge Co. *v.* Butler, 2 Gray, 130.
10. Pickup *v.* Thames Ins. Co., 3 Q. B. D. p. 600.
11. Compare the same judge in Anderson *v.* Morice, L. R. 10 C. P. 58 (1874), Abrath *v.* No. East. Ry. Co., 11 Q. B. D. 440 (1883), and Davey *v.* Lond. & S. W. Ry. Co., 12 Q. B. D. 70.
12. Caldwell *v.* New Jersey Co., 47 N. Y. 282, 290.

13. See *ante*, p. 49.

14. Dorr *v.* Bank, 128 Mass. p. 358; Page *v.* Osgood, 2 Gray, 260.

15. See *ante*, p. 50.

16. See *ante*, pp. 46, 55.

17. Powers *v.* Russell, 13 Pick. 69, 76.

18. Sperry *v.* Wilcox, 1 Met. 267.

19. Jones *v.* Stevens, 5 Met. 373, 378, Hubbard, J.

20. Jennison *v.* Stafford, 1 Cush. 168.

21. Delano *v.* Bartlett, 6 Cush. 364, 368. It may well be doubted whether this case rests upon the true analysis of the substantive law; but it is still followed in Massachusetts, *e.g.*, in Perley *v.* Perley, 144 Mass. 104 (1887), and, to some extent, elsewhere.

22. Wilde *v.* Armsby, 6 Cush. 314, 319.

23. See *ante*, p. 53.

24. Noxon *v.* DeWolf, 10 Gray, 343, 348.

25. Morgan *v.* Morse, 13 Gray, 150.

26. The opinion goes on: "In this sense it was manifestly used in this case. The attention of the court was not called to the distinction between that evidence which was sufficient to impeach and overcome a *prima facie* case, and that which was necessary to sustain the issue on the part of the plaintiff. . . . It would have been more correct for the court to have instructed the jury that the report of the auditor in favor of the plaintiff was *prima facie* evidence, and sufficient to entitle him to a verdict, unless it was impeached and controlled by the evidence offered by the defendant. But we see no reason to believe that the instruction given was not properly understood, or that the defendant was in any way aggrieved thereby." See also the difficult exposition in Wilder *v.* Cowles, 100 Mass. 487 (1868).

27. See *ante*, p. 49.

28. Bentham, Works. vi. 214. "This topic [the *onus probandi*] . . . seems to belong rather to Procedure than to Evidence." [See note 2 above].

# 8

# On Presumption and Burden of Proof

## C. P. Ilbert

*Presumptions.*—A presumption in the ordinary sense is an inference. It is an argument, based on observation, that what has happened in some cases will probably happen in others of the like nature. The subject of presumptions, so far as they are mere inferences or arguments, belongs, not to the law of evidence, or to law at all, but to rules of reasoning. But a legal presumption, or, as it is sometimes called, a presumption of law, as distinguished from a presumption of fact, is something more. It may be described, in Stephen's language, as "a rule of law that courts and judges shall draw a particular inference from a particular fact, or from particular evidence, unless and until the truth" (perhaps it would be better to say "soundness") "of the inference is disproved."[1] Courts and legislatures have laid down such rules on grounds of public policy or general convenience, and the rules have then to be observed as rules of positive law, not merely used as part of the ordinary process of reasoning or argument. Some so-called presumptions are rules of substantive law under a disguise. To this class appear to belong "conclusive presumptions of law," such as the common-law presumption that a child under seven years of age cannot commit a felony. So again the presumption that everyone knows the law is merely an awkward way of saying that ignorance of the law is not a legal excuse for breaking it. Of true legal presumptions, the majority may be dealt with most appropriately under different branches of the substantive law, such as the law of crime, of property, or of contract, and accordingly Stephen has included in his *Digest of the Law of Evidence*[2] only some which are common to more than one branch of the law. The effect of a presumption is to impute to certain facts or groups of facts a prima facie significance or operation, and thus, in legal proceedings, to throw upon the party upon whom it works the duty of bringing forward evidence to meet it. Accordingly the subject of presumptions is intimately connected with the subject of the burden or proof, and the same legal rule may be expressed in different forms, either as throwing the advantage of a presumption on one side, or as throwing the burden of proof on the other.

Thus the rule in Stephen's Digest, which says that the burden of proving that any person has been guilty of a crime or wrongful act is on the person who asserts it, appears in the article entitled "Presumption of Innocence." Among the more ordinary and more important legal presumptions are the presumption of regularity in proceedings, described generally as a presumption *omnia esse rite acta*,[3] and including the presumption that the holder of a public office has been duly appointed, and has duly performed his official duties, the presumption of the legitimacy of a child born during the mother's marriage, or within the period of gestation after her husband's death, and the presumption as to life and death. "A person shown not to have been heard of for seven years by those (if any) who, if he had been alive, would naturally have heard of him, is presumed to be dead unless the circumstances of the case are such as to account for his not being heard of without assuming his death; but there is no presumption as to the time when he died, and the burden of proving his death at any particular time is upon the person who asserts it. There is no presumption" (i.e., legal presumption) "as to the age at which a person died who is shown to have been alive at a given time, or as to the order in which two or more persons died who are shown to have died in the same accident, shipwreck or battle."[4] A document proved or purporting to be thirty years old is presumed to be genuine, and to have been properly executed and (if necessary) attested if produced from the proper custody. And the legal presumption of a "lost grant," i.e., the presumption that a right or alleged right which has been long enjoyed without interruption had a legal origin, still survives in addition to the common law and statutory rules of prescription.

*Burden of Proof.*—The expression *onus probandi* has come down from the classical Roman law, and both it and the Roman maxims, *Agenti incumbit probatio*,[5] *Necessitas probandi incumbit ei qui dicit non ei qui negat*,[6] and *Reus excipiendo fit actor*,[7] must be read with reference to the Roman system of actions, under which nothing was admitted, but the plaintiff's case was tried first; then, unless that failed, the defendant's on his *exceptio*; then, unless that failed, the plaintiff's on his *replicatio*, and so on. Under such a system the burden was always on the "actor."

In modern law the phrase "burden of proof" may mean one of two things, which are often confused—the burden of establishing the proposition or issue on which the case depends, and the burden of producing evidence on any particular point either at the beginning or at a later stage of the case. The burden in the former sense ordinarily rests on the plaintiff or prosecutor. The burden in the latter sense, that of going forward with evidence on a particular point, may shift from side to side as the case proceeds. The general rule is that he who alleges a fact must prove it, whether the allegation is couched in affirmative or negative terms. But this rule is subject to the effect of presumption in particular cases, to the principle that in considering the amount of evidence necessary to shift the burden of proof regard must be had to the opportunities of knowledge possessed by the parties respectively, and to the express provisions of statutes directing where the burden of proof is to lie in particular cases. Thus many statutes expressly direct that the proof of lawful excuse or authority, or the absence of fraudulent intent, is to lie on the person charged with an offense. And the Summary Jurisdiction Act 1848 provides that if the information or complaint in summary proceedings negatives any exemption, exception, proviso, or condition in the statute on which it is founded, the prosecutor or complainant need not prove the negative, but the defendant may prove the affirmative in his defence.

## Notes

From C. P. Ilbert, "Evidence" in *Encyclopædia Britannica*, 11th ed., vol. 10 (New York: Encyclopædia Britannica, 1910). Notes in square brackets are by HVH. The orthography of the original has been preserved.—Eds.

1. [Sir James Stephen, *Digest of the Law of Evidence*, 3rd ed. (London: McMillan, 1877).]
2. [Stephen, *Digest*.]
3. ["All things [are presumed] to have been done rightly."]
4. [Stephen, *Digest*, article 99.]
5. ["Proof lies with the plaintiff."]
6. ["The need for proof lies with him who asserts not with him who denies."]
7. ["The defendant by pleading becomes a plaintiff."]

# PART 2

# CONTEMPORARY DEVELOPMENTS

Reflecting the influence of Whately and inspired by legal practice, contemporary studies of argumentation rely on conceptions of presumption and burden of proof to either identify or establish principles for the conduct of parties engaged in arguments. These principles allocate roles to arguers, determining which parties are to produce reasons and evidence supporting their position and which need only respond with questions, doubts, objections, and (possibly) counterarguments. The simplest and most widely accepted view holds that where a presumption favors one party to a disagreement, a burden of proof falls to the other party or parties. Across the literature, there is widespread agreement that the allocation of probative burdens provides the basic structure within which productive argumentation can be conducted. Nicholas Rescher puts the matter this way: "The workings of the conception of burden of proof represent a *procedural or regulative principle of rationality* in the conduct of argumentation, a ground rule, as it were, of the process of rational controversy—a fundamental condition of the whole enterprise."[1] However, when one goes beyond this important consensus, one encounters a maze of differing interpretations and applications, some complementary and some conflicting, each of which illuminates the topic from a different perspective.

A fundamental difference concerns the status of the "burdens" allocated to advocates. Many authors share Douglas Ehninger and Wayne Brockriede's view that probative burdens are to be distributed based on the practical needs of parties engaged in persuasive argument. Generally, the beliefs, commitments, policies, and institutions that persons hold and occupy are resistant to change. Parties advocating change need to recognize a presumption favoring the status quo and accept the "burden" of providing reason and evidence designed to induce others to change. Most argumentation theorists hold that the "burdens" of primary importance to the structure of productive argumentation are in fact dialectical obligations. Where an advocate has the burden of proof, she owes a defense of her position to parties entitled to raise questions, doubts, objections, criticisms, and counterarguments.

Ehninger and Brockriede's exposition of this view is also a bridge from the classical Whatelian treatments of presumption and burden of proof to more modern developments. They take presumption to be, figuratively, a preoccupation of the ground that someone else wants to stand on.[2] Presumptions are of two kinds: natural and artificial. Whereas natural presumptions are based on the existence, for example, of institutions, practices, and values, artificial presumptions (e.g., the presumption of innocence) are established by agreement. Ehninger and Brockriede take "presumption" to be a descriptive term, a mere label that identifies the present order of things, setting the stage for debate. There is no associated evaluation because, for example, the established practice may be good or corrupt, and the accused person may be innocent or guilty. Burden of proof, by contrast, is an evaluative concept. The evaluation criticizes the present order of things and recommends an alternative order of what should be the case. But because of its evaluative nature, the burden of proof involves risk: either the criticism proffered of the existing order, or the particular alternative proposed, may be rejected. Accordingly, Ehninger and Brockriede define the burden of proof as "the risk involved in advancing the proposition" that challenges a presumption.[3]

To make good on the challenge, an arguer has a further burden of going "forward with the debate."[4] What Ehninger and Brockriede mean by that phrase is that it is up to the side wishing to challenge the presumption-holder to give a proof showing that its alternative view of how things should be is justified. Failing to meet this burden is to default. This concept of going forward with the debate is intimately tied to another concept, that of a *prima facie* case, one that "any reasonable judge would consider strong enough to stand, unless or until refutation is offered against it."[5] If the challenger succeeds in making a *prima facie* case against the side with the presumption, then the burden of going forward with debate is shifted to the presumption holder. The latter must now either dispel the argument just given or present a new *prima facie* argument in defense against the challenger. If successful, the burden returns to the challenger. In the context of debate, this back-and-forth can continue "until the evidence and proofs have been exhausted or a predetermined time limit has expired."[6] The party thought to have achieved a "preponderance of proof" in the exchange of arguments is the winner of the debate. Ehninger and Brockriede's discussion moves past Whately's, first by giving a more general account of how burdens are shifted by *prima facie* arguments, and further by distinguishing the burden of proof from the burden of going forward with debate. This distinction, or one very much like it, is also found in Rescher's *Dialectics*, wherein he distinguishes initiating or probative and evidential burdens of proof.[7]

Among the theorists who regard burdens of proof as obligations, many hold that probative obligations are properly distributed according to *onus probandi*: "The one who asserts must prove." For those who adhere strictly to this maxim, presumptions have no role to play in the allocation of probative obligations. Other theorists follow Whately and hold that burdens of proof are allocated in relation to presumptions. The issue between these two orientations comes to a head in pragma-dialectical approaches to the study of argumentation, represented here by the essay of Frans H. van Eemeren and Peter Houtlosser. Pragma-dialecticians study argumentation through the lens of an ideal model for the conduct of critical discussions. Within this framework burdens of proof are distributed according to *onus probandi*, and pragma-dialecticians adhere strictly to that maxim in their analysis of simple disputes wherein one party asserts a standpoint and another expresses doubts regarding it; here only one party has asserted a proposition, so the maxim is thought to suffice for the purposes of allocating probative responsibility. However, in mixed disputes, where an asserted standpoint meets with a denial of the assertion and/or alternative standpoint, pragma-dialecticians resort to the concept of presumption to allocate burdens of proof among contending parties. Here, both parties have a burden of proof, and "the problem concerns in which order the standpoints are to be defended." To resolve this matter, van Eemeren and Houtlosser turn to the conventions which constitutionally organize the dispute. Many institutional settings, for example, have procedural conventions for allocating probative burdens. Outside such settings, van Eemeren and Houtlosser argue, the conventions which, *à la* Searle, constitute specific speech acts have pragmatic implications enabling analysts to appropriately assign probative burdens in reconstructing argumentation as a critical discussion. The applicable convention in this connection, they argue, is the Interaction Principle,[8] which generally prohibits the performance of any speech acts that are not acceptable to the interlocutor. Accordingly, where a speaker executes a speech act in the absence of indications that she is not fully conforming to the interaction principle, the proposition she has expressed is presumably acceptable. Where there is indication that the speaker is not conforming to this principle, as in making an accusation that inherently and manifestly anticipates nonacceptance of an allegation, and her interlocutor does articulate a contradictory standpoint, then the protagonist incurs a burden of establishing the acceptability of her speech act, that is, a burden of proof.

To generalize this pragmatic account, van Eemeren and Houtlosser postulate that it is reasonable to let the presumption of acceptability remain with a speaker as long as the speaker's speech act does not go against the prevailing *pragmatic status quo*, that is, as long as it conforms to the list of premises that can be reconstructed as commitments. So, in a sophisticated view of presumption and burden of proof as procedural considerations, *onus probandi* only distributes probative obligations in the simplest of exchanges; elsewhere, procedural considerations make the allocation of probative obligations contingent on the prior presumptive agreements between the participants.

We should notice an important difference between dialectical and rhetorical approaches to presumption and burden of proof.[9] Dialectical traditions tend to situate or design argumentation for regulated settings in which the roles and duties of advocates are constrained by rules and conventions. Dialecticians look to legal conceptions of presumption and burden of proof and corresponding judicial practices as models of argumentation constrained by institutional rules, and in so far as they are influenced by such models, they attempt to design idealized procedures of regulated dialogues and abstract models for the conduct of "productive" argumentation. Rhetorical approaches, in contrast, tend to focus on presumptions and probative burdens as they play out in the messier world of day-to-day arguments, especially public argumentation in civic decision-making settings. The role of rhetorically oriented argumentation theorists then is to sharpen and clarify the capacity of practitioners to recognize proper presumptions and allocate burdens of proof accordingly. Reflecting this orientation, rhetorical conceptions throughout much of the modern period were articulated in connection with designing pedagogical exercises in the form of debates aimed at cultivating a student's ability to recognize presumptions and accept and discharge burdens of proof. Thus, rhetorically oriented scholars have sought to identify and clarify the presumptions that do and properly should operate in day-to-day public discourse.

As contemporary scholars have found independent purchase for investigating these structural components of argumentation, considerable skepticism has been voiced about the light judicial concepts and practices can shed on the larger world of argumentation. This skepticism has been reinforced by the difficulties jurists have encountered in their own understanding and utilization of these concepts. Richard Gaskins's stated goal in "The Juridical Roots of Presumptions and Burdens of Proof" is "to clarify the rhetorical functions of burdens of proof by focusing on the legal system."[10] For example, in cases where lack of evidence renders a definitive conclusion impossible, the proof burden may be a burden of persuasion on risk of nonpersuasion. A proof beyond reasonable doubt still is not conclusive, but a proof-burden rule may settle that an argument of this strength is determinative to win the case, or that arguments presenting less information will lose the case. Suppose the level at which a certain substance is toxic to humans in unclear. Legislation may stipulate that levels below a certain point will be presumed nontoxic. Showing that the level is below the specified point is sufficient to show nontoxicity. The presumption is established. Legal argument thus contrasts with scientific or ethical debate, which may leave the question open. The law may have spoken with finality, but the question may still be open in the "court of public opinion."

Also from the rhetorical perspective, James Crosswhite analyzes the pair *presumption/burden of proof* as key for understanding the dynamics of argumentation. In his view, the possibility of shifting the burden of proof by appealing to presumptions "is a power that shapes the rules whereby arguments proceed and the standards by which they are evaluated."[11] In order to defend this view, Crosswhite argues against Gaskins's criticism of the role of presumptions and burdens of proof in everyday argumentation. Namely, Gaskins had criticized the use of these notions outside the realm of law, because, in his view, they amount to an illegitimate means to try to "gain control over indeterminate questions of fact and value."[12] According to Gaskins, Chaïm Perelman and Lucie Olbrechts-Tyteca's *The New Rhetoric* proposes an alternative theory of argumentation that appeals to presumption and shifting the burden of proof. The bulk of Crosswhite's argument explains that Perelman's observation that there are areas of deliberation that cannot be subject to demonstrations *more geometrico* is not a plea for relativism but is rather Perelman's reason to look for new techniques of argumentation that could enable people to actually "'gain control' of questions of fact and value even when such matters cannot be determined with certainty."[13] According to Crosswhite, the main misunderstanding of Gaskins's reading of *The New Rhetoric* is his belief that Perelman's theory of argumentation is based on the procedures of law rather than on a robust conception of justice. As Crosswhite points out, the rule of justice in Perelman's model is a demand to treat like cases alike, and it is this rule that provides a measure of the strength of arguments: "Our hypothesis is that [. . .] strength is appraised by application of the rule of justice: that which was capable of convincing in a specific situation will appear to be convincing in a similar or analogous situation."[14] Following Perelman's insight, Crosswhite holds that, in areas of knowledge for which the methods of logic lose ground, the dynamics of argumentation can still be shaped and sanctioned by the notions of burden of proof and presumption. The ability of argumentation to deliver good results is then based on the assumption that, at least at times, communities have been right. For, as Crosswhite points out, Perelman had renounced grounding argumentation on the chimera of a pure reason, untouched by any tradition. Instead, from this point of view, judgments about values and facts in conditions of uncertainty can only be based on precedent: communities' background of this type of knowledge makes the weight of precedents possible and allows presumptions to play their role as provisional warrants for new cases.

G. Thomas Goodnight's essay on the liberal-progressive and conservative political presumptions,[15] updated for this volume, argues for an amended version of the Whatelian idea that a presumption favors the status quo and that the burden of proof falls to advocates of change. This version of presumption, Goodnight argues, sits well with a conservative ideology; liberally oriented advocates, by contrast, are guided by a presumption favoring innovation and change. To understand the distribution of burdens in the public realm, Goodnight analyzes how presumptions have been constructed over time to favor left and right leaning politics. These two set positions on permanence and change, Goodnight observes, constitute the "political orientation that offers a vibrant dialectic of centrist public argument and political debate."[16] Goodnight's essay, a classic among rhetorically oriented studies of argumentation, has had and continues to have a liberating impact on our understanding of presumption and burden of proof as the structural determinates within which argumentation is realized in public political discourse. In this revision of his original paper, Goodnight enlarges his account of presumptions to encompass their role in counterpublic discourses that arise outside the center of political debate. Here, arguers critique mainstream politics and established presumptions; their presumptions are oppositional and mistrustful of the limited range of presumptions embedded in established left-right public argumentation. One set of presumptions thus works against another set in the search for what deserves testing, what standards to apply, and how public argumentation should proceed.

Nicholas Rescher's seminal account of the work that presumptions and burden of proof do in epistemically oriented dialogues interweaves both dialectical and philosophical perspectives. It is the source of much contemporary dialectical interest in presumption and burden of proof and is also a barometer of their larger importance when it comes to argumentation as a source of knowledge, responsible decision making, and well-founded self-knowledge. For Rescher, "It is worthwhile to study the process of disputation closely because it offers—in miniaturized form, as it were—a vivid view of the structure and workings of the validating mechanisms which support our claims to knowledge."[17] Turning his attention to the process of disputation with this epistemic interest, Rescher finds that the inferential links underlying many knowledge claims are "*presumptive* rather than deductively airtight. [...] [This] means that in *dialectical* (as opposed to *deductive*) reasoning an assessment of the cognitive standing of a thesis can never leave its probative origins behind altogether."[18] Drawing on traditions of legal discourse, medieval dialectics, Whately's contributions, and modern intercollegiate debates for conceptions of dialectical tools, Rescher provides a reasonably comprehensive sketch of the structure presumptions and burdens of proof afford to a well-ordered dialogue. His construction of this process is moderately abstract and idealized, to the point that it could not be realized in practice without a corresponding set of institutional rules.[19] Rescher's sketch of the roles presumptions and burdens of proof play is familiar to argumentation theorists and instructive to anyone seriously undertaking study of these topics. The process (dialogue) is initiated by a proponent who categorically asserts a thesis she proposes to defend; the initiating burden of proof lies with her throughout the dialogue. By contrast, during the exchange the evidential burden of proof may shift back and forth as the proponent provides reason and evidence to establish what seem to be good reasons supporting her position. In the end, if the proponent sustains a *prima facie* case, she will have provided presumptive reason to accept the proposition she propounds. Presumption figures in this account as a feature of the status of the proposition sustained by a *prima facie* case. Rescher's account contains an interesting view of what counts as a *prima facie* case, what standard a body of argument must meet to merit presumptive status, that is, to stand good until overturned. This criterion, Rescher says, comes from outside the dialogue. It is the standard of plausibility.

Writing from the perspective of informal logic, James B. Freeman in "The Significance of Presumptions in Informal Logic" holds that a good argument is based on acceptable premises, which are relevant to its conclusion and constitute grounds adequate for accepting or believing that conclusion. His question, then, is: What are acceptable premises? What premises can serve as the starting points for argument? Like Perelman and Rescher, Freeman recognizes that argumentation can only be possible if some premises are accepted without further questioning, and he adopts a strong view that not only includes presumptions among the starting points for argument but also attempts to explicate premise acceptability in terms of the concept of a presumption. In addition, Freeman holds that our understanding of argument needs a concept of presumption to identify the force of arguments based on defeasible premises. Freeman notices that a conception of presumptions as starting points for arguments needs to square with the widely held view that presumptions are inferences. Accordingly, he distinguishes between a "statement's *being* a presumption and *justifying* that it has that status."[20] Following Rescher, Freeman takes a presumption to be a proposition that stands good until challenged. Accordingly, what appears to a person visually has, in Freeman's view, the immediate status of a presumption and retains that status until some defeating objection is raised—until, for example, someone objects that this person has recently ingested a hallucinogenic mushroom.

Freeman rejects legal conceptions of presumption on the ground that they are merely stipulated, and he likewise rejects what he describes as a rhetorical conception of presumption as grounded in little more than the psychological dispositions of audiences. In their place, Freeman advances an epistemological conception tying the presumption for a claim to sources that vouch for it. The range of vouching sources is quite wide: the deliverances of memory and the senses, common knowledge and expert opinion, personal testimony, and so on. In Freeman's view, considerations are tied to presumptions by a cost/benefit analysis based on epistemic evaluations. If certain considerations seem to adequately vouch for a claim, if no defeating objections are present, and if the cost of further investigation would not be warranted, then the claim should be accorded presumptive status. Freeman maintains that this conception of presumption accommodates both those propositions that are to be accepted as starting points for arguments and those that attain presumptive status through supporting arguments. For Freeman, inquiry into what considerations properly vouch for presumptive claims is an exercise in applied epistemology and points to a field of inquiry properly termed "informal logic." Hence, if premise acceptability is understood as premise justification as analyzed through presumption, our investigation of this concept is an instance of doing epistemology. Informal logic then is a branch of epistemology seeking to identify and justify criteria or canons for judging arguments to be epistemically good, and to delimit the practice whereby the epistemic goodness of arguments can be certified. The concept of presumption leads informal logic to this self-understanding. Seeing this connection discloses a major significance of presumption for informal logic.[21]

David Godden also delves into the logic of presumptive propositions, arguing that in "Presumably, $p$," the qualifier should not be understood as expressing an epistemic modality but rather one appropriate in practical reasoning. He notes that there are many modal qualifiers and asks whether "presumably" could be reduced to certain others, eliminating any need to develop a special theory of presumption. His thesis is that, when used epistemically, "presumably" can be reduced to other modalities; at the same time, it has a unique use in practical reasoning. Godden notes that "presumably" has been used to classify statuses when dealing with "default entitlement to standing commitments, and for conclusions supported by provisionally adequate cases."[22] In each of these cases, however, he argues that "presumably" may be properly substituted by the modalities "plausibly" or "defeasibly." Default entitlements are either dialectical (participants will agree to allow some statements to have presumptive status at the beginning of a dialogue so that reasoning can proceed from them) or epistemic (the sources or features of these claims give them presumptive status). Regarding epistemic default entitlements, Godden argues that we hold such claims because we believe we have good reasons for them and grant this entitlement to the claims of others, except in cases of disagreement. Hence, to advance a default commitment does not impose on an objector a burden to challenge the commitment. Godden finds support for his view in that we need "not attribute presumptive acceptability to standing commitments, since our entitlement to them does not impose an obligation of a reverse burden of proof upon objectors."[23] Rather, the modality we use here should be "plausibly," which "conveys a tentative, defeasible but actionable entitlement [but] does not connote the reverse burden of proof characteristic of presumptions."[24]

Provisionally adequate cases deal with arguments that, while they do not conclusively establish an entitlement for their conclusions based on their premises for which there is an entitlement, do constitute a *prima facie* case. Godden grants that one can appropriately characterize these arguments as rendering the conclusion presumptively acceptable but objects that if this is all one claims, one could just as well have used "defeasibly." To attempt to reduce "presumptively" to "defeasibly" disregards that presumptive acceptability can be justified by other than epistemic considerations, namely practical considerations, specifically the need to move an argument forward, as Edna Ullmann-Margalit has shown. A statement for which at present there is not sufficient evidence for epistemic justification may be counted acceptable for nonepistemic reasons connected with the goal of the discussion. Why then, Godden asks, should "presumably" be regarded as an epistemic modality? Furthermore, "a perfectly serviceable account of presumption as a nonepistemic modality is ready at hand," namely Ullmann-Margalit's. To presume that $p$ is to proceed as if $p$ were the case rather than taking $p$ to be the case. The force of "Presumably, $p$" is practical rather than epistemic.

Douglas Walton's essay marks a transition from the dialectical and logical interest in presumptions and burdens of proof to a perspective more concerned with the theory of speech acts. In his essay "The Speech Act of Presumption by Reversal of Burden of Proof," he sets out to do three things: (1) to distinguish presumption from other closely related concepts, (2) to refine the speech act analysis of presuming, and (3) to explain the relation of speech acts to the reversal of burden of proof.

Walton first distinguishes assumptions, assertions, presumptions, and presuppositions based on the roles they can play in conversational dialogues. The simplest is an assertion. The protagonist immediately incurs a burden of providing supporting evidence for an assertion if asked to do so. Burdens of proof invariably accompany assertions. A presumption is different. It is taken for granted as accepted by both parties unless the respondent comes up with some reason to reject it. That is, with presumptions it is the respondent who has a burden of proof and who must either accept the presumption or give an argument for not accepting it. An assumption is weaker than an assertion. It can only be allowed in dialogue with the consent of both parties, usually on the anticipation that it might lead somewhere interesting. Assumptions are tentative and can be easily withdrawn. Whereas assertions, presumptions, and assumptions are all forward-looking in a dialogue (because they have consequences for subsequent turns), presuppositions are backward-looking to an earlier turn. For example, at any stage in a dialogue the claim that Jones had been dishonorably discharged from the military requires an accepted step at an earlier turn to the effect that Jones was a member of the military. The earlier step is a presupposition of the latter step.

Walton identifies four kinds of conditions that must be satisfied in giving an analysis of the presumption of speech acts: the preparatory condition, the placement condition, the retraction condition, and the burden condition. The preparatory condition requires that the participants are engaged in a dialogue in which a certain proposition, A, would be useful. The placement condition is that A is introduced by the proponent and becomes a commitment of both parties unless the opponent can offer sufficient reason to reject A (the opponent has the burden of proof). By the rejection condition, the opponent can withdraw their commitment to A at any time provided they have good evidence against it. Finally, the burden condition is something made especially conspicuous by dialogue theory: it is that an assumption, A, must be allowed to remain tentatively accepted at least until the proponent has had a chance to show its utility in moving the discussion forward.

Imagine a dialogue in which a grandson is claiming his inheritance from his grandfather who has been long missing. The executors of the grandfather's estate refuse to comply with the request, demanding that the grandson should offer sufficient evidence that the grandfather is deceased. They thus saddle the grandchild with a burden of proof. However, the grandson can reply with the legal presumption that someone who has not been heard from in seven years is to be presumed dead. He thus shifts the burden back to the executors by having introduced a recognized presumption into the dialogue. It is this kind of situation Walton has in mind when he speaks of reversing the burden of proof by the speech act of presumption. There are then two ways to shift a burden of proof in dialogue: by introducing a presumption or by satisfactorily meeting the burden of proof.

With Ullmann-Margalit's paper, we move from a primary focus on rhetoric and dialectic to issues considered from a philosophical perspective, including informal logic. Both her paper here and her earlier paper "On Presumption"[25] are philosophical analyses of presumption. She does not speak of presumptions *simpliciter*, but of *presumption formulae*, *presumption-raising facts* and *presumed facts*. In her account, presumption formulae express *presumption rules* of the form: given that $p$ (the presumption-raising fact) is the case, you shall proceed as if $q$ (the presumed fact) were the case, unless or until you have (sufficient) reason to believe that $q$ is not the case. These rules are issued to persons "engaged in a process of practical deliberation whose resolution materially depends [. . .] on an answer to the factual question of whether $q$ is or is not the case."[26] In this respect, Ullmann-Margalit underlines, presumption rules are not inferences per se but are licenses to proceed. The paper included in this volume illustrates her proposal by shedding light on the analysis of Grice's Cooperative Principle[27] (CP) as a presumption governing the interpretations of utterances rather than as a principle governing the production of utterances. Her contention is that, so understood, CP turns into an *Interpretative Presumption of Cooperation*, whose justification is based not only on inductive-probabilistic considerations having to do with the evidence that, as a matter of fact, people tend to cooperate in the way Grice describes, but also with a two-tiered normative consideration having to do with (1) "with the question of which sort of error is morally or socially more acceptable: acting on $q$ when not-$q$ is in fact the case, or vice-versa"; and (2) "with the moral or social evaluation of the regulative effect on people's behavior of the presumption rule's being instituted and operative."[28] By means of this account of CP, Ullmann-Margalit is in a position to justify Grice's intuition that communicative cooperation is not only a fact but also something rational to do and to expect from others. In addition, by means of her account of presumptions, Ullmann-Margalit is also able to show that there are three different ways in which appeals to the normal are made: (1) as the presumed fact, (2) as a justifying consideration, and (3) as the premise in a presumptive inference.

For her part, Lilian Bermejo-Luque considers that the pair presumption/ burden of proof cannot ground the evaluation of argumentative procedures when it comes to their ability to justify our claims. In her view, the source of epistemic normativity does not spring from the rules that sanction argumentative dialogical procedures but rather comes from what she takes to be the constitutive correctness conditions of the speech act of arguing.[29] Thus, from a linguistic-pragmatic perspective, Bermejo-Luque somehow agrees with the rhetorical tradition in considering burdens of proof not as epistemic obligations but as practical requirements that have to do with parties' needs to persuade others of their views by giving reasons for them. In this respect, she criticizes not only dialogical foundationalism (i.e., the thesis that certain views are backed by presumptions in their favor, so that those holding these views are, in principle, relieved of arguing for them), but also dialogical egalitarianism (i.e., the thesis that any view must be argued for, if so required by an opponent). This is because, in her view, the question of determining who must give reasons for her claims cannot be settled independently of a substantive assessment of the initial plausibility of each claim. For Bermejo-Luque, the general principle "[she or] he who asserts must prove" is inadequate as a guide for communicative exchanges, even if they aim at truth and knowledge.

Accordingly, Bermejo-Luque's interest in presumptions is not focused on the way argumentative procedures are supposed to be developed but on the way acts of arguing that include expressions of the form "I presume that $p$," "*p*, I presume," and "Presumably, *p*" are to be analyzed and assessed. In previous works, she has suggested that the semantics of these expressions is key for understanding the difference between presumptions and presumptive inferences. Particularly, she characterized presumptions as a type of constative speech act that can be explicitly performed by using a performative expression such as "I presume." Following the analogy with assertions, Bermejo-Luque contends that "if asserting that *p* is behaving so as to count as meaning that *p* is true, presuming that *p* is behaving so as to count as meaning that it is reasonable to assume that *p*."[30] So understood, a paradigmatic presumption would be the famous sentence "Dr. Livingstone, I presume," and it would be a kind of speech act that can enter either as a premise ("this is business as usual, I presume; so, I should be ready") or conclusion ("she always phones if she cannot come; therefore, I must still wait, I presume") in an act of arguing. At any rate, in Bermejo-Luque's view, presumptions would not be "more able to shift the burden of proof to an opponent than is any other tentative claim to truth." In turn, she holds, presumptive inferences would be inferences having presumptions as their warrants, so as to sanction the use of an epistemic modal such as "presumably"—much in the same way in which, in her account, warrants that are necessary/probable/plausible sanction the use of epistemic modals such as "necessarily," "probably," or "plausibly."[31]

Finally, Fred J. Kauffeld deals with the pair presumption/burden of proof (or *probative obligations*, as he prefers to call them) as a matter of the pragmatic normativity of communication. But in contrast with other normative pragmatic proposals such as pragma-dialectics, Kauffeld's bottom-up approach does not seek to establish rules for conducting argumentative exchanges; rather, he attempts to *discover* these rules in the analysis of different types of speech acts that are characteristically performed in argumentative communication. In his contribution to this volume, he focuses particularly on the speech acts of *proposing* and *accusing*, offering an analysis of Martin Luther King Jr.'s "Letter from Birmingham Jail" to illustrate the dynamics of incurring, discharging, and shifting probative obligations.

Kauffeld criticizes dialectically oriented approaches for having adopted an "unduly narrow" construction of these obligations. For, in his view, these obligations are not epistemic but pragmatic, as they stem from the pragmatic conditions and consequences of performing certain communicative moves, whether they are part of procedures that aim at truth and justification or not. According to Kauffeld's pragmatic account, we incur probative burdens by merely performing certain speech acts—characteristically, those that usually initiate argumentation. Thus, for example, the norm of assertion involves the supposition that speakers are committed to speak truthfully and that they are responsible for the truth of what they say. In Kauffeld's view, this is precisely the reason why there is a special relationship between presumptions and probative obligations. This relationship has to do with the fact that the pragmatic force of presumptive inferences involves a distribution of responsibilities, rights, and obligations in conversations, dialogues, discourses, and other human interactions. For example, because speakers making assertions proper have the burden not only of speaking truthfully but also of having made a reasonable effort to ascertain the rational foundation of what they say, addressees can presume not only that speakers are sincere but (derivatively) they can also presume that what a speaker says when making an assertion proper is true. As Kauffeld points out, "in favorable circumstances, the fact that $S$ says that $p$ and thereby engages a presumption of veracity provides $A$ with adequate reason to believe that $p$."[32] In such cases $S$ does not encounter a burden of proof. However, in other circumstances, this presumption is too vague to justify the rational and empirical adequacy of the proposition $S$ has advanced. In such cases $S$ may undertake a probative obligation to induce skeptical consideration of her views. In this respect, Kauffeld's proposal would render more specific the principle "she or he who asserts must prove."

Kauffeld's proposal seeks to clarify the nature of the relationship between presumptions and probative burdens, not only in terms of its normative pragmatic framework but also its function in persuasive discourse. In his view, the need of providing reasons is not merely instrumental to the possibility of persuading our addressees but an obligation proper, although a pragmatic type of obligation instead of an epistemic one. In everyday argumentation we incur a variety of such obligations, and the possibility of discharging them explains not only the persuasive force of our performance but also the realignment of probative obligations in communicative exchanges—that is, the shifting of the burden of proof.

It is a commonplace that at least three disciplines study argumentation: rhetoric, dialectic, and logic.[33] Joseph Wenzel[34] sees rhetoric as concerned with addressing messages to audiences to win their acceptance of certain claims. Dialectic investigates how parties to a discussion may use rules of procedure to regulate their exchange to constitute a critical discussion to bring about critical agreement. Logic lays out and proceeds to evaluate arguments for cogency: are the premises acceptable and so connected to the conclusion that they render the conclusion acceptable? None of the essays in this part of the book are concerned solely with just one of these perspectives. The early chapters (Ehninger and Brockriede to Goodnight) are clearly concerned with rhetoric but also with the shape that recognition of presumption and burden of proof give to communication. Dialectic invariably intrudes wherever ordered discussion is wanted. The next set of chapters (from Kauffeld and Freeman's essay on Rescher to Godden) focuses more predominantly on the epistemological and dialectical aspects of presumption and burden of proof. But the dialectical considerations become connected to logical questions in the hands of Freeman and Godden. The last group of essays (from Walton to Kauffeld) is primarily concerned with the speech act of presuming as it occurs in dialectical contexts, but they also lean on epistemological ideas. It is fair to say, then, that these essays also belong to communication theory, and so by extension to rhetoric.

Whether coming from the rhetorical and dialectical perspectives or the logical and philosophical, or the communicative, these essays connect the concepts of presumption and burden of proof with a host of other concepts. Thus, they provide a spectrum of viewpoints, some mutually supporting and others dissenting, on presumption and burden of proof and their interrelations with perspectives on argument.

Fred J. Kauffeld

James B. Freeman

Lilian Bermejo-Luque

## Notes

1. Nicholas Rescher, *Dialectics: A Controversy-Oriented Approach to the Theory of Knowledge* (Albany: State University of New York Press, 1977), 30.
2. Douglas Ehninger and Wayne Brockriede, *Decision by Debate* (Toronto: Dodd, Mead, 1973), 83 (this volume, p. 103).
3. Ehninger and Brockriede, *Decision by Debate*, 85 (this volume, p. 106).
4. Ehninger and Brockriede, *Decision by Debate*, 85 (this volume, p. 107).
5. Ehninger and Brockriede, *Decision by Debate*, 85 (this volume, p. 107).
6. Ehninger and Brockriede, *Decision by Debate*, 85 (this volume, p. 108).
7. Rescher, *Dialectics*, 27.
8. F. H. van Eemeren and R. Grootendorst, "The Study of Argumentation from a Speech Act Perspective," in *Pragmatics at Issue: Selected Papers of the International Pragmatics Conference, Antwerp, August 17–22, 1987*, ed. J. Verschueren (Amsterdam: John Benjamins, 1991), 1:164; and F. H. van Eemeren, *Strategic Maneuvering in Argumentative Discourse: Extending the Pragma-Dialectical Theory of Argumentation* (Amsterdam: John Benjamins, 2010), 225–26.
9. See Michael Leff, "Rhetoric and Dialectic in the Twenty-First Century," *Argumentation* 14, no. 3 (2000): 241–54; and Michael Leff, "Rhetoric and Dialectic in Martin Luther King's 'Letter from Birmingham Jail,'" in *Proceedings of the Fifth Conference of the International Society for the Study of Argumentation*, ed. F. H. van Eemeren, A. Blair, C. A. Willard, and A. F. Snoeck Henkemans (Amsterdam: Sic Sat, 2003), 671–77.
10. Gaskins, "Juridical Roots," this volume, p. 129.
11. Crosswhite, "Inertia in Argumentation," this volume, p. 142.
12. Richard Gaskins, *Burdens of Proof in Modern Discourse* (New Haven, CT: Yale University Press, 1992), 37.

13. Crosswhite, "Inertia in Argumentation," this volume, p. 146.

14. Chaïm Perelman and Lucie Olbrechts-Tyteca, *The New Rhetoric: A Treatise on Argumentation*, trans. John Wilkinson and Purcell Weaver (Notre Dame, IN: University of Notre Dame Press, 1969), 464. Quoted by Crosswhite, "Inertia in Argumentation," this volume, pp. 149–50.

15. G. Thomas Goodnight, "'The Liberal and the Conservative Presumption: On Political Philosophy and the Foundation of Public Argument," in *Proceedings of the Summer Conference on Argumentation*, ed. Jack Rhodes and Sara Newell (Falls Church, VA: Speech Communication Association, 1980), 304–37.

16. Goodnight, "Liberal-Progressive and Conservative Presumptions," this volume, p. 171.

17. Rescher, *Dialectics*, 3.

18. Rescher, *Dialectics*, 8.

19. Rescher, *Dialectics*, 30.

20. James B. Freeman, "Significance of Presumptions," this volume, p. 197.

21. Freeman's view is further developed in *Acceptable Premises: An Epistemic Approach to an Informal Logic Problem* (Cambridge: Cambridge University Press, 2005).

22. David Godden, "Analyzing Presumption," this volume, p. 207.

23. Godden, "Analyzing Presumption," this volume, p. 212.

24. Godden, "Analyzing Presumption," this volume, p. 212.

25. Edna Ullmann-Margalit, "On Presumptions," *Journal of Philosophy* 80, no. 3 (1983): 143–63.

26. Ullmann-Margalit, "Some Presumptions," this volume, p. 234.

27. H. P. Grice, "Logic and Conversation," in *The Logic of Grammar*, ed. D. Davidson and G. Harman (Berkely: University of California Press, 1975), 64–75.

28. Ullmann-Margalit, "Some Presumptions," this volume, p. 235.

29. Lilian Bermejo-Luque, *Giving Reasons: A Linguistic-Pragmatic Approach to Argumentation* (Dordrecht: Springer, 2011), 40–51.

30. Lilian Bermejo-Luque, "Being a Correct Presumption vs. Being Presumably the Case," *Informal Logic* 36, no. 1 (2016): 1–25.

31. Bermejo-Luque, *Giving Reasons*, 170–79.

32. Fred J. Kauffeld, "Rhetorically Oriented Account," this volume, p. 261.

33. Today, many might support adding a fourth: computer science, specifically artificial intelligence.

34. Joseph Wenzel, "Jürgen Habermas and the Dialectical Perspective on Argumentation," *Journal of the American Forensic Association* 16, no. 2 (1979): 83–94.

# 9

# The Anatomy of a Dispute

Douglas Ehninger and Wayne Brockriede

When men are brought face to face with their opponents, forced to listen
and learn and mend their ideas, they cease to be children and begin to live
like civilized men.

—Walter Lippmann

## A Hypothetical Example

It is a hot August afternoon. Mr. N on his way home from the office comes
to the bus stop and, finding a single spot of shade just large enough to cover
him, steps into it gratefully. Soon Mr. A, a fellow worker, approaches and, seeing the only spot of shade already occupied by Mr. N, resigns himself to wait-
ing in the sun. A certain order of things—a certain pattern of relationships
among Mr. N, Mr. A, and the spot of shade—is thus established and persists
until the bus arrives.

But now suppose that instead of being a peaceful, timid soul, Mr. A is an
aggressive, belligerent individual, and that he attempts to push Mr. N out of
the shady spot, by words or manner challenging him to retain it. Under these
circumstances, one of two reactions is possible: (a) Mr. N may let the challenge pass, and move as Mr. A desires, so that a new pattern of relationships is
established, with Mr. A now in the shade and Mr. N out in the sun. (b) Mr. N
may try to repel Mr. A's aggression, with the result that blows are exchanged
and a fight develops.

Either way, two facts are to be observed: (a) Mr. N and Mr. A want the
same spot of shade, a spot too small for both of them to occupy at once; and
(b) when Mr. A attempts to push Mr. N out of the shade he takes a certain
risk, a risk on which he has to make good if he is to achieve what he wants,
and even, perhaps, avoid physical harm to himself. For Mr. N may respond to
A's shove by knocking him down and beating him soundly. Then Mr. A would
not only fail to win the place in the shade, but might sustain injuries, as well.

Now let us vary the story in one respect. Assume that the altercation between Mr. N and Mr. A, instead of involving shoves and blows, is confined
to words.

In this new situation, Mr. A, on approaching the bus stop, might say: "By rights, N, that spot of shade belongs to me." Again, Mr. N has two courses of action open to him: (a) He may reply, "Yes, that is so," and move out of the shady spot, allowing Mr. A to occupy it; or (b) he may answer, "I deny this spot of shade belongs to you. Prove that such is, indeed, true."

Three observations are to be made about this second version of the story:

1. Although less direct physical danger may be involved in the verbal declaration than in the shove, Mr. A still takes a risk when he asserts that the shade by rights belongs to him, for, unless his claim is to be idle talk, he must be able to prove the necessity, expediency, or justice of the state of affairs he seeks. This, too, is a "risk," not only because failure to make good his claim means that it will be impossible for A to achieve the goal he seeks, but also because defeat may cause him to lose status in the eyes of N and of the community as a whole, so that in the end he will be less well off than before.

2. The verbal assertion, no less than the physical blow, is an agitating force. It has the effect of stirring up and throwing into turmoil what had previously been a static and ordered situation, a situation which, it may be assumed, would have remained static had the challenge not been issued.

3. The verbal assertion, no less than the physical blow, specifies the particular reordering—the new pattern of relationships—that A believes should replace the old order. It says that instead of N being in the shade and A in the sun, A should be in the shade and N in the sun.

## Presumption, Burden of Proof, and Burden of Going Forward with the Debate

Keeping these points in mind, one must consider two concepts that are of the greatest importance in understanding what happens when contending parties engage in a debate. They are *presumption* and *burden of proof.*

As the two versions of the story about Mr. N and Mr. A showed, the battle of fists and the battle of words arose for the same reason: Mr. N was occupying a particular piece of ground that Mr. A believed N should not be on.

In this respect, the story is completely typical. Every debate that ever has or ever will take place concerns, if not an actual, at least a figurative piece of ground. One of the disputants *preoccupies*—figuratively stands upon—an idea, interpretation, or value that the other thinks he should not be occupying. Indeed, unless some actual or figurative piece of ground is preoccupied, there can be no debate. There is no established order or pattern of relationships that may be challenged. The situation is chaotic or formless and hence not subject to reordering. There is nothing to argue about, no matter concerning which the parties can disagree. For a debate to occur, the occupancy of a piece of argumentative ground must be contested. Here, as at many other points in a description of debates and verbal disputes, the analogy to a physical order or event is both close and pertinent.

The technical term for the preoccupation of a piece of argumentative ground is *presumption*. The party who at the beginning of the debate stands upon the disputed ground—in our example, Mr. N—is, therefore, said to have the presumption.

Presumption is, however, neither more nor less than such preoccupation. As a concept, it makes no evaluation of the situation it labels. To say that one of the parties to a dispute has the presumption does not mean that the ground which he occupies is occupied legitimately or illegitimately or that he should or should not be standing on it. The term only describes a situation that exists and points out the prevailing order of things by declaring that one of the disputants stands at a particular place within that order.

*Natural and Artificial Presumption.* As a description of an existing system of relationships, presumption may be either *natural* or *artificial.*

Natural presumption reflects things as they are viewed in the world about us. If an argument involves a belief concerning existing institutions, practices, customs, mores, values, or interpretations, the presumption is automatically in favor of that belief simply because the institutions, etc., are thought to exist.

Artificial presumption, on the other hand, is the result of ground arbitrarily assigned, a preoccupation by agreement rather than by the present order of things. That a man brought to trial is to be presumed innocent until proved guilty is an example of presumption of this second sort.

The point to bear in mind, however, is that neither natural nor artificial presumption evaluates. The former does not say that a belief about existing institutions, practices, customs, mores, values, or interpretations is intrinsically good or even better than anything that might be substituted for it. Presumption merely recognizes that the belief now stands on the ground that any alternative belief would have to occupy. Nor does the artificial presumption of innocence mean that an accused man is more apt to be innocent than guilty, or that the judge thinks him innocent, or that most men brought to trial are not guilty.[1] Here the presumption is only a man-made convention, invoked so that an order may be established and debate proceed. The accused must be placed on some piece of ground to begin with; and American legal tradition assumes that the interests of justice and expediency will best be served if he is assigned the ground of "innocence." In short, presumption is always descriptive, never evaluative.

## Burden of Proof

Whereas presumption is the preoccupation of argumentative ground, burden of proof is the obligation devolving upon the party who advances a statement—or, as it is called when formally worded, a *proposition*[2]—that challenges that occupancy. In most debates outside the courtroom, the burden of proof is twofold. It entails (a) showing that the person, idea, institution, or practice now occupying the disputed ground should not be there; and (b) specifying what person, idea, institution, or practice should be there. Hence, burden of proof both criticizes the present order and recommends a new one, the specific content and scope of the "burden" being determined by the wording of the proposition that is advanced. (In the hypothetical case outlined above, for example, Mr. A would have to prove (a) that Mr. N should not be in the spot of shade, and (b) that he, Mr. A, should be.)

Unlike presumption, which merely describes, burden of proof evaluates and recommends. Instead of reporting what is, it declares what should be. And because it does evaluate, assuming the burden of proof involves taking the risk described [above.[3]]

There is no risk in description. Descriptions are merely reports, and as such accurate or inaccurate, complete or incomplete, clear or unclear. But when the debater criticizes and recommends, he takes the risk that he will not be able to prove his criticism justified or his recommendation sound. The burden of proof may, therefore, most accurately and usefully be defined as *the risk involved in advancing the proposition*.

## The Burden of Going Forward with the Debate

Having defined presumption as the preoccupation of a piece of argumentative ground and burden of proof as the risk involved in advancing the proposition, we return to Mr. A and Mr. N.

All was calm and at rest—in technical language, the "universe" of the bus stop was quiescent—until Mr. A declared, "By rights, N, that spot of shade belongs to me." By advancing this proposition A disturbed the situation initially. Moreover, his proposition specified the exact burden of proof that A, as the party standing outside the disputed ground, must now be prepared to assume.

But the proposition alone did not start the dispute. Had Mr. N, without replying, surrendered the shady spot to A, no interchange would have taken place, even though a proposition had been advanced. Instead, a new order would have been established quickly and peacefully. The debate began only when N answered A's challenge by saying, "I deny this spot of shade belongs to you. Prove that such is, indeed, true."

This reply, operating in conjunction with A's challenge, produced the controversy, by forcing A to do more than mouth assertions. Now he was required to produce proof to support the proposition he had advanced.

If, for instance, at this point A were to say, "I have no proof. Let's just forget the whole matter," he obviously would fail to make good on the risk he took in initiating the dispute. Under these circumstances, not only would any impartial judge be forced to declare against him, but, as a practical matter, he would lose all hope of gaining the desired place in the shade. Therefore, if he is to attain the end for which he began the debate in the first place, A must now make good his claim. He must do as N asks and present proof designed to show its expediency and justice. In other words, he must go *forward with the debate*. Unless he does so, obviously his case will fail.

This obligation of going forward with the debate is a new and additional one, quite distinct from the risk A took in advancing his original proposition. Of course, if he had not challenged N, he would not now be called on to carry the debate forward. But it was not merely the advancing of the proposition that gave rise to the new burden. What directly motivated this second obligation was not A's challenge, but N's response. Had N not answered, the obligation would not have risen. Had N answered differently from the way he did, the obligation would have assumed a different form. But since N did deny the challenge in the fashion stated, A is now called on to make good his claim by proving that the shady spot is "by rights" his.

*Prima Facie Case.* The first thing A must do in discharging his obligation of going forward with the debate is to make out what is technically called a *prima facie case*[4]—that is, *a case that any reasonable judge would consider strong enough to stand, unless or until refutation is offered against it.* If A cannot make good his claim at least to this extent, he can hardly expect a further hearing. To have any validity at all, his case must at the minimum be able to stand by itself.

But making out a *prima facie* case is only the first step involved in carrying the debate forward. In a second, and equally important, phase of this process, N as well as A participates. For when A has successfully made out a *prima facie* case, his obligation is for the moment discharged. Now N must bestir himself. If he wants to maintain his place in the shade, he must counter A's *prima facie* case strongly enough so that it can no longer stand without additional support, or without A's showing the invalidity or irrelevance of N's attacks upon it.[5]

Assuming that N does attack successfully, the burden of going forward then shifts back to A. It is once more his duty to offer proof or refutation so that his *prima facie* case may be reconstituted and his cause strengthened. But A's action only calls for a new response from N, to which A must again reply. And so the debate proceeds, with each party alternately bestirring the other into action, until the evidence and proofs have been exhausted or a predetermined time limit has expired. Then he who by this process of alternating action and counteraction has achieved a preponderance of proof, thus establishing his "right" beyond the point where it can reasonably be disputed, may be awarded the decision.

The importance to each party of this alternating obligation to carry the debate forward may be seen by supposing the arrival of the bus at various stages during the course of the controversy between N and A. If, for example, the bus arrives after A has issued his challenge but before he has an opportunity to develop a *prima facie* case, any reasonable judge, being called on to decide the dispute at this point, would have to declare in favor of N. If, however, it arrives after the *prima facie* case is completed and before N has an opportunity to reply, the award would have to be for A; if after a successful attack upon that case, for N; etc. Not until both sides have had a fair and equal chance to present all of their proofs, or an agreed time limit is exhausted, is a final or summary decision possible.

*The Burden of Proof Does Not Shift.* A discussion of the difference between the burden of proof and the burden of going forward with the debate requires attention to a frequently misunderstood matter.

While the burden of going forward with the debate constantly shifts back and forth between the contesting parties, the burden of proof does not. From beginning to end it always rests with him who challenges the existing order. Unlike the burden of going forward, it is not a subsequent or contingent obligation. Rather, the burden of proof represents the risk involved in originating the action by advancing the proposition in the first place. Since the challenger puts forward the proposition, he must accept as his permanent and unshiftable obligation the task of making good on whatever risk it entails.

Moreover, this obligation requires that the challenging party maintain his proof throughout the debate at a level above equilibrium. Unlike the defendant, he cannot be satisfied with a balance or standoff. Although a draw in proof may subject the existing order to severe tests and put it on its mettle to defend itself, in the end it leaves that order unaltered, with the original occupant still in control of the contested ground. To make good his claim the challenger must do more than threaten or annoy; he must effect a rearrangement.

Consider, again, the dispute at the bus stop. N may maintain the existing order of himself in the shade and A in the sun simply by parrying or countering the attempts of A to alter it. He need not show cause why the situation should not be altered. A, on the contrary, must offer affirmative proof why it should. In conducting his defense of the present order N must, of course, from time to time go forward with the debate by advancing proof or refutation. This requirement, however, represents only a temporary shift in the center of gravity of the controversy, not a shift in the fundamental obligations of the parties. These obligations remain constant. A must strike and maintain throughout a level of proof sufficiently above equilibrium to effect the rearrangement he desires. This margin of proof above equilibrium represents the unshiftable obligation he assumed in initiating the action. Hence, another way to define the burden of proof is to say it consists of such a margin.

## Notes

Reprinted from Douglas Ehninger and Wayne Brockriede, *Decision by Debate* (New York: Dodd, Mead, 1973), 81–87. Notes in square brackets added by HVH. The orthography of the original has been preserved.—Eds.

1. Richard Whately, *Elements of Rhetoric* (London: 1828), 1.3.2 (this volume, p. 45).
2. See Chapter 14. [Chapter 14 has the title "Analyzing the Proposition."]
3. [Described earlier in the first section of this essay.]
4. See the definition of "case" on p. 233 of Chapter 15. ["A debate case may be defined, therefore, *as a structure of proofs a debater selects to substantiate his claims on the issue of a controversy for the purpose of influencing the beliefs of a particular audience.*"]
5. See James M. O'Neill, Craven Laycock, and Robert L. Scales, *Argumentation and Debate* (New York: The Macmillan Company, 1917), 33–38.

# 10

# A Pragma-Dialectical Analysis of the Burden of Proof

Frans H. van Eemeren and Peter Houtlosser

## The Pragma-Dialectical Approach to Argumentation

During the past three decades, the study of argumentation has seen a remarkable revival of both dialectic and rhetoric. There is at the same time some debate about their status and mutual relationship. Johnson, for one, is not sure about whether dialectic is a "free-standing discipline"; he seems inclined to assign dialectic a supplementary role. Leff sees a separate place in argumentation theory for dialectic beside rhetoric. Where these authors both perceive dialectic in the first place as an addition to logic or rhetoric, we view dialectic as the heart of the study of the argumentative process of critically testing opinions.[1]

By making use of dialectical insight taken from critical rationalism and dialogue logic, van Eemeren and Grootendorst have developed a procedure for resolving differences of opinion by testing standpoints critically.[2] In agreement with Barth and Krabbe's requirements of problem-validity and conventional validity,[3] no moves are allowed that are inconsistent or in any other way interfere with the resolution process or that do not cohere with the point of departure as defined by the arguers. We favor a pragma-dialectical approach that situates argumentation in a pragmatic context of instrumental action within a dialectical procedural framework. Among the theoretical tools for substantiating the pragmatic dimension of this approach are speech act theory, discourse analysis, and the Gricean theory of practical rationality.

The dialectic and the pragmatic dimensions of our approach are jointly given shape by four metatheoretical principles. Unlike Rescher[4] and Biro and Siegel,[5] who define argumentation in their epistemological approaches as "plausible justification of theses" and "reasonable justification of beliefs,"[6] following the *principle of functionalization* pragma-dialecticians conceive argumentation as a complex speech act aimed at justifying or refuting a standpoint to convince the interlocutor of the acceptability or unacceptability of that standpoint.

By relying on commitments ensuing in argumentative discourse from what has been said explicitly or implicitly, thus following the *principle of externalization*, we find ourselves in agreement with Mackenzie and Staines. They also argue that an argument "directly affects, not belief or opinion, but public commitment."[7] As Hamblin observed,[8] our saying commits us, whether we believe what we say or not. We also agree with Hamblin[9] that commitments can be incurred simply by putting on the appropriate linguistic performance—in our terms, by performing the appropriate speech act. In the critical discussion we envisage, the participants' aim is to convince each other by making use of their own and each other's commitments.[10]

Walton and Krabbe[11] note that a dialogue is enabled to move forward because the participants are willing to take on commitments in a collaborative way. This observation captures the mutual coordination that, following the *principle of socialization*, is expressed in the way we situate the performance of speech acts in a dialogical context where the need for anticipating and responding to the (presumed) reactions of the other party determines the progress of the discourse. By indicating "agreement or disagreement with a preceding remark of the other speaker," the participants build up their commitment stores. As Walton and Krabbe rightly observe, to know what a party is committed to should be equal to knowing what that party should do, or not do, to live up to this commitment.[12] There must therefore be rules of procedure for performing speech acts that specify for each discussion stage under which conditions certain commitments are incurred or deleted from a participant's commitment store, from the beginning of the discussion in the confrontation stage to its termination in the concluding stage. In establishing procedural rules for resolving a difference of opinion, we provide, following the *principle of dialectification*, standards for the conduct of argumentative discourse that regulate critical interaction.[13]

In this way, we are in perfect agreement with Rescher's recommendation to move "from the plane of the [. . .] descriptive and ontological to that of the [. . .] regulative and methodological."[14] Our dialectical standards are more inclusive, and also more differentiated, than the logical standard of formal validity and the preservation of truth.[15] Dialectical soundness is what can be maintained in a party's commitment store without leading to any justified accusation of logical or pragmatic inconsistency. With Barth and Krabbe,[16] we are among those who speak of a reasonable result of a discussion when this result has been reached by arguing *ex concessis*. In other words, we opt for a pragmatic way out of the Münchhausen trilemma:[17] our pragmatic angle warrants us to stop the process of argumentation at the point where acceptance by the other party is assured.

## The "Burden of Proof" as a Procedural Concept

Argumentative discourse can only be critically evaluated in a theoretically justified way if the discourse has first been adequately analyzed.[18] This requires a method of analysis that is systematic and leads to general and sustained pronouncements rather than merely *ad hoc* observations. Starting from the pragma-dialectical point of departure, the analysis of argumentative discourse can be envisioned as a methodical reconstruction of the process of resolving the difference of opinion contained in the discourse. Our method of analysis is to lead to an "analytic overview" attuned to enabling a sound critical evaluation. The model of a critical discussion can serve as a heuristic instrument for reconstructing the discourse in such a way that it becomes clear which function the various speech acts fulfil and which commitments they create.

The way in which in an argumentative exchange the burden of proof is divided sets the stage for the interactional patterns that may develop in the discourse. The concept of "burden of proof," which has received a lot of attention since the involvement of Richard Whately, is therefore crucial in the analysis of argumentative discourse and consequently in argumentation theory. We shall explain our pragma-dialectical perspective by answering several pertinent questions, starting with the fundamental question *why a division of the burden of proof is necessary.*

In our view, a division of the burden of proof is necessary in the first place for methodological reasons. Like Rescher,[19] we consider the burden of proof a procedural concept, which serves the critical rationalist purpose of testing the tenability of a standpoint by carrying through the appropriate testing procedures as systematically, perspicuously, efficiently, and thoroughly as required. A critical discussion aimed at resolving a difference of opinion concerning the acceptability of a standpoint can only be resolved if the division of the burden of proof is clear and the parties comply with this division. We therefore implemented the principle of socialization in the opening stage of the critical discussion by regulating the mutual coordination of the critical procedure in a "burden of proof rule"[20] that regulates how the *onus probandi* regarding a standpoint is distributed in the most perspicuous way. In this way, the concept of "burden of proof" serves the "division of labor of argumentation."[21] In terms of formal dialectics, one could say that the dialogue can move forward only if the participants are taking on commitments in a collaborative way.[22] In attributing a purely methodological status to the concept of burden of proof, we differ from others who appear to attribute epistemological, ideological, ethical, or even moral qualities to assuming the burden of proof.

It is clear that there should be a division of the burden of proof. The next question, however, is: *a burden of proof for what?* In answering this question, we regard argumentative discourse as consisting of the performance of speech acts, each type of speech act creating its own commitments, and only some specific commitments creating a burden of proof. From the perspective of a critical discussion, in assertive speech acts—or speech acts to be reconstructed as assertives—two types of commitment are to be distinguished, which have different procedural consequences. First, there are assertives advancing a standpoint or an argument that in the course of the discussion becomes a substandpoint. These assertives create the specific commitment that constitutes a burden of proof. Second, there are assertives performed to establish a starting point for the discussion. These assertives create commitments that can be used in the argumentation and concluding stages of the discussion. They have the same function as the formal dialectical concessions, albeit that in a critical discussion such concessions are made by both parties and the commitments they create can be used both in defending and attacking a standpoint. Since these assertives can only serve as a starting point when—and because—they are mutually agreed upon, they do not carry a burden of proof.

*What does having a burden of proof involve?* In the pragma-dialectical perspective the burden of proof for a (sub)standpoint is the obligation to defend the standpoint once challenged to do so, that is, to justify or refute the opinion expressed in the standpoint. This implies an obligation to give an adequate rejoinder to the critical response of the other party, that is, to argue the case concerned as thoroughly and extensively as the antagonist's criticisms require. Where Johnson[23] includes dealing with contradictory or otherwise alternative standpoints in the protagonist's burden of proof, the presence of such alternative standpoints makes the dispute in our approach "mixed"—or even "multiple." Then similar conditions for a burden of proof apply to the other party. According to our principle of externalization, only those objections need to be dealt with by the protagonist that are somehow advanced in the discussion, whether explicitly, implicitly, or indirectly.

*Under which conditions is there a burden of proof?* The obligation to defend a standpoint always applies and holds fully until the protagonist has complied with his obligation to defend his standpoint or has retracted the standpoint. There are, nevertheless, some practical restrictions. In both a nonmixed and in a mixed dispute, maintaining the burden of proof does not make sense when the protagonist has earlier defended his standpoint successfully against the same antagonist starting from the same point of departure. Starting a critical discussion is also a waste of time when no joint point of departure can be established.[24]

*Who has the burden of proof?* Which task is assigned to whom is, in our approach, a matter of procedural agreement concerning the division of labor in a critical discussion. Unless it is explicitly agreed otherwise, the burden of proof is on the side of those whose standpoints are challenged by the other party. Throughout the discussion, the division of the burden of proof can, at certain points, become more diversified. As Walton and Krabbe observe, "some commitments are initially set or undertaken, and other commitments are [. . .] incurred along the way."[25] In our approach, the latter comprise both the commitment to defend the reasons in defense of the standpoint that have been challenged—and thus have become substandpoints—and the commitment to reply to the critical reactions advanced in challenging the argument schemes that connect these reasons with the standpoint at issue. Rescher[26] and Walton[27] proclaim that the protagonist's advancing a *prima facie* argument for his initial standpoint shifts the burden of proof to the other party. In our view, this amounts to a transfer of argumentative duties from one party to the other: a "shift of initiative" rather than a "shift of burden of proof."[28] In a nonmixed dispute it is up to the antagonist to ask pertinent critical questions regarding the protagonist's argument; in a mixed dispute the other party's attack will be more severe.

In a nonmixed dispute, only one party has advanced an initial standpoint. This party is also the only party that has an obligation to defend. In a mixed dispute, where two parties have advanced contradictory standpoints, each party has an obligation to defend its own standpoint. The problem is: in which order are the standpoints to be defended?

In Whately's view, the burden of proof lies in such a case on the side of him who would dispute a "presumption," so that the issue of who should start the defense is decided in favor of the party whose standpoint has the highest degree of presumption. In epistemological approaches, such as Rescher's, the crucial issue is "how readily the thesis could make its peace within the overall framework of our cognitive commitments."[29] Presumption is then conceived as a cognitive and epistemic category: the one assertion has presumption because it is more plausible than the other. In Rescher's opinion, "in most probative contexts, there is a standing presumption in favor of the usual, normal, customary course of things,"[30] which he characterizes as "the cognitive status quo."[31] When Rescher refers to "the usual course of things" in plausible assessment, his words seem to echo those of Perelman and Olbrechts-Tyteca in their *Nouvelle rhétorique*.[32] According to the pragmatic view of Ullmann-Margalit,[33] the issue is not so much concerned with "ascertaining the facts as with proceeding on them." Her procedural consideration concerning the "comparative convenience with which the parties can be expected to produce pertinent evidence" has to do with the question "of what presumption will be the most useful to adopt as an initial step in the process of deliberation [. . .], quite apart from the question whether the conclusion to which [this] adoption [...] points is likely to be true."[34] In a similar pragmatic vein, we have developed our own solution to the problem of the order of defense in a mixed dispute, which we shall explain in the next section.

Another important question to be answered is: *what means can be used to meet the burden of proof?* In to our pragma-dialectical approach, the only means of meeting the burden of proof is advancing argumentation. The argumentation can be single, but, depending on the further critical reactions to the use of a particular argument scheme and the counterarguments of the other party, it may also become multiple, coordinatively compound, subordinatively compound, or some combination of those.

In advancing argumentation, the protagonist may—and may only—make use of the starting points that have been established in the opening stage of the discussion. Two kinds of distinctions can be made with respect to these starting points. First, there is a distinction between starting points that consist of material commitments ("premises") and starting points that consist of formal commitments ("discussion rules"). Second, there is a distinction between explicit starting points and implicit starting points. The explicit starting points are mutually agreed upon; they may, as avowed commitments, not simply be revoked. The explicit starting points have a similar status as the propositional commitments that Hamblin,[35] Barth and Krabbe,[36] and Walton and Krabbe[37] call "concessions." The implicit starting points are assumed to be inherent in the discussion context; as contextual commitments, they are liable to rejection but must be maintained if they have successfully passed the appropriate "intersubjective identification procedure" instigated by the party that does not accept them at face value.[38]

In the pragma-dialectical approach, the rationale for using certain starting points is a pragmatic one.[39] A starting point is acceptable if it is by intersubjective agreement accepted as such by the parties, irrespective of whether the reason for their acceptance is epistemological, ethical, ideological, juridical, esthetical, or other. As we have emphasized before, argumentation does not deal only with matters of truth and plausibility but also with policy matters, moral issues, etc. An epistemological perspective such as Rescher's can therefore at best cover only part of argumentative reality, thus excluding an abundance of important issues from "argumentative space."

*When has the burden of proof been discharged?* In practice, one can sometimes get rid of the burden of proof because of incidental circumstances, such as the antagonist abandoning his doubt without any critical consideration or the death of the protagonist. The burden of proof has only really been discharged when the standpoint has been sufficiently defended in the critical discussion and can be maintained while the opposition must be withdrawn. A well-defined procedure is required to achieve this result in an orderly fashion and in a finite number of steps.

Like Rescher, we find it necessary that in what we call the opening stage of the discussion the parties jointly determine what the rules are.[40] Unlike in Rescher's approach, in the pragma-dialectical approach the rationale of the rules lies in their "problem-validity" for the purpose of critically testing the acceptability of standpoints. Among the pragma-dialectical rules are those for the use and the correct application of argument schemes and for critically responding to argument schemes. However complex the argumentation—due to the critical reactions—may be structured, every separate argument is by means of a certain argument scheme connected with the main standpoint or a substandpoint and needs therefore to be tested on its own merits. In pragma-dialectics, this testing takes place in accordance with a fixed procedure. A crucial role in the testing procedure is played by the critical questions associated with the argument scheme used by the protagonist. These questions differ for causal argumentation, comparison argumentation, and symptomatic argumentation. Only by responding to all relevant critical questions, by adding a (subordinative, coordinative or multiple) extension to the argumentation, can the protagonist discharge his (possibly cumulated) burden of proof. The pragma-dialectical critical questions are not identical with the "objections" an arguer should respond to according to Johnson.[41] As a matter of course, critical questions are not equal to counterarguments and do not involve any burden of proof, however "serious" they may be.

The burden of proof has been discharged only when all relevant critical questions asked by the antagonist have been answered in a way that is deemed sufficiently thorough by the antagonist and no unanswered critical questions remain. Then, the required constellation of arguments has been advanced completely in the argumentation and the argumentation is accepted, so that Govier would speak of an "exhaustive case."[42]

## A Pragmatic Solution of the Problem of the Order of Defending Opposite Standpoints

We shall now explain how we intend to complete our pragma-dialectical analysis of the burden of proof with a pragmatic solution of the problem concerning the order in which two opposing standpoints regarding the same issue are to be defended in a mixed dispute. As we indicated in the previous section, various kinds of solutions have been proposed in the various treatments of this particular burden of proof problem: epistemological, juridical, ethical, et cetera. In our pragma-dialectical approach we opt for a more general stance. We think that the way in which this problem is to be resolved depends in the first place on the institutional practice or context in which the discussion takes place.

The opening stage of a critical discussion is designed precisely to accommodate the kinds of procedures and conventions that are operative in the various institutional practices and contexts. There are practices that are genuinely institutional, such as criminal court procedures and parliamentary debates, and where fixed procedures determine how issues of order should be decided. There are also practices where no fixed procedures exist, but where nevertheless certain conventional rules are operative that agree with the goals of the practice concerned. In a broader perspective, all everyday verbal interaction can be regarded as institutional in the Searlean sense that performing speech acts is a form of institutional, rule-governed behavior and specific types of speech acts in specific kinds of exchanges are subject to specific kinds of conventions.[43] If no genuine institutional procedures are operative in the context in which a discussion takes place, these specific kinds of conventions provide a *pragmatic rationale* for deciding on issues such as order of defense. We intend to explain what this pragmatic rationale consists of and how it can account for a certain decision on the order of defending when two opposite standpoints are advanced.

We start by presenting two dialogues in which the parties advance opposing standpoints, and in which the first speaker requires the second speaker to defend his opposite standpoint first. The standpoint that introduces the issue is represented in italics. In the first dialogue, this standpoint involves an implicit accusation:

(1)

1 S1: My purple vase!
2 S2: Yes, what a pity, isn't it?
3 S1: *You dropped it!*
4 S2: I did not!
5 S1: Make me believe you didn't.
6 S2: I beg your pardon?!

In the second dialogue, the standpoint is an informative assertive:

(2)

1 S1: Jan is leaving for Warsaw tomorrow.
2 S2: When exactly?
3 S1: 10:00 a.m.
4 S2: I shouldn't think so . . .
5 S1: Why not?
6 S2: As far as I know, the train departs every odd hour.

In a pragma-dialectical reconstruction of these dialogues as a critical discussion, the dispute can in both cases be characterized as *mixed* because the parties take opposite positions in regard of an issue: in dialogue (1), the issue is whether S2 has dropped the vase; in (2), the issue is whether the train leaves at 10:00 a.m. In both disputes both parties have a standpoint of their own. Consequently, in both cases both parties have an obligation to defend their standpoints.[44] There is a problem, however. Temporarily or definitively (we cannot tell), the party whose standpoint is put forward first shifts the burden of proof to the other party, but this shift seems in case (2) more or less legitimate, but certainly not in case (1).[45] We think that we will be able to explain this difference by examining how in ordinary argumentative discourse a burden of proof is acquired and what the pragmatic rationale for attributing such a burden of proof can be.

Reconstructing what people say and intend to convey in argumentative discourse as a series of moves in a critical discussion, as is the aim in pragma-dialectics, amounts to an explicit analysis of these people's "dialectical" commitments to certain propositions. Such an analysis can only be achieved if the dialectical commitments of the parties involved in the discussion can be derived from the "pragmatic": commitments that are inherent in the way in which they have expressed themselves in the discourse, whether explicitly or implicitly. These pragmatic commitments can be traced by making use of insight provided by theories of language use that focus on how mutual obligations are incurred and acquitted in verbal communication and interaction, such as the Searlean speech act theory and the Gricean theory of rational exchanges.

In the first place, Searlean speech act theory and Gricean theory of rational exchanges can be called upon to explain the rationale for attributing certain pragmatic commitments to the participants in argumentative discourse. As Jackson[46] observes, the Gricean maxims, in particular the Maxim of Quality ("Do not say what you believe to be false or that for which you lack adequate evidence"), support the general presumption that an assertion advanced in the discourse—and in our opinion this also goes for other types of speech acts—is acceptable. According to Jackson, this presumption is cancelled only if the interlocutor (1) has independent reason to doubt that the assertion is indeed acceptable, or (2) that the speaker is indeed behaving in a cooperative way, or (3) if the context indicates that the speaker himself deems his assertion less acceptable for the interlocutor.[47] Ullmann-Margalit expresses basically the same idea when she says that from a legal perspective an assertion being "presumptively acceptable" means that the interlocutor *is entitled to regard it as acceptable*.[48]

In our view, the presumption of acceptability needs to be grounded even more fundamentally in a genuinely normative principle, such as the Interaction

Principle postulated by van Eemeren and Grootendorst.[49] They state this principle as a general prohibition against the performance of any speech acts that are not acceptable to the interlocutor. Unlike the Gricean maxims, the Interaction Principle involves a real requirement. A violation of this principle does not encourage alternative interpretations of what is said. On the contrary, such a violation obstructs the normal course of the interaction and can even lead to sanctions.[50] Anyone who performs a speech act is committed to complying with the requirement involved in the Interaction Principle, and this commitment gives rise to the presumption that the speech act that was performed is indeed acceptable. This presumption is similar to the presumption that motorists who approach a red traffic light will obey the traffic rule and stop their cars.

Until there are clear indications of the opposite, the interlocutor is thus entitled to regard the speech act performed by the speaker or writer as acceptable. If, however, there *are* indications that the speaker or writer *has not fully committed himself* to the requirement involved in the Interaction Principle, the situation is different. When, for instance, a speaker makes it known in advance that he anticipates opposition from his interlocutor, and—following up on this— the interlocutor does indeed express opposition to the speech act concerned, then the presumption shifts to the interlocutor. To regain the presumption of acceptability, the speaker must adduce evidence that his speech act is acceptable after all. In other words, he has acquired a burden of proof. Only after the speaker has succeeded in acquitting himself of this burden does the presumption shift back to his position. If the interlocutor then intends to maintain his opposition, he, in turn, should acquit himself of the burden of proof for his opposite position. This is the only way in which he can regain the presumption for his opposition.[51]

We think that this analysis can be taken a step further by observing that it is reasonable to let the presumption of acceptability remain with a speaker as long as the speaker's speech act does not go against the prevailing pragmatic status quo. This means that his speech act may not be at odds with the set of premises that are mutually shared by the parties involved in the interaction. This set of premises represents the "pragmatic" status quo because it refers not to warranted beliefs or the general state of knowledge in a certain field, as in the "cognitive" or "epistemic" status quo, but to the list of premises that the particular parties involved in the discourse explicitly or implicitly accept and that define their *interactional relationship* in the *interactional situation at hand.* The pragmatic status quo is challenged as soon as one of the parties involved performs a speech act that is inconsistent with the shared premises, for example because the state of affairs presupposed by its identity or correctness conditions conflicts with one of more of the commonly accepted premises.

When may a speech act be assumed to be inconsistent with one or more mutually shared premises? We think that Kauffeld's analyses of the way in which a burden of proof is incurred in every day verbal interaction can be of help in answering this question.[52] In Kauffeld's view, it depends primarily on the nature of the speech acts concerned when people engaged in verbal interaction incur a burden of proof and on what the burden of proof involves. This means that the illocutionary point of a speech act and the implications of having made this point in a felicitous way are of decisive importance.

In our view, Kauffeld's account has the merit of complementing concerns with dialectical obligations in ideal situations with a pragmatic concern about the way in which burdens of proof are assumed in everyday verbal interaction. He achieves this complementation by showing how the performance of certain speech acts, namely, proposing and accusing, can endow the speaker with certain *probative obligations*.[53] We think that Kauffeld's approach can be generalized and applied to all verbal interaction by means of speech acts. In our outline of how we think such a generalization can be realized, we adapt Kauffeld's idea that certain speech acts may have implications that—possibly or presumably— go against the interlocutor's interests.[54] Our adaptation amounts to taking Kauffeld's idea to mean that a speech act may have implications that go against the interlocutor's view of the interactional relationship between the speaker and the interlocutor encompassed in the present pragmatic status quo.

According to our adapted account, a proposal would invite an adjustment of what the interlocutor until then took to be the shared expectation of how the interactional relationship between the communicators should be in the future; an accusation invites an adjustment of what the interlocutor so far regarded as the shared view of the relationship between them. In our conception of a pragmatic status quo, this would mean that both a proposal and an accusation have implications that are likely to be inconsistent with the list of mutually shared premises—or at least with what the interlocutor supposed the list to be.

Searle's taxonomy of speech acts may be of help in determining which types of speech acts may have implications that run counter to the interlocutor's view of his current interactional relationship with the speaker. "Commissives," for instance, can generally be expected to have implications that agree with the interlocutor's view of the interactional relationship between the speaker and the interlocutor. "Directives," on the contrary, can easily have implications that disagree with the interlocutor's view. Prototypical commissives such as promises do not, as a rule, introduce actions that the interlocutor will think inconsistent with agreed-upon desirables; however, with prototypical directives such as requests this may very well be the case. There is at least one class of speech acts in Searle's taxonomy that contains *both* types of speech acts. This is the class consisting of "assertives." Some assertives are designed to provide the interlocutor with information that he did not possess before but that is expected to be consistent with what he already knows, such as "informing" and "explaining." There are also assertives, however, that aim to make the interlocutor accept a view that he did *not* accept before and that *cannot* be expected to be consistent with what he already accepts, such as "claiming" and "accusing."[55]

Now that we have explained what we mean by a *pragmatic status quo* and how we can determine whether a speech act may be considered to violate this status quo, we return to the problem of the order in which two opposing standpoints are to be defended in a mixed difference of opinion.

In the pragma-dialectical view of argumentative confrontation, the speech act that initially introduces the issue can acquire the status of a standpoint in a dispute in two ways: either the person who performed that speech act makes it clear that he anticipates that the interlocutor will not accept this speech act at face value, or the interlocutor makes it known that he is not prepared to accept the speech act at face value by performing a counter speech act.[56] In the first case, there is no presumption attached to the initial speech act, because the speaker or writer makes it clear from the start that this speech act may *go against the prevailing pragmatic status quo* between himself and the interlocutor. In the second case, the speech act concerned initially *has* a presumptive status, because for all the speaker or writer knows—and also for all we know—this speech act *does not violate the prevailing pragmatic status quo*. This presumptive status is, of course, canceled when the interlocutor opposes this speech act with a counter speech act.

Let us assume for a moment that the interlocutor opposes the speaker's initial speech act with a counter speech act, not only in the second case we discussed but also in the first situation, in which the speaker has made it clear that he anticipates such opposition. The interlocutor's reaction then agrees completely with this anticipation. Both cases can now be regarded as involving the kind of interactional situation of maximal opposition that can pragma-dialectically be reconstructed as a mixed dispute: the two parties have assumed contradictory standpoints and each party has a duty to defend its own standpoint. All the same, there is an important difference between the two interactional situations. In the first case, the standpoint that initiated the dispute has no presumptive status from the start, whereas in the second case it has. And the interlocutor's opposition has a presumptive status in the first case, but not in the second. In the second case it is, after all, precisely the interlocutor's opposition that first challenges the pragmatic status quo that is up to then supposed to prevail.

What are the implications for handling the burden of proof of this discrepancy between these two different interactional situations in a mixed dispute?

In the previous section, we argued that the burden of proof consists of an obligation for a party in a dispute to defend its standpoint if challenged to do so, but we also mentioned an additional, procedural obligation that Hamblin pointed out earlier and referred to as the *burden of initiative*.[57] Besides having an obligation to defend a standpoint, having a burden of initiative implies in our perspective an obligation to defend this standpoint *at this particular juncture* of the discussion. Distinguishing between the obligation to defend a standpoint and the obligation to defend it at this juncture of the discussion allows for the existence of an interactional situation in which a certain party has an obligation to defend a standpoint but is not required to acquit itself of this obligation now. That is, at a particular juncture, a party that has advanced a particular standpoint does not have the burden of initiative.[58]

It is precisely the additional obligation of having the burden of initiative that makes for the difference in the burden carried by the parties in the two cases we just discussed. In the first case, the speaker has both an obligation to defend his standpoint and an obligation to start the defense. In the second case, he does have an obligation to defend his standpoint, but not an obligation to defend it immediately. He is only required to defend his standpoint after the interlocutor has defended *his* standpoint. Whereas the *order* in which the two standpoints are to be defended coincides in the first case with the order in which they have been put forward, in the second case it does not. The latter of the two dialogues we presented at the beginning of our chapter is, not coincidentally, an example of the interactional situation in the second case:

1 S1: Jan is leaving for Warsaw tomorrow.
2 S2: When exactly?
3 S1: 10:00 a.m.
4 S2: I shouldn't think so . . .
5 S1: Why not?
6 S2: As far as I know, the train leaves at 9:20.

The first speaker's assertion (in turn 3) has acquired the status of a standpoint because of the second speaker's opposition (in turn 4). Nevertheless, the presumptive status of the first speaker's assertion is preserved because at the stage in which it was performed there were no indications that he had performed a speech act that could be regarded as going against the prevailing pragmatic status quo; consequently, this speech act cannot bestow a burden of initiative on him. First, the interlocutor should justify his opposition. Once he has done so, the first speaker's assertive loses its presumptive status and this speaker is obliged to accept the burden of initiative. Then he cannot escape any longer from defending his assertive against the interlocutor's opposition.

## Conclusion

In this paper, we have explained what a pragma-dialectical approach to argumentation in terms of speech acts, commitments, mutual coordination, and procedural rules amounts to in the analysis of the burden of proof. We have addressed the central questions of why there should be a burden of proof, what it applies to, to whom it is to be assigned, what it involves, under which conditions it is activated, by what means it can be discharged, and when it is met. We have done so in a critical rationalist vein, attuned to furthering the most systematic, perspicuous, economic, and thorough process of resolving a difference of opinion by testing critically the tenability of a standpoint. In addition, we have given substance to our pragmatic solution of the problem of the order of defense in a mixed dispute. Our claim was that a burden of proof is incurred as soon as a speech act goes against a prevailing pragmatic status quo. We specified the concept of a pragmatic status quo in terms of a list of premises that are explicitly or implicitly accepted by the people who are having a dispute and that define their current interactional relationship. Criteria for determining whether a burden of proof is incurred can, in our view, be established by exploiting the idea that the performance of particular types of speech acts may have implications that go against the interlocutor's view of this interactional relationship. Decisions on the order in which two opposite standpoints must be defended can thus be justified by giving a truly pragmatic interpretation of the burden of proof concept that differentiates between a conditional obligation to defend a standpoint and a burden of initiative.

## Notes

1. F. H. van Eemeren and Rob Grootendorst, *Speech Acts in Argumentative Discussions: A Theoretical Model for the Analysis of Discussions Directed towards Solving Conflicts of Opinion* (Dordrecht: Foris/Mouton de Gruyter, 1984); and M. A. van Rees, "Comments on 'Rhetoric and Dialectic in the Twenty-First Century,'" *Argumentation* 14, no. 3 (Spring 2000): 255–59.

2. Van Eemeren and Grootendorst, *Speech Acts.*

3. E. M. Barth and E. C. W. Krabbe, *From Axiom to Dialogue: A Philosophical Study of Logics and Argumentation* (Berlin: Walter de Gruyter, 1982), 21–22.

4. N. Rescher, *Dialectics: A Controversy-Oriented Approach to the Theory of Knowledge* (Albany: State University of New York Press, 1977).

5. J. Biro and H. Siegel, "Normativity, Argumentation and an Epistemic Theory of Fallacies," in *Argumentation Illuminated*, ed. F. H. van Eemeren, R. Grootendorst, J. A. Blair, and C. A. Willard (Amsterdam: Sic Sat, 1992), 85–103.

6. We prefer to use the terms "tenability" or "acceptability," to keep the basic theoretical apparatus free from epistemic associations. Surprisingly, coming from

antirelativists, Biro and Siegel claim that "an argument aims at, and a good one succeeds in, leading an inquirer or an audience from some proposition(s) whose truth or justifiedness *they accept* to others whose truth or justifiedness they will *see themselves as* having good reasons to accept on its basis" (Biro and Siegel, "Epistemic Theory," 92).

7. J. MacKenzie and P. Staines, "Hamblin's Case for Commitment: A Reply to Johnson," *Philosophy and Rhetoric* 32, no. 1 (1999): 35.

8. C. L. Hamblin, *Fallacies* (London: Methuen, 1970), 264.

9. Hamblin, *Fallacies*, 16–17.

10. Hamblin's idea of a *commitment store*—which is similar to Lorenzen's *set of concessions*—and the accompanying *commitment rules* are an invaluable addition to this way of theorizing: they make it possible to determine what each participant is committed to at each particular discussion stage. This is exactly the kind of externalization we are aiming for.

11. D. N. Walton and E. C. W. Krabbe, *Commitment in Dialogue: Basic Concepts of Interpersonal Reasoning* (Albany: State University of New York Press, 1995), 9.

12. Walton and Krabbe, *Commitment in Dialogue*, 17.

13. Van Eemeren and Grootendorst, *Speech Acts*; and F. H. van Eemeren and Rob Grootendorst, *Argumentation, Communication, and Fallacies: A Pragma-Dialectical Perspective* (Hillsdale, NJ: Lawrence Erlbaum Associates, 1992).

14. Rescher, *Dialectics*, 40.

15. Van Eemeren and Grootendorst, *Argumentation, Communication, and Fallacies*.

16. Barth and Krabbe, *From Axiom to Dialogue*, 63–65.

17. H. Albert, *Traktat über kritische Vernunft*, 3rd ed. (Tübingen: Mohr, 1975).

18. Such a critical evaluation presupposes that ordinary arguers will, at least in principle, be inclined to comply with standards like those of a critical discussion. See F. H. van Eemeren, B. Meuffels, and M. Verburg, "The (Un)Reasonableness of the *Argumentum ad Hominem*." *Language and Social Psychology* 19, no. 4 (December 2000): 416–35.

19. Rescher, *Dialectics*, 30.

20. F. H. van Eemeren and P. Houtlosser, "Strategic Maneuvering with the Burden of Proof," in *Advances in Pragma-Dialectics*, ed. F. H. van Eemeren (Amsterdam: Sic Sat, 2002), 23–24.

21. Rescher, *Dialectics*, 25.

22. Walton and Krabbe, *Commitment in Dialogue*, 9.

23. R. H. Johnson, "Differences between Argumentative and Rhetorical Space," in *Argumentation and Rhetoric*, ed. H. V. Hansen, C. W. Tindale, and A. V. Colman (St. Catharines, ON: OSSA, 1998), available online in the OSSA 2 Conference Archive at http://scholar.uwindsor.ca/ossaarchive/; and R. H. Johnson, "More on Arguers and Dialectical Obligations," in *Argumentation at the Century's Turn*, ed. H. V. Hansen, C. W. Tindale, and E. Sveda (St. Catharines, ON: OSSA, 1999), available online in the OSSA 3 Conference Archive at http://scholar.uwindsor.ca /ossaarchive/.

24. We agree with Rescher that it should always be possible to refer to a "common ground" that determines "what is to count as evidence" (*Dialectics*, 30). We do not agree, however, that this common ground is necessarily "impartially fixed": we leave it to the parties involved to choose their own points of departure.

25. Walton and Krabbe, *Commitment in Dialogue*, 50.

26. Rescher, *Dialectics*, 28.

27. D. N. Walton, "Burden of Proof," *Argumentation* 2, no. 2 (May 1988): 233–54.

28. Here we connect with Hamblin. In his system for dealing with (mixed) disputes, Hamblin relies solely on the "somewhat simpler concept of initiative" (*Fallacies*, 274).

29. Rescher, *Dialectics*, 39.

30. Rescher, *Dialectics*, 30–31.

31. Rescher, *Dialectics*, 36.

32. C. Perelman and L. Olbrechts-Tyteca, *La nouvelle rhétorique: Traité de l'argumentation* (Paris: Presses Universitaires de France, 1958.)

33. E. Ullmann-Margalit, "On Presumption," *Journal of Philosophy* 80, no. 3 (1983): 143–63.

34. Ullmann-Margalit, "On Presumption," 146. Although adopting a presumption clearly prejudges an issue, according to Ullmann-Margalit, it may be seen as rational in a twofold sense: in any particular instance the presumption is open to rebuttal, and the bias it promotes is independently justifiable. In pragma-dialectical terms, the former would mean that a starting point can be revoked; this, however, is only allowed when it can be shown by offering counterevidence that this starting point is, after all, not acceptable. The latter would mean that institutional or other contextual support must be available.

35. Hamblin, *Fallacies*, 257ff.

36. Barth and Krabbe, *From Axiom to Dialogue*, 56.

37. Walton and Krabbe, *Commitment in Dialogue*, 133.

38. F. H. van Eemeren and R. Grootendorst, *A Systematic Theory of Argumentation: The Pragmatic-Dialectical Approach* (Cambridge: Cambridge University Press, 2004). Our contextual commitments are akin to Walton and Krabbe's "veiled" or dark-side commitments in their *Commitment in Dialogue*, even though the latter are associated with nonexternalized states of mind and are not related with any speech acts (compare Mackenzie and Staines, "Hamblin's Case for Commitment").

39. In argumentative practice, too, the arguers' orientation seems pragmatic rather than epistemological. Gaskins observes that "for pragmatists truth is 'the evolving product of a properly constituted research community' and that, in a similar spirit, the authority and legitimacy of the (American) judicial process is based on the integrity of its procedures rather than any privileged access to truth." See R. H. Gaskins, *Burdens of Proof in Modern Discourse* (New Haven, CT: Yale University Press, 1992), 25–26.

40. Walton and Krabbe point at a favorable consequence of spelling out the rules of dialogue in the opening stage of the discussion: "Your commitment tends to be made more specific as well, for when precise rules of argument are spelled out, the

means you can use to defend your point of view are narrowed down" (*Commitment in Dialogue*, 46).

41. Johnson, "Argumentative and Rhetorical Space."

42. T. Govier, "Arguing Forever? Or: Two Tiers of Argument Appraisal," in Hansen, Tindale, and Colman, *Argumentation and Rhetoric*.

43. J. R. Searle, *Speech Act: An Essay in the Philosophy of Language* (Cambridge: Cambridge University Press, 1969).

44. In a critical discussion, advancing a standpoint implies assuming a conditional obligation to defend the position expressed in that standpoint. When two opposing standpoints are advanced by different parties, both parties are required to defend their position.

45. In (2) it would indeed have been odd if S2 would in turn 6 have said that S1 should first prove that the train leaves at 10:00 a.m.

46. S. Jackson, "Fallacies and Heuristics," in *Analysis and Evaluation: Proceedings of the Third ISSA Conference on Argumentation*, ed. F. H. van Eemeren, R. Grootendorst, J. A. Blair, and C. A. Willard (Amsterdam: Sic Sat, 1995), 2:257–69.

47. Jackson, "Fallacies and Heuristics," 258.

48. In the law, the notion of presumption is applied to situations in which something is an "impending issue." What to do, for example, when someone has been absent for more than seven years: Should this person be declared dead or not? For legal purposes, it is then presumed that this person is dead. Ullmann-Margalit emphasizes this feature when she says that "[p]resumption entitles deliberators to make an assumption *that they are otherwise not entitled to make*" ("On Presumption," 148). Jackson's use of the notion of presumption conforms to the legal use on the condition that the acceptability of a speaker's assertion can be considered an "impending issue." What to do when someone has said something: accept it or not? The presumption is: accept, unless there is something that weighs against it.

49. F. H. van Eemeren and R. Grootendorst, "The Study of Argumentation," 151–70.

50. The Gricean maxims, which are Jackson's basis for the presumption of acceptability, are not rules in the same sense. Unlike violating a "real" rule, violating a maxim does not lead to any sanctions but rather to an interpretation of the speaker's meaning that is different from the literal "utterance meaning" (assuming the Cooperation Principle still applies). Thus, in a Gricean perspective, the fact that the Maxim of Quality is *not* violated does not warrant the conclusion that what the speaker asserts is presumptively acceptable. Given that none of the other maxims are violated either, and, again, that the Cooperation Principle still holds, it is only warranted to conclude that nothing else was meant than was literally said.

51. Rescher, *Dialectics*, 28.

52. F. J. Kauffeld, "Presumptions and the Distribution of Argumentative Burdens in Acts of Proposing and Accusing," *Argumentation* 12, no. 2 (1998): 245–66; and "Pivotal Issues and Norms in Rhetorical Theories of Argumentation," in *Dialectic and Rhetoric: The Warp and Woof of Argumentation Analysis*, ed. F. H. van Eemeren and P. Houtlosser (Dordrecht: Kluwer Academic, 2002), 97–118.

53. "[I]n many kinds of illocutionary act, S does not, at least not typically, engage a larger obligation to provide, on demand, reason and evidence vindicating the truth and adequacy of her primary utterance. [. . .] But, other things being equal, where S makes a proposal or levels an accusation, she cannot responsibly dismiss an addressee's demand for proof" (Kauffeld, "Pivotal Issues," 104, italics by the author). For empirical confirmation of this theoretical observation in as far as it concerns "accusing," see F. H. van Eemeren, B. Garssen, and B. Meuffels, "'I Don't Have Anything to Prove Here': Judgements of the Fallacy of Shifting the Burden of Proof," in van Eemeren et al., *Analysis and Evaluation*, 281–84.

54. In his analysis of proposing, Kauffeld claims that the major reason for having to justify an act of proposing is that the one who proposes something is supposed to have good reasons for what he proposes, and if he aims at having his proposal accepted he should inform the interlocutor of these reasons. In his analysis of accusing, Kauffeld suggests that a major reason for having to justify an act of accusing is that the accused party has a right to deny the accusation and can only do so properly if the accuser has provided reasons for his accusation.

55. The declaratives, in particular "language declaratives" such as definitions and specifications, are likely to be open to the same problem as the "expressives."

56. See F. H. van Eemeren, "For Reason's Sake: Maximal Argumentative Analysis of Discourse," in *Argumentation: Across the Lines of Discipline. Proceedings of the Conference on Argumentation 1986*, ed. F. H. van Eemeren, R. Grootendorst, J. A. Blair, and C. A. Willard (Berlin: Walter de Gruyter, 1987), 201–15; and Peter Houtlosser, "Indicators of a Point of View," in *Advances in Pragma-Dialectics*, ed. F. H. van Eemeren (Amsterdam: Sic Sat, 2002), 169–84.

57. Hamblin, *Fallacies*, 274.

58. This is, in fact, a different way of making Rescher's well-known distinction between an I(nitial)-burden of proof and an E(vidential)-burden of proof (Rescher, *Dialectics*, 27).

# 11

# The Juridical Roots of Presumptions and Burdens of Proof

RICHARD GASKINS

The absence of proof is not the same thing as proof of absence.
—US Secretary of Defense Donald Rumsfeld

## Burdens of Proof in Public Discourse

Leading up to the American invasion of Iraq in 2003, international diplomacy became mired in controversy over Saddam Hussein's weapons of mass destruction. The "WMD" debate played itself out in scholarly legal journals, in the United Nations Security Council, and in the world media, where the response to Saddam Hussein would hinge on a massive public inference based, by necessity, on the absence of proof. As competing camps reached the moment when this inference would be definitively made, they offered a full display of discursive strategies, none more powerful than allocating the burden of proof. Burdens of proof and their close relations, presumptions, are often consigned to the shadows of public debate, blending softly into the rhetorical background. In this case, however, as the international stakes grew higher, and as the need to resolve the WMD question turned into high drama, these elusive devices were suddenly thrust onto the world stage.

If one accepts that prior to 2003 available information about Iraq's WMD was at best inconclusive, how were prudent nations supposed to respond? Given his odious history, was Saddam Hussein guilty until proven innocent? Alternatively, did international norms require compelling evidence of an imminent threat before military intervention would be justified? But just how "compelling," and how "imminent"? After 9/11, when several nations found themselves engaged in an unprecedented war against terror, did the normal presumption against military intervention suddenly shift the other way? But where do "normal" presumptions come from, and exactly when does the burden of proof shift? Despite the difficulty of these questions, would postponing judgment not constitute a judgment in its own right? Finally, who decides all these questions, and under what canons of public inference?

Students of public discourse will scrutinize the Iraq WMD debate for many years to come. Some provocative lessons have already been suggested by official investigations and by partisans in the heat of electoral contests. Beyond the factual question of whether such weapons even existed, investigators have drawn attention to "assumption trains" and "groupthink" that may have contributed to startling intelligence failures. Putting these investigations aside, however, I am less concerned with assigning fault than with exploring basic juridical elements of public inference. My goal is to clarify the rhetorical functions of burdens of proof by focusing on the legal system—the arena of public discourse where such devices are most widely acknowledged. Even in law, where public inferences are regularly performed by courts, legislatures, and executive agencies, it takes some effort to assess the subtle power of proof burdens. By the end of this chapter you should have acquired some useful terms for analyzing public controversies like the WMD debate. There are few better examples of dueling burdens of proof in public discourse.

Although their precise functions require careful study, proof burdens are found in many venues of legal argument. The diversity of functions and venues is important for distinguishing several kinds of proof burdens, including their presence in legal "presumptions" and "default rules." Lawyers do not own these concepts exclusively; virtually all fields of public discourse share similar strategic practices. But the legal system remains the traditional place where these practices are explicitly labeled, debated, codified, and allocated. Clarifying the juridical roots of proof burdens is useful for definitional purposes, but the concepts surveyed here can be extended by analogy to discursive practices found throughout the public realm, including science, ethics, and public affairs. From law we learn how proof burdens get assigned to specific actors, and how they may suddenly be shifted to different actors under certain conditions. Law also offers the intriguing model of a public forum where final judgments are authoritatively delivered and respected. Most legal judgments are contested strenuously along the way, but at the end of the process they present themselves as legitimate, definitive, and beyond further appeal within the legal domain. One reason to examine juridical elements in public discourse is to weigh this ideal of finality in the face of human controversy, uncertainty, ignorance, and value diversity.

Legal proceedings illustrate the vital but often tacit inference strategies found throughout the public sphere. These broader inferences rely heavily on juridical components, whether they are embedded in generic rules of social conduct, disciplines of inquiry, default values, or conventions of discussion and casual interaction. Inferences in this larger sense are endemic to any deliberative public life. They lend shape to social experience, and they punctuate key changes in that experience. Indeed, collective inferences penetrate all the way down to the very perception of bedrock facts in any community of inquiry. They lie inert within social habits and cultural practices, and they become the pivots on which social and political changes may suddenly turn. Standing behind such inferences, in all their varieties, are the powerful juridical elements associated with burdens of proof.

## Legal Functions of Proof Burdens and Presumptions: Basic Definitions

In law *the burden of proof* is a ubiquitous but elusive device with several distinct functions. In everyday legal proceedings, it is an operating rule that blends into the background—much like the default settings in computer programs, with which it has some striking parallels. Within the field of law itself there is surprisingly little commentary on how proof burdens actually work; even academic experts on Evidence have mapped only a small part of the total field. Lawyers often think of the "burden of proof" as basic stage directions that say which party must speak first, or who must step forward with specific kinds of evidence. But its ultimate effect on the entire legal system is far greater than it first appears, and students of argument can profit from exploring its more ambitious legal functions.

Solving the matter of "who speaks first" is indeed one important function, often referred to by lawyers as *the burden of production*, or *the burden of going forward*. While common sense may want to assign this function to the accuser or plaintiff in standard cases, there are also occasions when law reverses the norm and requires the defendant to "come forward" with evidence—or lose the case. For example, the defendant may sit on vital business records or complex medical information, without which the plaintiff cannot get the case truly started. Or perhaps the plaintiff manages to present just enough information to raise a potential argument (a "prima facie" case, as in a case alleging possible employment discrimination), and law then imposes on the defendant the burden of producing further evidence in mitigation. This sort of proof burden may be more onerous than it sounds, as parties maneuver carefully (often in pretrial skirmishing) to shift the cost of "going forward" onto their adversaries. But from the standpoint of the entire legal system, it is simply a device for getting relevant evidence into the trial record, from whatever source, in the most efficient manner. It operates primarily in the controlled domain of trial courts (or pretrial negotiation).

But now suppose that neither party has enough evidence to resolve the legal matter clearly. No one really knows, for example, exactly when the common environmental contaminant PCBs may cause cancer in humans, especially for exposures below a certain threshold; and individual cancer patients may find it impossible to produce clear evidence that their cancers were caused by specific exposures, however well-documented. When both sides lack clear proof on the core issue of disease causation, who wins the case? Should such cases be resolved individually in separate courtrooms, or collectively at the level of legislation? Students of public discourse should pay close attention to this second major function of the burden of proof: what lawyers call *the burden of persuasion*, or *the risk of nonpersuasion*. These technical terms refer to the distinct chance that arguments presented before judge and jury will fail to support any relevant inference, whether guilt or innocence in criminal trials, or the presence or absence of liability in civil cases. The reasons for nonpersuasion may be many, ranging from the lack of evidentiary facts to the mysteries of jury psychology, and to the inherent ambiguities of legal standards and public values. Nonpersuasion can even be calibrated by degrees, as in the criminal trial requirement of "proof beyond a reasonable doubt."

For individual disputes, allocating the risk of nonpersuasion compensates for the fundamental uncertainties of litigation, allowing the judicial system to reach determinate outcomes in the absence of complete information. While this burden plays an essential strategic role in individual trials, it operates more widely throughout all parts of the legal system: at the levels of legislation, constitutional law, even international law. Wherever the legal system faces barriers of uncertainty, ambiguity, or value conflicts, allocating the risk of nonpersuasion allows the law to deliver concrete results. It is the law's essential response to *ignorance*: a decision rule for drawing inferences from the absence of knowledge—or at least complete or sufficient knowledge. In public discourse, where tacit juridical practices abound, struggles over proof burdens are mainly about who carries the risk of nonpersuasion.

*Presumptions* are flexible tools for adapting the risk of nonpersuasion to a wide range of legal purposes. Presumptions are thus to be found not only in judicial trials, but throughout the entire legal system. Most people outside the legal profession imagine the courtroom as the main center of legal conflict—especially criminal trials, where the "presumption of innocence" represents a heightened form of nonpersuasion ("proof beyond a reasonable doubt"). Popular television programs remind us that prosecutors must meet this heavy burden of proof and that defendants can win without supplying any evidence whatever. (In civil trials, the burden initially falls on the plaintiff but is measurably lighter in weight.) Dramatic as these courtroom encounters may be, however, they represent only a tiny portion of legal disputes. Indeed, considering the breadth of social conflicts and legal concerns in this country, full courtroom trials are a statistical rarity. Moreover, trials are heavily constrained by legal rules originating in other parts of the legal system. Some of these constraining rules come from appeals courts dealing with questions of fair process. (Enforcing the presumption of innocence in criminal trials is the ultimate responsibility of appeals courts, which control the principles for applying the presumption.) In addition to appeals courts, presumptions are created by legislatures, by executive authorities, and by judges who interpret the substantive rules of common law. Thus, all legal rules that apply to business and commercial activity, to property and the environment, indeed nearly all laws associated with the regulative state take part—by formulating presumptions—in allocating the risk of nonpersuasion. Procedural and substantive legal rules from all sources, including constitutional law, contain a vast network of legal presumptions, often working behind the scenes.

Presumptions codified in all these sources tell courts and other legal authorities how to allocate, calibrate, and shift burdens of proof in concrete cases. They set up what may also be called *default rules*, which structure debates by determining in advance what words can be uttered, what arguments will count, and who loses the dispute if not enough information enters the field. In law these presumptions and default rules are richly dynamic, in contrast to the dry assumptions of formal logic. In deductive logic a "presumption" plays a static, abstract role: to represent the purely given or counterfactual premise in a formal inference. In law this "premise" becomes an active burden affecting all parties to future legal contests. The scope of legal presumptions is thus not simply deductive, nor even "pragmatic" in the language of speech-act theory; rather these presumptions inject *strategic* elements into public debate. As default rules they shape discourse strategies in situations where evidence is shallow or nonexistent, where ambiguities of fact or principle may dominate the discussion, and where serious value conflicts would otherwise make it difficult for law to reach determinate conclusions.

In legislation, presumptions put people on notice about how burdens of proof may affect their legal rights and responsibilities. These default rules about evidence and proof tell people specifically how the courts will cope with problems of uncertainty. For example, the legislature may stipulate that a chemical pesticide like DDT shall be presumed toxic to humans, in the absence of clear proof to the contrary. Similar preemptive rules may come from appeals courts, as for example the judicial rule that a rare form of cancer, mesothelioma, is presumptively caused by exposure to asbestos. Under federal legislation, any sovereign nation that has been listed by the US State Department as "supporting terrorism" is presumed to be civilly liable for terrorist acts carried out by groups it has indirectly supported—even without any "smoking gun" evidence that it knew anything about the specific acts. In short, presumptions allow the legal system to draw inferences by default in situations where relevant or sufficient evidence may be lacking. There are some situations in which the presumptive loser in a legal battle may overcome the presumption with some kind of evidence (known as "rebuttable presumptions"). In other cases, presumptions are not rebuttable, but rather "conclusive." Put another way, some default rules are permeable, while others solidify into the defining character of the legal system.

The central mission for law is to make principled decisions even in the face of partial or inadequate evidence—as so many times it must. Proof burdens (and especially the risk of nonpersuasion) determine in advance where the buck must stop. In contrast, it is honorable for the research scientist or the practical ethicist to say, following good-faith inquiry, "I don't know the answer here, and thus will move on to the next problem." The legal system rarely has that option: as an institution law offers the public a distinct and valuable type of finality, albeit only after a full course of adversarial debate, appeals, and reversals.

Default rules in the legal process thus project the authority of law into its definitive results. Someone wins, and someone loses. This deliberative finality remains a distinctive accomplishment of legal institutions, even though many legal decisions are highly unpopular in some circles, as in the case of abortion rights in the United States. Similarly, during the 2000 US presidential election, the Supreme Court was widely criticized for its decisive finding that Florida's electoral votes belonged to George W. Bush; nonetheless, its authority was treated as final by both winner and loser. To this day there remain pockets of popular resentment against the Supreme Court's historic decisions on school prayer and race discrimination. But the authority of law achieves finality within its broad public domain, even if the contest is sometimes transferred to higher venues of morality or to lower venues of political opposition. Once the law has spoken, the losing party must concede legal defeat. If the loser tries to shift the debate to other spheres—to morality, economics, politics, or history—the search for victory will continue, but with little hope for public closure. The ultimate function of proof burdens is to enable the law to speak its mind with finality. It is this distinctive accomplishment that draws our attention to juridical elements in other arenas of public discourse, especially at moments of high drama in the "court of public opinion."

The juridical capacity to reach final conclusions despite uncertainty offers an essential working model for students of modern rhetoric. It is not enough for rhetoricians to dwell on pragmatic discourse rules that would facilitate mutual dialogue or ideal speech conditions. In a complex society where mankind yearns for definitive answers to murky questions, everyday rhetorical practices are destined to draw heavily on the same strategic devices found in legal systems. The rhetorical functions of proof burdens do not observe any sharp division between "law" and "life." Indeed, there may well be juridical categories embedded in the deepest patterns of human thought, through which we resolve our most profound uncertainties of cognition and being. We need not treat these philosophical questions here; instead, we will examine how burdens of proof reach across the legal system through elaborate structures of presumptions.

## Resolving Ambiguities of Public Life: Some Applications

Legal systems hold wide jurisdiction over human conflicts, and not simply through the famous American propensity to litigate disputes. Litigation is just one part of the law's broader role in resolving conflicts, which is better described as shaping the default presumptions under which people and organizations operate. Legal rules fall into various *structures of presumption*, which set default values for weighing and discarding evidence in concrete situations. In effect, these structures create social priorities by balancing legal rules against each other. Structures of presumption thus provide practical *working rules* that allow people and organizations to cope with ambiguous laws, uncertain facts, and indeterminate norms that surround nearly all common activities. Surprisingly, among the working rules studied by sociologists, economists, political scientists, philosophers, and historians (not to mention legal scholars), burdens of proof remain almost entirely neglected. Yet they operate powerfully, if often tacitly, throughout the public sphere.

Along with reducing ambiguity, structures of presumption also encourage perpetual conflict. When you cannot resolve a dispute by mutual consent, your next best strategy may be to shift the burden of proof onto your opponent. The argument that "I win, because you cannot prove your case" has spread across the entire landscape of public discourse. Its success depends entirely on the power of presumptions to filter, dilute, or blunt the intended relevance of "evidence" presented by the party that is forced to meet the burden of persuasion. There will always be "some" evidence on offer—maybe even quite a lot of it. But to meet the terms of presumptions, that evidence must be persuasive enough to satisfy norms that are highly demanding, or even unattainable. We can describe these dynamics in a brief survey of four distinct situations: individuals relying on private contracts, government agencies seeking to implement legislation, federal courts seeking to implement constitutional values, and international bodies seeking to establish international norms.

*Contractual Ambiguity.* A web of presumptions surrounds the enforcement of private contracts, which are voluntary agreements between individuals, firms, and other entities seeking to meet their respective goals through collaboration. Disputes may arise when the parties come to disagree over the meaning of contract terms, especially considering novel circumstances. To take an extreme but intriguing case, the last owner of the World Trade Center in New York City held an insurance policy that promised compensation up to a limit of $3.5 billion of damage to his twin buildings, for any single adverse "event." Everyone concedes that the two hijacked planes on 9/11 caused total damage to both structures, but was this just a single event, or rather two separate events? A simple question, perhaps, but it makes the difference between an insurance settlement of $3.5 billion and $7 billion. This problem has almost nothing to do with evidence, but rather points to a bizarre gap in the insurance contract, which, in hindsight, failed to spell out the parties' expectations in this most unlikely contingency. While the massive stakes here are scarcely typical of contract disputes, this is a vivid reminder that contracts never cover all possible contingencies in advance. There will always be unforeseen events, definitional puzzles, and other ambiguities to stir up adversarial conflicts between the contracting parties. Sometimes the difference is worth a big fight.

The case of the World Trade Center insurance may seem to call out for Solomonic compromise. Splitting the difference would be numerically convenient, but it is not automatically preferred in contract law. The legal approach is to apply default rules of contract interpretation, as though they were part of the original bargain. Contract law thus gives the parties an opportunity to negotiate in advance about the structure of enforcement presumptions. Presumptions can also be inferred from the patterns of contract language as well as from past decisions in similar legal cases: all these sources may yield default rules to resolve disputes if and when conditions suddenly change. For example, the parties may have used language that hedges their promises with words like "normally," "generally," "unless otherwise specified," "unless circumstances change." Any language of this sort can serve as the pivot on which default presumptions will suddenly shift the advantage to the other side.

The strategic purpose in such disputes is to become the winner by default, with an argument that says, whatever the factual circumstances, "My interpretation of the contract is correct, unless the other side proves that it isn't." Or, more simply, "I win, unless he can prove that he wins"—where the actual threshold for meeting the burden of persuasion can be set very high. If favorable contract language seems to be lacking for my purpose, then the strategy calls for me to find self-serving analogies in other legal cases and to present them as "precedents" with presumptive force in the instant case, unless my opponent can prove they are wrong. The libertarian proponents of "freedom of choice" hope to see contract disputes resolved through the default settings of the contracts themselves, even by imputing layers of inferred terms of agreement. Their opponents look for default rules outside the actual bargain: in other court opinions, or in statutes. Both methods allow strategic actors to compete for favorable presumptions, and thus to sway the whole legal inference in their direction. That is about all one can do in the dispute over the 9/11 insurance claim, where the choice between "one event" and "two events" might otherwise come down to a coin toss. From favorable presumptions, the skillful advocate hopes to prevail by means of default reasoning. This perspective leaves little rhetorical space for traditional "evidence" and factual matters in general. The precise factual issues that are contested in law are generally the same facts that trigger shifts in opposing layers of presumption. What matters is avoiding the risk of nonpersuasion, and factual disputes are themselves shaped by that overriding strategy.

*Policy Ambiguity.* While contract disputes are sometimes contained within the language of the contract itself, they are also drawn into further uncertainties, ambiguities, and value conflicts commonly found in public policy. When "working rules" for a complex society are expressed in legislation, they inevitably reveal gaps between the *general language* of statutory rules and *specific problems* at the concrete level of implementation—gaps that can be closed only by presumptions. Some implementation problems start with basic definitions. For example, environmental laws protecting the "habitats" of endangered species have been challenged to set the exact area limits for protecting a particular creature—a demand that may well exceed the powers of environmental science in concrete cases. At a more general level, critics have also questioned whether "habitat" includes the vast migration lands over which rare species might pass. Does the law mandate habitat protection wherever the notorious spotted owl might choose to fly? Does it protect every narrow tributary and wide expanse of river potentially open to the tiny fish known as the snail darter? The answers to these questions depend on the structure of presumptions, which may be implied by statutory language or read back into that language by administrative bodies or appellate judges.

Even when definitional problems have been resolved, statutory rules are destined to conflict with each other, and with larger legal principles. When the legal system stumbles over such conflicts it must set priorities, often described as striking some kind of "balance" between opposing rules. For example, the same environmental statute that protects the habitats of endangered species may contain further mandates, including rules to minimize the costs of compliance. There are also higher constitutional rules that protect certain property rights held by owners of habitat land. How does law "balance" these potentially conflicting rules? As with metaphors of proof burdens, the image of balancing suggests that the scales of justice can be construed strictly as a quantitative device. In reality, the law performs this balancing act by invoking a nested structure of presumptions, organized into default relationships.

These problems are not the result of sloppy drafting. Statutory schemes of any complexity cannot avoid the need to balance conflicting norms. Some laws try to reduce ambiguity in advance by formulating specific presumptions: declaring, for example, that a "habitat" for any protected species is presumed to include the larger ecological system on which the immediate "habitat" is dependent. The law might further hedge its presumption by saying that habitats will "normally" include the larger system, or that the presumption can be rebutted under certain conditions, including hardship for the landowner. Other possibilities include words to the effect that hardships for the landowner should be considered "whenever possible." Most statutes, however, simply ignore the ambiguities of general language. Adding these qualifying phrases and hedges is a common task for appeals courts or administrative agencies. Given the inevitable gaps in statutory language, the parties in a concrete dispute will urge the appeals courts to adopt explicit presumptions to help seal their victory. As part of ongoing legal strategies, interest groups make similar arguments to administrative agencies (the Department of the Interior, the Environmental Protection Agency) and to congressional committees. As ambiguities emerge within rule systems, the law expects one of its bodies to impose a structure of presumptions through which the legal system can complete its job of drawing final inferences in specific cases.

At first glance, disputes based on policy ambiguities may seem to turn largely on factual evidence. Certainly, the US Endangered Species Act has sparked lengthy disputes about data, and evidence of some kind is a constant element in every strategic battle. But more important than any quantity of evidence is the prior selection of norms guiding the inference process. Evidence does not exist in a strategic vacuum; its value depends on the prior allocation and weight of the risk of nonpersuasion. The metaphor of "proof burdens" is thus misleading if it suggests that factual evidence alone can resolve public disputes— if only enough evidence can be found and properly introduced. Factual evidence will be deemed clear, sufficient, and persuasive only when it can be measured against a modestly demanding norm. We may know everything we want to know about the spotted owl or the snail darter, but no amount of natural biology can tell us whether its migration plans or mating habits compel some costly compromise with the economic welfare of landowners. It is not surprising, therefore, that parties engaged in policy disputes seek the advantage found in favorable presumptions. Each side wants to avoid the burden of proving precisely why, under a default structure of competing norms, it should not lose the case. Victory in such disputes requires mastering the structure and idioms of argument through presumptions.

*Ambiguity of Legal Principles.* This analysis leads to the paradox that "burdens of proof" are not primarily concerned with "proof" as such. Leave aside the relatively simple "burden of production"—at least when it concerns proof that is readily accessible, awaiting only the initiative of one party or the other to bring it into play. Burdens of proof compensate for the *absence* of proof, enabling the legal system to draw final inferences in cases by assigning the loss to the party whose evidence is deemed "insufficient." This chronic absence of evidence is a by-product of complex legal rules in a dynamic society. The rules found in contracts, in statutory systems, and even in the Constitution must all be implemented in particular situations, amid public conflict and social change, and in situations that no lawmaker could have reasonably foreseen. Implementation requires the legal system to make final inferences in the face of definitional uncertainties, normative indeterminacy, value conflicts—in short, "ambiguities" of many types. The solution lies not simply in demanding factual evidence but in creating a default structure of presumptions. The stakes in this process can be substantial, as parties to a dispute strive to become winners by default reasoning. Their strategic purpose is to let their opponents bear the risk of nonpersuasion.

Constitutional arguments rest on the same strategic concerns. Leading cases over the past century have flowed directly from judicial variations on the *presumption of constitutionality*. Especially in recent decades, the US Supreme Court has used, stretched, and shifted this key presumption with great virtuosity. Over time, by reallocating and recalibrating the burden of overcoming this presumption, the court has given itself enormous flexibility while maintaining the façade of doctrinal consistency. The presumption of constitutionality is the central premise in reviewing actions taken by other branches of government, whether the legislature (federal or state) or the executive. To be sure, these cases also draw on mountains of factual testimony and expert evidence. But what counts in the court's final inference is how all this material relates to a carefully layered structure of presumptions, which can suddenly shift the advantage to either side.

In a pair of 2003 cases involving affirmative action policies at the University of Michigan, the Supreme Court justices were bitterly divided as to how the presumption of constitutionality should be allocated. For the past several decades, whenever states have used explicit racial categories in any official policy, the court has scrutinized their actions under a *reverse* presumption—in effect, a presumption of *un*constitutionality. To borrow a phrase from criminal law, the Supreme Court treats all racial classifications in statutes as guilty (i.e., unconstitutional) until proven innocent, and the burden of persuasion placed on state officials is nearly absolute. Against this background, affirmative action has become a polarizing issue for the court, as some justices believe that the presumption should revert to its historic permissiveness when states use racial classifications in socially benign ways. In other words, in affirmative action cases some justices would restore the conventional presumption of constitutionality for state policies. In early 2003, when the nine justices seemed split into nearly equal factions espousing these two opposing presumptions, legal observers found it hard to predict how the Michigan cases would come out. Despite mountains of evidence placed into the record, the legal outcome would depend entirely on the structure of presumptions. In the end, a single centrist judge held the balance of power in allocating presumptions. Justice O'Connor seemed to split the difference between camps by voting with the majority, in one case, to strike down one of the university's policies using the presumption of unconstitutionality but *upholding* the other policy under the very same presumption. One might even say that "proof" made the difference in the case where affirmative action was upheld, as Justice O'Connor found that the University of Michigan Law School had managed to overcome the "strict" presumption against its practices. Her action may also have been strategic opportunism within the court, by conceding one victory to state affirmative action programs without clearly changing the structure of presumptions. However one explains her approach, the other justices remained polarized at the level of dueling presumptions. They saw the available "proof" as sustaining their prior selection of norms, including the decisive allocation of presumptions.

Justice O'Connor used similar pragmatic methods in the 2004 Supreme Court cases reviewing President Bush's authority to detain "enemy combatants" in the aftermath of 9/11. In essence the court had to balance the authority claimed by the president, resting in part on his inherent constitutional power as commander in chief, with equally strong principles of due process for incarcerated prisoners. In the Supreme Court, as in the lower courts, decisions in these enemy combatant cases had very little to do with factual evidence, and everything to do with how much "deference" each justice was prepared to give the president in his post-9/11 war on terror. The language of deference is one way for the court to calibrate the presumption of constitutionality in favor of the president's authority to act; the degree of deference determines the weight of principle to be overcome by the challenger's evidence. The nine justices found numerous gradations for expressing this presumption of presidential authority, ranging from treating it as nearly irrebuttable to shrinking it down to the reverse onus that rests with the prosecution in a standard criminal case. The dominant opinion from Justice O'Connor handed the president a substantial presumptive advantage, suggesting that enemy combatants themselves might even carry the burden of proving that the president's factual case was weak. Although these cases are technically not part of the criminal law system, the new doctrine puts enemy combatants into a virtual "guilty until proven innocent" status. This does not say in so many words that the president asserts his war authority by default, but his chances of prevailing are certainly strengthened by the court's new structure of presumptions.

*Ambiguity of International Norms.* We now return to the Iraq-WMD controversy for some summary comments. The Iraq debate unfolded as though it were concerned primarily with raw evidence about the extent of WMD in Saddam Hussein's regime. Contention focused on the site reports of international inspectors, while the Americans presented the Security Council with satellite photographs and detailed intelligence reports and the Iraqis contributed computer discs with tens of thousands of documents. Behind this façade of evidence, the more critical contest was being fought to shape the structure of presumptions, under which *any* evidence (including, inevitably, the "absence of evidence") would be subsumed. Each side wanted to control the public inference as to whether an invasion was warranted. Months after American-led troops entered Iraq, this contest of presumptions continued, with all sides sticking close to their prewar positions. The absence of evidence only increased the pressure on each camp to assign the burden of proof to its opponent. Even though the invasion actually took place, the continuing battle over presumptions allowed the adversaries to harden their positions, thus preparing the actors strategically for the next such world controversy.

From a rhetorical perspective, even more important than the absence of evidence in this controversy was the absence of consensus among powerful international actors. There were too many goals being advanced, not all of which were ultimately compatible. The United Nations Charter itself recognizes an inevitable tension between each nation's right of self-defense and the strong desire to control military conflict through international law. This tension was sharpened by diverse geopolitical goals of powerful countries. The changed circumstances of 9/11 led some of these countries, especially the United States, to challenge the prevailing structure of presumptions in the international law of armed conflict. The resulting conflict over norms utterly dominated the battles over evidence, lending a hard strategic edge to the search for proof.

The highest drama surrounding debates on evidence and norms is reserved for the question of who finally decides on the structure of presumptions. If strategic conflict points toward resolution in the guise of juridical inference, who holds the authority to make that inference? Within the American legal system such authority belongs largely with appellate judges, who have mastered the rhetoric of building stolid deductive judgments upon a shifting structure of presumptions. As a cultural matter Americans defer to this power with astonishing fidelity, although we hear persistent complaints about "judicial activism." There are no comparable cultural patterns in the international legal arena, but surely one element in the Iraq-WMD controversy was the desire by some nations to lodge that judge-like final authority in the United Nations Security Council. Even more remarkable, then, are the many juridical elements found in general public discourse, especially burdens of proof and their related practices. Even without the brute decisional authority found in American law, the court of public international opinion is the scene of strategic conflict that yearns for juridical closure. As for American law, the sheer plurality of norms in a dynamic society means that underlying conflicts are never finally closed. Discrete legal battles can be officially settled, but they survive in the discursive contests of morality, politics, and international relations.

# 12

# Inertia in Argumentation

## *Nature and Reason*

JAMES CROSSWHITE

## Introduction

Presumption and burden of proof issues play a unique role in argumentation studies. Particular argumentative methods and techniques may advance or deter a line of reasoning, but burden and presumption issues decide when a line of reasoning is needed at all. There is little doubt that burden and presumption issues are hugely influential in determining the outcome of conflicts. In law, most burden and presumption issues are typically decided well before trials proceed and in fact must be decided for trials to go forward. Once the burden and presumption issues are decided, some cases resolve themselves.

And so being able to shift the burden of proof or change presumption is a power that seems to be qualitatively different from the power of ordinary argumentative techniques. For it is a power that shapes the rules whereby arguments proceed and the standards by which they are evaluated. Other kinds of arguments take place within the framework established by burden and presumption. Burden and presumption govern argumentation, make it possible, limit and define its outcome.

## The Burden-Shifting Society

In many institutionally governed argument fields, burden and presumption provide relatively stable frameworks for argument. In many cases, no one attempts to shift burdens, and no one attempts to change reigning presumptions. Where burden and presumption structures remain unchallenged, one has a great deal of agreement that the issues have been decided fairly and so one has a certain stability of institutions and practices. So, it is not surprising that in *Burdens of Proof in Modern Discourse*, Richard Gaskins finds that in situations of deep uncertainty, in times of doubt about foundational matters of burden and presumption, burden shifting becomes a more common technique of argumentation. It is a dream of argumentation theory to be a social theory, to find social forms to be determined by the kinds of arguments that are signally persuasive for the groups in question. Gaskins gives a wonderful example of such an attempt, finding a way to measure social uncertainty by, first, identifying what kinds of argumentative strategies are taking power and second, by actually coming to critical judgments about a society because of the frequency and the occasions of burden shifting.

Douglas Walton has a corrective response to Gaskins's theoretical zealotry. He points out that the shifting of burden that goes with the argument from ignorance is not at all simply a fallacy but a very reasonable adaptation to practical situations of complexity in which fairly quick decisions are needed. The ability to formulate an argument for a course of action when a course is required and no one else seems able to formulate an argument is hardly a sign of cultural decay; it is a sign of a creative and practical mind that has adapted to a situation.

However, it is not clear that Gaskins and Walton are speaking of exactly the same thing. It is one thing to use the argument from ignorance in a situation in which a choice must be made based on the best line of reasoning available within a very limited amount of time. It is another to resort to burden shifting that does not require an explicit argument from ignorance. For example, when Gaskins discusses Kant's antinomies, he is more concerned with the problem that presumption is entirely vulnerable to being challenged at any point, even when arguments have been offered on each side. And timeliness is not an issue in the situation of Kant's antinomies. In addition, burden issues regard more than simple arguments from ignorance; they also regard standards such as "beyond reasonable doubt," or "by a preponderance of evidence." And presumption in law seems to work across the line between argument from ignorance and burden issues, with presumption in argumentation in general often taking on an even broader meaning.

I want to shed some light on this unique issue of burden and presumption by exploring *The New Rhetoric*'s approach to the subject. Chaïm Perelman and Lucie Olbrechts-Tyteca agree with Walton that there is nothing strictly fallacious about the argument from ignorance—since in the end they don't have much tolerance for the concept of a fallacy at all. There are argumentative techniques and there are countertechniques. And, like Walton, they are usually keen on showing the rational dimension of what many people would call fallacies. However, they also seem to see what Gaskins sees—the unusually important role that presumption plays in argumentation. In fact, I believe that their account of presumption is enormously subtle, and capable, I think, of explaining what truth there is in Walton's and Gaskins's approaches to the issue.

## Gaskins's Attack on *The New Rhetoric*

Richard Gaskins deploys a critique of *The New Rhetoric* as an important part of the argument of his book on *Burdens of Proof in Modern Discourse*. His arguments against its approach run like this. First, the treatise's theory is weak because it depends on shifting the burden of proof. This is especially troubling to Gaskins because the authors include no developed account of burden shifting or presumption in their theory. That is, *The New Rhetoric* makes an argumentative move for which it cannot account. Further, when the treatise does speak of presumption, outside of situations in which presumptions are institutionalized, presumptions are completely up for grabs. Here Gaskins goes for the aorta of what he calls Perelman's "humanistic idealism." "The major barrier to restoring rhetoric to intellectual respectability has been its history of troubled association with relativism [. . .] the price of Perelman's 'freedom' could be the utter loss of standards, fixed principles, and other forms of authority."[1]

The major difficulty with Gaskins's analysis is that he concerns himself only with a very abstract version of Perelman and Olbrechts-Tyteca's argument—one he finds in the last paragraph of *The New Rhetoric*. Here is the passage:

> Only the existence of an argumentation that is neither compelling nor arbitrary can give meaning to human freedom, a state in which a reasonable choice can be exercised. If freedom was no more than necessary adherence to a previously given natural order, it would exclude all possibility of choice; and if the exercise of freedom were not based on reasons, every choice would be irrational and would be reduced to an arbitrary decision operating in an intellectual void. It is because of the possibility of argumentation which provides reasons, but not compelling reasons, that it is possible to escape the dilemma: adherence to an objectively and universally valid truth, or recourse to suggestion and violence to secure acceptance for our opinions and decisions. The theory of argumentation will help to develop what a logic of value judgments has tried in vain to provide, namely the justification of the possibility of a human community in the sphere of action when this justification cannot be based on a reality or objective truth.[2]

And here is the next sentence, the final sentence in *The New Rhetoric*, the one that Gaskins leaves out: "And its starting point, in making this contribution, is an analysis of those forms of reasoning which, though they are indispensable in practice, have from the time of Descartes been neglected by logicians and theoreticians of knowledge."[3] Remember this sentence; I will return to it shortly.

Gaskins judges this passage and in fact the entire project of *The New Rhetoric* as follows: "As a subtle example of argumentation in its own right, based entirely on affirmative inferences from negative assertions, this passage illustrates a central paradox in Perelman's approach. It all boils down to a hypothetical proposition, using an argument form strangely absent from Perelman's compendium: if formal models of reasoning lead to abhorrent practical results, then the new rhetorical model must be embraced as a valid alternative."[4] Now if this were what Perelman's argument "boils down to" then he wouldn't have had to team up with Lucie Olbrechts-Tyteca, and they wouldn't have had to write *The New Rhetoric*, which includes, beside the last paragraph, five hundred-plus pages of framework and starting points theory and, of course, a very large argument by example that includes an analysis of around fifty distinct techniques of argumentation. This analysis, say Perelman and Olbrechts-Tyteca, explicitly in the very last sentence of their treatise, is the starting point of the justification of the possibility of free human community in the sphere of action when certainty is not available.

However, this does not stop Gaskins from pursuing his straw rhetorician. To continue the earlier passage:

> One could respond to [Perelman's] eloquent plea by asking whether Perelman's model of rhetoric—in addition to being something useful and inspirational—is also valid, true, correct or rational. But from Perelman's point of view this question misses the purpose of the whole rhetorical enterprise: to liberate us from all such inaccessible criteria of categorical judgment [. . .] But even more important, the new rhetoric has not even prevailed according to its own rhetorical standards. Some permissive spirit or contingent license is necessary to keep it alive as an option for further deliberation. In short, something like a presumption of validity-until-proven-false haunts Perelman's basic argument [. . .] Perelman's move follows the grand strategy of shifting the burden of proof. Whereas for centuries the onus weighed heavily on would-be challengers to formal logic, Perelman's argument reverses that presumption.[5]

There are two kinds of difficulty in Gaskins's critique of *The New Rhetoric*. First, there is a problem with Gaskins's concept of burden of proof and with the argumentative strategy he employs. Second, there is a related problem with his understanding of *The New Rhetoric*'s rhetorical theory. Gaskins's concept of burden of proof goes way beyond any usual account of what the phrase means. For Gaskins, it does not have to do directly with what standards of proof must be met by arguers. Neither does it have to do, at bottom, with who shoulders the burden of having to argue, or with what party the presumption rests. Instead, as he says, "Among the many dialectical functions performed by the courts, I have singled out their administration of burdens of proof. By purposely expanding this concept beyond the set of technical rules found under

146 / James Crosswhite

that label in the major textbooks on legal evidence, I mean to include the entire range of practices by which courts gain control over indeterminate questions of fact and value."[6] Gaskins develops this expanded concept and then carries it well beyond the courts, finding in public discourse in general and in theories of reason especially many different kinds of attempts to "gain control over indeterminate questions of fact and value."[7]

However, if any attempt to "gain control" over these questions in conditions of uncertainty is taken to be burden shifting, then the entire sphere of argumentation *The New Rhetoric* analyzes and out of which it argues is going to be a sphere of burden shifting. This might be a half-plausible claim if one reduced *The New Rhetoric* to a truncated and abstract version of one of its arguments—as Gaskins does in his citation of the book's last paragraph. However, it is much less plausible if one acknowledges that Gaskins's charge is just what *The New Rhetoric*'s many examples of techniques of argumentation are there to refute—that when there are no established procedures for achieving finality in argumentation people have nothing to resort to but irrational burden-shifting struggles. *The New Rhetoric*'s many examples show that people really do "gain control" of questions of fact and value even when such matters cannot be determined with certainty. Gaskins's greatly expanded notion of burden of proof makes the real argument impossible to join. From Gaskins's viewpoint, *The New Rhetoric*'s account of how we reason in conditions of uncertainty can be *about* nothing more than, and can itself *be* nothing more than, burden shifting. Again, as long as one doesn't look at *The New Rhetoric*'s real argument in its detail, one can make this charge seem half-plausible.

The other difficulty with Gaskins's approach is that he misunderstands *The New Rhetoric*'s argument fairly completely. He believes that Perelman and Olbrechts-Tyteca are trying to model and ground their theory of argumentation on juridical procedures whose complexities they misunderstand. He misses the fact that *The New Rhetoric* is finally grounded in a concept of justice, not in the procedures of law. Gaskins believes that *The New Rhetoric*'s argument is negative, an argument about the inability of formal theories to account for reasoning, and so ignores the real substance of the treatise's case. And Gaskins believes that the book's discussion of presumptions in its account of how specialized audiences reason exhausts what it has to say about the matter. To show how far wrong Gaskins has gone, it is going to be necessary to show what *The New Rhetoric*'s real account of these matters is.

## Inertia and Reason in *The New Rhetoric*

At critical junctures in *The New Rhetoric*, the authors resort to naturalistic metaphors. No juncture is more critical than when they formulate the concept of "inertia." Inertia is the foundation of the rule of justice,[8] which is in the end itself the measure of the strength of arguments—the treatise's version of a validity criterion. How is it that inertia is the foundation of justice and reason? What strange trick allows a treatise devoted to reason and freedom to rest finally on a metaphor relating to a force of physics? It's an interesting story, and one that puts the issues of burden and presumption in a remarkable light.

The main discussion of inertia takes place in part two of *The New Rhetoric*, which is concerned with the starting points of argumentation—that is, with a background that must be in place for argumentation to proceed. Part of this background is fixed and is not arguable: facts and truths, for example. Part of it is fixed for particular audiences but not for others—values and hierarchies, for example. Presumptions occupy an interesting in-between place—they enjoy a universal acknowledgment, but adherence to them, although universal, can vary by degree. And so, adherence to presumptions can be strengthened or weakened by way of argumentation. Presumptions usually regard what is likely or probable—for example, the presumption that other people are telling us the truth. We usually have to have reasons to doubt people's truthfulness; the presumption lies on the side of truthfulness. Of course, there are times when this presumption's power can be drastically reduced by arguments to the contrary—usually by arguments that point out what is not normal about the situation in which the presumption might be made or that calls the underlying assumption about what is normal into question. Perelman and Olbrechts-Tyteca mention other common presumptions in this section: the presumption that actions reveal the character of the person, the presumption that what is said to us is somehow of interest to us, and the presumption that actions can be understood and explained. Such presumptions about what is normal rest, they say, on a reference group of what are taken to be normal people. Such presumptions are both universally held—and they can be strengthened and weakened by argumentation.

We can easily see why Gaskins might focus on the weakening and even collapse of presumption as a signal indicator of social dissolution, the decline of reason, and the cause of adversarial eristics. Much reasoning—especially in law—depends on what one can reasonably take for granted about human behavior. The more agreement there is about this, the easier it is to proceed with argumentation; the less agreement, the more burdens and presumptions become matters of argument themselves. Think of the presumptions of heterosexuality and of able-bodiedness and of the social conflict around whether these presumptions are warranted—which is, as Perelman and Olbrechts-Tyteca point out—a conflict about who is in the reference group from which the concept of the normal is derived.

However, what is most interesting about presumption in *The New Rhetoric* is that it is thought of as a natural phenomenon. Presuming is not simply an action we take but a condition for life and reason. Here is one of the critical passages: "In most cases [. . .] a speaker has no firmer support for his presumptions than psychical and social inertia which are the equivalent in consciousness and society of the inertia of physics."[9] This is a remarkable equivalence, since inertia has a place of such primacy in physics. Inertia is responsible in a profound way for what regularity and order there are in physics—for the intelligibility of the physical world. Perelman and Olbrechts-Tyteca are claiming that there is something like this same force operating to give reason and society what order and intelligibility they have. A primary inertia-like force sustains presumption. This view of a natural force operating in reason is worlds away from Gaskins's account of the arbitrariness he finds in Perelman's account. Here is Gaskins: "It is not surprising that Perelman treats presumptions as isolated parochialisms, rather than as broad cognitive or strategic forces. For him presumptions are simply localized biases or prejudices, characteristic of discrete groups but certainly not binding on the community as a whole."[10]

However, let me quote *The New Rhetoric* on inertia a little further:

It can be presumed, failing proof to the contrary, that the attitude previously adopted—the opinion expressed, the behavior preferred—will continue in the future [. . .] According to Paulhan, the strange thing about our condition is that it is "easy to find reasons for strange acts, but difficult to find them for ordinary acts. A man who eats beef does not know why, but if he gives up beef forever in favor of frogs or salsify he will think up a thousand proofs, each more ingenious than the last." Inertia makes it possible to rely on the normal, the habitual, the real, and the actual and to attach a value to them, whether it is a matter of an existing situation, an accepted opinion, or a state of regular and continuous development. Change, on the other hand, has to be justified [. . .][11]

In short, those who advocate for change bear the burden of proof. There is a host of issues to be explored in this passage. The world of the fact/value distinction is completely overcome here by the way inertia attaches a value to the real, the actual, the normal, the habitual. This means, as Perelman shrewdly notes, that change has a "devaluating effect." It "shakes social confidence," because inertia grants a value to the way things are.[12]

However, the most important move in Perelman's account is where this psychical and social force of nature takes on a property not shared by the physical world. In physics, inertia is a force that is continuous in space and time; it is not translated over breaks in time or space. In reason and society, matters are different: it is through inertia that the technique of the closed case is extended, so to speak, into the technique of the precedent. The only difference between the repetition of a precedent and the continuance of an existing state is that in the former the facts are seen as discontinuous. With this very small shift in perspective, we can still see inertia at work: "it is as necessary to prove the expediency of changing behavior when confronted with the repetition of a situation as it is to prove the utility of changing an existing state of affairs."[13] This is an insightful account, but I am not convinced that this is a small shift in perspective. For it is the power of discontinuity in the working of inertia that allows for the force of precedence to take hold, and this is directly connected to the relation between inertia and justice, as we shall see.

One reaches *The New Rhetoric*'s center of gravity at a remarkable passage on the strength of arguments. The passage occurs in the middle of a section titled "Interaction and Strength of Arguments," in which an essential identity of reason and justice is highlighted.[14] According to *The New Rhetoric*, the *strength* of arguments has a special philosophical status. The strength of arguments cannot be discovered empirically. It cannot be measured psychologically or through any kind of social scientific research. The conceptual origin of the strength of arguments lies in what *The New Rhetoric* calls a "dissociation." The dissociation here is between the *normal*, in the sense of the usual, and the *norm*, in the sense of the normative, something regulative and not just descriptive, a standard. This dissociation makes possible the important distinction between effectiveness and validity. Some arguments may be effective as a matter of fact and yet not be strong or valid. Valid arguments are strong arguments. Their strength is not a simple matter of effectiveness but is rather a de jure validity.

What then, according to *The New Rhetoric*, is the ground of what it calls "validity" or strength? It is one thing to have a logical distinction; it is another to have grounds for making the distinction in practice, with actual cases. Here is the answer: "The normal, as well as the norm, is definable only in relation to an audience whose reactions provide the measure of normality and whose adherence is the foundation of standards of value [. . .] The superiority of the norm over the normal is correlative to the superiority of one audience over another."[15] This is not an unexpected answer. Earlier in the treatise, the authors develop the idea at some length in the section on "The Universal Audience."[16] Across several sections, they develop at length the processes and criteria for constructing universal audiences; the idea has received much attention and has led to a lively controversy.[17]

In this discussion of strength and validity, though, Perlman and Olbrechts-Tyteca go a little further and ask: "What guarantees this validity? What provides the criterion for it?"[18] They are reaching here for a clearer definition of the universality that belongs to a universal audience. And they answer: "Our hypothesis is that [. . .] strength is appraised by application of the rule of justice: that which was capable of convincing in a specific situation will appear to be convincing in a similar or analogous situation."[19] That is, universal audiences generally follow precedents. They bend to the law of inertia. They recognize norms. This is a striking passage for close readers of *The New Rhetoric* because here the universal audience is identified with a specific argumentative technique: the rule of justice, which itself is grounded in this unusual idea of inertia. This is the core of *The New Rhetoric*'s philosophy of argumentation: reason is justice.

The quasinatural force of inertia grounds presumption in its most fundamental form: change must be justified. However, inertia as *The New Rhetoric* conceptualizes it is also capable of supporting a more far-reaching presumption of justice—that a change that violates precedent must be justified, and more generally that precedents can be used in arguments. Here one glimpses again the ethical heart of *The New Rhetoric*'s project. The presumption of justice is a presumption of fairness and equity, and the rule of justice is the rational means by which equity is protected.

In its abstract form the rule of justice states that people in similar situations should be treated similarly, that situations that are alike should be treated alike. A teenaged brother and sister murder their father. The rule of justice says that we should treat this murder like any other murder. However, we can argue that the act and situation are not like most murders. The teenagers are young. Their action came only after years of violent abuse by their father. The children had reason to fear imminent violent actions, and so on. Without the presumption of the rule of justice, supported by inertia, none of these arguments would be available.

However, Perelman knew early on that the formal rule of justice was not sufficient to make this presumption of equity concrete enough to reach decisions in difficult cases. People would always argue about whether actions or situations were relevantly similar. In his positivist phase, he had attempted to solve this problem abstractly and formally, through conceptual analysis. However, this led him to a famous impasse. The only way to reach conclusions about real cases was to make value judgments about the concrete details of cases: young people should be treated differently from adults in criminal cases. At a certain level of suffering from violence, preventive counterviolence is justified, and so on. But Perelman despaired of being able to justify these kinds of statements philosophically. He tried to find a logical ground for "value judgments," but could not. Some appeal to tradition, or precedents, or values seemed to be necessary. He came to recognize that the positivist project had isolated itself from the resources it required.

The principle of inertia puts the philosopher of reason back into the world, a world rich with precedents, full of decisions that have actually been made, a world ordered already by substantive decisions about when actions and situations are and are not alike. This is true not only in juridical matters, in which laws and customs and regulations are assumed to be just by the mere fact of their existence, but it is true, too, in the way past decisions and judgments within families and friendships and organizations work by inertially powered presumptions of equity to make reasoning possible in accord with the principle of justice.

## The Argument of *The New Rhetoric*

However, not only does presumption play this central role within the theory of argumentation that *The New Rhetoric* offers; it also plays a central role in *The New Rhetoric*'s own basic argument. Recall that Gaskins charged that *The New Rhetoric*'s argument was primarily an argument from ignorance, one based on inferences from negative assertions—since formal logic cannot solve practical problems of reasoning, then rhetoric is the right approach. Since dogmatism and skepticism have intolerable practical consequences, we should follow the path of the rhetorical tradition to return to reason. These are simply not *The New Rhetoric*'s main arguments. Rather, the treatise takes the limits of formal reasoning and the undesirability of skepticism and dogmatism as givens. They receive attention only for a short space at the beginning of the treatise as a way of accounting for the motivations of the project. The real question is: given the limitations of formal logic and the undesirable consequences of dogmatism and skepticism—all fully evident in the postwar milieu in which Perelman and Olbrechts-Tyteca wrote—what is the alternative? Is there an alternative? The burden of the argument in *The New Rhetoric* is to show that there is such an alternative.

But how does the argument proceed? Does Perelman use a strategy for which he himself cannot account, as Gaskins charges? No. Perelman's formative critical action was to move from asking the question about how value judgments could be logically justified within a positivist framework to abandoning the intellectual context and community within which such a question had force at all. One would not make meaningful progress within that context. One cannot build a meaningful world out of nothing, or out of pure logical relations. Perelman retained some of the positivist program. He believed that the aspiration for universality was an aspiration for nonviolence, for peace. He believed that some conception of reason was essential for this project. However, he could not see how positivism could provide a ground for reasoning about substantive conflicts, about social goods, about the kinds of disagreements that could lead to violence.

Perelman's 1945 positivist essay, *On Justice*, refers to only eight other authors. There is only one citation to a work that is older than fifteen years. In the first sixty pages of *The New Rhetoric*, there are one hundred sixteen citations, and the authors cited span millennia. The sea-change could not be more evident. *The New Rhetoric* is a book of examples that support a case—examples not simply of argument theorists but of arguments themselves and their forms and their authors. *The New Rhetoric* describes the discovered techniques and forms of reasoning, and in doing so it also allies itself with a historical community of argumentation. Further, Perelman and Olbrechts-Tyteca also rediscovered the rhetorical tradition—its theories and its practices. The examples of argumentation in *The New Rhetoric*, which make up most of the book, both establish the case and highlight the new community of deliberators and theorists to which Perelman and Olbrechts-Tyteca turned when Perelman abandoned the positivist framework.

Within a positivist framework, precedents do not exist as such; they are simple antecedents. They need logical justification to have any rational force. But to live in this kind of world, to believe that there are no precedents, no already existing agreements about values, is not to live in the real world of human beings. Within a new rhetorical framework, and in a human world, the world of real history, precedents are inertially energized and authorized and work across time. This is the human world to which *The New Rhetoric* returns— a world with not only a rich store of values and precedents but also a world with people who share the aspiration for universality and nonviolence. For *The New Rhetoric*, it was just an undeniable fact that people do often settle their disputes nonviolently, through reasoning and argumentation. And the case made by *The New Rhetoric* is that these arguments grounded in a common conception of what is good can have strength and not just effectiveness. Even further, *The New Rhetoric* also establishes that there has been a transhistorical and transcultural tradition of people who have developed theories about this kind of reasoning and argumentation, about its social and political and personal importance, its inherent inclination toward peace, and its conception of reasoning as a kind of justice. This tradition becomes for *The New Rhetoric* part of the new context, the new framework. Perelman and Olbrechts-Tyteca join these interlocutors in an inertial frame of reference and attempt to win for them the presumption.

So Gaskins is not only wrong about the supposed relativistic burden shifting of *The New Rhetoric*; he misses more or less completely the contributions of the treatise. However, Gaskins is in some ways right to call burden shifting a kind of sign of social dissolution and to connect it with a decline of reasoning and an increase in eristics. Perelman himself addresses the need this creates and we will come to that at the end. But, first, it should be clearly acknowledged that the burden-shifting social disruption to which Gaskins points can be destructive or it can creative or progressive, or it can be all these things. In a 2017 article in *The New York Times Magazine*, Emily Bazelon, very rarely a defender of traditional positions, makes a case for the traditional norms that govern US presidential practices. These norms are not laws, but they are something like a set of precedents or unwritten rules that traditionally govern presidential action. She is concerned about President Trump's frequent flouting of these unwritten rules, to which the media respond with words like "unprecedented" or "unusual" or "startling." In her article, Bazelon struggles to find the right language for something she experiences as social dissolution—and wrongness. However, Trump seems to be a skilled burden-shifter whose aim is precisely to shake things up by taking "unprecedented" action, and he has many defenders in this. One of Bazelon's phrases for "dissolution" is "erosion of norms," and her worry is about what happens when the erosion has gone too far, when erosion repair is obviously needed. Her answer seems to be that laws will be created to address the breakdown caused by the erosion of norms. But Bazelon is clearly not at ease with this, and her Gaskins-like discomfort is obvious, even though she is usually on the more norm-breaking side herself. She describes—and enacts—quite well that moment of social dissolution at which it becomes difficult to argue effectively.

A more positive account of "dissolution" can be found in a 2016 forum in *Political Geography* on the study of police power and violence. In an article titled simply "Burden of Proof" (a commentary on Mat Coleman's "State Power in Blue"), Nisha Shah makes the case that the study of racialized police power operates with certain presumptions and burdens that occlude the sources of racialized police violence. The *study* of policing is thus *itself* a central feature of the "blue wall" that seems to shield police from scrutiny and accountability. This feature of the wall prevents any inference from mere racial disparities to racial discrimination; effects are not evidence. And effects that are generated across a variety of people and practices and places have no obvious single source, no clear focus for accountability. Proof of intent would be evidence, but intent is elusive in such wide effects, and can hide, say Coleman and Shah, in training and in evidentiary practices. Thus, they say, the burden of proof should not require the establishing of intent. The burden must be shifted away from the paradigm of the intent of individuals to the "practices and their effects that come to exist in routine ways." The "blue wall" does not hide individual intent, but functions as "a seemingly neutral part of police practice" to hide the source of racial disparities in policing. This shift and this method of inquiry become, according to Shah, "a way to submit into evidence the effects controlled for by the data and kept out of the law courts."[20]

This is clearly a creative and potentially progressive form of burden shifting. Here, in fact, burden shifting is the solution to an intransigent problem concerning reasoning and evidence. It should also be pointed out that this is work motivated and supported in part because of early twenty-first century demonstrations against racialized police violence that were sometimes violent and often strongly eristic in their discursive mode. Since eristic discourse is one sign of Gaskins's "dissolution," chiefly signaled by burden shifting, it is important to recognize its potentially positive features, too. Walton described this productive feature of eristics in *The New Dialectic*, where he wrote that eristic struggles can serve to air grievances and lead to increased mutual understanding.[21]

One challenge that Perelman took up after *The New Rhetoric* was not Gaskins's challenge to give presumption its proper due, but the opposite: to explain how one can ever move beyond the conservatism and what appears to be the injustice of the force of inertia. In his 1964 Genoa lectures, in the lecture on "Justice and Justification," he asks: "Is it possible in the practical realm to transcend the aspirations of a political community?"[22] This takes things to a clearly philosophical level. Burden shifting might be one way to change certain social goals or values, but burden shifting only functions effectively when social life is already undergoing change. Perelman is asking about the possibility of confronting such matters philosophically—and not just Minerva-like retrospectively.

In his final Genoa lecture, on "Justice and Reason," Perelman poses this question in a different way, by asking whether there is such a thing as a philosopher's mission, whether it is possible to reason in a way that is not simply reliant on presumptions or willful burden shifting. In this context, Perelman cites Husserl's dictum that "philosophers are the civil servants of humanity."[23] They are not simply legislators or judges or social activists. Philosophers, says Perelman, must imagine law for the whole of humanity and not some particular group. This challenge puts enormous strains on Perelman's central concepts of universality, inertia, and justice, but these are just the matters that Perelman judged to need addressing after finishing *The New Rhetoric*, in which the concepts of inertia, presumption, and precedent play such important roles.

## Notes

1. R. Gaskins, *Burdens of Proof in Modern Discourse* (New Haven, CT: Yale University Press, 1992), 36.
2. Quoted in Gaskins, *Burdens of Proof*, 31–32.
3. C. Perelman and L. Olbrechts-Tyteca, *The New Rhetoric: A Treatise on Argumentation*, trans. J. Wilkinson and P. Weaver (Notre Dame, IN: University of Notre Dame Press, 1969). Originally published as *La nouvelle rhétorique: Traité de l'argumentation* (Paris: Presses Universitaires de France, 1958), 514.
4. Gaskins, *Burdens of Proof*, 32.

5. Gaskins, *Burdens of Proof,* 32–33.

6. Gaskins, *Burdens of Proof,* 37.

7. Gaskins, *Burdens of Proof,* 37.

8. Perelman and Olbrechts-Tyteca, *The New Rhetoric,* 218–19.

9. Perelman and Olbrechts-Tyteca, *The New Rhetoric,* 105.

10. Gaskins, *Burdens of Proof,* 34.

11. Perelman and Olbrechts-Tyteca, *The New Rhetoric,* 105–6.

12. Perelman and Olbrechts-Tyteca, *The New Rhetoric,* 106.

13. Perelman and Olbrechts-Tyteca, *The New Rhetoric,* 107.

14. Perelman and Olbrechts-Tyteca, *The New Rhetoric,* 460–65.

15. Perelman and Olbrechts-Tyteca, *The New Rhetoric,* 463.

16. Perelman and Olbrechts-Tyteca, *The New Rhetoric,* 31–35.

17. I have tried to summarize and address this controversy in J. Crosswhite, "Universalities," *Philosophy and Rhetoric* 43, no. 44 (2010): 430–48.

18. Crosswhite, "Universalities," 464.

19. Crosswhite, "Universalities," 464.

20. N. Shah, "Burden of Proof," *Political Geography* 51 (August 2016): 88.

21. D. Walton, *The New Dialectic: Conversational Contexts of Argument* (Toronto: University of Toronto Press, 1998), 185.

22. C. Perelman, *Justice* (New York: Random House, 1967), 70.

23. Perelman, *Justice,* 72.

# 13

# The Liberal-Progressive and Conservative Presumptions

## *On Deliberation, Debate, and Public Argument*

### G. Thomas Goodnight

America and the democracies of the West have long celebrated public address. Elected representatives and private citizens have taken to the public forum to defend themselves, advance community interests, and offer resolutions for action. This essay constructs public argument as a scene in which deliberations play out in debates, and presumptions are at work. As a concept, presumption finds a place in studies of informal logic, institutional thinking, and politics. Presumptions in public argument become articulated, used, reinforced, and modified in ways that build points of time. The political articulation of presumption persists as a resource for invention, a division among advocates on a resolution, and a repertoire of argumentation for articulating party division and unity. The presumptions of public argument are anchored in a constitutional act that sets the boundaries and outlines procedures for public debate at election time and among the duties of governance.[1] The status of argument as presumption is crucial to a democracy because it underwrites the processes of deliberation when policy questions arise. Sometimes the prudent course presumptively resides in line with keeping the status quo as is or with small changes. The constitutional theory of presumption is tied to centrist public deliberation, yet it also reaches to extremes of right- and left-wing discourses and social movements This essay proceeds to (1) posit the characteristics and limits of public argument; (2) evaluate alternative definitions of presumption; (3) define the liberal-progressive and the conservative presumptions; (4) examine the articulation of American political practices as boundaries; and (5) fashion a constructive critique of centrist civic exchange from counterpublic standpoints of the right and left.

## Public Argument

In large measure, the nature, value and limits of public argument is a legacy from ancient Greece. Speaking to the value of free knowledge, free expression, and free ballot, Pericles said: "We alone regard a man who takes no interest in public affairs, not as a harmless; but as a useless character; and if few of us are originators, we are all sound judges of a policy. The great impediment to action is, in our opinion, not discussion, but the want of that knowledge which is gained by discussion preparatory to action."[2] Aristotle's reflection on deliberative logos points to the kind of practical intelligence guiding public argument and consequently furthering the interests of the polis. While such knowledge could not attain the certainty of *theoria*, its virtue resided in generating tested, probable knowledge directed towards the concrete situation, grasping the circumstances in their infinite variety.[3] Aristotle finds political speaking to be advisory; it urges us to do or not do something.[4] Hence, its domain is the possible and its objective is to address what should be done hereafter.[5] Aristotle's views of rhetorical argument, lodged at the juncture of ethics and politics, are rooted in a particular cosmogony with race, class, and gender restrictions. Nevertheless, three assumptions carry forward into modern understandings of deliberative practices: (1) Speech serves to distinguish the advantageous from harmful, and hence the right from the wrong.[6] If speech cannot lead to a better course of action, despite the difficulties of disagreement, then deliberation is fruitless. (2) Each situation has a good, which intelligent inquiry can hope to discover.[7] If there is no hope that a single best alternative can be discovered, or at least one better alternative sifted from many, then any preferential decision could be accepted or rejected without deliberation. (3) In the long run, the best interests of the individual are served by advancing the interests of the entire community. If there is no link between the interests of the individual and common goods, then public deliberation becomes irrelevant to decisions about future conduct. In principle, public deliberation assumes importance because it can produce and evaluate alternative courses of collaborative conduct relevant to the well-being of the individual and community.

The Western tradition has not always placed such trust in the results of practical discourse. Still, from time to time the supporting ideas of *prudentia* and *eloquentia* have been reaffirmed as necessary to generate knowledge concerning practical conduct in the world of human affairs. For example, Vico writing on behalf of the humanistic tradition issued a defense of the *sensus communis*, practical wisdom, which he believed to be "not nourished on the true but on the probable."[8] He goes on, "The *sensus communis* is the sense of right and of the common good that is to be found in all men; moreover, it is a sense that is acquired through living in the community and is determined by its structures and aims."[9] Thus, Vico sought to dismantle Cartesian rationalism with the old *topica*. As Gadamer concludes: "This is the art of finding arguments and serves to develop the sense of what is convincing, which works instinctively and ex tempore and for that very reason cannot be replaced by science."[10] According to Gadamer, Thomas Reid echoes Vico's belief that language rather than abstractions characterizes speaking and thinking. He affirms practical intelligence generating knowledge to "direct us in the common affairs of life"[11] [...] "providing a cure for the 'moon sickness' of metaphysics."[12] Aristotle and Vico found practical intelligence to be a form of prudential wisdom. In contrast to Machiavellian realism, Gadamer concludes, the *sensus communis* expresses "the basis of a moral philosophy that really does justice to the life of society."[13]

The idea of a community guided by common sense articulated in public argument may have its most contemporary roots in the evolution of the nineteenth-century Republican tradition. The practices of public argument were assembled into restricted democratic institutions in the new world.[14] Enshrined in the foundation myths of Western democracies and protected by constitutional law is the norm that a free people through public deliberation can determine its own course of government through holding public institutions and officials accountable. This presumption makes for a decisive difference between, say, the revolutionary traditions of France, with their peculiar distributions of authority and the United States, where authority in principle is held accountable to publics.[15] Public institutions put into practice public policy. The discourses of public policy are argumentative, a subject is affirmed, criticized, contested, and subject to dissent by citizens. Policy discourses struggle to legitimate planning, practice, and access as well as justify change, revision, and renewal. Public policy debate is a core feature of citizen performance in a democracy. Twentieth-century Americans articulated this idea into a social theory of knowledge and practice. Argument skill sets of problem-solving are cultivated by education in schools to support plural but shared forms of living, discipline-based professions, and the performances of citizenship.[16] The Constitution subordinated some groups, too, thus, the painful routes to change, equality, and reform remain incomplete and continue to goad citizen action.

The common sense of contesting publics appears in the performances of a great variety of unfinished political projects to ground, interpret, and entangle constitutional law-making, professional codes, and community practices. How is it that democratic debate held where advocates contest opinions, interests, and policies, assures even a workable, much less the best outcome in the long run? Charles Sanders Peirce reaffirmed the value of "critical common sense." He established the reason for an inclusive politics of opinion formation—thus transforming Aristotle's more limited notion of excellence and virtue of the individual into the participation of citizens in discussion.

> Human opinion universally tends in the long run to a definite form, which is the truth. Let any human being have enough information and exert enough thought upon any question, and the result will be that he will

arrive at a certain definite conclusion, which is the same that any other mind will reach under sufficiently favorable circumstances. [. . .] There is, then, to every question a true answer, a final conclusion, to which the opinion of every man is constantly gravitating. He may for a time recede from it, but give him more experience and time for consideration, and he will finally approach it. The individual may not live to reach the truth; there is a residuum of error in every individual's opinions. No matter; it remains that there is a definite opinion to which the mind of man is, on the whole and in the long run, tending. On many questions the final agreement is already reached, on all it will be reached if time enough is given. The arbitrary will or other individual peculiarities of a sufficiently large number of minds may postpone the general agreement in that opinion indefinitely; but it cannot affect what the character of that opinion shall be when it is reached.[17]

In short, Peirce believed that individual opinions formed through a process of critical deliberation leads in the long run to a true consensus. This concept broadens the Aristotelian perspective by opening and exposing to criticism all opinions that cannot withstand inquiry of "a community of inquirers infinite in number, and capable of carrying an inquiry for an infinitely long time."[18] So important was this concept of a community of free inquiry to the evolution of enlightened self-government, that Walter Lippman concluded, "it is not possible to reject this faith in the efficacy of reason and at the same time to believe that communities of men [and women] enjoying freedom could govern themselves successfully."[19]

Peirce provided the justification for a process of public argument that invites a copious range of opinions and multiple debates through adhering to processes of free inquiry and expression. On the other hand, John Dewey sought to discover the memberships of finite, concrete, and organized publics. The United States, with its various strands of nationalities, creeds, and cultures never knew the homogeneity of the Athenian polis. Consequently, in America the enthymematic basis for argument lacked a common fund of prudential wisdom. The Greek orator could rely on shared topics, common ends, and living memories to undergird discussions in the polis, however heated. The common means and ends of American publics were nowhere as clearly present. Peirce's idea of an ideal "community of inquiry" could provide a principle for democratic discussion and debate, but not the necessary glue of practical interests for evaluation of what is expedient or inexpedient for alternative communities of interest. "Why could Dewey find no identifiable and articulate contemporary public? Because, he thought, there was not a community—and because the arts of communication sufficient to form community were absent."[20] Disillusioned with the failure of the Progressive movement to sustain a national public, Dewey considered the prerequisites for advancing the self-interests of a democracy. Lloyd Bitzer quotes Dewey: "Without communication the public will remain shadowy and formless, seeking spasmodically for itself, but seizing and holding its shadow rather than its substance. Till the Great Society is converted into a Great Community, the Public will remain in eclipse."[21] Bitzer's conclusion follows a long tradition of scholars who have sought to increase the competence of public advocates and the quality of public advocacy. "The formation of the public requires community; and community requires the sharing of rich symbols, interests, and ideas by means of communication."[22]

Aristotle could assume that audiences would know and defend arguments drawn from the common fund of the Athenian polis, however rancorous a debate. A modern, more heterogeneous culture, however, faces the problem of identifying and articulating appropriate publics. Without advocates who discover and essay common interests and without audiences capable of evaluating alternative interests or ends, public argument may be stretched to the realms of egoistic posturing, mimetic rivalry, and flashy entertainment. Fallacies do spring to view, especially when elections are hotly contested and expensively produced. No matter how compelling the "horse race," public argument persists and remains at work in citizen deliberations.

Public arguments shape into deliberative engagements when presumptions are brought into play to inform citizens of the risks to proposed resolutions for action. If argument in general "aims at a choice among possible theses" as Perelman and Olbrechts-Tyteca claim,[23] and if a "public," as Bitzer contends, "is a community of persons who share conceptions, principles, interests and values, and who are significantly interdependent,"[24] then a private disagreement becomes a public argument when the consequences of choice go beyond the interlocutors (and perhaps even the immediate audience) to involve the interests in a community, made common by the consequences of decision. When such disputes enter a forum with more or less specific procedures and traditions of airing and adjudicating disagreement, public argument becomes civic debate. When successful, public argument generates prudential knowledge guiding the constitution of communities. Public argument works best, normatively speaking, if (1) the future is held to be undecided; (2) good reasons can present and support evaluations of options for collective conduct; (3) individual judgment and action are relevant to the options discussed; (4) the process adheres to freedom of inquiry and expression in the long run perfecting consensus; and (5) a community of common interests can be discovered and articulated through discourse. From a realistic standpoint, public argument emerges from the historical accumulation and contemporary practices of political disputes over policy and power; from a critical view, public argument performances are accountable to counterfactual tests, holding to common account those advocates whose justifications for enacting or changing policies are but gloss and glitter laid over privilege and special interest.

## The Liberal and the Conservative Presumptions

Adverse to the terrors of extremism, twentieth-century American political parties have typically, though not always, been pulled within a centrist orbit and stretched elliptically. Many modern disciplines, including communication studies, emerged during an era of "Progressive Reform," a curious urban movement that oscillated between left and right-leaning politics, largely in favor of finding pragmatic solutions to what were asserted to be the social problems of the era. Scientific problem-solving through public discussion and debate was the prized objective of educating a democratic citizenry. To this end, the Progressives called for voters to take a "middle-of-the-road" position, a common course that would avoid the naked self-interest of politics on the one hand and the endless repetitions of ideological praxis on the other.[25] During this period of economic and population growth, many issues previously accorded deliberation in the public sphere were entrusted to the "impartial" expertise of institutional hierarchies. Nevertheless, the great issue that troubled Dewey remains: how can publics on behalf of whose interests argument occurs be discovered, defined, educated, and sustained? Presumption plays multiple, key roles in the answer. Democratic orientations to public argument have at their core a set of beliefs, feelings, and readings that set presumptions in more or less consistent ways. Presumptions identify the normal course in a situation against which the proposals for policy must be tested. Presumptions have a provisional standard, since sometimes advocates demonstrate that the exception to the rule is useful in particular cases of justice, the common welfare, and the common defense.

American liberal and conservative political presumptions will be outlined as orientations to argument. An orientation is a symbolic cluster of views that draws equations and posits differences between supporters and opponents. Orientations are sites of invention and contestation. As invention, a political orientation creates a space where identification of policy is articulated, defended, and acted upon. As contestation, political orientations offer stasis points of opposition where burdens of proof remain unmet, inconsistent, posed as token response, or simply bad ideas whose time for rejection is at hand. "Liberal" and "conservative" are relative terms that travel over time. Every democracy has its divisions among elites, middle class, and folks at the lower end of the social and economic spectrum. The term "liberal" I deploy for this essay is grounded in the leftist orientations toward public policy discourses of the American New Deal and the Great Society. From time to time, public argument takes a vernacular form, particularly in identity politics that hitches affects to transcendence, from hate to hope. The term "conservative" is a rightest orientation in public debate that ranges from elite defenses of free-enterprise policies to populist resentments of state actions. Chamber of Commerce, Republican Party, and think-tank conservativism works sometimes in consonance with and occasionally in opposition to populist national, anti-immigrant, and xenophobic vernacular polemics. Conservatism in a postwar world is a complicated discourse.[26] Liberal discourse ranges from policy hearings, studies, and reports to performative oppositional gestures of disturbance, disruption, and transgression. The center is a contested ground where some groups and advocates on the extremes of public argument struggle to undermine legitimacy, take power from the middle, and stretch the political mainstream. Public argumentation and debate energize the circuits of disagreement, contestation, and antagonism among citizens and others who identify with a nation and its range of missions.

In the public arguer's world, choice is uncertain, but prior thought and experience lead to expectations of what normally constitutes the accepted, approved, or beneficial courses of conduct and its contraries. "Presumptions," Perelman and Olbrechts-Tyteca observe, are "connected with what is normal or likely."[27] If views are held as presumptions, then argument is possible. Exposure to new information, logical testing, and different ideas results in several possible outcomes: the confirmation, qualification, or complete overturn of presumption, or, alternatively, confusion, greater uncertainty, and further argument. Holding prejudgment as provisional, capable of modification, engages the arguer in a world where the future is not fully disclosed; this also protects the arguer from the compelling, sometimes violent world of the visionary who must ride a single truth to heaven or consign all to perdition. But such protection has its price. Because the arguer builds cases and accepts judgments on probable truth, the possibility of error is always present—just as the scientist who builds into experiments resistance to unsupported belief risks error. Because the arguer builds cases and accepts judgments on probable truth, the possibility of error is always present. Whether the kind, direction, and degree of risk is fathomed by inchoate intuition or by a well-defined philosophy, "being wrong" is always possible within a process that makes no *a fortiori* guarantee, at least in the short term, that any particular decision will be right.

Susan Langer conceptualizes this risk by reminding us that "every new insight is bought with the life of an older certainty."[28] Henry Johnstone Jr. explains that the tension between conserving old knowledge and changing to new knowledge is the very impulse of argument.[29] If presumptions are an outcome of balancing norm against exception, then any particular presumption exists within that tension between the premature denial of new knowledge—falsely retaining old prejudices—on the one hand, and the premature acceptance of what is offered as new knowledge—unwisely jettisoning tried-and-tested knowledge—on the other. Although this tension is implicit in every deliberative public argument, the reasons why some risks are taken and not others may not be fully understood or even rendered expressible. Over the long term, however, which decision-risks are accepted as routine and which are avoided in-so-far-as-possible discloses the standing of presumption for a person, profession, institution, and community. Presumption may be rendered articulate through historical understanding that reveals the kinds of risks accepted by a community, separating out core interests from the more peripheral. Presumption may be conceptualized in terms of theoretical understanding, as experts posit what risks ought to be incurred and which not. The life of public institutions includes rule-grounded logics that pit traditional versus innovative, formal versus informal choices among proof standards and decisions. Finally, presumption becomes expressive of individual choice as the typical interests of community and conceived directions of obligations, freedoms, rights, and duties are weighed and evaluated within the processes of argument itself.

If public argument is grounded in the risks of permanence and change, and if these risks catch up individuals in communities of common concerns, then public argument not only "jeopardizes" individual preferences but also extends to community involvement in both traditional fora (such as the old-style town meeting) and expert decision-making sessions where the public is represented as both potential support, client, and part of internal nonspecialized institutional change. In a dispute over a given resolution, deliberations may extend the traditional presumptions of an argument community, or it may be found that differences are too great to span. In the latter case, the community of interlocutors may repeat, vary, suspend, or fragment. Thus, in debate, argument puts at stake more than the outcome of a single resolution; at risk is the continuity and change of the community itself. At the end of the day, public argument always encounters in its discussion means and ends, even if the latter are not presented as surface contestation per se.

Perelman and Olbrechts-Tyteca's discussion of "abstract" and "concrete" values reveals the basis for opposing ends that are put at issue in all public argument. An abstract value is universal, "valid for all people and under all circumstances," such as "truth" or "justice."[30] They "can readily be used for criticism because they are no respecters of persons and seem to provide criteria for one wishing to change the established order," they write.[31] "A concrete value," by contrast, "is one attached to a living being, a specific group, or a particular object, such as the Church or France."[32] Because abstract values elevate the conceived ideal over that which exists, they are much easier to use when one wishes to renovate.[33] Concrete values characterize conservative argumentation while abstract values "manifest a revolutionary spirit."[34] Although these value orders are often brought into conflict, they are not necessarily mutually exclusive. Perelman and Olbrechts-Tyteca surmise: "It seems that there have always been people who attach more importance to one set than to the other; perhaps they form characterial families. In any case their distinctive trait would not be complete neglect of values of one kind, but subordination of these values to those of the other."[35] The value commitments become exclusive only in the perspectives of the revolutionary who holds that all conceived abstract values must be realized by complete change, and the reactionary who holds that conceived concrete values are the complete fulfillment of abstract values and no change or tolerance of exception can be worthwhile. At the extreme political ends, arguers committed to praxis discount rather than listen to others because difference of views becomes attributed to either corruption, naiveté, or hegemony. For those engaged in the broad realm of public argument the situation is different. The arguer must continually confront choices between permanence and change, concrete and abstract values, because the processes of public argument do not point in a univocal direction for minimizing error. Openness, listening, advocacy, and sympathy are all integral features of lively public debate.

Presumption functions as a balancing concept by minimizing the likelihood of a bad decision and its consequences, whether from the point of view of an individual, community, or special forum. Understanding the political points of view that explain the nature, degree, and direction of typically acceptable and unacceptable risks is the keystone for formulating a more adequate understanding of presumption. Upon what bases are preferences for the preservation of concrete values articulated? Upon what bases is a defense of abstract values viable? Moreover, when exceptions are made—and in public argument exception is often the rule—how are concessions to political positions with which one is not self-identified offered and made? These are the questions that will be answered in the next two sections, which sketch liberal and conservative presumptions. It must be noted at the outset, however, that although these presumptions are informed by political philosophy, they constitute only beginning places, possible analogies, or categories to work with in coming to terms with the actual play of contemporary politics.

## The Liberal (Progressive) Presumption

Historically, American liberalism has not maintained a consistent position on such issues as government power, economic regulation, and social welfare. Still, as Sibley observes, it has been continually characterized by commitments to "the high-order value of liberty; receptivity to change; openness to experimentation in social and political affairs; distrust of mere tradition as a guide; the possibility of rationality in collective life; and the potential for moral and political progress."[36] Distilling these characteristics, Plano and Greenberg define liberalism as: "A political view that seeks to change the political economic or social status quo to foster the development, and well-being of the individual. Liberals regard man as a rational creature who can overcome human and natural obstacles to a good life for all without resorting to violence against the established order. Liberalism is more connected with a method of solving problems than with a specific program."[37] This definition is not untypical. Virtually all characterizations of liberalism point to the assumption that change occurs inevitably and should be guided to the fulfillment of abstract values. Wolfe summarizes one early twentieth century liberal outlook: "The progressive welcomes and works for orderly and gradual changes which can be brought about by planned endeavor and the conscious direction of social evolution."[38] In order to understand the presumptive qualities of the normal beneficial course of affairs, a question must be answered: why does the pursuit of abstract values typically guide prudent choice? The following synthesizes a case for change, drawing upon several liberal political perspectives.

For the progressive presumption, actions associated with change are generally held as prudent. The progress of society depends upon those who find social problems "susceptible of constant modifications" and plan change. "Abstract values"—the goals toward which improvement tends—enable the individual to take action through conceptualizing ways to improve society, ultimately providing humanity's "rational control of [its] collective destiny."[39] The term "rational" here is used in a transcendent rather than imminent sense, as in opposition to unjustified permanence. To maintain an institution because of some claimed intrinsic value is normally risky because "amid the ceaseless change that is inevitable in a growing organism, the institutions of the past demand progressive readaptations."[40] Consequently, the risk of the unknown—of rejecting a true proposition or accepting a false one—resides in the multiplication of arbitrary decisions that perpetuate a stagnant, constricted, and mindlessly arbitrary social order. Stemming from the historic beginning of liberalism, originally a movement to expand freedom by challenging rationally the authority of the antiquated English system of jurisprudence, the progressive-liberal is haunted by the actions of a decadent yet powerful reactionary regime whose hypocritical elites victimize all who would speak the truth, hence rendering society incapable of improvement.[41] This view of change has been explained in terms of assumptions about human nature, law, knowledge, and social action.

Following Rousseau and others, human nature is conceived to be, initially, typically good for all individuals but malleable to its environment and, so, susceptible to both degradation and improvement. The truly evil person is the exception rather than the rule. The problem that typically confronts society is that most people are kept from realizing their capabilities because of complacency; they have been conditioned to believe that a state of affairs is tolerable and not susceptible to change. In the name of petty self-interest, citizens give up the greater freedom to which they are entitled. The law, for the most part, was something created under conditions less modern and should be regarded as continually susceptible to scrutiny for violating abstract values of fairness, equality, and justice.[42] In Bentham's view, the common law is filled with fictions and crusty traditions that serve as impediments to a more just order.[43] Given better laws, there is no fundamental reason why prejudicial attitudes cannot be erased. That which threatens all laws is not too much, but too little, change.

The progressive-liberal's view of knowledge reinforces a commitment to change. The progressive venerates reason.[44] The true test of an individual is whether the latest method, technique, or theory can pierce the prejudices of the past. If reason is given a limited role, truth suppressed, facts ignored in favor of outdated sentiments, then citizens cannot adapt to changing conditions and thus suffer unnecessarily. Because the progressive-liberal feels a responsibility to this generation, he or she will often evaluate policies from the point of view of function and practice. The past generation is past and cannot have faced precisely the same problems; moreover, it did not have the knowledge currently available. Given that knowledge is ever expanding, it becomes a duty to make use of the new opportunities and forge a better world. As a result, the liberal impulse is outer-directed. So long as the individual adheres to the canons of logic and the pursuit of the common good, he or she is not in need of perfecting.

From this view of knowledge stems a vision of collective action. If knowledge is ever-widening, better, and more relevant now than in the past, then everything can be subject to some improvement. To reply that these claims represent a minority point of view is not to say they are unacceptable, because the masses as a rule are uneducated, superstitious, and misled. Once they become aware of the better world, then they will follow. Even if the motives of those who would argue for maintaining past courses of action are sincere (which most often they are not, because apologists usually gain from protecting the status quo), to assume that something should be left alone because no further improvement can be brought about is the rare exception.[45]

The fervor for reform sometimes, but not always, pushes the liberal into the radical camp; the necessities of revolutionary action contradict many of the values progressives cherish. But the liberal is somewhat more willing to use government for the common good than those who adamantly oppose federal policy, no matter how great the social need and cost-effective the government intervention. Consequently, the battle is waged on the grounds of incremental improvement, and the improvement tends to take a definite direction—extending individual opportunity.[46] For twentieth-century liberalism this has meant reforms that employ government as a tool to drag down the barriers of social discrimination and reduce human suffering. Toward this end, the liberal sees the Constitution as an affirmative document interpreted somewhat expansively to curb social prejudice through programmatic legislation that creates a more level playing field within and among communities.

The progressive does not see the same barriers to the use of power as a conservative. Should a policy work well at the state or local level, then it can and should function as a model for change on a wider basis. The individual or local decision maker is more likely to be out of touch with the complex demands that make up an interdependent society whose externalities require common intervention.[47] If a more sophisticated body of decision makers do not act, then local injustices remain and the local remains a site where transregional or transnational forces must overcome more limited programs. In any society, the opportunities for government to bring relief to the poor and suffering are virtually unlimited. Moral duty and common sense demand that public policy pursue the abstract values of fairness and equality.

## The Conservative Presumption

American conservatism is in the peculiar position of a political outlook defined largely as devotion to laissez-faire government, a negative view of the Constitution, a strict historical-constructionist interpretation of law, and a dismissive attitude toward executive governance. "Bureaucracy" as a demeaning term replaces the idealistic "civil service." Consequently, some of its contemporary causes, such as balanced budgets, saving free enterprise from government regulation, and extreme opposition to social policy—such as health care—take on characteristics of the neoconservative economic revisions of the liberalism of classical economics. Plano and Greenberg characterize conservatism as: "Defense of the status quo against major changes in political, economic, or social institutions of a society. The general conservative position on issues has been fairly consistently opposed to governmental regulation of the economy and civil rights legislation, and in favor of state over federal action, fiscal responsibility, decreased government spending, and lower taxes."[48] Rather than grounding conservatism in any particular issue, it may be better to accept William Safire's definition of a conservative as a "defender of the status quo who, when change becomes necessary in tested institutions or practice, prefers that it come slowly and in moderation."[49] Consequently, the conservative presumption is in favor of the maintenance of social structures and processes, "thought, belief, and culture, practically as they happen to be at that time."[50] At the federal government level, activist conservatives become articulated as attacking executive branch administration, pulling back commitments on social programs, cutting budgets, defunding enforcement agencies, blocking states' efforts to advance regulation and change. When occupying the presidency, conservatives undo government obligations by executive order, perverse appointments, or deliberate neglect of duties. Again, the questions arise over why concrete values and permanence are valued generally over abstract values and change. Indeed, the very concreteness of values are stressed by dismantling and undermining government operations in the name of recommitting to a status quo ante.

In distinguishing political right from left, Bernard Brock et al. argue that the liberal accepts cultural drift and gears policies toward controlling that drift. In contrast, the conservative rejects the drift and the institutional changes that follow. "[Conservative] policies are aimed at slowing down the drift or maintaining social policies in spite of it. These social policies are usually predicated upon the premise that it is possible to prevent these changes from taking place."[51] "Drift" to the conservative is neither inevitable nor portentous of good opportunities; rather, change causes uncertainty and is a prelude to instability. As Edmund Burke said, "It is with infinite caution that any man ought to venture upon pulling down an edifice which has answered in any tolerable degree for ages the common purposes of society, or on building it up again without models or patterns of approved utility before his eyes."[52] Lincoln captured this spirit when he wrote that "Conservatism is adherence to the old and tried against the new and untried."[53]

Conservatives hold that actions associated with "permanence" are generally prudent because concrete values are overall preferable to destabilizing, premature abstract calls to social justice. This position harkens back to natural law, a social perspective that acknowledges that there are certain institutions born into history that incarnate the best of human (or sometimes divine) values. To invoke action sanctioned by traditional institutions is to maintain the tested and true course of civilization. Change and abstract values have a place, of course, by and large an antecedent one. Because individual talents and desires are contingent, each person comes to express social choice from a private vantage point.[54] Balancing notions of change against true understanding of the common good is everyone's right and responsibility. To elevate competing concepts of change in the name of abstract values, however, is to risk collapse. Stemming from the historical origins of the movement as a reaction to the French Revolution, the conservative nightmare appears in the convulsive phantasmagoria of subversion, revolution, and aftermath.[55] The risk of the unknown is the possibility that self-restraint may be abolished. As Peter Viereck contends, "He who irresponsibly incites revolutionary mob emotions against some minor abuse within a good tradition may bring the whole house crashing down on his head and find himself back in the jungle—or its ethical equivalent, the police state."[56]

Conservative advocates hold that mankind is not naturally good or selfless.

In any age the altruistic citizen is an exception because the great majority conceive of collective order in relation to self-driven, short-term personal benefit. The masses are often misled to trust those who desire greater power; differences are eroded and those who demand change raise the specter of class warfare in their calls for social betterment. The Law was created by good citizens (although with some imperfections intermixed). The Constitution is not an affirmative tool of change for the conservative; rather, it is a bulwark to protect hard-won freedoms against those who would seek change. Any bad law impugns all other good ones; presumption is set high against new legislation, if it changes the law too much or expects too much of social reordering as a consequence.[57] No program, however well-intended, can be expected to work if it cuts too deeply against the grain of tradition.

The conservative's suspicion of change is supported by a conception of knowledge. The conservative venerates tradition. The true test of any generation is whether it can live up to those who have achieved prior cultural heights. If tradition is ignored and the authority of accumulated knowledge flaunted or condemned, then a generation remains unrooted and feckless.[58] The conservative has pessimistic expectations for new schemes of learning, the leveling of culture, and the likelihood that a new generation will have the self-discipline to master self-restraint and sustain the best of tradition. If tradition is ignored, authority arbitrary, decorum rent asunder, the accumulated wisdom of the ages may perish in a single era.[59] Knowledge is not cumulative, and the conservative has pessimistic expectations for the likelihood of great new insights in a single generation. The individual should seek to perfect him or herself, to be inner-directed rather than supportive of notions claiming to be reforms. Populist conservative movements, too, hold these sentiments; but they add anger to the affective aspects of presumption—that whatever change is underway is not to their short or long-term benefit.

Reform is more often than not the naiveté of idealists or the last refuge of scoundrels. If each person's knowledge is limited, a flickering in time, then claims to a better world are often the result of misunderstanding rather than new insight. Even if the advocate can convince the majority that new ideas are preferable, this is not a sign of truth since the public is easily misled. Even if the advocate's motives are in the right place (which most often they are not), only the test of time is sufficient to weigh the quality of social values. Populist conservatives condemn others (such as noncitizens, ethnicities, gender groups) for problems and project blame onto elite, expert organizations that manage private capital and government programs.

Not all change is derided. To do so the conservative would have to deny human yearning to achieve greater perfection—and the collective pursuit of abstract values. Totalitarian measures taken by reactionaries are found intolerable. Yet there is a direction toward which acceptable change tends. Kirk argues that the conservative stands for the return of "individual responsibilities": even if in the name of "freedom" one must risk "security."[60] Thus, reforms least risky to the conservative are ones that are aimed at trimming unnecessary programs, that is, acts that have inhibited individual initiative by replacing individual initiative with some collective, governmental schemes. These schemes inhibit crucial freedoms necessary for a just social order. Additionally, the addition of domestic and military police powers is presumed to be necessary because a sense of security does not come easily in a world where change is identified with specious advantage and aggressive threats.

Social order is construed to be the natural relation among people who, within the limits of their own imperfections, try to work out personal problems, and, if collective action is necessary, convince their family, community, or region to act. A government which ignores this sequence even in the name of a greater good will not be successful or desirable. If the rule is not at the minimal level of agreement, then the individual is less likely to recognize a program or law as necessary or beneficial.[61] If this is the case, arbitrary laws will either be ignored or co-opted. The conservative stands ever vigilant to Utopian-like schemes proposed again and again by real and imagined liberal counterparts.

## Liberal and Conservative Presumption: A Criticism

David Spitz summarizes the liberal and conservative presumptions at the most basic level: "The central issue between conservatives and liberals may be simply: can society be governed by the light of immutable 'right principles,' as conservatives insist, or is the search for 'right principles' chimerical, as liberals argue. By placing values in terms of nearer or further approximation, change can be guided or continued in more propitious ways."[62] From a foundational position, political presumptions move from personal preference to greater ambits of reflection. The liberal ontology posits that human nature has intrinsic dignity. Limits are the products of environments that can be changed; material interventions create the routes to self-fulfillment, and maximizing talent brings society closer to abstract values. The liberal epistemology is sometimes found in application of reason through empirical experimentation leading to a wider sense of present obligations, since problems and solutions can be found to have measurable outcomes. The liberal axiology is a positive view of the decency of all people, and the Constitution is seen an instrument of social change and improvement. Change is the key trope of contemporary liberalism. Since all seems in flux, guiding change toward abstract values is key to the liberal consensus formation.

Conservative politics presents a different orientation. Ontologically speak-

ing human motives remain essentially stable. Whether one centers conservatism in religious notions of original sin or economic motives of self-interest,
the human condition does not change from generation to generation. Epistemologically, knowledge is rooted in tradition that teaches that culture is
fragile, perishable, and difficult to sustain. Axiological action must be taken
when norms of social or legal conduct are flouted, ignored, or put in jeopardy
by those who profess abstract values with naive idealism or worse motives. The
state functions best when accountability and the law are reinforced by private
and public police powers.

The positions described above are only presumptions because each orientation admits of an exception to the rule. For liberals, permanence is vener-
ated in terms of questions of human dignity: human rights, basic freedoms
that protect privacy and community from government intrusions on cultural
issues or social denials of freedom. Stagnation in social reform is to be feared,
for if the diversity toward which change is ever tending is disrupted by con-
strictions on freedom, then the nightmares of a totalitarian state may come.
For conservatives, change has a place. Since human motives are what they are,
programs that defend the concrete value of the nation are necessary. Occasionally, it is even necessary to act pre-emptively in the name of security interests.
This leads to change in two directions: first, reduction of unnecessary government programs and spending; second, increases in the quality and variety of
security, whether police or military, seem useful to guard against threats from
those who practice aggression or who slyly disguise power as reform on the national and international stages.

If the liberal and conservative presumptions are viewed as set preferences
on permanence and change, each constitutes a political orientation that offers
a vibrant dialectic of centrist public argument and political debate. Over the
course of a political career, candidates and entrenched politicians achieve a
reputation as a liberal or a conservative or maverick by virtue of the positions
advanced and defended. So, too, institutions and audiences participate in establishing and acting in relation to shifts in presumptions. The presidency of
Richard Nixon, for example, appears to be a progressive jaunt in environmental policy, even though he worked day and night to retard and coopt leftist
movements; the second term of Barack Obama, similarly, does not appear to
pursue great leftist goals, but he did use executive orders to retard conservative
roll backs and advanced international collaboration and justice.

Presumptions can be located by informal logic or critical thinking in the
contexts of individual preference, institutional rule, or audience predisposition.
When these strands of presumption are braided, one can find a fuller sense of
the public argument in context constituting democratic debate. Centrist public argument entwines individual, institutional, and audience presumptions in

networks of exchange that come to assemble a middle ground and push op-posing interlocutors to the extreme. Put differently, centrist arguers claim to occupy the ground of "common sense" for a range of issues (legislative, elec-toral, epideictic, and/or forensic). This is not as easily accomplished as it would seem, for the centrist must at once occupy a ground that captures majority opinion without cutting off the enthusiasm that forms the base of active po-litical support.

To analyze contexts in practice, it is necessary to explore how issues develop and fuel the passions of party actors, agents of public institutions, and civic audiences. Presumption identified with specific individuals comes from asso-ciations claimed with professions, institutions, and communities. These are articulated in interests or causes championed by an individual and/or a party or group. Presumption identified with institutions is shaped by knowledge of long-standing and recent decisions that have been made in following or diverg-ing from standing rules of procedure and policy practices and goals. Presump-tions concerning audience involve how publics champion certain social norms and promote values across policy choices. In each situation of public argument, those engaged in debate and controversy are engaged in the multi-dimensional field of invention. The field offers bases for political analysis and development of strategic argument justifying a broad consensus and depriving opponents of the same standing. When bound together, the presumptions powerfully iden-tify, legitimate, and motivate political action. More often, though, there is a strain between center and periphery that requires artful rhetorical arrange-ment. The outcomes of such concatenations are sometimes an odd mix of bun-combe, where politicians in power represent themselves as "the change" and those out of power celebrate their lack of training, experience, and good will— on the grounds of pretending to not be politicians.

No one would have doubted at election time that Ronald Reagan was a strong conservative; he had been proclaiming a single message throughout his career. So too no one would doubt that Bill Clinton was a liberal, or at least more left-leaning than his congressional critics. Yet each manipulated pre-sumption to his own benefit. While Reagan claimed to be for small govern-ment, reduced government spending, and a lower deficit, nevertheless to meet a conservative presumption (military spending), he massively increased the fed-eral deficit—while claiming that Democrats were responsible. Not to be out-done, Clinton, while claiming to support liberal causes like diversity in the military, gun control, and choice, coopted the crime issue, voucher/teacher competency, workfare, reduced government size, abolishing the deficit, and other conservative issues that had characterized the Reagan revolution. Both were popular public presidents; both brought on themselves attacks from the far left and right. Liberals were able to stem some reductions in poverty programs during the Reagan era; conservatives did achieve a House victory in 1994. However, by offsetting blame in Reagan's case and straightforwardly creating a pragmatic blend of popular issues in Clinton's, these presidents created successful strategies for two-term administrations.

Critical analysis of presumptions exhibits the ways in which politics changes in practice through emphasizing unique combinations of personal identity, institutional necessity, party loyalties, and the common weal. American politicians need be neither logically consistent nor bound ideologically to any given set presumptions, of course, but the coherence required to develop or envelop political movements and forge election and governing strategies requires analyzing presumptions as constituting a field in which democratic deliberation arranges institutions, publics, and identities in movement from past to future. Presumptions can be converted into data, stripped of context, and reissued as propaganda. The permanent campaign turns discourse about governance into simulated-belligerent event quarrels. Weaponizing acts of governance erodes the glue that holds together the constitutional process of federalism and checks and balances together, of course. New media operations increasingly platform incoherent event contests and filter authoritarian discourses (disparaging tweets, slogans, public opinion polls), thereby networking ecologies of parasitic argument onto citizen deliberation. Antidemocratic modes of message generation, targeting, and distribution—social media—exhibit tendencies to corrode public argument and thereby threaten communities of deliberative practices requisite to democracy globally.

## Counterpublics and Critique of Presumptions

Not all public argument is centrist. Sometimes public argument pushes beyond the debates whose dynamics feature accepted norm and expedient exception. Critique or "critical rhetoric" denounces centrist presumptions as limiting freedom, lacking candid direction, misdirecting attention to sham differences and the like. Praxis of this sort, I assume, eventually aims at undermining confidence in the assumptions upon which a deliberative model of the public sphere is erected, hence advancing "freedom."[63] For a centrist model, public argument works best when alternatives are undecided; capable of free expression; vital to a community's interest; and differences are openly discussed and made comprehensible to those engaged in the process of argument. Mirroring these conditions of deliberation, critique brings into discursive form alternative questions. Do the representations of options for debate conceal more than they reveal? Is it time for a sweeping political movement that contests whether all the interests are actually presented for debate? Is genuine participation encouraged? For a number of audiences, the articulation of issues may be less inviting than off-putting; and the consequences of policies may not be understandable by anyone at all. Public arguments in the form of radical critique from the right often are couched as the story of a Golden Age of the public sphere—a providentially inspired, constitutional founding moment—and its consequent decline. The decline of the Roman republic figures into this mix from time to time. Radical critique from the left is couched as a dystopian story fitting the present out as a dark time, when perpetual injustices among classes, perpetuated by false consciousness, remain cemented through hegemonic control enforced by the police powers of the state. The charges of evil and tales of trauma are distinct, of course, but they do highlight social injustice concerns for those opposing centrist public argument. Wedge issues demand an either/or decision and so promote polarization, corrosive of public trust but useful in different ways to extremists and centrists alike.

The presumptions of public argument are challenged from time to time by determined populists or by progressive social movements. Social movements generate wider ambits of public argument that oppose centrist politics by asserting claims to be excluded or misrepresented from actual matters central to public interest. Counterpublics to the right take the form of seditious groups that rebel against taxes, form secret societies, and assemble into watches and militias. Counterpublics to the left engage in walks, demonstrations, sit-ins, and queer performances in strategic urban spaces. People huddle in safe spaces to imagine action under conditions of surveillance and oppression. Counterpublics are groups that, if not completely enclaved, are separated either by social convention or personal choice in relation to an identity that is in the process of being claimed outside the norms of left and right conventions. These conventions constitute norms of value that are taken for granted.[64] At the extreme left, praxis drives words to release consciousness into a utopian future not subject to argumentation. Being open to disagreement can only weaken the will and tempt one to betrayal. At the extreme right, original sin and an Edenic fall shadow the present. For the radically predisposed, counterarguments are but temptations that undermine resolve; thus, perforce, opposing views are always venally intended, if not downright evil. Indeed, spokespersons may articulate radical views as strategic discourse, marking the range of acceptable public argument as broader than the debates at issue, pushing candidates to take otherwise risky moves. However extreme oppositional contestation may be, it too contributes to democratic debates. Public argument only finds its limits when talk turns to violence. In political acts of violence, the peaceful transfer of power itself is placed in jeopardy. Perhaps this is why polemical breaches of civility and performance of street opposition themselves go into the mix of public controversy.

The presumptions of a counterpublic sphere are oppositional. Oppositional presumptions are animated by objections, acts of argument that themselves may not be fully articulate and so deemed irrelevant to the ambit of discussion under way. Objections take shape because it is presumed that centrist advocates do not include sufficiently the interests of stakeholders whom they claim to represent. Further it is presumed that expressive (discursive, visual, gestural) alternatives to conventional deliberative norms need to be brought into play to disrupt the taken-for-granted legitimacy of fora for debate. The search for alternative forms may take shape as the arguments of forerunner elites, public intellectuals, or celebrities-turned-advocates, who identify changes in civic participation as prerequisite to a fuller discussion. Disruption may take place through populist performances of disruption, display, and gatherings. Whether elite or popular, all counterpublics share presumptions against trusting the prevailing range of disagreement, the rules of decorum, and the representation of identities. Counterpublic presumptions factionalize. Debate repeats, renews, replays over questions of who owns the rights to identify injuries, articulate the needs for an enclave, and speak as a subaltern. Critique links identification to opposition through the assertion of difference. Difference-oriented public arguers (academic critics and professional politicians alike) find ways to reverse normative presumptions that define debate for a centrist public sphere. Absent violent revolution or repressive purge, a citizenry and its fellows engaged in public life utter objections that bring change to centrist public actors. Democratic contestation, antagonism, and confrontation always places the peaceful transfer of power at risk. Of course, mainstream political parties can imitate the spectacle of transgressive display and supplement everyday debate with spectacle.

## Conclusion

Orienting presumptions offer resources and hazards to democratic performance, process, and practice. To identify presumption in a public argument is to search for (1) that side of a question that deserves testing before it is accepted, (2) the standards of proof that must be met to consider the test a success, and (3) how the debate proceeds reflexively—should the outcome of a deliberation prove to be precipitous, untimely, or in error. Should one change one's personal habits, identity, and efforts or continue on the proven path? Should levels of acceptability be set high or low for changing the established wisdom of the community, the practices of an institution, or a field's state-of-the-art standards of classification and judgment? Finally, should citizens and fellow life-world members ask for more or less change in belief and action, given the status quo? The liberal and conservative presumptions articulated in political discourse lend insights into the justifications for distributing necessary relief or justified benefits that arguments must test in relation to the times. The working relationship of setting shared standards, thresholds, and tests of presumption are reinforced if—and only if—the question of who gets the benefits and absorbs the costs of an outcome that either falsely rejects a probably true conclusion or wrongly accepts a false positive become articulated through inquiry into issues and advocacy of an election or policy extension or change.

In the model of centrist political argument, risk is set in such a way that a politician can generally stand on principle while admitting to "common sense" in an effort to coopt opposing points of view. Principle provides a fund of differences from the opponents, while expediency provides a place to occupy a broad central position. Such argument may factionalize at election time, as advocates try to test and stretch the middle, drawing opinion further to the right or to the left. Policy discourse as it appears in debates offers a rich archive of study for the workings of presumption linked to elections and party maintenance and change. Social movements and counterpublics arise when the presumptions of centrist debate leave unaddressed major questions for people driven historically to the edges of democratic practice. Argument enters into worlds of civic engagement through presumptions put into play in public discussions, debates, and addresses.

# Notes

An earlier version of this essay, "The Liberal and the Conservative Presumption: On Political Philosophy and the Foundation of Public Argument," was delivered at the first joint meeting of the Speech Communication Association and American Forensic Association at Alta, Utah, 1979. It was subsequently published in the *Proceedings of the Summer Conference on Argumentation* (Falls Church, VA: Speech Communication Association, 1980).—Eds.

1. D. H. Zarefsky and V. J. Gallager, "From 'Conflict' to 'Constitutional Question': Transformations in Early American Public Discourse," *Quarterly Journal of Speech* 76, no. 3 (1990): 247–61.

2. Thucydides, *History of the Peloponnesian War*, bk. 2, trans. Benjamin Jowett, accessed November 27, 2014, https://ebooks.adelaide.edu.au/t/thucydides/jowett/book2.html.

3. H.-G. Gadamer, *Truth and Method*, 2nd ed., trans. J. Weinsheimer and D. G. Marshall (New York: Continuum, 1999), 21.

4. Aristotle, *Rhetoric*, in *Basic Works of Aristotle*, ed. W. R. Roberts and R. McKeon (New York: Modern Library, 1941), 1358b, 8.

5. Aristotle, *Rhetoric*, 11358b, 13–15.

6. J. H. Randall, *Aristotle* (New York: Columbia University, 1960), 254.

7. Randall, *Aristotle*, 252.

8. Gadamer, *Truth and Method*, 21–22.

9. Gadamer, *Truth and Method*, 22.

10. Gadamer, *Truth and Method*, 21.

11. Thomas Reid, quoted in Gadamer, *Truth and Method*, 25.

12. Gadamer, *Truth and Method*, 25.

13. Gadamer, *Truth and Method*, 25.

14. V. L. Parrington, *Main Currents in American Thought: An Interpretation of American Literature from the Beginnings to 1920* (New York: Harcourt, Brace, 1927), 1:2–26.

15. J. Taylor, *Modern Social Imaginaries* (Durham, NC: Duke University Press, 2004), 109–42.

16. J. Dewey, *Democracy and Education: An Introduction to the Philosophy of Education* (New York: Macmillan, 1916); J. Dewey, *The Public and its Problems* (Denver: Swallow, 1927); J. Dewey, *How We Think: A Restatement of the Relation of Reflective Thinking to the Educative Process*, rev. ed. (Boston: Heath, 1933).

17. Charles S. Peirce, "Fraser's *The Works of George Berkeley*," in *The Essential Peirce: Selected Philosophical Writings*, ed. Nathan Houser and Christian Kloesel, vol. 1, *1867–1873* (Bloomington: Indiana University Press, 1991), 89.

18. R. J. Wilson, *In Quest of Community: Social Philosophy in the United States, 1860–1920* (New York: John Wiley & Sons, 1968), 52.

19. W. Lippman, *Essays in the Public Philosophy: On the Decline and Revival of Western Society* (Boston: Little Brown, 1955), 33.

20. L. Bitzer, "Rhetoric and Public Knowledge," in *Rhetoric, Philosophy, and Literature: An Exploration*, ed. D. M. Burks (West Lafayette, IN: Purdue University Press, 1978), 80.

21. John Dewey, *The Public and Its Problems*, quoted in Bitzer, "Rhetoric and Public Knowledge," 80.

22. Bitzer, "Rhetoric and Public Knowledge," 80.

23. C. Perelman and L. Olbrechts-Tyteca, *The New Rhetoric: A Treatise on Argumentation*, trans. J. Wilkinson and P. Weaver (Notre Dame, IN: University of Notre Dame Press, 1969), 62.

24. Bitzer, "Rhetoric and Public Knowledge," 27.

25. D. W. Grantham, *The Progressive Era and the Reform Tradition* (Indianapolis, IN: Bobbs-Merrill, 1964); H. W. Allen and J. Clubb, "Progressive Reform and the Political System," *Pacific Northwest Quarterly* 65, no. 3 (1974): 130–45; R. Hofstadter, *Anti-intellectualism in American Life* (New York: Knopf, 1962).

26. M. J. Lee, *Postwar Words That Made an American Movement* (East Lansing: Michigan State University Press, 2014).

27. Perelman and Olbrechts-Tyteca, *The New Rhetoric*, 71.

28. S. Langer, *Philosophy in a New Key: A Study in the Symbolism of Reason, Rite, and Art*, 3rd. ed. (Cambridge, MA: Harvard University Press, 1957), 294–95.

29. H. W. Johnstone Jr., "Some Reflections on Argumentation," in *Philosophy, Rhetoric and Argument*, ed. M. Natanson and H. W. Johnstone Jr. (University Park: Penn State University Press, 1965), 4–5.

30. Perelman and Olbrechts-Tyteca, *The New Rhetoric*, 77.

31. Perelman and Olbrechts-Tyteca, *The New Rhetoric*, 79.
32. Perelman and Olbrechts-Tyteca, *The New Rhetoric*, 79.
33. Perelman and Olbrechts-Tyteca, *The New Rhetoric*, 77.
34. Perelman and Olbrechts-Tyteca, *The New Rhetoric*, 79.
35. Perelman and Olbrechts-Tyteca, *The New Rhetoric*, 77.
36. M. Q. Sibley, *Political Ideas and Ideologies: A History of Political Thought* (New York: Harper and Row, 1970), 490.
37. J. C. Plano and M. Greenberg, *The American Political Dictionary*, 4th ed. (Hinsdale, IL: Dryden Press, 1976), 12–13.
38. A. B. Wolfe, "Conservatism and Radicalism: Some Definitions and Distinctions," *Scientific Monthly* 17, no. 3 (1923): 230–31.
39. Sibley, *Political Ideas and Ideologies*, 500.
40. J. Morley, *On Compromise* (New York: Macmillan, 1891), 125.
41. Morley, *On Compromise*, 125–26.
42. D. Spitz, *Essays in the Liberal Idea of Freedom* (Tucson: University of Arizona Press, 1964), 127.
43. Sibley, *Political Ideas and Ideologies*, 492.
44. D. J. Manning, *Liberalism* (New York: St. Martin's, 1976), 16.
45. Manning, *Liberalism*, 16.
46. H. K. Givertz, *The Evolution of Liberalism*, rev. ed. (New York: Collier Books, 1963), 353–57.
47. Givertz, *The Evolution of Liberalism*.
48. Plano and Greenberg, *American Political Dictionnary*, 14.
49. W. Safire, *Political Dictionary* (New York: Random House, 1978), 137.
50. Wolfe, "Conservatism and Radicalism," 12.
51. B. L. Brock, J. W. Chesebro, J. F. Cragan, and J. Klumpp, *Public Policy Decision-Making: Systems Analysis and Comparative Advantage Debate* (New York: Harper Collins, 1973), 47; and B. L. Brock, M. E. Huglen, J. F. Klumpp, and S. Howell, *Making Sense of Political Ideology: The Power of Language in a Democracy* (New York: Rowan and Littlefield, 2005).
52. Edmund Burke, *Reflections on the French Revolution*, in *The Harvard Classics*, ed. Charles W. Elliot (New York: P. F. Collier and Son, 1909–1914).
53. H. Sperber and T. Trittschuh, *American Political Terms: An Historical Dictionary* (Detroit, MI: Wayne State University Press, 1962), 76.
54. R. Kirk, "Prospects for a Conservative Bent in the Human Sciences," *Social Research* 35, no. 4 (1968): 580–92.
55. R. M. Christenson, A. S. Engel, M. R. Jacobs, and H. Waltzer, *Ideologies and Modern Politics* (Nashville, TN: Thomas Nelson & Sons, 1972).
56. P. Viereck, *Conservatism Revisited: The Revolt against Revolt, 1815–1949* (New York: Scribner, 1949), 11.
57. Kirk, "Prospects for a Conservative Bent," 43.
58. Kirk, "Prospects for a Conservative Bent," 42.
59. Kirk, "Prospects for a Conservative Bent," 42.
60. Kirk, "Prospects for a Conservative Bent," 121.

61. I. L. Horowitz, *Ideology and Utopia in the United States, 1956–1976* (New York: Oxford University Press, 1977), 136.

62. Spitz, *Liberal Idea of Freedom*, 89–90.

63. R. E. McKerrow, "Critical Rhetoric: Theory and Praxis," *Communication Monographs* 56, no. 2 (1989): 91–111.

64. R. A. Asen and D. C. Brouwer, "Introduction: Reconfiguration and the Public Sphere," in *Counterpublics and the State*, ed. R. A. Asen and D. C. Brouwer (New York: State University of New York Press, 2001), 1–34.

# 14

# Rhetorical and Epistemological Perspectives on Rescher's Account of Presumption and Burden of Proof

FRED J. KAUFFELD AND JAMES B. FREEMAN

### Rhetorical and Epistemological Aspects of Rescher's Account

Nicholas Rescher provides a particularly well-developed theoretical formulation of the contribution made by presumption and probative obligations to rational disputation. His dialectical account is of rhetorical interest both for the light it sheds on the importance of presumptions and probative obligations in the conduct of productive reason-giving and for the pragmatic rationale it offers for the allocation of probative obligations based on "natural" presumption outside "artificial" institutional contexts.

Where Whately takes an analogy to the law's conception of presumptions and probative obligations as a heuristic directing attention to everyday common-sense presumptions related to probative obligations, Rescher takes the legal formulation as his model for the roles these concepts and corresponding practices play in dialectical disputation. Rescher is less interested in refining day-to-day argumentation than in developing an epistemically satisfying model for what he calls "rational inquiry." "It is worthwhile to study the process of disputation closely," he maintains, "because it offers—in miniaturized form, as it were—a view of the structure and workings of the validating mechanisms which support our claims to knowledge."[1] Accordingly, Rescher first provides an abstract model for rational disputation and then transforms this model from "a methodology of controversy to one of inquiry."[2] Although Rescher's focus on the use of dialectical methodology in intellectual/theoretical inquiry does not directly address the normative structure of everyday argument, his account is nevertheless of considerable rhetorical interest.

From a rhetorical perspective, Rescher's account sheds light on the pragmatic value of these practices in argumentation and affords a pragmatic rationale for using presumptions as a basis for distributing probative obligations. Unfortunately, as we shall see, his account focuses on rational inquiry as ideally conducted in scholarly communities and leaves open just how such practices can be and are conducted in the messier domains of day-to-day argumentation outside communities explicitly committed to rational inquiry in intellectual/ theoretical domains.

Rescher strongly affirms the importance of presumption and the burden of proof as practices essential to the conduct of rational controversy, that is, argumentation in which reasons acquire force commensurate with their capacity to withstand critical scrutiny. "The workings of the conception of burden of proof," he maintains, "represent a *procedural or regulative principle of rationality* in the conduct of argumentation, a ground rule, as it were, of the process of rational controversy—a fundamental condition of the whole enterprise."[3] With respect to presumptions, he writes, "The idea of presumptive truth must thus play a pivotal role in all such various contexts where the notion of a "burden of proof" applies. The mechanism of presumption thus accomplishes a crucial epistemological task in the structure of rational argumentation."[4] Supposing that Rescher's affirmation of the procedural importance of presumptions and burdens holds for epistemically satisfactory rational disputation, we might cautiously suppose that these concepts and practices are important to the conduct of epistemically optimal day-to-day argumentation.

Drawing on the principles and rules that regulate legal argumentation, Rescher identifies three roles played by presumptions and probative obligations in the methodology of rational disputation. First, they manage the introduction of evidence into the argumentation. The party (or parties) with the burden of proof has the obligation of substantiating its assertions with reason and evidence; other parties can fulfill their roles by simply expressing their doubts. Rescher accepts a twofold legal division into (1) the burden of an initiating assertion and (2) the evidential burden of further reply. In (1) the basic rule is "whichever side initiates the assertion of a thesis within the dialectical situation has the burden of supporting it in argument." This burden, according to Rescher (and most legal authorities), remains constant throughout the proceedings. (2) is relevant to situations in which apparently weighty considerations have been adduced in support of an assertion; here, the opponent of that contention has the "burden of further reply." This burden "of going forward with evidence on a particular point" may shift from side to side as the dialogue unfolds.[5] This is an important and difficult distinction.

Second, presumptions provide starting points for argumentation. It cannot be the case, Rescher observes, that every proposition introduced in defense into a disputation carries with it a burden of proof. Were that the case, argumentation could not get under way, as each proposition introduced would be challenged and no starting points could be found. Presumptions, as tentatively acceptable propositions, provide starting points for the defense of propositions that do carry a burden of proof.

Third, identification of presumptions and probative obligations affords a basis for identifying the rational (persuasive) force of evidence and arguments introduced into a disputation. If argumentation is to have a point, Rescher maintains, it must be possible to identify when the proponents of a thesis have discharged their probative obligations. That can be done in terms of the concept of a *prima facie case*—a body of reason and evidence with sufficient weight to reverse the presumption that imposed the burden of proof and therefore realign the prevailing probative obligations. Rescher holds that it "makes sense to speak of a 'burden of proof' only in the context of established rules regarding the discharge of such a burden."[6] Accordingly, argumentation "is pointful as a rational process only if the extent to which a 'good case' has been made can be assessed in retrospect on a common, shared basis of judgment—be it agreed or imposed."[7] What would be required to provide a *prima facie* case will vary depending primarily on whether the arguer bears an initiating burden or the evidential burden of further reply and on the strength of corresponding presumptions. Thus, British law has one standard of proof for criminal cases (proof beyond a reasonable shadow of doubt) and another for civil cases (on the balance of probabilities). Generally, in disputation, he maintains, "what is sufficient in shifting the burden of proof will hinge on the inherent seriousness of the contention at issue."[8]

According to Rescher, presumptions and probative obligations afford a principled basis for introducing and eliciting the arguments required to defend a controversial proposition; they also enable identification of (provisional) standards for assessing the overall rational/persuasive adequacy of those arguments. Rescher's claims in this connection need to be handled with some caution. It seems clear that he identifies three kinds of functions necessary to the conduct of rational disputation and inquiry. Moreover, he provides good reason to suppose that practices involving the allocation of probative obligations on the basis of presumptions can fulfill these functions. Whether those practices are the only, and hence the pragmatically essential, means of doing so remains unclear. Still, presumptions and probative obligations would, on Rescher's account, have this potential utility in all domains in which arguments (reasoning given under conditions of doubt and disagreement) occur. This would include day-to-day argumentation as well as the intellectual/theoretical sphere of Rescher's rational inquiry. Therefore, we may suppose that Rescher alerts us to the pragmatic importance of presumptions and probative obligations in argumentation that manifests the force of reasons on the basis of their epistemic quality.

But the claim that practices developed in what Rescher identifies as artificial institutions—that is, courts of law, formally regulated disputations, and competitive debates—have normatively similar functions in "natural settings" outside formal regulation opens the door to Sidgwick's challenge to Whately. Sidgwick denies that the institutionalized practices of the courts are a viable model for extralegal argumentation because day-to-day argumentation does not occur in a context where there are authorized rule givers. This pointed objection underwrites his denials (1) that presumptions provide a reliable guide to the allocation of the burden of proof and (2) that "burdens" of proof are obligations. These challenges to Whately's views raise a very serious question, which any rhetorical account of probative *obligations* must address. While allocations of the "burden of proof" in institutionally regulated procedures involve more problems and difficulties than is generally recognized, the genesis, parameters, and consequences of institutionally sanctioned distributions of the "burden of proof" are relatively clear-cut matters. They are governed by authorized and carefully promulgated traditions, interpreted and applied by duly empowered judges, and enforced by institutional sanctions. How, outside the courts and similar institutions and in the conditions under which day-to-day arguments are conducted, can these obligations be incurred in the absence of official formulation and sanctions? This question—Sidgwick's challenge—must be faced by accounts generated within a rhetorical perspective, but it applies with equal force to dialectically oriented views of presumption and the burden of proof offered as applicable to day-to-day argumentation. Here Rescher's work provides significant, though limited, guidance.

In addition to identifying the generic potential of presumption and probative burdens as epistemically significant means for managing argumentation, Rescher also address issues related to what we must clarify if we are to comprehend how related practices operate outside institutional contexts. First, Rescher takes pains to address questions regarding how the concepts and practices developed in what he describes as artificial institutions need modification and amplification in order to function properly in the natural settings of rational inquiry. His adaptations in this connection are enlightening. Second, he addresses the question of how, outside artificial institutional frameworks, presumptions can have normative force relative to probative obligations.

Rescher's adaptation of "artificial" legal regulations to norms governing rational disputation in "natural settings" advances two conceptual refinements. The first offers significant clarification of the concept of presumption and the range of practices that fall within the scope of that concept. The second speaks to the difficulty of identifying parameters for a "prima facie case" in argumentation outside of artificial institutional regulation.

Rescher, along with most legal and scholarly authorities, holds that presumptions are inferences that stand good unless and until they are overturned by parties who accept the burden of proof. This conception opens the all-too-often ignored question of what grounds warrant such inferences. With respect to the presumptions recognized in institutional contexts this question has a relatively unproblematic answer: presumptions are inferences warranted on grounds specified by institutionally sanctioned rules. But that answer has little purchase as regards presumptions at large. In response to this question Rescher draws a distinction between (1) conventional presumptions that may rest on rules specific to an institutional forum and/or on agreements negotiated or imposed at the outset of a formal disputation and (2) "natural presumptions fixed by purely probative consideration of evidential weight and intrinsic plausibility."[9] In this connection Rescher provides an extended discussion of plausibility as "the extent of our cognitive inclination towards a proposition—of *the extent of its epistemic hold upon us* in light of the credentials represented by the bases of its credibility. The key issue is that of how readily the thesis in view could make its peace within the overall framework of our cognitive commitments."[10] Natural presumptions in rational disputation and inquiry, then, may be warranted by "the reliability of sources which vouch for them," the probative strength of confirming evidence, and thesis-warranting principles such as simplicity, regularity, uniformity, and normalcy.[11]

Rescher then uses this conception of natural presumption to articulate the requirements for *prima facie* cases in disputations and inquiry outside artificial institutional settings. He recognizes that in law and other artificial settings, determination of what qualifies as a *prima facie* case—a "good case"—is fixed by "purely conventional rules." "However," he writes, "in the dialectic of rational controversy 'natural' presumptions are the determining guide. Here a winning position is reached by the proponent when every initiating burden of proof has been discharged by him. This circumstance is realized when all the pertinent contentions have been carried back in the process of evidentially supportive argumentation to theses that stand in the status of presumptive truths not only in the first analysis, but in the final analysis as well, because no adequately weighty counterarguments against them are forthcoming within the dialectical context of the dispute."[12] This appears at first to be a very strong requirement. To establish a "prima facie" case, it seems, the proponent must provide presumptive answers to all relevant doubts and objections. However, Rescher qualifies this rather stringent requirement by making presumptive adequacy relative to the purposes of the argumentation.

> Our policies of presumption are justified through their purposive efficacy in facilitating realization of the inherent purposes and objective of the domain in which they are instituted. [...] [T]hese principles of presumption find their justification, insofar as they indeed are justified, through the common consideration that their operation is pragmatically effective.
> There are indeed differences in the ways in which the presumptions of different domains are validated—for example, as between law and ordi-

nary discourse. But these differences all stem from the same underlying source: the specific manifold of purpose that underlies and defines the enterprise at issue.[13]

Thus, what is required to establish a *prima facie* case depends on the domain in which the argumentation is conducted. Rescher recognizes three distinct domains: (1) an essentially intellectual/theoretical domain, where the issue is primarily a matter of having certain beliefs; (2) "the essentially *practical* issue of espousing certain *actions* (viz. accepting that X is to be done)"; and (3) the complex domain in which issues of *methodology* (tools, procedures, policies, rules for action, etc.) arise in "Janus-faced" fashion looking "both in theoretical and practical directions."[14]

As Rescher adapts institutionally artificial legal conceptions of presumption and the burden of proof to their use in the larger world of rational inquiry, he amplifies the former by enriching the grounds for presumptive inferences to include "natural presumptions" based primarily on estimates of plausibility and attempting to clarify what in the "natural" contexts of rational inquiry can qualify as a *prima facie* case. We may doubt whether these adaptations adequately encompass the richness of everyday argumentation, but they alert us to two important considerations relevant to our rhetorical interest in such arguments: What are the grounds for presumptive inferences in the complex sphere of day-to-day argumentation? And how are the parameters of probative obligation established on an everyday basis?

Turning now to the answer offered by Rescher's position to Sidgwick's challenge, Rescher does not, to our knowledge, directly address Sidgwick. However, he does regard the *burdens* of proof within the scope of his interests to be *obligations*: "What stops a presumption from being a mere assumption or hypothesis is the aspect of compulsion—be it juridically or rationally mandated—inherent in the fact that a presumptive principle normatively makes a normative stipulation regarding *what is to be done*. Assumptions after all are free options—one can make them or not as one is minded. A presumption by contrast is grounded in the compelling authority of the law in the one case and of the demands of reason on the other."[15] And he does attempt to show how such obligations can arise outside the courts and other "artificial" institutional settings. In Rescher's account, Sidgwick's challenge emerges as a question of what warrants the practices of relying on "natural presumptions" in rational inquiry. Rescher sees such questions as a matter of the pragmatic rationales for rules that have evolved within communities committed to rational inquiry in intellectual/theoretical domains.

Rational inquiry, in Rescher's view, may be conducted by individuals working more or less on their own, but it is a fundamentally communal endeavor undertaken by persons who share a "cognitive enterprise" committed to the priority of rational processes. Specifically, "probative standards are person-indifferent; they are inherently public and communal. The testing standards of convincingness relate not to what convinces me or you as idiosyncratic individuals, but to what is convincing in general. [. . .] The very conception of duly validated knowledge-claims relates to publicly established interpersonally operative standards. To abandon these in favor of some putatively personalized standards of inquiry—withdrawing to the use of private criteria, however well intentioned—is to secede from the community of rational reasoners and to abandon the project of rationality as such."[16]

Probative standards within this community of "rational reasoners" rest on pragmatic considerations. They answer the question: What inferential policies enable us to best approximate the truth in an uncertain world? The normative force of such standards rests ultimately on their pragmatic utility. "The 'ought' in 'Men ought to be rational' is in the final analysis a *prudential* [. . .] certainly not a *moral* ought. That is, one should be rational *if one is to be effective and efficient in the realization of one's chosen objectives* (whatever they may happen to be). The constraints to rationality are not those of *morality*, but those of *purposive efficacy*. Accordingly, the rationale for subscribing to the established ground rules of probative procedure in inquiry ultimately lies in the domain of prudence and intelligent self-interest."[17]

Drawing on his analysis of the contributions made by practices involving presumption and the burden of proof to rational disputation, Rescher concludes that corresponding practices are pragmatically necessary in rational inquiry. In his view, "The crucial linkage between presumption and rationality rests on the underlying thesis that a warranted presumption is one which should carry weight with the rational man, and the rational man is prepared to accord to presumptions the weight that is their just due."[18] He holds that "in refusing to give to the standard evidential considerations the presumptive and prima facie weight that is their established value on the market of rational interchange, the skeptic [. . .] is in fact profoundly irrational"; he adds that a "refusal to acknowledge the ordinary probative rules of plausibility, presumption, evidence, etc." places one outside "the enterprise of rational discussion and the community of rational inquirers."[19]

According to Rescher, then, respect for the proper weight of presumptions and corresponding acceptance of probative obligations are normative requirements for membership in the community of rational inquirers. Those requirements are warranted by the pragmatic value of practices involving presumptions and burdens of proof in the central project of that community: "the general process of reason in the pursuit of truth."[20] General principles regulating the use of presumptions and burdens of proof are apparent from reflec-

tion on the contributions those practices make to rational disputation; conformity to those principles is a pragmatically sanctioned normative requirement
of rational inquiry.[21]

Viewed from our rhetorical perspective regarding presumption and probative obligations in day-to-day arguments, Rescher's account helpfully points
out the contributions that practices involving presumption and probative obligation can make to epistemically satisfying consideration of defeasible propositions. His claim that rational disputations about defeasible propositions require practices that manage reason-giving discourse in these ways suggests that
some practices involving presumptions and probative obligation are needed if
day-to-day argumentation is to accord to reasons the persuasive force commensurate with their rational quality.

Beyond this (vague) implication that presumption and probative obligations
have significant work to do in day-to-day argumentation, Rescher's adaptation
of "artificially" determined conceptions to "natural" conceptions operating in
rational inquiry is also little more than suggestive. His observation that outside
"artificial" institutional contexts we need to attend to the grounds that warrant
presumptive inferences, properly directs us to give serious consideration to the
structure of ordinary presumptive inferences. However, his claim that "natural"
judgments of plausibility may be true for a great many presumptions does not
exhaust the presumptions that figure significantly in day-to-day argumentation. The possibility of serious day-to-day argumentation depends upon the
kinds of regard persons have reason to attribute to each other in circumstances
of doubt and disagreement. Accordingly, presumptions having to do with mutual respect for personal interests, concerns, fairness, and similar issues, can be
expected to figure prominently in that discursive domain. Such presumptions
fall outside the scope of Rescher's characterization of "natural presumptions."

Similarly, his discussion of the parameters of a *prima facie* case in extralegal
contexts points to an important line of investigation for our effort to delineate
the normative character of day-to-day argumentation. How is it that ordinary
probative obligations acquire mutually recognized limits, such that they are
discharged by apparently adequate argumentation? At the outset, we cannot
suppose that such limitations are agreed to as a matter of commitment to the
standards of argument maintained by an ideal community of rational inquirers. Commitments to reasonableness and rationality certainly play important
roles in day-to-day argumentation, but in that hurly burly domain they have
not the paramount status Rescher attributes to them as the singular commitment guiding rational inquiry.

This latter point has serious implications for Rescher's account of the normative status of presumption and probative obligations in "natural" settings.
Here we encounter the limitations of his focus on rational inquiry. There are

significant and relevant differences between the ideal theoretical/intellectual domain of inquirers singularly devoted to the reasoned pursuit of truth and the rough-and-ready world of day-to-day argumentation. Part of his defense of the normative aspect of natural presumptions does seem to be broadly correct. Where in what he identifies as the domain of practical affairs and of methods, we have practices that it is reasonable to presume rest on some more-or-less coherent and efficacious practical calculations whose existence can be traced over time, that would also be true of practices involving presumptions. However, on Rescher's own account, one cannot infer from this "evolutionary" rationale that the practices involving presumption in the intellectual/theoretical domain—where argumentation is conducted within a community devoted to rational inquiry—are warranted by principles that generalize to ordinary day-to-day argument, which for the most part occurs in the domains Rescher describes as concerned with practical affairs and with methods. Not only do the latter involve constraints related to the temporal necessity to take action (which are in principle held in abeyance in the intellectual/theoretical domain), in the practical domain of every day argumentation, even among persons who value the importance of good reasons and rationality, it is frequently the case that persons are prudently and reasonably reluctant to consider reasons for adopting courses of action, policies, and methods that do not initially strike them as agreeable. In the domain of day-to-day argumentation, presumption and probative obligation have more and different work to do than Rescher requires of them within the gentle confines of a community devoted to rational inquiry.

Overall, from our rhetorical perspective, Rescher's account highlights the contributions that practices involving presumption and probative obligation can make to the epistemically satisfying consideration of defeasible propositions. At many points it seems that similar practices may make analogous contributions to day-to-day argumentation. The latter also deal with defeasible propositions under conditions of doubt and disagreement. Moreover, the idea that probative obligations in rational inquiry rest on pragmatic rationales might well extend to day-to-day argumentation. However, without careful analysis of day-to-day argumentation on its own terms, we are left in the position of utilizing Rescher's account by the use of slippery analogies between (to use Rescher's terms) discourse in the rational theoretical/intellectual domain to discourse in the practical domain.

## Epistemological Questions

The previous section sees Rescher's account of presumption and burden of proof as having both rhetorical and epistemological dimensions. Rhetorically, presumptions and probative obligations afford a basis for identifying the rational (persuasive) force of evidence and arguments. But this force is deemed sufficient when the argument is sufficient to constitute "a *prima facie case*—a body of reason and evidence" sufficient to reverse the burden of proof. Spelling out just what constitutes sufficient "reason and evidence" presupposes criteria to determine just when a burden of proof has been discharged. Identifying such rules when they have not otherwise been agreed upon is an epistemological task.

In Rescher's discussion, epistemological concepts play a central role in developing presumption and burden of proof. Presumptions and probative burdens let us identify "epistemically significant means for managing argumentation." To recall, while institutional or conventional presumptions are based on the rules of an institution, rational presumptions are "fixed by probative considerations of evidential weight and intrinsic plausibility." Again, the notion of plausibility deals with the credibility of sources and epistemic conceptions such as "simplicity, regularity, uniformity, normalcy" are epistemic notions. Outside of institutional contexts in which rules determining presumption are stipulated, presumptions are determined by the "demands of reason" (which is an epistemic authority), more specifically the requirements to satisfy "the pragmatic rationales for rules which have evolved within the community (communities) committed to rational inquiry."

Given this understanding of the epistemic nature of presumption and burden of proof, that they are connected to persuasive force, what is left to say about these concepts from an epistemological viewpoint? The discussion in the first section opens up a number of epistemological questions, in particular about natural presumptions and probative obligations, that is, those not arising from constructed systems of rules such as the law. Just when are burdens of proof discharged in natural contexts? What do the notions of evidential weight and intrinsic plausibility mean in these contexts? How does one assess source reliability and plausibility in such cases? Where natural rules are available, which may be maintained by pragmatic considerations, just how are these rules identified and their pragmatic motivations understood? These are tantalizing questions for the epistemologist.

Just why should an epistemologist find them fascinating, or the lack of a specific answer to them in particular cases frustrating? Presumption is the hallmark of acceptability. As I have said in my book *Acceptable Premises*, a statement is acceptable just when there is a presumption in its favor.[22] Likewise, acceptability may be a hallmark of justified belief. But justification is a central epistemological concept. One may accept a statement because one has some evidence for it. This is epistemic acceptance. To be justified, one needs sufficient evidence of the right sort. This is epistemic acceptability. To shift the burden of proof from one side to the other, certain conditions must be satisfied. Rescher's discussion tantalizes the epistemologist by not telling us explicitly what the conditions are when the transfer is to be based on natural epistemic reasons. His discussion then identifies where epistemic work needs to be done in order to arrive at epistemic conditions of establishing a presumption for some claim, and also for when the epistemic burden of proof has not yet been discharged. How does this emerge from Rescher's discussion?

As pointed out in the first section, Rescher distinguishes between the initiating burden of proof and the burden of going forward with the disputation. A person puts forward a claim that some may find questionable. He now has an initiating burden of proof to defend that statement. He initially discharges this burden satisfactorily by presenting a *prima facie* case for this claim. The burden is shifted to his interlocutor to rebut the case. She presents a *prima facie* rebuttal. The burden is shifted back to the original proponent to present a *prima facie* counterargument or counterrebuttal. The exchange may shift back and forth until either one side or the other presents a case that the opposing side cannot rebut successfully, or the interlocutors run out of time. But now the questions for the epistemologist are clear. Just what are the natural epistemic reasons for an initiating burden of proof? Just when has an interlocutor given a satisfactory *prima facie* case? When does the last contribution in a dialectical exchange constitute an *ultima facie* case?

Rescher sketches what presumption may mean in four given contexts: law, disputation, debate, and theory of knowledge. His descriptions ably illustrate his concept of burden of proof, how it may be discharged, and how that move of discharging may be defeated. In each case, a principle of presumption is in effect a material inference rule. From an assertion of a certain sort, one may take it, that is, accept, a further statement. In law, from someone's not having been heard from for over seven years, we may take it that the person is dead. In disputation, there is a presumption for certain types of evidence. For example, from common knowledge attesting that $p$, we may take it that $p$. In debate, the presumption is for the status quo. From the fact that the gate is almost always locked at sunset, we may take it that the gate will be locked following sunset this evening. In theory of knowledge, there is a presumption for the senses and memory, among other sources. From remembering seeing the whale at the aquarium yesterday, we may take it that there was a whale at the aquarium yesterday. In all these cases, imagining the premise to be true gives one good reasons for expecting the conclusion to be true in the imagined world. Imagining situations where defeating evidence rebuts the move from premise to conclusion may also be straightforward.

These four examples of such basic exchanges provide straightforward illustrations but raise epistemic questions for a statement of general criteria for correctly carrying out the evidential burden of further reply. The proponent makes an assertion and supplies a putative reason for it. What are the criteria by which the rational adjudicator can say that this reason constitutes a *prima facie* case and that the burden has been shifted to the challenger to present rebutting counterconsiderations? Likewise, where the opponent does present rebuttals, what are the epistemic criteria for a rational adjudicator to grant that the opponent has shifted the evidential burden of proof back for the proponent to reply? Adducing rebuttals may make it rhetorically incumbent on one's interlocutor to respond. Not responding might be taken as a sign that one could not respond in a satisfactory way. But for the burden shifted to be an *evidential* burden of proof, the interlocutor's contribution must constitute a *prima facie* case, that is, one "whose evidential weight is such that—in the absence of countervailing considerations—the 'reasonable presumption' is now in its favor."[23]

To judge that the burden has been shifted, one must be able to say what we mean by measuring evidential weight. Rescher's notion of "evidentially sufficient contention" (ES), "a contention that succeeds in effecting a shift in the burden of proof with respect to the thesis on whose behalf it is brought forward,"[24] does not answer our question. If anything, it raises two questions. There must be a "substantial presumption of truth" for such ES contentions and "the evidential force they are able to lend to the thesis in whose behalf they are adduced [must be] sufficiently weighty that the burden of proof is shifted in its favor."[25] But what is this substantial force and how does one ascertain that it is substantial? Again, what is this evidential force? According to Rescher, it is variable. Different contexts require different degrees of force to shift the burden of proof such as the familiar proof beyond reasonable doubt versus proof on balance of probabilities. But noting these considerations does not clarify just how one ascertains evidential weight in a given case.

Rescher claims that burden of proof is not "a strictly *logical* concept," but "a *methodological* one."[26] This methodological or dialectical nature may be indicated by certain rules concerning what is admissible in building up a case for an assertion, in what statements may be enlisted as basic (undefended) premises. The rules specify that "certain categories of contentions [have] evidential weight."[27] For example, our rules of presumption may license us to assert statements describing how things usually are as basic premises. These statements are simply given evidential weight by the rule. The rule itself seems to require no justification. Likewise, rules of presumption may license certain inferential moves. When is evidence sufficient to defeat a defeasible inference rule? Surely these are legitimate epistemic questions inspiring us to go beyond being content with saying that a statement or inference rule is simply authorized by some presumption.

Rescher does not leave us without direction here, for he introduces a discussion of plausibility. "Presumption favors the most *plausible* of rival alternatives—when indeed there is one. This alternative will always stand until set aside (by the entry of another, yet more plausible, presumption)."[28] Plausibility, Rescher claims, is a natural as opposed to artificial or conventional route to determining presumption. How then may one assess plausibility? According to Rescher, there are three criteria: the authority (i.e., reliability, competence) of the sources vouching for the claim, the strength of evidence supporting the claim, and the degree to which the claim satisfies such plausibility principles as simplicity, regularity, or uniformity with other cases,[29] i.e., these principles being the same as those that textbooks routinely include as criteria of scientific explanation.[30] Of course, one can object that since the second of these criteria involves supporting strength, applying these principles to determine plausibility and then using plausibility to assess argument strength is circular. As presented here, it is. Explaining whether we have only the appearance of circularity that could be dispelled by a deeper analysis is beyond our scope in this paper.

In connection with concluding his discussion of presumption, Rescher suggests a possible direction for this analysis. Suppose a proponent puts forward one or more initiating assertions, but in the course of the dialectic argues for each of them, answering *all* of the opponent's challenges. We could say that the proponent had covered every point. There is a presumption for each of his initial premises, and he has transferred that presumption to his initiating theses. Such a case would certainly be stronger than one that left some point "uncovered." Can strength, then, be explicated in terms of how well an assertion is covered? We leave that as a further epistemological question that Rescher's discussion directs us to answer.

What then does this investigation into Rescher's account of presumption and burden of proof reveal about how the rhetorical and epistemological perspectives in his account of these issues are related? If rhetoric is concerned with persuasion, with moving the addressees of some communication to accept a thesis, we may distinguish types of persuasion. As we have seen, rational persuasions are grounded on pragmatic rationales. If our goal is to approximate truth as closely as possible, we are constrained by certain requirements. In particular, we must recognize when an assertion raises a burden of proof, when there is a presumption for a reason given to discharge that obligation, and when the reasons put forward constitute a *prima facie* case for the assertion claimed. These considerations have rhetorical interest since they spell out conditions for when a discourse is rationally persuasive in discharging a burden of proof. The rationales are pragmatic because, assuming these questions are properly addressed, they advance us toward our goal of approximating the truth. Why do some assertions make probative obligations incumbent on the party who makes them? Why is there a presumption for other assertions put forward to satisfy these probative obligations? How does one tell how well or strongly these obligations have been satisfied?

Just how may these questions be answered? In some cases, institutions, such as the law, may provide answers. In others, we may need to turn to rational inquiry involving natural presumptions. Within communities of rational inquirers, rules have evolved for answering these questions with the pragmatic motivation of best approximating the truth. As the rules of rational inquiry go beyond formal, institutional rules in allocating presumption and burden of proof, so everyday argumentation may require us to inquire further. But as the rationales for rational inquiry are pragmatic and epistemological, we may expect this to be true also of the allocation of presumptions and burdens of proof in this even wider sphere. Rhetoric raises the necessity of recognizing presumption and burden of proof in rational persuasion. Epistemology investigates why this persuasion is rational persuasion.

## Notes

The coauthors prepared their sections of this paper independently of each other. The original intention was to include an extended discussion of Nicholas Rescher's views on dialectical argumentation in the introduction to part 2 of this book, with Fred Kauffeld writing from the rhetorical perspective and James Freeman from the epistemological perspective. Kauffeld's summary of Rescher's views proved far too extensive, however, for an introductory overview. Hence, it was decided to introduce a separate essay completely devoted to a discussion of Rescher's views, in which Kauffeld's mini-essay would be bolstered by Freeman's analysis. This essay is the result. Before his passing, Kauffeld read the entire paper in draft and indicated his approval. Freeman subsequently made minor modifications to his part of the essay in response to a reviewer's comments. We trust that Professor Kauffeld would continue to approve. —Eds.

1. Nicholas Rescher, *Dialectics: A Controversy-Oriented Approach to the Theory of Knowledge* (Albany: State University of New York Press, 1977), 3.

2. Rescher, *Dialectics*, 47.

3. Rescher, *Dialectics*, 30.

4. Rescher, *Dialectics*, 34.

5. Rescher, *Dialectics*, 27.

6. Nicholas Rescher, *Presumption and the Practice of Tentative Cognition* (Cambridge: Cambridge University Press, 2006), 30.

7. Rescher, *Dialectics*, 43.

8. Rescher, *Dialectics*, 29.

9. Rescher, *Dialectics*, 38.

10. Rescher, *Dialectics*, 38–39.

11. Rescher, *Dialectics*, 39–41. For a fuller account of Rescher's discussion of the locus of presumption, see James Freeman, *Acceptable Premises: An Epistemic Approach to an Informal Logic Problem* (Cambridge: Cambridge University Press, 2005).

12. Rescher, *Dialectics*, 43.

13. Rescher, *Presumption*, 51.

14. Rescher, *Dialectics*, 106.

15. Rescher, *Presumption*, 34.

16. Rescher, *Dialectics*, 60.

17. Rescher, *Dialectics*, 99.

18. Rescher, *Dialectics*, 78.

19. Rescher, *Dialectics*, 95.

20. Rescher, *Dialectics*, 46.

21. Rescher's account of natural presumptions based on commitments made by members of a community devoted to rational inquiry is similar in some respects to a view of "dialectical obligations" advanced by the informal logician Ralph Johnson working in conjunction with his colleague Tony Blair. According to Johnson, a party who intends to persuade addressees by providing them with reasons incurs a two-fold obligation: first, an obligation to provide good reasons for the proposition she wants accepted, and a second, dialectical, obligation to provide satisfactory answers to all significant doubts, objections, and/or counterarguments which she encounters and of which she is otherwise aware. She incurs this obligation, Johnson maintains, by engaging in the very act of advancing persuasive argument to a member of an idealized community of arguers.

22. Freeman, *Acceptable Premises*, 21.

23. Rescher, *Dialectics*, 28.

24. Rescher, *Dialectics*, 28–29.

25. Rescher, *Dialectics*, 29.

26. Rescher, *Dialectics*, 29.

27. Rescher, *Dialectics*, 30.

28. Rescher, *Dialectics*, 38.

29. Rescher, *Dialectics*, 41.

30. See Irving M. Copi and Carl Cohen, *Introduction to Logic*, 12th ed. (Upper Saddle River, NJ: Pearson/Prentice Hall, 2005), 519–22.

# 15

# The Significance of Presumptions in Informal Logic

## The Need for Presumptions in Informal Logic

It is a commonplace in informal logic circles that for an argument to be logically cogent, its premises must be acceptable, relevant to its conclusion, and constitute grounds adequate for accepting or believing that conclusion. Govier names these the ARG conditions.[1] (They hark back to Johnson and Blair's three basic fallacies—irrelevant reason, hasty conclusion, and problematic premise.)[2] The issue of premise acceptability is especially acute for the basic premises of an argument, that is, those premises which are not argued for, at least in the context of the argument being presented. Even if the basic premises of a given argument are found acceptable on the basis of previous argument, that argument will have basic premises. At some point the regress will stop. Informal logic must address the question of acceptability for premises not defended by argument. It must also address why certain patterns of argument, which in many instances are Toulmin's warrants,[3] are adequate to at least *prima facie* transfer acceptability from premises to conclusion. Under what circumstances do the premises of an argument constitute grounds adequate for accepting the conclusion? Informal logic, then, should endeavor to provide principled criteria for acceptable basic premises and adequately grounded inferences, and procedures to determine and certify whether or not premises are acceptable and constitute adequate grounds for the conclusions inferred from them.

Surely if an agent's inference pattern instanced a valid deductive inference rule and I recognized its validity, I should find the move logically adequate. Surely also if a basic premise were indubitable for me, either because it was logically necessary and I recognized its necessity, or because it described some state of affairs to which I had internal access—for example, that I was currently being appeared to greenly, that premise should be acceptable for me. But are these the only conditions under which basic premises and inference patterns are acceptable? That they are constitutes one type of classical foundationalism.[4] As I have argued in *Acceptable Premises*,[5] classical foundationalism is too

strict to provide a proper account of basic premise acceptability and leads ultimately to skepticism. How may we argue properly from indefeasible premises about our experience together with premises logically necessary to statements describing states of affairs in the external world, their nomic relations,
or their value? Certainly, we cannot deduce such statements from necessary
truths and protocols of experience. But such statements concerning events or
conditions in the external world, their nomic relations, and value express the
issues we may be most concerned to reason about, to come to a justified position concerning what we should believe or do.

I believe that basic premise acceptability may be explicated through a concept of presumption. Put briefly, premises should be acceptable when there is
a presumption in their favor. More precisely, acceptability is a ternary relation
between a statement, a challenger in a dialectical situation, and a point in that
situation reflecting or constituting an epistemic position for that challenger. A
statement will be acceptable for a challenger at a point in a dialectical exchange
just in case there is a presumption for it from her point of view, given the evidence she is aware of. There will be a presumption from her point of view just
in case anyone aware of the same evidence she is aware of would either have
to concede the statement or present an argument against it.[6] In legal terms,
there will be a presumption for a statement when the burden of persuasion for
making that statement has been satisfied for the triers of fact. By making an assertion requiring evidence, the proponent has raised the initiating burden of
proof. By presenting sufficient evidence, the proponent has convinced the triers
of fact, discharging this burden. (Compare the definitions of burden of persuasion given by the Legal Information Institute and by McCahey.)[7] My understanding of presumption owes a significant debt to Rescher.[8] He makes the
point that in building an argument for a claim which has initiated some dialectical exchange, it must be possible in principle for the proponent to bring
forward some assertions which will not at that point be questioned or challenged but which will be allowed to stand as evidence in the case he is building: "In rational controversy, there must always be some impartially fixed common ground determining what is to count as evidence. This leads straightway
to the topic of *presumption.*"[9] The assertions which the proponent may bring
forward without challenge at a given point are presumptions and constitute
acceptable basic premises.

Applying Rescher's discussion of presumptions to explicate criteria for the
acceptability of basic premises requires some clarification. Rescher cites some
jurisprudential discussions in which presumptions are inference rules or conclusions drawn in accord with certain inference rules: "The French *Code civil*
defines 'presumptions' as: 'Consequences drawn by the law or the magistrate
from a known to an unknown fact.'"[10] Ilbert says, "A presumption in the or-

dinary sense is an inference [. . .] A legal presumption [. . .] may be described, in [Sir James] Stephen's language, as 'a rule of law that courts and judges shall draw a particular inference from a particular fact, or from particular evidence, unless and until the truth' (perhaps it would be better to say 'soundness') of the inference is disproved."[11] If presumptions are to be inference rules or what is drawn in accordance with inference rules, how may we speak of *basic* premises as being presumptions or having presumptions in their favor? This characterization of presumption also raises the question of how the status of the known fact as known fact or evidence as evidence on which presumptions are based is to be characterized.

To resolve this puzzle, we need to make a distinction between a statement's *being* a presumption and *justifying* that it has that status.[12] Suppose I am appeared to in the manner of a tree in full green leaf outside my office window. To my knowledge, I am not subject to hallucinations nor am I aware of any distorting factors in my environment which would create the mirage of a tree. I have no reason to question the general reliability of sensory perception or to think I am subject to wishful thinking.[13] That is, in the normal course of events when I am appeared to perceptually in a certain way and am aware of no evidence of abnormal facts, the best explanation is an external cause of that perception. Now on the basis of my sensory experiences, in the absence of defeating considerations, I form the belief that there is a tree in full leaf outside my office window. I form the belief in the basic way. I do not *argue* that there is a tree outside my office window from premises that I am having certain sensory experiences together with premises asserting that no defeaters are operating or that I am aware of none. I form the belief on the basis of my nonpropositional sensory evidence. However, since I am aware of this nonpropositional evidence—since in the normal course of affairs my perception is reliable and I am aware of no defeaters—my belief is justified and there is a presumption for it from my point of view.

On the other hand, to justify that the claim had this presumptive status for me I would need to cite the factors of my experience which we have just been noting. However, my not being able to give this justifying argument would not mean that I would not be justified in holding this belief or that it did not have presumptive status for me. My awareness of the evidence is sufficient for justification. There may then be a presumption for basic premises, in particular when they express basic beliefs formed in the light of appropriate evidence absent defeaters. From my point of view, these premises are acceptable until appropriate defeating evidence comes to light. They have the status of presumptions as Rescher has characterized it. "They are able to stand provisionally—i.e., until somehow undermined."[14]

Notice that not every statement having presumptive status need be a basic premise. A statement may gain presumptive status when defended by or supported by appropriate reasons. Although a proponent's initial claim may be controversial and he incur a burden of proof in putting the claim forward, a proponent may so satisfactorily discharge that burden that it would now be incumbent on the challenger to argue why the claim should not be accepted. The burden of proof would be shifted to the challenger to make a reply. But what must be the relation between premises and conclusion for the argument to transfer presumption status from premises to conclusion? We would not expect such arguments in general to be deductively valid. But their premises must constitute grounds adequate for accepting their conclusions, at least provisionally or as presumptions. That is, they must make a *prima facie* case, being in Rescher's words "evidentially sufficient"[15] to effect this shift. The principles of evidential sufficiency would be principles of presumption transfer. We need the concept of presumption in informal logic because we need an account of the conditions under which basic premises are properly basic or acceptable, and defeasible arguments present grounds adequate for their conclusions.

## Sources of Presumption for Informal Logic— Law and Rhetoric as Candidates

Again, as Rescher points out, the concept of burden of proof and thus also of presumption "is at root a legal conception."[16] As such, legal contexts furnish us with many examples of presumption. But from the informal logic point of view these examples may be problematic. Consider the familiar legal presumption, at least in Anglo-American law, of innocence in favor of the accused. Although in a legal proceeding this places the burden of proof on the prosecutor, there could still be significant doubt concerning whether the accused *in fact* was innocent before the prosecutor makes a *prima facie* case for his or her guilt. If one were engaging not in the regulated dialogue of a judicial proceeding, but in an informal persuasion or inquiry dialogue,[17] the legal presumption would seem inappropriate to certifying that the claim "the accused is innocent" is an acceptable basic premise. Likewise, that in law from the fact that a person has not been heard from for seven years we may take it that the person is dead, that is, legally dead, may we also take it that *in fact* the person *is* dead? Does the premise create a presumption for this conclusion?

The problem with relying on a system of statue law for providing an account of presumption appropriate for general argument evaluation is that statute law is stipulative. It is established by the decisions and actions of legislative bodies in enacting certain laws. Such bodies may lay down presumptions and burdens of proof by fiat. But can premise acceptability or evidential weight be a matter of stipulation? Do certain conditions become criteria of good argument—

some of the criteria at least—simply by the declarations of legislative bodies? What are we to say then if different systems of law allocate presumptions and burdens of proof in different ways?

Sproule has argued[18] that Whately's thought in introducing presumption and burden of proof into rhetorical theory underwent a development whereby these concepts, originally legal, were transformed into rhetorical notions.[19] In the rhetorical sense, presumptions are determined by certain audience predispositions. That audiences would be prepared to accept certain statements, prefer certain interpretations or arguments, to accord deference or credibility to certain sources of information, would afford a presumption for these claims— including those endorsed by these sources.[20] In the eyes of the audience, there would be a presumption for these statements if used as basic premises or presented as conclusions of arguments instancing favored inference patterns (where the premises were also accepted), or backed by credited sources of information.

These presumptions are not grounded in stipulations but in facts about the psychology of audiences, discoverable through empirical research. But the fact that certain statements are accepted in general by a particular audience, that certain forms of argument are found persuasive, or certain authorities respected does not in itself render these statements acceptable, these arguments sufficiently weighty in evidence to establish their conclusions, or the vouching authorities properly respectable. It may be prudent for a rhetor to take these factors into account in presenting a persuasive argument, but they do not address the normative concerns of informal logic. Here the issue is not whether a statement or form of argument is accept*ed* but whether it is accept*able*, that is, whether one is justified in accepting it. To frame an understanding of presumption adequate from that perspective, we shall need to turn to a further source.

## The Epistemic Approach—Sources of Belief and Their Presumptive Reliability

In *Dialectics*, Rescher indicates that there are further "loci" of presumption beyond the law. Both disputation and debate recognize a presumption in favor of matters of common knowledge or opinions of properly qualified authorities or experts.[21] In addition, within the theory of knowledge a longstanding tradition maintains a presumption for memory and the senses.[22] What I find salient here is that these grounds tie presumption for a claim to the source or sources which may vouch for it. Memory and sense perception are personal sources, belief-generating mechanisms of the person who may be asked to accept some claim. If I remember putting away the silverware, then my memory vouches for the claim "I put away the silverware." If I perceive a tree in full green leaf outside my office window, then my sense perception vouches for the claim that "there is a tree in full green leaf outside my office window." Common knowledge and expert opinion are interpersonal sources which may vouch for claims. Perhaps speaking of common belief rather than common knowledge is more accurate. Each society transmits to its members, in particular to those growing up in the society, a stock of beliefs concerning significant events and figures in its history, concerning the way the world works at least ordinarily, and concerning values. No one individual can be identified as the source of these claims or their sole transmitter in a given case, as a witness may vouch for claims as a matter of personal testimony or a news organization reporter may transmit the observation reports of others. One's society or culture vouches for a body of claims which become the common inheritance of members of that culture, at least at a certain time. Authorities or experts, by contrast, *are* individuals who vouch for claims.

How are presumptions for claims tied to sources which vouch for those claims? Suppose I am asked to accept a certain statement—to take it as a premise for further deliberation about what to believe or do. Ordinarily I shall be aware of at least one source which vouches for that claim. If the source is presumptively reliable and I am aware of no defeater of its reliability in this particular instance, and the estimated disutility of my gathering further corroborating evidence would be greater than the estimated disutility of my mistakenly accepting that claim,[23] then there is a presumption for that statement from my current perspective. The pragmatic issue of the cost of accepting a statement or gaining further evidence may be regarded as an epistemic issue.[24] Whether a source is presumptively reliable and what are the defeaters of that presumption—what are the conditions or circumstances which require setting aside that presumption—are epistemic matters, issues which can be argued on epistemological grounds. Hence, the presumptions the sources create by vouching for certain claims are epistemic presumptions. They are grounded in our understanding of what it means to be justified in believing or accepting a given proposition.

For example, suppose I am appeared to in a certain auditory way. Not only may my experience be described as being aware of certain sounds, but I also immediately form the belief that these sounds have an external cause. Suppose I have learned that sounds such as these are caused by a certain type of event—say a passing bus. Consequently, through sensory perception I come to believe that a bus is now passing. If my auditory perception is presumptively reliable and I am aware of no defeaters of that presumption—for example I am not aware of having grown hard of hearing so that what is the roar of a huge tractor trailer sounds like the rumble of a passing bus, or I am aware of no one trying to play a record of a bus going past my house in order to deceive me, or I am aware of no compulsion to believe that a bus is passing, and no foreseeable disaster would ensue on my mistakenly accepting that a bus was passing—then there is a presumption from my perspective that a bus is passing on the street in front of my house.

We may give an epistemological argument that auditory perception—indeed sensory perception in general—is presumptively reliable. With Reid,[25] we may argue that forming such beliefs as that, in some sense of cause, an external event or object has caused certain auditory impressions and, given certain learning on our part, that the cause is of a certain type, are matters of our constitution. Such beliefs are first premises or first principles from which we reason, basic premises we may put forward to support or justify further claims, but not in themselves ordinarily in need of justification. Although the perceptual skeptic may question the reliability of sensory perception, with Hume he abandons his skepticism as soon as he leaves his study—suggesting that his skeptical questioning is not in good faith. If he argues that our senses are not presumptively reliable because they could be mistaken, with Reid we may reply that his reasoning confuses a demand for incorrigibility with a demand for reliability. Why should we trust only those sources of belief such as introspection when applied to the immediate contents of our consciousness, or reason when recognizing relations between ideas or concepts, and not our other standardly reliable basic belief-generating mechanisms although they may be mistaken on certain occasions? The demand for certainty above reliability is not itself obvious, and the skeptic incurs an undischarged burden of proof in making this requirement.

Identifying what sources, both personal and interpersonal, may vouch for a claim and whether or under what circumstances these sources are presumptively reliable constitutes the second part of this study on acceptable premises.[26] The discussion culminates in detailing a procedure of epistemic casuistry. Although one may come to a belief for which there is an epistemic presumption immediately or in a basic way—without inference to a propositional conclusion from propositional premises—and thus we may be justified in holding that belief, justifying the belief requires argument. To present a justifying argument, I believe we should address three questions:

(1) What type of statement is it?
(2) What source (or sources) vouch for it?
(3) Does this voucher create an epistemic presumption for the statement?

We may group personal sources of belief according to the types of statement they vouch for. Reason is the form of *a priori* intuition which vouches for necessarily true claims. Memory, sense perception, and introspection vouch for extensional descriptions of conditions or states of affairs. Statements involving intentional or interpretative claims (for example, claims of certain physical or causal necessity or possibility) are matters of intuition of various sorts. Finally, evaluative claims concerning the right and the good are vouched for by moral sense and moral intuition. In each case we can argue that the personal belief-generating mechanism is presumptively reliable (at least in certain employments) and detail conditions under which that presumptive reliability is rebutted. Indicating that this presumptive reliability is not rebutted in these circumstances or that pragmatic considerations do not require our seeking further evidence completes the argument.

Other persons may advance statements of any of these sorts—necessarily true statements, extensional descriptions, intentional interpretations, or evaluations—and one may come to believe such statements on their word. Whether their word is genuine testimony which would confer a presumption upon it from the receiver's or challenger's perspective again concerns various circumstances and conditions, in particular whether the proponent is presumptively reliable to speak on these issues and whether there is a presumption that he or she is speaking sincerely. By taking these factors into account, we may justify that there is a presumption in favor of a statement from a particular person's point of view. Given the factors entertained in making this justification, this will be an epistemic presumption.

I believe that presumption in this sense is precisely the notion of presumption which informal logic needs to explicate premise acceptability—specifically the acceptability of basic or undefended premises.[27] An argument for whose premises there is an undefeated presumption, in the sense we have developed here, is an argument whose premises are acceptable. Should the argument transfer that presumption to the conclusion, surely the argument would give us good reason to accept the conclusion and be a good argument in the sense of argument goodness appropriate to informal logic.

Although this may be speculative, the sense of presumption we have developed may also be applicable, in at least some cases, to determining whether the premises of an argument are adequately connected to its conclusion. An argument will instance a warrant in Toulmin's sense. But corresponding to that warrant or inference principle will be a suitably qualified quantified conditional statement. Should there be a presumption for this conditional statement from one's point of view, then there should be a presumption for the corresponding warrant. Provided that this warrant is not rebutted, the presumption for the premises should be transferred to the conclusion.

I have thus identified the significance of the concept of presumption in informal logic. Epistemic presumption is at the heart of understanding premise acceptability and may be central to understanding connection adequacy. Presumption has a further significance dealing with the very self-understanding of informal logic. If epistemic presumption, an epistemological concept, is at the core of informal logic evaluation, what exactly is informal logic? I turn to that question in the next section.

## Epistemic Presumption and the Self-Understanding of Informal Logic

A commonly recognized consequence of taking soundness (deductive validity together with true premises) as the criterion of argument goodness—logical as opposed to rhetorical or some other sort of goodness—is that logic cannot give a complete answer to whether an argument is good. With the exception of those basic premises which are logically determinate, logic cannot pronounce on whether the premises are true or false, since the question is extralogical. One must turn in many instances to empirical investigation, in others perhaps to moral or other forms of insight. Broadening the concept of argument goodness to include both arguments which are deductively valid and inductively strong does not affect the issue of logic's being able to evaluate premises. It is not in the purview of logic to gather the evidence on which judging the truth of the premises depends. By contrast, on the informal logic criteria of acceptability, relevance, and ground adequacy, where acceptability is understood in terms of presumption, one need seek no further information to determine whether a premise is acceptable from a given person's point of view than the evidence of which that person is already aware. A judgment of whether there is a presumption for a statement from a person's point of view is a judgment of whether the evidence available to that person *prima facie* justifies believing or accepting that statement.

Consider the questions constituting the practice of epistemic casuistry. "What type of statement is it?" This is a semantic question. By virtue of understanding the language in which a statement is expressed one should recognize whether it is logically determinate or whether it is a contingent description, interpretation, or evaluation. "What source or sources vouch for it?" Remember that presumption as we understand it is a ternary relation between a statement, a receiver or challenger in a dialectical situation, and a point in that situation. To ask what sources vouch for a statement is not to ask for a search for sources but to ask the challenger to take stock of the sources of which she is currently aware. Which, if any, of her personal belief-generating mechanisms vouches for this statement? What other persons (the proponent or perhaps further individuals) vouch for the claim?

"Does this voucher create a presumption for this statement?" Consider these questions: What evidence (for example, sensory experiences) is the challenger aware of? Are the personal sources presumptively reliable? Is the challenger aware of factors certifying the presumptive reliability of those giving their word? Is the challenger aware of any defeater of this presumptive reliability? How does one determine expected cost? As Clarke points out, this will ordinarily be the result of freehand estimates. But such estimates will consider the challenger's awareness of *prima facie* signs of the intrinsic badness of mistakenly accepting the claim versus gathering further information together with her estimates of the likelihood of these results. Again, the information pertinent to judging whether there is a presumption for a statement from the challenger's perspective concerns factors in the challenger's current awareness.

The issues on which a judgment of presumption rests are issues pertaining to the extent and quality of the evidence of which a challenger is aware. Does that evidence justify her believing or accepting a given claim? But justification is an epistemological notion. Hence, if premise acceptability is understood as premise justification as analyzed through presumption, our investigation of this concept is an instance of doing epistemology and the practice of epistemic casuistry is an exercise in applied epistemology.[28] Informal logic then is a branch of epistemology seeking to identify and justify criteria or canons for judging arguments to be epistemically good and to delimit the practice whereby the epistemic goodness of arguments can be certified. The concept of presumption leads informal logic to this self-understanding. Seeing this connection discloses a major significance of presumption for informal logic.

## Notes

1. T. Govier, *A Practical Study of Argument* (Belmont, CA: Wadsworth, 1985), 60–61.

2. R. H. Johnson and J. A. Blair, *Logical Self-Defense* (Toronto: McGraw-Hill Ryerson, 1977), 12–29.

3. S. Toulmin, *The Uses of Argument* (Cambridge: Cambridge University Press, 1958), 98–100.

4. Locke's foundationalism is more generous than the version I have just sketched. Locke admitted acceptable inductive patterns of inference and the acceptability of conclusions inferred inductively.

5. J. B. Freeman, *Acceptable Premises: An Epistemic Approach to an Informal Logic Problem* (Cambridge: Cambridge University Press, 2005), ch. 1; and J. B. Freeman, "Why Classical Foundationalism Cannot Provide a Proper Account of Premise Acceptability," *Inquiry: Critical Thinking Across the Disciplines* 15, no. 4 (1996): 17–26.

6. Compare R. C. Pinto, *Argument, Inference, and Dialectic* (Dordrecht: Kluwer, 2001), 3–4.

7. J. McCahey, "The Burdens of Persuasion and Production," *Proof: The Journal of the Trial Evidence Committee* 16, no. 3 (2008): 8; Legal Information Institute, "Burden of Persuasion," Cornell Law School, https://www.law.cornell.edu/cfr/text/12/108.10.

8. N. Rescher, *Dialectics: A Controversy-Oriented Approach to the Theory of Knowledge* (Albany: State University of New York Press, 1977).

9. Rescher, *Dialectics*, 30.

10. Rescher, *Dialectics*, 30, note 7.

11. Rescher, *Dialectics*, 31. See also Ilbert, "On Presumption and Burden of Proof," this volume, ch. 8.

12. This parallels Alston's distinction "between one's *being* justified in believing that *p*, and one's *justifying* one's belief that *p*." William Alston, "Concepts of Epistemic Justification," *Monist* 68, no. 1 (1985): 58.

13. That is, I am not aware of any factors that would contravene Plantinga's conditions for warrant. See Alvin Plantinga, *Warrant and Proper Function* (New York: Oxford University Press, 1993), 19.

14. Rescher, *Dialectics*, 34.

15. Rescher, *Dialectics*, 28.

16. Rescher, *Dialectics*, 25.

17. D. Walton, *Informal Logic: A Handbook for Critical Argumentation* (Cambridge: Cambridge University Press, 1989), 10.

18. J. M. Sproule, "The Psychological Burden of Proof: On the Evolutionary Development of Richard Whately's Theory of Presumption," *Communication Monographs* 43, no. 2 (1976): 115–29.

19. I understand that Sproule's understanding of Whately is subject to challenge. We cannot enter into this dispute here. It does not gainsay the fact that one can identify a rhetorical sense of presumption and burden of proof.

20. Compare Sproule, "Psychological Burden of Proof," 122.

21. Rescher, *Dialectics*, 36–37.

22. Rescher, *Dialectics*, 37.

23. This latter clause presents the pragmatic dimension of premise acceptability as developed in J. B. Freeman, "The Pragmatic Dimension of Premise Acceptability," in *Anyone Who Has a View: Theoretical Contributions to the Study of Argumentation*, ed. F. H. van Eemeren, J. A. Blair, C. A. Willard, and A. F. Snoeck Henkemans (Dordrecht: Kluwer Academic, 2003), 17–26.

24. I owe this view to D. S. Clarke Jr., *Rational Acceptance and Purpose: An Outline of a Pragmatist Epistemology* (Totowa, NJ: Rowman and Littlefield, 1989), 79–85.

25. See R. E. Beanblossom and K. Lehrer, eds. *Thomas Reid's Inquiry and Essays* (Indianapolis, IN: Hackett, 1983).

26. See Freeman, *Acceptable Premises*, chs. 6–10.

27. It is the burden of my entire monograph *Acceptable Premises* to substantiate this claim.

28. For further thoughts on this theme and references to authors holding similar views, see J. B. Freeman, "The Place of Informal Logic in Philosophy," *Informal Logic* 20, no. 2 (2000): 117–28.

# 16

# Analyzing Presumption as a Modal Qualifier

### David Godden

## Presumption as a Modal Qualifier

Minimally, presumption is a modal qualifier for claims used in reasoning and discourse. When true, sentences of the form "Presumably, $p$" indicate the presumptive status of $p$. This presumptive status, while something less than truth or unqualified acceptability, marks $p$ as having a defeasible but default and actionable acceptability. Thus, utterances of the form "Presumably, $p$" qualify or mitigate a speaker's commitment to $p$ while asserting $p$'s presumptive status.[1]

Presumptive status is standardly explained in terms of burden of proof. As Rescher describes it, "A presumption indicates that in the absence of specific counterindications we are able to accept how things 'as a rule' are taken as standing, and it places the burden of proof upon the adversary's side."[2] Accepting this basic notion, we may adopt Pinto's definition of "presumably" as a modal status: "A proposition or statement has the status of a presumption at a given juncture of an interchange if and only if at that juncture any party who refuses to concede it is obliged to present an argument against it—that is to say, is obliged either to concede it or to make a case against it."[3] So conceived, the modality of presumption may be understood as making particular allocations of probative entitlements and obligations. Regarding entitlements, a presumptively acceptable claim may be taken to be the case in the absence of countervailing reasons; thereby may be used as a premise in further reasoning and discourse. Regarding obligations, those who deny the entitlements arising from a claim's presumptive acceptability are obliged to make some reasoned case against $p$'s presumptive acceptability.

By redistributing probative obligations and entitlements across discursive standpoints, Hahn and Oaksford observe that presumptions "favor certain substantive outcomes" over others.[4] This raises the question of whether presumptions do so in reliable, or truth-conducive ways. Are presumptions engineered to track truth? Is "presumably" an epistemic modality? The answer here will determine how presumptions (that is, presumed claims) ought to be treated in reasoning and argumentation—for example, what sorts of entitlements they license, what obligations they occasion, and what kinds of inferences may generate, and be based on, them.

Next, "presumably" takes its place among a long list of qualifiers, for example: "necessarily," "certainly," "defeasibly," "probably," "all things considered," "plausibly," "perhaps," "hypothetically," etc. These expressions have a dual function in reasoned discourse. First, when used in utterances they serve to modify a speaker's commitment, or express their propositional attitude, to some claim. Second, as constituents of sentences they operate to mark and track the logical, epistemic, deontic, discursive, or other modal status of propositions. Whether used as commitment markers or modal operators, qualifiers may be operationalized as making assignments of probative entitlements and obligations upon rational actors according to their discursive standpoints.

These other modalities occasion a second question: is the modality *presumably* different from these others, and if so, how? That is, can a reductive account of presumption be offered by explaining uses of "presumably" in terms of (some disjunctive combination of) other modalities? The theoretical significance here is whether any special analysis of presumption is required. For example, if "presumably" amounts to nothing more than marking the defeasible acceptability of some claim (because, e.g., a *prima facie* case has been made for it), then the modality *presumably* might be reduced to the modality *defeasibly* without loss of content. As such, no special theory of presumption or presumptive inference would be required.

The modality of presumption, then, presents two theorical questions. First, is *presumably* an epistemic modality? And second, is it reducible to some other modality? This chapter undertakes to answer both questions. The thesis is that, while some standard accounts of presumption treat it as an epistemic modality, properly understood it is not. When treated as an epistemic modality, presumption is reducible to other epistemic modalities, particularly *defeasibly* or *plausibly*. Yet, when understood as a modality in practical reasoning, as suggested by Edna Ullmann-Margalit,[5] *presumably* can be analyzed as a unique modality that plays a distinct role in reasoning and argument.

The chapter proceeds as follows. The first section ("Presumption as a Distinct Epistemic Modality") reviews two versions of a standard account of presumption, due to Douglas Walton and Nicholas Rescher, on which *presumably* is held to be a distinctive modality that may be properly used in epistemic contexts.[6] The second section ("What Presumption Isn't [or Needn't Be]") considers two uses of presumption as an epistemic modality licensed by such theories: as default entitlement to standing commitments, and for conclusions supported by provisionally adequate cases. I argue that both uses of "presumably" reduce to some other epistemic modality. Moreover, I contend that the first use does not satisfy a standard analysis of presumption according to which a positive burden of production (e.g., to produce negatively relevant evidence or counter-vailing reasons) is required for presumption-rebuttal. The third section ("Presumption as a Modality in Practical Reasoning") argues that the uses of "presumably" as an epistemic modality made by these theories are not properly warranted by the pragmatic considerations offered in justifying those usages. Then, drawing on the theory of Ullmann-Margalit, I present a nonreductive analysis of *presumably* in which it is a nonepistemic modal qualifier for claims used in practical reasoning. My conclusions are offered in the final section.

## Presumption as a Distinct Epistemic Modality

Standard accounts of presumption permit epistemic uses for the modality *presumably*. Rescher explicitly contrasts his view with those of theorists (such as Ullmann-Margalit) who "see presumption as merely an action-guiding device," objecting that "while practice is indeed at issue with presumption, this can also include the practice of information management—of epistemic or cognitive procedure." Contending that "warranted presumption [...] is an *epistemic* category," Rescher distinguishes between cognitive presumptions whose purpose is "filling in gaps in our information" and practical presumptions whose function is "guiding our decisions regarding actions."[7]

Walton's position is more circumspect. Presumptions enter his theory as a type of defeasible commitment. "When a presumption is brought forward by a proponent," Walton writes, "the burden is on the respondent to refute it, or otherwise it goes into place as a commitment."[8] He also holds that presumptive arguments convey probative merit from premises to conclusion. "The [presumptive, schematic] argument serves a probative function whereby probative weight is transferred from premises to the conclusion."[9] Yet, while the qualifier "presumably" modifies the *extent* of an arguer's commitment to a claim, Walton does not use it to distinguish the *type* of an arguer's commitment or entitlement. Commitments, including qualified commitments, are available for use as premises in further argument regardless of whether the commitment was established on the basis of a dialectical considerations (e.g., discursive concession), practical considerations (e.g., instrumental reasoning), or epistemic considerations (e.g., strictly evidential reasons). Particularly in cases of dialogue shifts or nested dialogues, changes in dialogue type can mean that any commitment amounts to an epistemic commitment. For example, were a negotiation dialogue to shift to an inquiry (e.g., into some factual matter bearing on some policy), that a commitment was initially established by negotiation (e.g., due to some compromise or trade-off made by the negotiating parties) does not restrict the uses that can be made of it when the goals of the dialogue change to a truth-directed inquiry. Rather, what Walton tends to restrict are the kinds of *moves* that may be made in dialogues of different types. But, if *commitments* hold in place through shifts in dialogue type, then any commitment can become an epistemic commitment and *presumably* becomes an epistemic modality.

J. Anthony Blair has claimed that "presumptive reasoning/argument represents a *sui generis* class of reasoning/argument."[10] Citing several examples of "schematic" argument types, Blair argues that they are characterized by a distinctive set of features differentiating them from deductive and quantitatively probabilistic arguments.[11] If correct, presumptive warrant represents a distinct standard of connection between premises and conclusions or between grounds and claim. As such, the modality *presumably* ought, similarly, to be unique and irreducible to other modal qualifiers.

Such a position accords with Walton's characterization of schematic arguments as "presumptive" and "plausibilistic."[12] Walton, Reed, and Macagno write that, while argumentation schemes include deductive reasoning patterns, "they also include forms of reasoning that are [. . .] more tentative in nature and need to be judged circumspectly by reserving some doubts. Such reasoning is presumptive and defeasible. This kind of reasoning is only plausible and is often resorted to in conditions of uncertainty and lack of knowledge. Presumptive reasoning supports inference under conditions of incompleteness by allowing unknown data to be presumed."[13] On this view, the defeasible quality of inferential connection at work in presumptive arguments is best understood in rough-hewn, qualitative terms, and is best evaluated using schematically indexed critical questions designed to "stress-test" stereotypical points of default.

Rescher also explains presumptive reasoning in plausibilistic terms: "Presumption favors the most *plausible* of rival alternatives."[14] He agrees that presumptive arguments are not articulable or assessable quantitatively: "The plausibility of a thesis will not be a measure of its *probability*—of how likely we deem it."[15] Rather, plausibility is explained in terms of coherence. The plausibility of a thesis "reflects the prospects of its being fitted into our cognitive scheme of things in view of the standing of the sources or principles that vouch for its inclusion therein. [. . .] The key issue is that of how readily the thesis in view could make its peace within the overall framework of our cognitive commitments."[16]

On these views, presumption is a distinct modality that, having some status in theoretical as well as practical reasoning, is at least partly epistemic. Presumptive warrant constitutes an irreducible standard of support that confers a defeasible but default and actionable acceptability, operationalized as a local shift in burden of proof, on presumed claims.

# What Presumption Isn't (or Needn't Be)

Consider now two discursive, epistemic statuses typically classified as presumptive on such accounts: (1) default entitlement to standing commitments and (2) conclusions supported by provisionally adequate cases. I argue that a reductive analysis of each use of "presumably" is available in terms of the alternative modalities *plausibly* and *defeasibly*, and, indeed, that *presumably* doesn't properly apply to the former.

Presumptive acceptability, or default entitlement, is sometimes ascribed to select claims or rules. Dialectical theories typically take the fact of acceptance of, or agreement upon, claims in an initial commitment set of statements to confer presumptive acceptability upon them. Since they are not in dispute, they may be unproblematically drawn upon as resolution resources in situations of disagreement. Foundational epistemic theories typically identify sources or features that are claimed to confer presumptive warrant on basic, noninferred beliefs.

The reasoning involved goes something like this: Reasoning and argumentation do not *generate* acceptability (justification) *ex nihilo*; rather, they only *transmit* acceptability from inputs to outputs via rules. Unless these inputs and rules are initially acceptable, the justificatory activity of reasoning cannot begin. Paths of reasoned support (justification) cannot be circular, since the acceptability of premises must be epistemically prior to, and independent of, that of any conclusion based upon them. Nor can paths of justification be infinite, since claims whose acceptability has yet to be established cannot confer acceptability upon claims inferred on their basis. So, responding that the acceptability of inferential inputs is based on some prior act of reasoning does not answer the justificatory challenge but only pushes the regress back. This line of thinking results in the foundationalist view that at least some claims and rules must "wear their acceptability on their sleeves"—if only initially, defeasibly, and tentatively.

It should be admitted that our acts of reasoning must, as a matter of practical necessity, begin somewhere. Ordinarily we begin in the epistemic situation in which we find ourselves, with the epistemic resources we have at hand, and we make additions and corrections to our beliefs as we discover particular instances of ignorance or error. We may even reconceptualize our view of the terrain, shifting our whole frame of reference so as to gain a better understanding of what there is and how it "hangs together." Yet, that this is our epistemic lot does not warrant conferring the status of presumptive acceptability to all—or even some select subset of—the claims in our current belief set.

That a claim, *p*, is presumptively acceptable confers upon it a status of acceptable-by-default and places a positive burden to make a case against *p* (or against *p*'s presumptive acceptability) upon all those who would not accept it.

But no such burden exists for those who would doubt or deny any claim in our existing commitment set—not even ourselves! Granted, ordinarily we only revisit the acceptability of our present beliefs, that is, address the question of whether we should make any changes to them when faced with some reason to do so. Yet, while objectors to a presumption must *show cause*, that is, provide some *reason* counting against the presumption, all that is required to challenge our entitlement to a standing commitment is to call it into question—to raise doubt, to demand reasons, to withdraw commitment, any of which may be done without bringing any directly negatively relevant evidence to bear.[17]

To appreciate this point, consider Aijaz, McKeown-Green, and Webster's distinction between *attitudinal* and *dialectical* burdens. When unchallenged, our shared or background commitments do not have dialectical burdens, understood as a requirement to "*provide* sufficient evidential support for one's position," attached to them—yet we still bear an attitudinal burden, or a requirement to "*possess* sufficient evidential support for one's position."[18] Challenges to standing commitments only require shifting a standing, attitudinal burden to a dialectical one—that is, challenging a party to *produce* what it must already *possess*: its warrant, or entitlement, to some view. Practically such demands typically occur on the basis of some reasonable and particular doubt; when frequent, general, and unmotivated, such demands exhibit a skeptical frivolity. Yet epistemically they needn't be occasioned only by negatively relevant evidence specific to the claim challenged. Rather, the obligation to possess adequate warrant for our beliefs is a standing one, and a paradigmatic criterion for possession of adequate warrant is that we are able to produce it on demand.

Further, let us grant that typically we are both correct and justified in thinking that *overall* our beliefs are reliable and that we had some sufficiently good reason for adopting the particular beliefs we have. Yet, when challenged to demonstrate our entitlement, that we already accept the claim should not count as a reason in favor of its acceptability.

The mere availability of cognitive attitudes other than our own rationality obliges us to have some sufficient reason for the view we elect to retain rather than adopt some other view in its stead.[19] And, as fallible knowers, we ought to recognize that at least some of our standing beliefs are false or unwarranted. The problem, epistemically speaking, is we don't know *which*. The hope is that argumentation and critical inquiry are self-correcting procedures, reliably sorting good commitments from bad. The acceptability of our commitments, then, is best understood as a consequence of their standing at the *end* of our rational and argumentative undertakings, not their status at the *beginning*.

To sum up: While our ordinary epistemic practices demonstrate that we typically proceed on the basis that we are epistemically entitled to our existing commitments, this is normally done on the basis of good reasons. Ordinarily we rightly take ourselves to possess adequate warrant for our views, and, except in cases of disagreement, we normally confer this same entitlement upon others, while recognizing that each of us has a standing obligation to possess this warrant and may be called upon to produce it more-or-less on demand. Thus understood, this practice does not attribute presumptive acceptability to standing commitments, since our entitlement to them does not impose an obligation of a reverse burden of proof upon objectors.

Instead, *plausible* seems a modality that more aptly and accurately describes our entitlements and obligations concerning our standing commitments. Rescher explains plausibility as the fit, or coherence, particular claims have within the overall framework of our cognitive commitments. While plausibility conveys a tentative, defeasible but actionable entitlement, it does not connote the reverse burden of proof characteristic of presumptions, whereby objectors must either concede the claim or make some positive case against it. Rather, in cases of disagreement where each disagreeing party maintains one of several individually plausible but mutually incompatible views, no view is presumptively acceptable and each party must produce their attitudinal warrant for their standing view. Thus, plausibility is a more epistemically egalitarian modality for standing commitments, which better accords with our epistemic practices in cases of challenge and disagreement.

Next, the modality *presumably* is sometimes used to mark claims in reasoned discourse that have *some* probative merit, just not *enough* to meet some applicable threshold of acceptability. So-called "presumptive" arguments (e.g., informal schematic arguments) are typically described as making *defeasible, provisional*, or *tentative*—rather than *conclusive*—cases for their conclusions. As such, commitment to the conclusions of presumptive arguments should be tempered accordingly. Walton writes: "Presumption requires a notion of provisional commitment, not characterized by an obligation to defend the proposition in question, if challenged."[20] Similarly, Rescher introduces the notion of presumption by saying: "To *presume* in the presently relevant sense of the term is to accept something in the absence of the further relevant information that would ordinarily be deemed necessary to establish it."[21]

Both Rescher and Walton develop their accounts of presumption in terms of *pro tanto* reasoning and argument. Rescher uses the notion of a *prima facie* case, writing: "To make out a *prima facie* case for one's contention is to adduce considerations whose evidential weight is such that—in the absence of countervailing considerations—the 'reasonable presumption' is now in its favor, and the burden of proof [. . .] is now incumbent on the opposing party."[22] Walton uses the notion of an insufficient but plausible inference: "A presumption may be defined as a plausible inference based on a fact and a rule as premises, where the premises are insufficient to support the conclusion in accord with the link of warrant presenting the argumentation scheme joining the premises to the conclusion, and where a further boost is needed to gain a proper acceptance of the conclusion."[23] These accounts share the notion of a "provisionally adequate case,"[24] which Rescher introduces to capture the idea of an argument that may offer the best available reasons at the time but is nevertheless insufficient to conclusively establish its conclusion or otherwise falls short of some applicable standard of adequate support.

Sometimes, we may rely on tentatively accepted conclusions supported by provisionally adequate cases. As with standing commitments, that claims supported by pro tanto reasoning be qualified as *presumptively* acceptable is not itself a problem. Given the foregoing explanations, the modality is perspicuous and readily applied in most cases.

Yet, if this is *all* that presumption amounts to, the label "defeasibly" applies just as readily. After all, this modality also connotes a defeasible, but default and actionable, acceptability. And, reducing such uses of "presumption" to *defeasibility* offers a robust analysis of presumptive acceptability by indicating the defeasibility conditions for the default acceptability of a presumed claim, thereby signaling how the reverse burden of proof may be discharged. Further, a probabilistic understanding of defeasible acceptability analyzes *tentative*, presumptive commitment as *partial* commitment, thereby highlighting that partial commitment to a claim entails partial commitment to its contradictory.

A more pressing objection is this. Positions advocating a usage of "presumably" as an epistemic modal qualifier typically don't restrict presumptive justification to epistemic justification. Quite the opposite. As a rule, presumptive justification *essentially* involves practical or methodological considerations. Specifically, presumptions are presented as licensed or warranted, in part, by the practical need to move forward with reasoned discourse at some stage, whether initially or when some impasse is subsequently reached.

The claim that tentative, presumptive acceptability may be warranted on the basis of otherwise insufficient evidence is often invoked when the practical exigencies of circumstance call for a resolution of reasoned dialogue. Walton, for example, writes: "A proposition can be tentatively accepted as having the status of presumption even though the evidence supporting it at that present point in the dialog is insufficient for accepting it. The reason for accepting it [is] typically a practical one."[25] Similarly, Rescher claims: "A cognitive presumption, stakes a claim that outruns the substance of actually available information; it is a proposition that, in suitably favorable circumstances, is accepted as true in the absence of any counterindications."[26]

Yet, as I have observed elsewhere, "the mere need to get on with things and bring an argumentative discussion to a close is not a good reason to distribute probative responsibilities one way rather than another. Instead, we require *prin-*

*cipled* reasons why a claim should be presumed when insufficient evidence is available."[27] What we tend to find, then, in such practical justifications of presumption is reference to some nonepistemic end of the discursive activity.

Rescher, for example, writes that "presumptions are validated by their functional efficacy within their operative context and not by their statistical accuracy [i.e., reliability]."[28] He elaborates: "The justificatory rationale of our presumptive practice is in the end pragmatic. [. . .] [T]he processes of justification— the way of going at it—is always one and the same: pragmatic efficacy in regard to the functional/purposive teleology of the particular domain at issue. And, given the pragmatic justification of presumptions, the domain of epistemic presumption is a crossroad where considerations of practical and theoretical reason intersect. Those epistemic presumptions are, in effect, practical policies justified by their serviceability in the furtherance of our cognitive interests."[29] Walton's dialogical theory of presumption provides an equally explicit statement of the practical and nonepistemic rationale for presuming. Generalizing Walton's language slightly, the last three conditions for a presumption that $p$ can be stated as follows:

(1) $p$ is not sufficiently warranted by the available evidence;
(2) there is a condition (e.g., a presumptive inference rule) that supplies an appropriate practical warrant for $p$ (in the circumstance);
(3) when this practical warrant is factored in, $p$ is sufficiently warranted to shift a local burden of proof to an objector.[30]

On each account, presumptions are insufficiently warranted by purely epistemic considerations. Rather, an essential design feature of presumption is that it is tied to, and partly justified by, some nonalethic discursive end. Often this is presented as the need to move reasoned discourse forward in some way. And, the obstacle presented as causing the stagnation of reasoned progress is typically a lack of available evidence or other epistemically determinative resources.

Yet, in situations where the only discursive values or ends are epistemic, a lack of available evidence is not so much an obstacle to progress as an indication that the right epistemic attitude in that circumstance is to suspend judgement. Generally, we should weight our credences according to the available evidence. The need to reach some conclusion beyond this (e.g., to take a decision or form a determinative judgment about the matter at hand) will be motivated by some nonepistemic end.

Yet, if the acceptability of a presumed claim is not sufficiently warranted on the basis of purely epistemic considerations, why treat *presumably* as an epistemic modality? Moreover, if it is admitted that we can consistently or coherently presume things that we *know* are not so,[31] why treat presumptions as having any role in epistemic discourse? Doing so seems to mismanage the epistemic risks involved in theoretical reasoning,[32] in ways that are entirely avoidable given that a perfectly serviceable account of presumption as a nonepistemic modality is ready at hand.

## Presumption as a Modality in Practical Reasoning

As distinct from the preceding accounts, Ullmann-Margalit has formulated an account of the modality *presumably* that reflects the inherently practical aspects of presumptive justification. Presumption, Ullmann-Margalit writes, "is concerned not so much with *ascertaining* the facts as with *proceeding* on them. [. . .] Presumption rules belong to the realm of praxis, not theory. Their point is to enable us to get on smoothly with business of all sorts, to cut through impasses, to facilitate and expedite action."[33]

Three important features of Ullmann-Margalit's account help us to avoid the confusions and bad epistemic risk-management that comes from mistakenly treating pragmatically justified claims as though they *thereby* have some positive epistemic status.

First, presumption rules—which are used to inferentially generate presumptively acceptable claims—have rule subjects, such that they are "directed to any person who is engaged in a process of practical deliberation whose resolution materially depends, among other things, on an answer to the factual question of whether $q$ is or is not the case."[34] In this way, presumptive entitlement is restricted to reasoners who are engaged with some specific set of practical concerns. Correspondingly, the probative obligations generated by presumptive entitlements are only binding upon subjects of the presumption rule—that is, those beholden to the nonalethic discursive goals backing the presumptive warrant. So restricted, presumptive entitlements and obligations do not extend beyond the scope of those immediate concerns involved in licensing the presumption. As such presumptions cannot be carried over into theoretical reasoning or even to practical reasoning about other matters.

Second, Ullmann-Margalit explicitly recognizes that, because the justification of presumptions is at least partly nonevidential, the status of presumptions is not epistemic. "Where one has reasons for belief sufficient for grounding the action, there is no deliberation problem: it is to pave the way to action in default of such reasons that presumption rules come about."[35] One needn't presume (although one *may* in the right circumstances) where one can know or reasonably believe. As such, *presumably* is clearly demarcated as a nonepistemic modality.

Finally, because of this, Ullmann-Margalit restricts the application of presumption rules to practical, deliberative reasoning. Presumptively warranted entitlements and their correlative obligations are similarly restricted. "The [presumption] rule entitles one to hold $q$ as true for the purposes of concluding one's practical deliberation on the impending issue; it neither requires nor entitles one to believe that $q$. [. . .] [A presumption] rule sanctions the practical passage from $p$ to $q$ while at the same time acknowledging the possible falsity of $q$."[36] In this way, the propositional attitude licensed by presumption is similarly nonepistemic: it is one of *proceeding as if* q, rather than *taking it that* q, or *taking* q *to be the case*. As such, although "presumably" indicates a propositional attitude, the attitudinal stance modified is one of commitment not belief.[37]

A position along the lines of Ullmann-Margalit's permits the modality *presumably* to do the rational work it is properly suited to do, while preventing its mislabeling the epistemic modal status of claims in theoretical reasoning and truth-directed discourse. It grants that "cognitive presumptions function as instrumentalities of rational economy,"[38] without mistaking those instrumentalities for actualities.

## Conclusion

In this chapter I have argued, in agreement with Ullmann-Margalit, that *presumably* is best understood as a nonepistemic modality, modifying commitment to—not belief in—a claim among agents engaged in particular, purpose-specific episodes of deliberative reasoning or discourse.

Accounts that treat *presumably* as an epistemic modality fail to distinguish it from other modalities, particularly *defeasibly* or *plausibly*. Discursively, each of these modalities functions to moderate commitment to the claims it qualifies; logically, each marks and tracks the modal status of the sentences they modify. Ordinarily, "defeasibly" and "plausibly" are applied in ways roughly equivalent to, or corrective of, the prescribed uses of "presumably" in the accounts considered. Furthermore, they may be operationalized to have the same rational and discursive effects as *presumably*—redistributing probative burdens across standpoints by shifting a local burden of proof with respect to some plausible or defeasibly acceptable claim.

Accounts like those critiqued in the chapter take a reductive approach to analyzing presumption—they effectively reduce the modality *presumably* to other discursive modalities. By itself, this is not a criticism. After all, to the extent that accounts of these other modalities are well worked out, reduction to them would neatly solve the analytical problem of specifying the nature of presumption. The point becomes critical when it is noticed that these accounts do not provide an exclusively epistemic basis for presumption, but also invoke practical considerations tied to nonalethic discursive ends. Yet, such accounts proceed to treat presumption as an epistemic modality.

This is the move that I claim is mistaken, misleading, and avoidable. It is mistaken because it operationalizes a modal status of a claim that is partly founded on practical considerations as an epistemic modality. Yet, doxastic, deliberative, and other discursive attitudes towards a claim may differ, since they may rely on considerations of different sorts. While deliberative attitudes may be based on practical, nonalethic considerations, doxastic attitudes, if held rationally, should be based solely on alethically oriented, epistemic (e.g., evidential, reliabilist) considerations. Mistakenly basing epistemic modalities on practical considerations misleadingly labels claims as having one epistemic status when their actual or proper status is quite different. Such mislabeling defeats the logical purpose of modal qualifiers that serve, in part, to manage epistemic and deliberative risk by marking and tracking the statuses that claims have been established to have in reasoning and discourse. Accuracy in labeling contributes to an inferential risk-rating and risk-management system that prevents errors in reasoning and argumentation. Such errors can occur when, for example, we mistakenly rely on a claim in our theoretical reasoning as though it had some epistemic status when in actuality it has only been established as having a comparable status in practical or deliberative contexts. Mislabeling of this kind is avoidable because other modal qualifiers are available to do the work of "presumably" in theoretical reasoning and discourse. The modal qualifier "presumably" may then be reserved for use in practical reasoning and deliberative discourse in a way that accurately reflects the practical foundations of presumption as a modality and discursive status. Adopting such a stipulative policy of use for "presumably," based on the analysis of presumption proposed herein, would help avoid ambiguity-based confusion and epistemic risk in reasoning and argumentation.

## Notes

1. On this point, L. Bermejo-Luque rightly treats allocutions of "presumably, *p*" as *constative*, rather than *performative*, speech acts. While the speech act of presumption (that is, of presuming that *p*) has felicity conditions for successful performance, those generally differ from the satisfaction conditions for the sentence "Presumably, *p*." ("Being a Correct Presumption vs. Being Presumably the Case" *Informal Logic* 36, no. 1 [2016]: 1–25.) Analogously, assertions can be made without their being either true or warranted. Since the presumptive status of a claim is not, generally speaking, established by its having been presumed, normative theories of presumption should concentrate not on acts of presuming (that is, kinds of claimings) but on the contents of those acts (that is, kinds of claims).

Viewed as singular speech acts, utterances of "presumably, *p*" are *assertions*—the burden remains with the assertor to establish that *p* is presumptively acceptable. Against at least some readings of D. Walton ("The Speech Act of Presumption," *Prag-*

*matics & Cognition* 1, no. 1 [1993]: 125–48), the burden of proof with respect to *p* is not shifted in making the speech act of presuming that *p*; rather, as Bermejo-Luque recognizes, the burden of proof is only properly shifted when the satisfaction conditions for the sentence "Presumably, *p*" are met, and seen to have been met by the discussants. If disputed, showing that these conditions are met remains the obligation of the one making the presumption.

2. N. Rescher, *Dialectics: A Controversy-Oriented Approach to the Theory of Knowledge* (Albany: State University of New York Press, 1977), 30; N. Rescher, *Presumption and the Practices of Tentative Cognition* (Cambridge: Cambridge University Press, 2006), 14.

3. R. C. Pinto, *Argument, Inference, and Dialectic* (Dordrecht: Kluwer, 2001), 3–4.

4. U. Hahn and M. Oaksford, "The Burden of Proof and Its Role in Argumentation," *Argumentation* 2, no. 1 (March 2007): 39–61, 41.

5. E. Ullmann-Margalit, "On Presumptions," *Journal of Philosophy* 80, no. 3 (1983): 143–63.

6. See D. Godden and D. Walton, "A Theory of Presumption for Everyday Argumentation," *Pragmatics & Cognition* 15, no. 2 (2007): 313–46, for a survey of theories of presumption, and P. Bodlović, "Dialogical Features of Presumptions: Difficulties for Walton's New Dialogical Theory," *Argumentation* 31, no. 3 (2017): 513–34, for a critical survey of the development of Walton's account of presumption.

7. Rescher, *Presumption*, 11, 23, 27.

8. D. Walton, *Argumentation Schemes for Presumptive Reasoning* (Mahwah, NJ: Lawrence Erlbaum, 1996), 29.

9. D. Walton, C. Reed, and F. Macagno, *Argumentation Schemes* (Cambridge: Cambridge University Press, 2008), 12.

10. J. A. Blair, "Presumptive Reasoning/Argument: An Overlooked Class," *Protosociology* 13 (1999): 56.

11. Blair, "Presumptive Reasoning/Argument," 51–55.

12. For example, Walton, *Argumentation Schemes*, 13; D. Walton, "Abductive, Presumptive, and Plausible Arguments," *Informal Logic* 21, no. 2 (2001); D. Walton, "A Dialogical Theory of Presumption," *Artificial Intelligence and Law* 16, no. 2 (June 2008): 209–43; D. Walton, *Burden of Proof, Presumption, and Argumentation* (Cambridge: Cambridge University Press, 2014), ch. 3.

13. Walton, Reed, and Macagno, *Argumentation Schemes*, 10.

14. Rescher, *Presumption*, 39; see also Rescher, *Dialectics*, 37–41.

15. Rescher, *Dialectics*, 38; Rescher, *Presumption*, 42.

16. Rescher, *Dialectics*, 38–39; compare Rescher, *Presumption*, 42.

17. In holding that schematic presumptive arguments can be rebutted by asking a critical question that has no positive burden of production for the questioner, Walton's theory implicitly acknowledges this point. If posing a critical question sometimes amounts only to asking "Why *p*?" then it is not clear how presumptive arguments shift a burden of proof to an objector.

18. I. Aijaz, J. McKeown-Green, and A. Webster, "Burdens of Proof and the Case for Unevenness," *Argumentation* 27, no. 3 (2013): 261 (emphasis changed).

19. D. Godden, "Teaching Rational Entitlement and Responsibility: A Socratic Exercise," *Informal Logic (Teaching Supplement)* 34, no. 1 (2014): 124–51.

20. Walton, *Argumentation Schemes*, 18.

21. Rescher, *Presumption*, 1.

22. Rescher, *Dialectics*, 28; see also Rescher, *Presumption*, 7.

23. Walton, "Dialogical Theory of Presumption," 234.

24. Rescher, *Dialectics*, 28.

25. Walton, "Dialogical Theory of Presumption," 234–35.

26. Rescher, *Presumption*, 27.

27. D. Godden, "Review of: D. Walton, *Burden of Proof, Presumption and Argumentation*," *Cogency* 7, no. 1 (Winter 2015): 102.

28. Rescher, *Presumption*, 9.

29. Rescher, *Presumption*, 63; see also pp. 53–55.

30. Walton, "Dialogical Theory of Presumption," 235, presents the conditions in the context of presumption in argument stating them as:

[i] The argument is not sufficiently strong, based only on the evidence supporting the [...] premises to shift a burden of production to the respondent's side. [ii] The presumptive rule has a practical justification in line with the goal of the persuasion dialog. [iii] The argument is sufficiently strong, with the practical justification counted in, to shift a burden of production to the respondent's side.

The remaining conditions are not relevant to the point being made.

31. Bermejo-Luque, "Being a Correct Presumption," 10.

32. D. Godden, "Presumption as a Modal Qualifier: Presumption, Inference, and Managing Epistemic Risk," *Argumentation* 31, no. 3 (2017): 485–511.

33. Ullmann-Margalit, "On Presumptions," 147.

34. Ullmann-Margalit, "On Presumptions," 147.

35. Ullmann-Margalit, "On Presumptions," 152.

36. Ullmann-Margalit, "On Presumptions," 149.

37. See D. Godden, "The Importance of Belief in Argumentation: Belief, Commitment, and the Effective Resolution of a Difference of Opinion," *Synthese* 172, no. 2 (February 2010): 397–414.

38. Rescher, *Presumption*, 27.

# 17

# The Speech Act of Presumption by Reversal of Burden of Proof

Douglas Walton

This chapter clarifies the connection between presumption and burden of proof by refining the speech act analysis modeling how the putting forward of a presumption in a conversational exchange essentially works by reversing the burden of proof already operative in the exchange. To help the reader really understand how presumptions work, three everyday examples and two legal examples of presumptions are given in the first section. Clarifications of terminology are offered in the second section, where presumptions are distinguished from assumptions, assertions, presuppositions, and defeasible reasoning. In the third section, a brief explanation of the relationship between presumption and burden of proof is given. In the fourth section, the theory that the speech act of making a presumption works essentially by reversal of burden of proof is explained and defended. In the fifth section, the theory is applied to the five examples previously givens in the first section.

## Five Examples of Presumptions

Art normally leaves the office to walk home every day at 4:00 p.m. Betty normally meets Art on Wellington Crescent at exactly 4:30 p.m. every weekday in order to give him a lift home. But sometimes they need to cancel this arrangement, for example if Art wants to walk all the way home, or if there is very bad weather. To make this arrangement work, it would be tedious if they had to phone each other every day to confirm pickup or not. For this reason, they have adopted the convention that if one does not hear from the other on any given day before 4:00 p.m., the presumption in place is that they will meet on Wellington Crescent at 4:30 p.m.

The second example, summarized from the more detailed account given in Walton's *Plausible Argument in Everyday Conversation*,[1] is often taken to be the classic case of a presumption. David Livingstone left England in 1866 on an expedition to try to find the source of the Nile. Subsequently, very little was heard of him, but he was thought to be in a certain area near Lake Tanganyika. Henry Morton Stanley reached this area in 1871 and saw a pale, gray-bearded white man wearing a navy cap in the center of a large crowd of tribesmen and Arabs who came rushing toward him. At that point, Stanley uttered his famous words, "Dr. Livingstone I presume."

In the third example, summarized below from the same book by Walton,[2] a memo was sent to all university faculty members from the library telling them that a large backlog of old examination papers no longer being used by students had piled up. The memo went on to say that unless the sender hears from any faculty that they still wish to keep these papers, the latter will be withdrawn from circulation.

The fourth example is presumption of death in law. For example, suppose that a person has disappeared, and no trace has been found of him. Should we assume that he is still alive, or after a number of years, can it be assumed that he is dead? In order to deal with issues concerning wills and estates, the courts in a particular jurisdiction may rule that a person is presumed to be dead for legal purposes if there has been no evidence that he is still alive for the last X years. In such a case, there is a presumption that the person is dead, even though there is no hard evidence to support it, apart from his having disappeared without a trace X years ago.

The fifth example is a kind of case often cited as an example in textbooks on evidence law. In this version[3] the plaintiff suffered a fall on a dark stairway in an apartment building. He sued the defendant, the building's owner, claiming that she did not keep the stairway in a safe condition, namely that the lighting did not work properly. To prove notice, the defendant claimed she had mailed a letter to the plaintiff informing him that several of the lights in the stairway no longer worked.

The legal ruling on the fifth example[4] was that the letter is presumed to have been received. A legal rule states that a letter properly addressed, stamped, and deposited in an appropriate receptacle is presumed to have been received in the ordinary course of the mail. Unless the presumption created by this rule is rebutted, the properly addressed, stamped, and deposited letter will be deemed to have been received in what is considered to be the ordinary amount of time needed in that delivery area.

## Distinguishing Presumptions from Related Notions

The first task of any theory of presumption is to distinguish between presumptions and associated notions such as assumptions, assertions, presuppositions, and defeasible reasoning. According to the account given in Walton's *Plausible Argument*, chapter 2, a presumption is a special kind of assumption that, like an assumption, needs to be backed up by evidence if challenged, but the burden of proof in the two cases is different. The proponent of an assumption has to give some argument to back it up if the respondent requires this prior to acceptance. In the case of a presumption, the burden of proof is the other way around. The proposition put forward with the presumption is taken for granted as accepted by both parties unless the respondent comes up with some reason for rejecting it.

An assertion is different both from an assumption and a presumption.[5] If an assumption is challenged, the proponent may reply that it's just an assumption, and she really has no evidence, at least right now, to back it up to make it acceptable by both parties. But she can still argue that it is worthwhile going ahead hypothetically with this assumption, because it will lead somewhere interesting. An assertion, on the other hand, carries with it an immediate burden of proof to either provide backup evidence or to immediately give up the assertion. Failure to do so means that the proponent can no longer hold it as an assertion, although she might still hold it as an assumption.

A presumption is different from a presupposition. To understand the difference, you have to visualize a dialogue sequence of questions and replies containing argumentation between two parties, conventionally called the proponent and the respondent. Such a dialogue essentially involves turn taking, so that as each party makes its move, the other party is expected to reply to that move in an appropriate way, after which the first party has a chance to reply to the reply, and so forth. Presupposition essentially refers to the sequence of moves prior to the particular move which is the case in point. For example, the question "Why did you kill the victim?" presupposes that there was a victim and that the respondent killed the victim. In other words, the asking of this question presupposes a prior sequence of dialogue between the two parties in which the respondent committed himself to the proposition that he killed the victim.[6] Hence we say that this proposition was a presupposition of the question.

Presumption, in contrast, is directed toward the future sequence of such a dialogue. The putting forward of a proposition as a presumption influences how the respondent can or must reply at the next move. If the respondent makes no move to deny the presumption, giving a reason for the denial, it will be assumed by all parties that the respondent accepts the presumption, and it will be lodged in place as a proposition henceforth accepted by the speaker and hearer. However, it leaves open the possibility that the hearer can deny that the presumption holds, provided that he can offer some reason supporting this denial. You could say that both presumption and presupposition have a certain structure as moves embedded in an orderly sequence of dialogue in which two parties are taking turns engaging in argumentation with each other.

Reasoning on the basis of accepting a presumption is a species of defeasible reasoning but is not the same thing as defeasible reasoning. Defeasible reasoning is provisional acceptance of the conclusion, where the argument used to derive the conclusion has at least one premise that is a generalization that is subject to exceptions. For example, consider the following argument: birds fly; Tweety is a bird; therefore, Tweety flies. This argument is classified as a defeasible one on the basis that if new evidence comes in informing us that although Tweety is a bird, Tweety is a penguin, Tweety is therefore a type of bird that does not fly. The argument still holds in general but is defeated as applied to the case in point, namely the case where Tweety is a penguin. Some would say that this argument is presumptive by claiming that the universal generalization that birds fly is only presumptively acceptable because it can be defeated in special cases, such as the case where Tweety is a penguin. However, this is not quite right. The universal generalization still holds, even though the argument defaults in the case where Tweety is a penguin.

A distinction might be drawn here between a broader and narrower sense of the term "presumption." In the broader sense, the Tweety example does represent what might be called presumptive reasoning. But it is not appropriate to classify the defeasible universal generalization that birds fly as a presumption, even though it can be made inapplicable by pointing to an exception in the given case. What this discussion suggests is that there is a broader sense of the term "presumption" in which all instances of defeasible reasoning are presumptive in nature, meaning that they can default if evidence comes in to show that they do not hold in a particular case at issue.

## Presumption and Burden of Proof

It has long been known that there is close connection between presumption and burden of proof,[7] but the precise nature of the connection proved to be elusive and slippery before its recent clarification in formal dialectical models of argumentation. Rescher wrote[8] that a presumption is not a form of evidence arising from factual knowledge, but rather something we take to be acceptable on a tentative basis in a situation where there is a lack of evidence for not accepting it. On his account, "a presumption indicates that in the absence of specific counterindications we are to accept how things as a rule are taken as standing."[9] On his theory, presumption needs to be understood in relation to two kinds of burden of proof.[10] The first kind is what he called the probative burden of proving an initiating assertion. Basically, this requires that when a participant in a dialogue makes a claim that is the subject of disputation representing the topic of a dialogue, he or she incurs a continuing burden of supporting it with an argument. Second, there is the burden of coming forward with the evidence.[11] This burden is also often called the burden of producing

evidence in law. What Rescher called the probative burden of proving an initiating assertion is comparable to what is called "the burden of persuasion" in law.

The probative burden of an initiating assertion remains constant during
the entire dialectical proceeding. This burden expresses the rule that whoever
initiates an assertion in a dialogue has the burden of supporting it with argument. The contrasting burden is called the evidential burden of further reply
in the face of contrary considerations. This burden of going forward with evidence shifts from side to side as particular moves are made in the course of the
dialogue as the argumentation proceeds.[12] Having defined burden of proof in
this dialectical fashion, Rescher went on to define presumption in the framework of a context of dialogue where burden of proof is operative.[13] Presumption is defined[14] as a device that shifts the burden of proof from one side to
the other during a disputation. Thus, if one side puts forward a claim in a case
where there is insufficient evidence to prove it, presumption can be used as a
device to gain tentative acceptance of the claim by shifting the burden of coming forward with evidence against the other side to provide counterevidence. If
the other side cannot provide such counterevidence, the claim should be held
tentatively acceptable to both sides, assuming that there is some evidence supporting the claim, and no stronger evidence refuting it.[15]

## The Speech Act of Making a Presumption

According to the dialectical theory of presumption presented in *Plausible Argument in Everyday Conversation*,[16] presumption is a kind of speech act in dialogue that is in the middle between assertion and assumption. When a proponent in a dialogue asserts a proposition, if the respondent asks for justification,
the proponent must either give an argument to justify the proposition or she
must retract the proposition. This requirement is often called the burden of
proof. What it means is that if you assert something, you are committed to the
truth or acceptability of what you asserted. Hence you are obliged to back it
up if you are challenged. This requirement then is a kind of rationality assumption that defines the nature of assertion as a speech act in dialogue. Assumption may be contrasted with assertion. You are free to assume any proposition
you like in a dialogue. There is no burden of proof attached. You can assume
that the moon is made of green cheese, for purposes of a discussion. There is
no "cost" or "burden" attached. Presumption is a dialectical notion that fits in
between assertion and assumption. If you presume that something is true, you
don't have to prove that it is true, or offer evidence to prove it. But you do have
to give it up if the other party can prove it is false. Simply put, the dialectical
function of a presumption is to reverse a burden of proof.

Others, including Rescher,[17] Ullmann-Margalit,[18] Cohen[19] and Freeman[20] appear to agree with this principle of presumption. Freeman's theory of presumptive acceptability[21] is based on a concept of presumption tracing back to the account given by Cohen,[22] which states that a presumption is a proposition that may be taken for granted in the absence of reasons against doing so.[23] Rescher[24] is broadly in agreement with this model of presumption when he writes that defeasible presumptions are closely interconnected with notion of burden of proof. In fact, he appears to be advocating the key defining feature of this model when he writes that defeasible presumption can be simply characterized as the reverse of an evidential burden of proof.

According to the dialectical theory of presumption presented in *Plausible Argument in Everyday Conversation*,[25] there are four kinds of conditions governing the operation of the speech act of presumption in a dialogue. The preparatory conditions state that a proponent and a respondent are engaged in a dialogue in which a proposition $A$ is a useful assumption. The placement condition states that $A$ is brought forward for acceptance by the proponent, that the respondent has an opportunity to reject $A$, and that as long as he fails to reject it, $A$ becomes a commitment of both parties. The retraction conditions state that the respondent can retract commitment to $A$ at any point in the succeeding dialogue, provided that he can give evidence to support such a rejection. But the retraction condition also states that the respondent is obliged to let the presumption stay in place in the discussion unless he can give such evidence. The burden conditions state two requirements. One is that at any given point in the dialogue, the proponent has the burden of showing that assuming $A$ has some practical value in moving the discussion forward. The other requirement is that past this point in the dialogue the respondent must let the presumption stays in place long enough for the proponent to make whatever use of it he has proposed.

In formal dialogue systems the speech acts are the locutions—such as making an assertion, asking a question, or putting forward an argument—that are permissible to make at each move of a dialogue. Each speech act in a dialogue has protocols that defines what kinds of moves are allowed and what kinds of responses that the other party in the dialogue is allowed to make immediately afterwards. Making a presumption can be defined as a distinctive type of speech act in a persuasion dialogue that is different from the simpler speech act of making an assertion. When a party in a dialogue makes an assertion, that party immediately incurs a burden of proof to provide an argument supporting the assertion if the other party questions the assertion. This requirement of fulfilling burden of proof stems from the global burden set at the beginning of the dialogue, but it is a local burden because it pertains to a specific move, or a local sequence of moves, during some segment of the argumentation stage.

The list of preparatory conditions, placement conditions, retraction conditions, and burden conditions[26] defines the protocols for the speech act of putting forward a presumption as well as the protocols for responding appropriately to it. This set of speech act conditions defines the notion of presumption itself by specifying the requirements on how a presumption has to be put forward, and on whether or not it is deemed to be acceptable at points in a dialogue later than the particular point where it was put forward. This set of defining conditions can be briefly summed up in the following five points:

(1) At some point in a dialogue a proposition can be brought forward by the proponent as a presumption, meaning that the proponent is asking the respondent to tentatively accept this proposition for the sake of argument.

(2) The proponent does not have to prove this proposition in order to make it acceptable as a presumption, but the respondent has the opportunity to reject it.

(3) However, the respondent can only reject this proposition as a presumption if he offers an appropriate argument against it.

(4) Essentially then, the local burden of proof for presumption is reversed from the normal distribution of the local burden of proof for the speech act of making an assertion.

(5) During the rest of the dialogue exchange, unless the respondent discharges the burden of proof to rebut the presumption, the proposition that is presumed stays in place as tentatively accepted by both parties.

The question remains open of how strong the rebutting argument needs to be in order to dislodge the presumption. This question is taken up in the last section of this chapter.

This dialectical model of shifting of the burden of proof by presumption can be summarized very simply. Presumption is like assertion except that the burden of proof is reversed. When you make an assertion, you are obliged to prove it. But when you make a presumption you are not obliged to prove it. You are only obliged to give it up if the other party can disprove it (or, on the other standard, give evidence against it). Those familiar with fallacies will immediately recognize a relationship between presumption and the argument known as the argument from ignorance—the *argumentum ad ignorantiam* in the logic textbooks.[27] This form of argument, better called the argument from lack of evidence, has the following argumentation scheme: $A$ has not been proven to be true (false), therefore, $A$ is false (true). Rescher[28] also appreciated the connection between the notion of presumption and the argument from lack of evidence. On his theory, presumptions arise from a situation of there being a lack of counterevidence to refute a claim even though there is insufficient evidence to prove it.

## Application to the Examples

In the first example, if neither person calls the other during the day, it is presumed that Betty will be in the designated location on Wellington Crescent at 4:30 p.m. that day, and that Art will leave work at 4:00 p.m. as usual, and so will arrive at Wellington Crescent by 4:30 p.m. In this case the presumption is put in place by the acceptance of an earlier general convention (rule) between the two parties. Unless one party contacts the other and cancels the conventional agreement temporarily for that particular day, it is assumed that the convention is to be taken as applicable by both parties on that day. Here, in the absence of evidence of any exception to the general rule, the convention adopted by both of them is taken to imply that the presumption holds.

In the second example it is interesting to conjecture what the evidential basis for the reasonableness of the presumption is. One basis was that it would be reasonable to expect that there would be very few or no other persons having the appearance of this person except Livingstone in this area at this time. Thus, even though it is possible that this person could be someone other than Livingstone, it is certainly a reasonable presumption that in fact he was Livingstone. The proposition that this man was in fact Livingstone is subject to some doubt, but the evidence supporting it is the basis of a defeasible argument for the conclusion. But even so, Stanley did not ask the individual whether he was in fact Livingstone or not. Perhaps for reasons of politeness he told the man that he was presuming that he was Livingstone. This left the respondent room to deny it, if in fact he wished to do so. But if he made no response of this sort, Stanley would draw the reasonable conclusion that it was indeed Livingstone whom he was facing.

The third example shows that the absence of evidence of anyone expressing disagreement with the proposal to withdraw the old examination paper from circulation will be taken as constituting support for going ahead. This use of a presumption shifts an evidential burden onto the disagreeing party to offer some reason why the papers should not be withdrawn.

In the fourth example, the problem is that it cannot be proved that the person is dead—for example, by finding the body. But legally it can be presumed that he is dead, based on a law in a jurisdiction specifying an unexplained absence over some conventionally accepted time period. Why is such a presumption reasonable to act on? There are two basic reasons. One is that if he were alive, then presumably there would be some evidence that he is alive. The other is that there is no such positive evidence. Hence, we draw the conclusion, by presumptive inference, that he is not alive, that is, that he is dead. Once again, this is an argument from negative evidence (ignorance, or absence of evidence) that shifts the evidential burden to the other side. Note that the argument is defeasible. If evidence turns up suggesting that the man is or might be alive, the presumption could be refuted.

In the fifth example, the two arguments, the plaintiff's and the defendant's, are pitted against each other. Since this is a civil case, all he has to do to win is to prove to the standard of the preponderance of the evidence that the defendant is liable for injuries he sustained while walking down a dark stairway in a building that she owned. This seems like a strong argument because it is supported by evidence that the lighting in the stairway did not work properly and therefore the stairway was unsafe. Moreover, as the owner of the building, the defendant is responsible for keeping the stairways in a safe condition. The structure of the sequence of argumentation composed of three subarguments is shown in figure 17.1.

How could the defendant produce a counterargument? If she could argue that she had warned the plaintiff that the stairway was unsafe, this could be a strong enough argument to defeat the defendant's argument. She did have such an argument, but there was a weakness in it. She could argue that she had mailed a letter to the plaintiff informing him that several of the lights in the stairway no longer worked. But the problem is that the statement that she had mailed such a letter, even with evidence backing it up, is only a probabilistic basis for concluding that the plaintiff actually received the letter and was therefore warned about the lights no longer working. However, because there is a presumption in law that a letter properly addressed, stamped, and deposited in an appropriate receptacle is presumed to have been received by the person to whom it was addressed, the landlord could argue that on a balance of probabilities the plaintiff did receive this letter. And if he did receive it, it can be presumed that he was warned that the stairway was unsafe because the lighting was not working.

If we look at the argument diagram for the defendant's argument shown in figure 17.2, we see that three arguments are involved in the main structure of the argumentation, labeled a1, a2 and a3. The first of these arguments, a1, has a defeasible *modus ponens* form, but one of its premises is questionable. Why would there be reason to believe that the defendant had informed the plaintiff that the lights no longer worked? The backup argument supporting this premise, a2, also has the defeasible modus ponens form, but one of its premises needs further support, namely, the claim that the plaintiff received the letter from the defendant. Here the defendant is in a weak position because

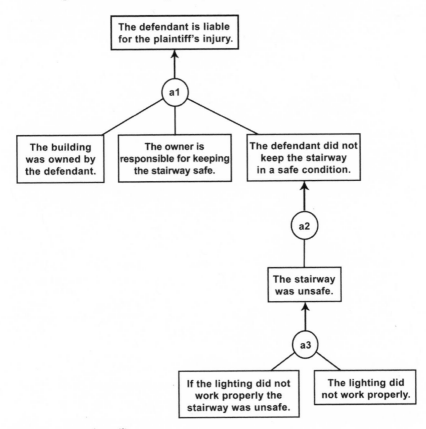

Figure 17.1. The plaintiff's argument

even though she might be able to support her claim that she mailed a letter to the plaintiff warning her that the lights no longer worked in the stairway, this claim is not enough to substantially support the conclusion that he actually received the letter. But here she can invoke the legal presumption stated in the other premise, to the effect that if one party has mailed a properly addressed, stamped letter to another, it is presumed that the other party received it. The argument based on these two premises, a3, may not be strong enough, however, to make the preponderance of evidence standard. It needs a boost in order for it to even be considered relevant. To provide this boost, argument a3 is considered to be an acceptable presumptive inference, and so it can take its place in the sequence of argument leading to the defendant's ultimate conclusion, the *stasis* proposition in the case.

Given that the presumption is acceptable, the argument as a whole might be strong enough to support the opposite conclusion, the proposition that the defendant is not liable to the plaintiff for the injuries he sustained while walk-

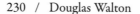

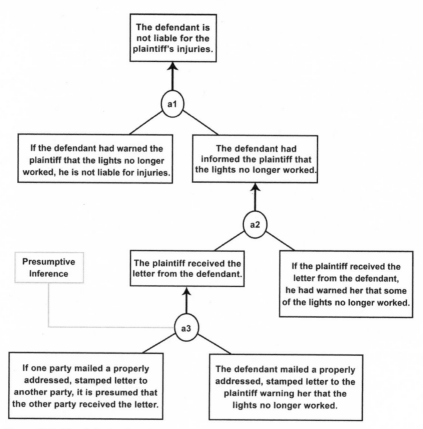

Figure 17.2. The defendant's argument

ing down the dark stairway in the building that she owned. The final outcome depends on which argument is stronger, the plaintiff's argument or the defendant's. That will be decided by the judge.

Notice however that the *modus ponens* argument a3 is not a deductive type of *modus ponens* argument, but a defeasible one. It could be that even though the lighting did not work properly, there might be some reason defeating the argument for the conclusion that the stairway was not safe. For example, it is possible that lighting from the room leading to the stairway sufficiently lighted the stairway so that it was arguably not unsafe under these conditions. The lighting in the stairwell not working does not give a conclusive reason for the claim that the stairway was unsafe.

In this case, then, the defendant's argument is not very strong because just because she put the letter in the mail, it does not follow by deductive logic that plaintiff received the letter, read it, and was warned. But it does shift a burden of proof to his side. Unless he can provide some evidence that he did not receive the letter, the defendant's argument, as imperfect as it is deductively, might stand a good chance of prevailing on a basis of the balance of probabilities.

## Rebutting Presumptions

How much evidence does it take to refute a presumption? Two theories of presumption have been offered in law on this matter.[29] According to the so-called Bursting Bubble (Thayer-Wigmore) theory of presumption, the presumption is cancelled by evidence challenging it. This theory says that presumptions are "like bats flitting in the twilight, but disappearing in the sunshine of actual facts."[30] It says that a presumption should have no effect once "rebutted" with evidence challenging the presumed fact. Suppose that the respondent did not challenge the proponent's proper addressing, stamping, and mailing of the letter, but testified that, during the whole period in question, he picked up and diligently read his mail each day and never saw the letter. On the Bursting Bubble theory, the presumption that the respondent received the letter is cancelled. The jury would now be left "to apply its sense of logic and experience" to determine whether the respondent received the letter or not.[31]

According to the other theory, the Morgan-McCormick theory, once a presumption is raised by its proponent, the burden of proof shifts to the opponent,[32] or otherwise the presumption stands. This theory holds that the Bursting Bubble theory gives too "slight and evanescent" effect to presumptions.[33] On this theory, "if the jury finds that the proponent properly addressed, stamped, and mailed the letter sufficiently in advance of the accident, the respondent must prove it more likely than not he received the letter or suffer a finding that he did."[34]

Thus, there are differing theories in law on how much evidence it should take to rebut a presumption. One approach requires that a presumption is refuted by any evidence offered by an opponent. The other says that the burden of proof shifts, and that the opponent has to disprove the presumption. The question of how much evidence it should take to rebut a presumption is a very interesting one for evaluating evidential weights in everyday argumentation outside legal settings. Using extensive case studies of complex arguments, Prakken and Sartor[35] and Walton[36] use graph structures, essentially argument diagrams along with other tools along with formal argumentation models to offer answers to this general question.

Basically, the evaluation of argumentation in given cases is weighed by the global burden of persuasion set at the opening stage, as well as other factors determined by the argument graph representing the structure of the sequence of argumentation around the local area where the presumption is operative. The graph links up the chain of argumentation in a given case, propagating the argumentation forward to the ultimate conclusion to be proved. Along the way, some propositions could be useful as premises but they are too weakly supported to meet the appropriate evidential standard of proof. Still, they carry some evidential weight and could be used if none of the parties in the dialogue care to dispute them. In such as case, the usual standard could be relaxed by the putting forward of a presumption reversing the burden of proof, according to the protocols of the model. So, whether a proposition is acceptable as a presumption depends on the burden of proof, which in turn depends on the standard of proof, on the weight of the evidence for it, and on the weight of the evidence against it. To sum up, conditions are right for putting it forward and even for accepting it as a presumption (1) if there is not enough evidence supporting it as a claim (assertion), (2) but there is some evidence supporting it, even if it is only negative evidence, and (3) there is no evidence against it.

## Notes

The author would like to thank the Social Sciences and Humanities Research Council for an award (Canada of Insight Grant 435-2012-0104), which supported the research presented in this chapter.

1. Douglas Walton, *Plausible Argument in Everyday Conversation* (Albany: State University of New York Press, 1992), 62.

2. Walton, *Plausible Argument*, 69.

3. Roger C. Park, David P. Leonard, and Steven H. Goldberg, *Evidence Law* (St. Paul, MN: West Group, 1998), 107.

4. Park, Leonard, and Goldberg, *Evidence Law*, 103.

5. Walton, *Plausible Argument*, 45.

6. Fabrizio Macagno, "Presupposition as Argumentative Reasoning," in *Interdisciplinary Studies in Pragmatics, Culture and Society*, ed. A. Capone and J. L. Mey (Cham, Switzerland: Springer, 2015), 465–87.

7. David M. Godden and Douglas Walton, "A Theory of Presumption for Everyday Argumentation," *Pragmatics and Cognition* 15, no. 2 (2007): 313–46.

8. Nicholas Rescher, *Presumption and the Practices of Tentative Cognition* (Cambridge: Cambridge University Press, 2006), 6.

9. Nicholas Rescher, *Dialectics* (Albany: State University of New York Press, 1977), 30.

10. Rescher, *Dialectics*, 27.

11. Rescher, *Presumption and the Practices*, 17.

12. Rescher, *Dialectics*, 27.

13. Rescher, *Presumption and the Practices*, ch. 3.

14. Rescher, *Presumption and the Practices*, 22.

15. Fabrizio Macagno and Douglas Walton, "Presumptions in Legal Argumentation," *Ratio Juris* 25, no. 2 (2012): 271–300.

16. Walton, *Plausible Argument*, 56–61.

17. Rescher, *Dialectics*; and Rescher, *Presumption and the Practices*.

18. Edna Ullmann-Margalit, "On Presumption," *Journal of Philosophy* 80, no. 3 (1983): 233–54.

19. L. Jonathan Cohen, *An Essay on Belief and Acceptance* (Oxford: Oxford University Press, 1992).

20. James B. Freeman, *Acceptable Premises* (Cambridge: Cambridge University Press, 2005).

21. Freeman, *Acceptable Premises*, 21.

22. Cohen, *Essay*, 4.

23. Godden and Walton, "Theory of Presumption," 329.

24. Rescher, *Dialectics*, 32.

25. Walton, *Plausible Argument*, 280–82.

26. Douglas Walton, "The Speech Act of Presumption," *Pragmatics and Cognition* 1, no. 3 (1993): 139–40.

27. Douglas Walton, "Presumption, Burden of Proof and Lack of Evidence," *L'Analisi linguistica e letteraria* 16 (2008): 49–71.

28. Nicholas Rescher, *Plausible Reasoning* (Assen: Van Gorcum, 1976); Rescher, *Dialectics*; Rescher, *Presumption and the Practices*.

29. Park, Leonard, and Goldberg, *Evidence Law*, ch. 4.

30. Park, Leonard, and Goldberg, *Evidence Law*, 109.

31. Park, Leonard, and Goldberg, *Evidence Law*, 110.

32. Park, Leonard, and Goldberg, *Evidence Law*, 111–12.

33. Park, Leonard, and Goldberg, *Evidence Law*, 111.

34. Park, Leonard, and Goldberg, *Evidence Law*, 112.

35. Henry Prakken and Giovanni Sartor, "A Logical Analysis of Burdens of Proof," in *Legal Evidence and Burden of Proof*, ed. Hendrik Kaptein, Henry Prakken, and Bart Verheij (Farnham: Ashgate, 2009).

36. Douglas Walton, *Burden of Proof, Presumption, and Argumentation* (Cambridge: Cambridge University Press, 2014).

# 18

# Some Presumptions

EDNA ULLMANN-MARGALIT

## The Explication of Presumption: An Outline

The *presumption formula* is "pres $(P, Q)$," to be read as "*P* raises the presumption that *Q*." (For example, a person's unexplained absence for seven years or more raises the presumption that this person is dead.) *P* is said to be the presumption-raising (generic) fact, *Q* the (generic) presumed fact. (Lower-case letters will stand for particular descriptions of states of affairs.) The presumption formula is said to *apply* in a certain concrete instance when the generic presumption-raising fact is instantiated in that instance. The presumption formula is interpreted as expressing a *presumption rule*, directed at the *rule subjects*. A rule subject is any person who is engaged in a process of practical deliberation whose resolution materially depends, among other things, on an answer to the factual question of whether $q$ is or is not the case. The rule is this:

> Given that $p$ is the case, you (= the rule subject) shall proceed as if $q$ were the case, unless or until you have (sufficient) reason to believe that $q$ is not the case.

Even though the presumption formula is propositional in nature ("the presumption that $Q$") and thus ostensibly about facts, it is concerned not so much with *ascertaining* facts as with *proceeding* on them. This praxis orientation (as opposed to theory orientation) is brought out by the rule interpretation. The presumption rule is not to be construed as involving an inference from the presumption-raising fact $P$ to the presumed fact $Q$. Rather, it is construed as sanctioning, for its subjects, the practical passage from $p$ to $q$: it enables the subject whose practical deliberation process is stranded on the factual question "$q$ or not $q$?" to get on and take action on the assumption that $q$, given that $p$. Thus, it functions as a means of extrication from unresolved deliberation processes; it supplies a procedure for decision by default.

The presumption-that-$q$ is rebuttable, however. The unless-or-until clause in the presumption rule is the *rebuttal clause*. The presumption that $q$ and the proceed-as-if-$q$ injunction corresponding to it are taken to be triggered *in the absence of* certain reasons for belief (i.e., reasons to believe that not-$q$). But once the deliberator is *in possession of* reasons for belief (that not-$q$), the presumption (that $q$) is rebutted and the injunction (to proceed as if $q$) is annulled. The weight of the reasons required for the rebuttal of a presumption varies with *the degree of strength* of the presumption.

If a presumption rule applies in a certain instance, it is there prior to the deliberation process and may at times preempt that process altogether. The situation may be pictured as involving scales which, owing to the presumption rule and the bias inherent in it, are tilted (toward the $q$ side) *to begin with*—hence the "pre-" of "presumption"—and where the balance can be reversed only when a certain weight is put on the other side.

So much for the explication. Now many interesting questions relate to the context of the *justification* of presumptions. This is taken to involve two distinct justificatory tasks. The first concerns the justification of there being a presumption rule—some presumption rule—in situations of a certain type, rather than there being no presumption rule in those situations at all. It is here that the role of presumption rules as a method of extrication is expounded. The second concerns the justification of the specific presumption espoused by the presumption rule: why this presumption rather than some alternative? It is here that the peculiar blend of considerations justifying a specific presumption is spelled out. This consists primarily, on the one hand, of inductive-probabilistic considerations (having to do with the likelihood of $q$, given $p$) and, on the other, of two-tiered normative considerations (having to do [a] with the question of which sort of error is morally or socially more acceptable: acting on $q$ when not-$q$ is in fact the case, or vice-versa; and [b] with the moral or social evaluation of the regulative effect on people's behavior of the presumption rule's being instituted and operative).

## Grice's Cooperative Principle

In this section[1] I propose to recast H. P. Grice's Cooperative Principle[2] as a presumption governing the interpretations of utterances rather than as a principle governing the production of utterances. My purpose in so doing is twofold: first, I believe that the reconstruction in presumptive terms is truer to the facts of the conversational situation, and, second, I believe it may offer a solution to a problem Grice himself poses, referring to it as "fundamental" (68) and confessing to be unhappy with his own answers to it.

The Cooperative Principle (CP)—"a rough general principle which participants will be expected (*ceteris paribus*) to observe"—is this:

Make your conversational contribution such as is required, at the stage
at which it occurs, by the accepted purpose or direction of the talk exchange in which you are engaged. (67)

Given that talk exchanges characteristically have some goal, or at least a mutually accepted direction, Grice contends that they will be profitable only on
the assumption that their participants in general observe the CP and its attendant maxims, which he proceeds to list and discuss.

The rendition of this principle as an Interpretative Presumption of Cooperation (IPC) will be this:

Your interlocutor's having uttered a sentence in a talk exchange in which
you are both engaged raises the presumption that the sentence is an appropriate contribution to the accepted purpose or direction of the talk
exchange.

This is the presumption formula. The way it is spelled out as a rule is this:

Given that your interlocutor has uttered $u$ in a talk exchange in which
you are both engaged, you shall proceed (i.e., interpret $u$) as if $u$ is an appropriate contribution to the accepted purpose or direction of the talk
exchange, unless or until you have (sufficient) reason to believe that it is
an inappropriate contribution thereto.

The presumption may of course be rebutted. This will happen once one has
what one judges in the circumstances to be sufficient reasons to believe that
one's interlocutor has violated one of the maxims of appropriateness, or opted
out, either explicitly or implicitly, of the conversational goal altogether. This is
not at all uncommon. (To the extent that one believes one's interlocutor to have
"flouted" a maxim, this will not rebut the presumption but will lead one instead, in Grice's spirit, to impute to one's partner a conversational implicature.)
The way I view the matter, this rule of IPC is a member, perhaps an hon-
orific member, of a class of interpretative presumptions that come to our aid
in resolving practical deliberations involving a bit of human behavior, either
verbal or nonverbal. Given on the one hand, the pressing and continuous need
for us to get on in situations of transaction with people, where we necessarily
have to base our actions (or reactions) on an ascription to them of certain intentions and motivations, and, on the other hand, the fact that people's inten-

tions and motivations are to us always a matter shrouded in some degree of doubt or uncertainty, the call for some interpretative presumptions as a useful extrication method is apparent.

We are dealing, then, not with situations in which a prescription—concerning the production of utterances—is being imposed upon the speaker, but rather in which a way out—from a potential interpretation problem—is being offered to the hearer. Incidentally, the main use to which Grice himself puts his CP, namely, that of characterizing the notion of conversational implicature, turns on the interpretation of utterances, not on their issuance: "The hearer is faced with a minor problem: how can [the speaker's] saying what he did say be reconciled with the supposition that he is observing the overall CP? This situation is one which characteristically gives rise to a conversational implicature" (69).

As for the justification of this specific IPC, as distinct from the justification of there being a presumption rule in this area to begin with, I take it to be grounded in the following considerations. First, there is the inductive-probabilistic consideration spelled out by Grice himself[3]:

> it is just a well-recognized empirical fact that people *do* behave in these ways; they have learned to do so in childhood, and have not lost the habit of doing so; and indeed it would involve a good deal of effort to make a radical departure from the habit. It is much easier, for example, to tell the truth than to invent lies. (68)

That is, according to Grice, when a person contributes to a conversation usually his contribution is indeed appropriate to its purpose or direction. But the last sentence in this quotation already touches on another justifying consideration: the determinateness consideration: once the need for a presumption rule in this area of interpreting one's interlocutors' utterances is recognized, there is little real choice in the matter of *which* presumption it should espouse. The presumption that the converser's contribution is appropriate is determinate and useful (*both* where its application in a concrete instance is straightforward *and* where it seems "flouted" and leads to the postulation of a conversational implicature). The presumption that it is *in*appropriate is so indeterminate (e.g., is it a lie? is it underinformative? is it irrelevant? and, if any of these, how? etc.) as to be quite useless as a guide for action (reaction, response).

And then there is also the two-tiered evaluative consideration. To begin with, to presume one's conversers' contribution appropriate is to take them as compeers, to reflect an attitude of respect for and trust in one's fellowmen and women. These attitudes are judged in our society desirable and laudable: it is after all no accident that people "have learned to do so in childhood" rather than to adopt the attitudes of disrespect, suspicion, or haughtiness that go with any contrary presumption. In addition there is the way the very fact that the IPC is known to be operative and prevalent itself serves to regulate behavior. If you know how your utterances are likely to be interpreted and if you care about the goals that are central to the conversation in which you are engaged and hence can be expected to have an interest in its being profitable, you will surely issue your utterance in such a way as to ensure that its interpretation turns out correct. Hence, you will comply with the CP and its attendant maxims. (Grice's own remark is very fitting here: "In any case one feels that the talker who is irrelevant or obscure has primarily let down not his audience but himself"; p. 69.) And to the extent that this effect which the IPC has on the production of utterances is judged to be a good thing, a socially valuable practice greatly facilitating—indeed perhaps even enabling—smooth verbal transactions among people, this constitutes the second tier of the evaluative justification of our presumption.

This leads me, finally, to Grice's Problem. It is put thus:

> a fundamental question about the CP and its attendant maxims [is] what the basis is for the assumption which we seem to make [. . .] that talkers will in general (*ceteris paribus* and in the absence of indications to the contrary) proceed in the manner which these principles prescribe.

Grice then expresses his dissatisfaction with the "dull but no doubt at a certain level adequate" answer (quoted earlier) that it is an empirical fact that people do behave in these ways, and proceeds to say this:

> I am, however, enough of a rationalist to want to find a basis which underlies these facts, undeniable though they may be; I would like to be able to think of the standard type of conversational practice not merely as something which all or most do *in fact* follow, but as something which it is *reasonable* for us to follow, which we *should not* abandon. (68)

It seems to me that within the framework of the reconstruction offered here, the "basis" Grice searches for is readily available. I shall sum it up in the form of two chains.

Grice's chain:

The Outset: we are often involved in talk exchanges; they are typically to some degree cooperative efforts; they typically have some purpose or direction that is recognized by the participants. (Let us agree to refer to the participant, who has an interest in pursuing the purpose or direction of the conversation and does not "opt out," as an *interested participant*.)

At this point the focus of attention is on the prospective interested *speaker*: a certain principle, the CP, is introduced, and the claim is put forth that, given the Outset, the speaker is expected to observe it.

The additional (allegedly empirical) observation: the CP is in fact generally observed.

The question: what is the basis of our assumption that people will go on observing the CP? Or more incisively: what is the reason—the rational reason—for observance of the CP?

Here Grice professes to be stuck with unsatisfactory answers. (He expresses [a] dissatisfaction with the idea that the observance of the CP and the maxims is "a quasi-contractual matter"; and [b] a belief that an answer will be forthcoming only once he is "a good deal clearer about the nature of relevance" [69].)

My chain:

The Outset: the same as Grice's.

At this point the focus of attention is on the (interested) hearer: it is recognized that he might typically be faced with an interpretation problem, and a certain prescription, the IPC, is introduced as offering a way out.

The IPC is then shown to be *justified*, i.e., to be well grounded in the appropriate variety of justifying considerations.

The additional (allegedly empirical) observation: the IPC is in fact operative and prevalent.

From here the attention shifts to the prospective interested *speaker*, and the chain continues as follows:

Given that the speaker recognizes that the IPC is operative and prevalent, he recognizes that his utterance is likely to be interpreted according to the IPC. We assume that he is an *interested* speaker, hence he has a reason to issue utterances whose IPC-governed interpretation will be correct. An interpretation of an utterance according to the Interpretative Presumption of Cooperation will be correct if and only if the utterance was issued in observance of the Cooperative Principle. From this it follows that the interested speaker has a good reason for observing the CP and its maxims. Or, if you will, it follows that it is reasonable for the speaker to observe the CP and its maxims.

As for its being *rational* too, I shall venture the following comment. It seems to me that any speaker who gears his utterances to the method likely to govern their interpretation is being reasonable. The question of rationality, I believe, concerns the interpretation method itself: I can easily think of downright crazy interpretative principles, which may nevertheless be imagined to work provided that both speaker and hearer cooperate with respect to them. What makes for rationality in our case, however, is, I contend, the nature of the considerations in which the IPC is grounded. The fact that our interpretative presumption is justified as it was shown to be, on the basis of both inductive-probabilistic and normative considerations, as well as the determinateness consideration, makes it, in my view, rational.

I conclude, then, that the conversational practice of interpreting utterances in accordance with the IPC and hence of issuing utterances in observance of the CP has been shown to be, indeed, "something which it is *reasonable* for us to follow, which we *should not* abandon."

## The Presumption of Normality

In the philosophical literature one occasionally comes across arguments involving presumptions (or: the presumption) of normality. I shall refer to a few of them presently. The use of this notion, however, is not sufficiently critical, and, consequently, several issues tend to be lumped together which ought in my view to be separated. I shall proceed then to introduce a distinction among three areas where normality may bear upon the notion of presumption.

*Normality as the Presumed Fact.* Given the rendering of the presumption formula "pres. $(P, Q)$" as "$P$ raises the presumption that $Q$," the presumed fact $Q$ may be that a certain (generically described) state of affairs (object, person, utterance, etc.) is normal. Normality here then is that which the presumption is about; the presumption-*raising* fact $(P)$ consisting of some background assumptions or some "frame"[4] description.

It should be noted that "normal" is ambiguous between the statistical sense of "the usual, the average, the most frequent" on the one hand, and the normative (so to speak) sense of "conforming to some standard or norm" on the other. Often these two senses mesh—after all it is the average, or that which is not extraordinary, which usually serves to fix the norm—but not always. (Thus, take a backward region where most of the population still suffers from glaucoma: is "the normal person" there glaucomatous or healthy?) This ambiguity may afflict the presumption of normality, and this may or may not be detrimental to its uses.

It is my suspicion that most cases where a presumption of normality is alluded to are not cases where the normality of something or someone is the presumed fact. I suspect, that is, that even where it appears that normality is that which the presumption is about, this appearance is misleading, or the use of the notion is misguided, and that the role normality plays in those cases is actually one of the two discussed next. One case that does seem to me to fall under the present category occurs in James W. Lamb's proposed analysis of knowledge in terms of justified presumption.[5] He puts forward a principle which he refers to as *the principle of the presumption of normality*, according to which "if subject $S$ knows proposition $P$ and has no reason for believing $P$ abnormal, then $S$ would be justified in presuming $P$ normal" (125). I find this principle problematic on various counts (for one thing, it is surely not the proposition, as distinct from either the utterance expressing it or—what seems closer to Lamb's intention—the circumstances of the state of affairs depicted by it, which can be believed normal or abnormal; besides, can one *know* an abnormal proposition?)[6] But this is beside the point, which is merely illustrative: it does seem that Lamb intends the normality of $P$ as the presumed fact.[7]

*Normality as a Justifying Consideration.* In her paper "Contextual Implication"[8] Isabel Hungerland talks about the presumption that in a situation of communication acts of stating are normal. Now this formulation is misleading if it is construed as follows: "$x$'s being an act of stating in a situation of communication raises the presumption that $x$ is normal." I submit that it is not the normality of certain acts of stating that is here presumed. The construal, rather, should be something like this: "an indicative sentence $x$'s being uttered in a situation of communication raises the presumption that the utterance of $x$ is an act of stating." Where normality plays a role here is in the justification of this presumption.

It is because utterances of indicative sentences in situations of communication are (allegedly) normally acts of stating that there is a presumption from an indicative sentence being uttered in a situation of communication to the utterance being an act of stating. Generally speaking, then, the presumption that $Q$ espoused by a presumption rule expressed by the formula "pres $(p, q)$" is often (partially) justified by the consideration that cases of $P$ are *normally* (i.e., commonly, most frequently, on average) cases of $Q$. Broadly speaking, this fits into the inductive-probabilistic realm of justifying considerations in which the justification of presumptions is grounded.

*Normality as a Premise in the Presumption Inference.* Consider the following question: what role does the fact that there is no reason to believe something abnormal play with regard to presumptions about that thing? I contend that this fact is indeed a factor in presumptions about the thing in question, but that it does *not* play the role of a presumption-raising fact with respect to the presumption that that thing is normal. In order to see the way this factor comes in let us consider the following rule of inference:

(1) pres $(P, Q)$
(2) $p$
Therefore, pres $q$

The conclusion that $q$ is presumed here follows from two premises, the first stating the presumption formula and the second asserting that the presumption-raising generic fact is instantiated in the concrete case in hand. The point now is that it may be argued that, if the inference is to go through, a third premise has to be added:

(3) $p$ is not abnormal.

Premise (3) may be interpreted to mean that there actually is evidence that $p$ is normal, or else that there is *bona fide* absence of evidence that $p$ is relevantly abnormal. Also, (3) may arguably be construed as a tacit rather than as an explicit premise. But in any case with regard to many presumption rules this may well be considered a necessary component of the total evidence required for the presumption rule to apply in the particular instance.

Thus, Mats Furberg[9] speaks of two kinds of conditions that have to be satisfied for a term $T$ to be flawlessly applied, the first being that a sufficient number of $T$'s criteria be satisfied, and the second consisting of what he refers to as certain *presumptions of normality* associated with $T$ (73–74, 178–79). The way I take this to be rendered is this: even where the presumption-raising fact is instantiated in a given concrete instance, i.e., a sufficient number of the criterial conditions associated with a given term $T$ are satisfied with respect to a certain object, the presumption that $T$ applies to this object will not go through if the object manifests freakish, extraordinary, miraculous, or otherwise abnormal behaviour.[10]

## Notes

Reprinted with permission from *How Many Questions: Essays in Honor of Sidney Morgenbesser*, ed. L. S. Cauman, I. Levi, C. D. Parsons, and R. Schwartz (Indianapolis, IN: Hackett, 1983), 451–73. The author's endnotes have been reformatted to fit the conventions of this volume. The orthogragphy of the original has been preserved.—Eds.

1. I am grateful to Avishai Margalit for having pointed out to me the relevance of the notion of presumption to Grice's discussion in the first place, and also for valuable discussions on the matter, as on most other matters dealt with in this paper, since.

2. H. P. Grice, William James Lectures, Harvard University, 1968, 2nd lecture.

Reprinted as "Logic and Conversation," in *The Logic of Grammar*, ed. D. Davidson and G. Harman (Berkeley: University of California Press, 1975), 64–75. All page references will be to the latter.

3. Grice, "Logic and Conversation," 68, refers to it as "dull." The reason is that he is considering it as a candidate answer to his question of what makes people issue their utterances in observance of the CP, and as *such* he finds it wanting. Within the present framework, however, this consideration serves as one among several justificatory considerations of the IPC, and, as such, even though possibly obvious, it is not dull.

4. For a useful statement of the notion of "frame," see Marvin Minsky, "Frame-System Theory," reprinted in *Thinking*, ed. P. N. Johnson-Laird and P. C. Wason (New York: Cambridge, 1977), 355–76.

5. James Lamb, "Knowledge and Justified Presumption," *Journal of Philosophy* 69, no. 5 (1972): 123–27.

6. For further criticism of this principle, as well as of Lamb's central argument, see William Morris, "Knowledge as Justified Presumption," *Journal of Philosophy* 70, no. 6 (1973): 161–65 (esp. 164).

7. It is possible, I think, to regard the legal presumption of sanity as a special case of the presumption of normality: a person brought to trial is presumed sane, that is, normal (in which sense?).

8. Isabel Hungerland, "Contextual Implication," *Inquiry* 3, nos. 1–4 (1960): 211–58.

9. Mats Furberg, *Saying and Meaning* (Oxford: Basil Blackwell, 1963).

10. On the issue of presumptions of reference, see Edna Ullmann-Margalit and Avishai Margalit, "Analyticity by Way of Presumption," *Canadian Journal of Philosophy* 12, no. 3 (1982): 435–52.

# 19

# On the Relationship between Presumptions and Burdens of Proof

LILIAN BERMEJO-LUQUE

## Introduction

The notion of presumption is usually explained in terms of the notion of burden of proof. Basically, the idea is that what characterizes presumptions in contrast with other types of tentative claims to truth—like predictions, conjectures, guesses, etc.—is their ability to shift the burden of proof to an opponent. The main goal of this chapter is to question this view. I would like to show, on the one hand, that presumptions are not more able to shift the burden of proof to an opponent than is any other tentative claim to truth, and on the other hand, that burdens of proof and presumptions involve different types of normativity. To this end, in the second section below, I point out that the Whatelian strategy of dealing with presumptions in everyday discourse by considering the role of legal presumptions is particularly problematic for those aiming at characterizing presumptions in terms of the notion of burden of proof. In the third section, I propose an account of ordinary presumptions as a certain type of constative speech act with constitutive correctness conditions. Following this account, I explain that for a presumption to shift the burden of proof to an opponent, it must operate within a context of dialogue. In the fourth section, I analyze two ways of thinking of a presumption as operative in a context of dialogue and explain that they correspond to two very different conceptions of the epistemological/argumentative role of presumptions. Finally, in the fifth section, I argue that the type of normativity that the notion of burden of proof sanctions is merely instrumental, so that meeting the burden of proof does not amount to any kind of epistemic obligation.

## The Traditional Account of Ordinary Presumptions

It is a commonplace that the notions of presumption and burden of proof are to be "aligned as pairs: a presumption favoring one side in [a] proceeding relieves that side of probative responsibilities and assigns the obligation of mustering evidence and reasoning to [the] other side of [the] contest."[1] Within the field of law, Francis Wharton, for example, said that "the term *præsumtio*, in its classical sense, means exclusively a rule of law adopted for the purpose of determining the burden of proof."[2] In fact, one of the most well-known legal presumptions, that is, the *presumption of innocence*, does not seem to play any role other than setting who has the burden of proof in a court trial. In this respect, it exemplifies the type of dialectical normativity that the notion of burden of proof seems to sanction.

This was the leading idea of Whately's seminal work on the issue: in his *Elements of Rhetoric*,[3] he took for granted a particular view of the legal notions of presumption and burden of proof as counterparts of each other, in order to provide an account of the normativity of everyday argumentative exchanges.[4]

However, a growing number of authors have criticized Whately's strategy of dealing with the ordinary notions of presumption and burden of proof in terms of the corresponding legal notions: within the field of law, presumptions have been considered "the slipperiest member of the family of legal terms, except its first cousin, 'burden of proof.'"[5] Besides, the similarity between ordinary and legal presumptions is far from evident.[6] As Gama-Leyva has observed, "Whately's description of the legal discourse on presumptions is very limited. He only cited two legal presumptions—namely the presumption of innocence and the presumption of property from possession—and he questionably took them as paradigmatic of the work of presumptions in law."[7]

Probably because of Whately's much influential work, philosophers and argumentation theorists have usually disregarded the distinction between *presumptions of law* and *presumptions of fact*.[8] However, the strategy of dealing with the everyday notions of presumption and burden of proof in terms of their legal counterparts does not favor the view that presumptions and burdens of proof are to be aligned as pairs. Actually, it is questionable that all presumptions of law can be seen as mere devices to settle the burden of proof. For, setting apart the presumption of innocence, the main role of presumptions of law does not seem to be procedural but substantive: most presumptions of law are devices for establishing facts in absence of full or proper evidence, not devices for determining each party's argumentative duties. Certainly, presumptions of law usually establish facts provisionally: that which is presumed stands as a fact until contradicted by (new) evidence, and this provisional character may explain why they look so tied to the notion of burden of proof—namely, because by settling facts provisionally, they appear as invitations to either accept what is presumed or provide evidence to the contrary, shifting in this way the burden of proof to the opponent. However, not all legal presumptions settle facts provisionally: this is the case, for example, of the *doli incapax* presumption, which unconditionally mandates the assumption that a defendant younger than a certain age is incapable of committing a felony. At least for such types of presumption it seems difficult to say that its main function is to determine who has the burden of proof in a dialectical exchange.

Yet, maybe things are different outside the realm of law: are presumptions of fact in that context better tied to the notion of burden of proof?

## Presumptions and Their Correctness Conditions

My main goal in this chapter is to show that the ordinary notions of presumption and burden of proof are orthogonal to each other rather than parallel. Less metaphorically, I would like to show that the normativity of presumptions is constitutive of something being a presumption at all, whereas the normativity of burdens of proof is merely instrumental: their authority to sanction argumentation depends on the ends that we pursue by deploying an argumentative procedure. Let me deal first with the everyday notion of presumption and its correctness conditions.

In previous work,[9] I have characterized nonlegal presumptions as a certain type of constative speech act that can be explicitly performed by using a performative expression such as "I presume." So understood, a paradigmatic presumption would be the famous "Dr. Livingstone, I presume" that Mr. Stanley pronounced when he met Dr. Livingstone in Tanganyika.

Following the analogy with assertions, I contended that if asserting that $p$ is behaving so as to count as meaning that $p$ is true, presuming that $p$ is behaving so as to count as meaning that it is reasonable to assume that $p$. In other words, a presumption that $p$ would be the speech act of putting forward $p$ as a reasonable assumption, and presuming that $p$ would be making the presumption that $p$. Thus, a presumption that $p$ would be *constitutively correct* if, at the time the presumption is made, $p$ is something reasonable to assume indeed.

On this account, presumptions can enter into inferences just as any other type of constative speech act: that is, they can be premises ("I presume that he is being sincere; therefore, we should deal with the issue by considering other hypotheses") and conclusions ("She didn't say anything to the contrary; so, we should wait a bit more, I presume"). Regarding the latter, good argumentation for a presumption that $p$ would be argumentation showing that it is reasonable to assume that $p$. Certainly, we can show that it is reasonable to assume that $p$ by showing that $p$ is actually true, or plausible, or very likely; but we can also show that it is reasonable to assume that $p$ by showing, for example, that doing otherwise would have undesirable consequences in some respect (like when we presume the probity of our students, or that soldiers will do their duty, even against evidence).

This said, making a presumption would not necessarily involve making inferences; at least, not in any idiosyncratic way. In this respect, my proposal diverges from the inferentialist accounts of Whately, Sidgwick,[10] and more recently, Ullmann-Margalit[11] and Hansen,[12] who characterized presumption as the status of a claim that results from a specific kind of inference linking a presumption-raising fact to a presumed consequence by means of a *rule of presumptive inference*. Contrastingly, in my proposed account, we can make presumptions much in the same way in which we make assertions, suggestions, conjectures, declarations, etc. For, although in principle we are supposed to have reasons for what we say and do, we can make any type of constative speech act without referring to our reasons for it. And just as we can interpret a speaker as having made an assertion even if we think that her assertion is wrong, we can interpret a speaker as having made a presumption even if we think that her presumption is wrong—which means not that we think that what she has presumed is false, but that we think that her very presuming this, that is, her putting forward this as something reasonable to assume, is wrong.

When an addressee accepts that there is a presumption in favor of a certain view, she accepts that it is reasonable to assume this view. But, of course, accepting that it is reasonable to assume that *p* is not the same as accepting that *p*. After all, despite the reasonability of assuming that *p*, it might be the case that not-*p*. Consequently, when we make a presumption, an opponent can try to either *defeat* it or *rebut* it. That is, as a countermove to a presumption that *p*, an opponent may argue against *p*—that is, against the issue itself—and thus try to defeat the presumption; or, alternatively, she can argue against the very presumption that *p*—and thus try to rebut the contention that it is reasonable to assume that *p*. Because of this, negating a presumption is a little more complex than negating an assertion: whereas there is only one way of negating a previous assertion—which is to assert that this previous assertion is false, we can negate a presumption such as "women like these things, I presume" either by holding that it is not reasonable to assume so (we *rebut* the presumption) or by holding that what is presumed isn't actually the case (we *defeat* the presumption). In this respect, presuming is also different from other speech acts in which a proposition is put forward as being less than certain—such as guessing, conjecturing, suggesting, predicting, foretelling, etc. For, in principle, these other speech acts can be opposed much in the same way in which we oppose a plain assertion, that is, just by questioning that the corresponding proposition is probable, or foreseeable, or plausible, or likely, etc.

On the other hand, normally, when we defeat a presumption, we consequently rebut it: if we offer good reasons against *p*, we normally show as well that it is no longer reasonable to assume that *p*. However, this is not always the case: an officer can have evidence against the view that a soldier will do his duty and still hold that it is reasonable to assume that he will do it.

Finally, in my model nothing precludes the possibility of making presumptions in nondialogical contexts, including *solo* reasoning and deliberation, where verbal presumptions have their corresponding mental counterparts—just as assertions, conjectures, promises, and other speech acts. Presumptions performed in thought alone are the mental events of deeming it reasonable to assume that something is the case. In this respect, my proposal also diverges from the dialectical approaches by Rescher,[13] Walton,[14] and Freeman,[15] who characterize presumptions as the status of certain speech acts in a context of dialogue.[16] Yet, my approach can also make sense of the idea of a presumption that $p$ as something that operates in a context of dialogue: in my account, this means that, in that context, parties accept that it is reasonable to assume that $p$.

## Two Approaches to the Study of Presumptions

Actually, I would like to show now that there are two ways of thinking of presumptions as something that operates within a context of dialogue, and that they underlie, correspondingly, two very different conceptions of the role that the study of presumptions is to play for the analysis and appraisal of argumentation.

Following Whately again, some authors have adopted what we may call a *God's eye* perspective towards presumptions. Whately himself claimed that certain presumptions are always in order, so that in any procedural exchange in which, for example, one of the parties is proposing a novelty, it is this party who has to give reasons for it. Whately's project in dealing with presumptions and burdens of proof was to provide a substantive, although general, account of which argumentations are sound, and which are unsound. Contemporary scholars following this approach, like Rescher or Freeman, have refrained from providing lists of (correct) presumptions; but they still think that the task of studying presumptions has to do with the task of substantively evaluating argumentation, not with the task of explaining how to appraise argumentation containing claims of the form "I presume that $p$," "$p$, I presume," or "Presumably, $p$." The idea is that once we, the evaluators, determine that "there is a presumption" favoring this or that view, we (not the parties themselves) are in a position to determine which party has the burden of proof and, therefore, how the argumentative procedure should be developed. From this perspective, if a presumption operates within a context of dialogue, then the party opposing the presumption has the burden of proof—whether parties themselves see things that way or not.

Notably, this approach requires the notion of presumption to be a normative one. That is, only correct presumptions would count as presumptions proper. For, as Freeman himself has noticed, if someone makes an incorrect presumption such as "slavery is morally permissible, I presume," his move should not shift the burden of proof to his opponent.[17] Such a normative conception of presumptions is indeed influenced by Whately's legal perspective: after all, presumptions of law are necessarily correct presumptions, if only because it is always (provisionally) reasonable to assume that which is (provisionally) mandatory to assume.

In the last section, I have questioned the strategy of dealing with ordinary presumptions and burdens of proof by considering the roles of the corresponding legal notions. But the truth is that thinking of presumptions this way makes sense within Freeman's project of determining premise acceptability: thus understood, presumptions would be good starting points for inquiry under uncertainty, which is also Rescher's reason for his interest in presumptions. This said, however, it must be noticed that, outside the realm of law, such normative conception of presumptions just shifts the bulk of the epistemological task of inquiring under uncertainty on to the metaphysical task of determining whether or not a presumption is a *real* presumption after all. Indeed, much would be gained if our epistemological models were in a position to discriminate which things are, as a matter of fact, reasonable to assume.

On the other hand, even if we had a mechanism to distinguish real presumptions from fake ones, it is still doubtful that we would have a means to settle how nonlegal argumentative exchanges should proceed. After all, within epistemology, the debate between dialogical foundationalists, who hold that some claims have a privileged status as starting points because there is a presumption in their favor, and dialogical egalitarians, who hold that any claim in a dialogue has the burden of proof, is far from having been settled.[18] In the next section, I am going to suggest that, in fact, this debate cannot be settled *a priori*.

Now, in contrast with this *substantive* notion of presumption, it is also possible to think of a presumption that *p* operating in a context of dialogue as an (eventually tacit) agreement among the parties regarding the reasonability of assuming that *p*. Thus understood, there are, in turn, two possibilities: on the one hand, we may be talking of presumptions that none of the parties in the context of dialogue opposes. This is the case, for example, when in a communicative exchange both interlocutors presume that they are using words with their usual meaning, or that they both are trying to be polite, cooperative, nice, etc.[19] Certainly, from a third-person point of view, we may think that such communicative presumptions are indeed correct; but what matters for them to play their function in communication is that participants themselves take them to be correct and behave accordingly. Importantly, regarding such communicative presumptions, the notion of burden of proof does not seem to play any role: in principle, in nonadversarial contexts, no one is required to give reasons for or against anything. In fact, if an interlocutor comes to think that what she was presuming in this respect does not hold any more, the communication may be diminished, or may become less friendly or less efficient, or it may just cease. But that's all: in nonadversarial dialogues, no party has any burden of proof, despite the fact that there may be presumptions going on and that there may be disagreement on them.

On the other hand, it is also possible that parties take it to be reasonable to assume that $p$, and yet one of them also questions that $p$. That is, certain presumptions may operate adversarially in a context of dialogue. For example, Alex and Bern plan to go to visit a friend without calling first, because they both presume that their friend will be happy to see them anyway. In this context, if Alex doesn't feel so sure about their friend's reaction after all, he may also feel that he has to give reasons for his doubts if he wants to persuade Bern to not go without calling first. He cannot expect Bern to just agree if he says, "shouldn't we have called him first?" precisely because a presumption to the contrary operates in their context of dialogue.

To see why such presumption is operative in their context for both participants, not just for one of them, imagine now that Alex and Bern are an old-fashioned couple that by no means presumes that you can pay visits without calling first. In this case, the operative presumption is that they cannot visit their friend without calling first. Thus, if Bern wants to visit their friend even though they haven't called him first, he will have to give reasons showing, for example, that, after all, their friend will be happy to see them anyway (and thus, defeat the presumption that they should have called him first)—or that they know their friend for too long to care about such a rule of etiquette with him (and thus, rebut that presumption). If Bern himself didn't agree that, in principle, it is reasonable to assume that they should have called their friend in advance, he wouldn't take himself to be in need of arguing for his view.

Certainly, when a presumption operates adversarially in a context of dialogue, it shifts the burden of proof to its opponent. Yet, again, it is only the participants' view that matters here, not our view as evaluators. After all, we can only determine which presumption is operating adversarially in a given context by considering which participant feels in need of giving reasons to make his case.

Importantly, however, there are many other speech acts that can also shift the burden of proof to the opponent when they both agree on them. This is the case with predictions, conjectures, guesses, and all those speech acts in which a proposition is put forward as less than certain. For example, it is because both Alex and Bern take it to be unlikely that they'll be hungry on their way to their friend's place that if Bern still thinks that they should take some snacks, he'll have to give reasons for it. In that case, Bern's point is not that despite it being reasonable to assume that they won't be hungry, they may be hungry after all. Rather, his point is that, in the unlikely event that they are hungry, it would be good to have something to eat. He agrees on the prediction *qua* prediction, but he refuses to take what is predicted for granted. If he had not agreed on the prediction, his point would have been that they have to take some snacks, not that it would be good idea to do so just in case.

No doubt we can show that a presumption that *p* is correct by showing that *p* is to be expected, or that it is plausible, or probable, or likely, etc., so that it is also reasonable to assume that *p*. But presuming that *p* is not the same as putting forward *p* as foreseeable, or plausible, or probable, or as an option to consider, etc. These are different types of speech acts, with their own constitutive correctness conditions, which is the reason why, for example, we cannot make sense of *predicting* that a soldier will do his duty and still hold that he won't do it, whereas we can make sense of presuming that a solider will do his duty and still hold that he won't do it. The strategy of characterizing any tentative claim to truth as a presumption is misleading.

## The Instrumental Normativity of Burdens of Proof

The ultimate goal of this chapter is to show that thinking of presumptions in terms of burdens of proof distorts our understanding of both notions. In my account, the normativity of presumptions—that is, that which makes a presumption right or wrong—is constitutive of something being a presumption at all. Now I would like to show that the normativity of burdens of proof is instrumental, which means not only that the question of determining who must give reasons for her claims cannot be settled *a priori*, but also that, outside the realm of highly conventionalized dialectical procedures, there is no real obligation of giving reasons, but only prudential requirements to do so that depend on the ends that we pursue with our communicative exchanges.[20]

Most authors agree that meeting the burden of proof is a type of *dialectical* obligation. But what type of obligation could this be? Suppose that a stranger knocks on the door of a magnificent house and a Latina woman opens it. The stranger says, "the housekeeper, I presume." According to the view defended so far, we should acknowledge both that the stranger has made a presumption and that this is not enough for shifting the burden of proof: in order to shift the burden of proof, the stranger's presumption has to be operative in the context; and, in my view, this means that both participants agree that it is reasonable to assume that the woman is the housekeeper—whether she is or not.

But suppose that the woman is not the housekeeper, and also that she is very concerned with the social and cultural rights of minorities, so that she not only disagrees with what the stranger presumes, but she also disagrees with his very presumption, as she takes it to be based on stereotypes.[21] In this case, wouldn't we say that the woman should at least respond that she is not the housekeeper? After all, in being addressed, she is somehow compelled to reply something, especially because if she doesn't say anything to the contrary, the stranger will normally interpret that she agrees with both his presumption and what he presumes.

Kauffeld has characterized the normativity of both presumptions and burdens of proof along these pragmatic terms.[22] Notably, the need for meeting this type of burden amounts to a practical requirement: responding one way or another to the stranger is a means of accomplishing communicative success via cooperation. Yet, the woman may refuse to cooperate with the stranger, and it is far from evident that we could accuse her of not being rational for doing so or of failing to meet an obligation proper.

Importantly, a requirement of responding would have also been on her side had the stranger asked a question or just introduced himself. Thus, this type of requirement does not necessarily come from a presumption. Moreover, this type of requirement cannot be an epistemic obligation, but is a mere condition of successful communication—that is, a condition that has to be met if we aim at having a good communicative interaction, given the fact that the context of dialogue in which it arises may have nothing to do with truth and knowledge.

So, at this point, we should better consider Rescher's characterization of burdens of proof as devices that pose real obligations in the pursuit of truth, whether we deal with *conventional* dialectical procedures—such as those deployed in a court trial or in a debate tournament—or *natural* dialectical procedures.[23]

No doubt, regarding conventional dialectics, the obligation of meeting the burden of proof comes as a prescription. For, although the rules for allocating the burden of proof may have a practical rationale, once these rules are settled for a certain type of conventional practice, they are mandatory. For this reason, within conventional dialectics, the question of determining who has the burden of proof can be settled *a priori*: conventional dialectical procedures provide criteria to decide who has to defend her position, regardless of our considerations about the initial plausibility of the claim under discussion.

But, can we say the same about burdens of proof in natural procedures? For Rescher, natural dialectics is the very pursuit of truth and knowledge, which, in turn, is the hallmark of epistemic rationality. Indeed, for Rescher, meeting the burden of proof is an epistemic obligation, not a merely instrumental requirement: after all, from a merely instrumental point of view, it may happen to be advisable not to try to meet the burden of proof and make evident that our position is untenable. Basically, the idea is that we must meet our burdens of proof because we would be epistemically irrational if we didn't.

According to Rescher, any procedure of natural dialectics is based "on the natural presumptions fixed by purely probative considerations of evidential and intrinsic plausibility."[24] However, as pointed out before, a presumption can only settle who has the burden of proof in a context of dialogue when it is operative in this context. But precisely for this reason, in case of disagreement about who has the burden of proof, appealing to presumptions cannot do the work: he who contends that the burden is on the other's side will also contend that the presumption (or the prediction, or the expectation, or any other tentative claim to truth, in general) is on his side; and this is exactly what the other party will deny. And considering the evaluator's point of view cannot solve the problem of settling who is rationally obliged to defend his standpoint: after all, would it be rational for a party to try to meet a burden that she doesn't think to be on her side?

Of course, as evaluators, we can have our own view in this respect, but this only means that we have taken sides with one of the parties, which means, in turn, that unless the other party offers good reasons, she won't persuade us of her views. But this is fair enough if she doesn't care: why should she be epistemically obliged to give reasons to persuade us?

In reality, the problem with the notion of burden of proof has to do not only with the way presumptions and other tentative claims to truth operate in certain contexts of dialogue but also with its allegedly epistemic normativity. Because of this, it affects not only the view of the dialogical foundationalist but also that of the dialogical egalitarian. For the principle "he who asserts must prove" makes sense as a means to secure the goals of certain argumentative exchanges: after all, if none of the parties were obliged to give reasons for their views, procedures may even not take place. But, so understood, such a principle only has a practical rationale, and for this reason, can only be compulsory within highly conventionalized practices. Outside of them, the need of giving reasons for our claims depends on the particular goals that we pursue in the contexts of our dialogues, not on the rules of the type of dialogue that, allegedly, we are engaged in. For, on the one hand, we are not rationally or epistemically obliged to deploy any type of dialogue in particular, not even when we pursue truth and knowledge. And, on the other hand, even if we are supposed to be engaged in a type of dialogue whose constitutive goals are truth and knowledge, meeting the principle "he who asserts must prove" may take us astray from such goals. This is the case, for example, if our interlocutors are not in a position to provide reasons for their claims—for example, because they are too young, or scared, etc. In such cases, the epistemological task may consist of building a plausible case together, instead of testing the plausibility of each other's claim by considering the reasons that each party is able to provide in its favor.

Rational controversy dialogues are not the only type of dialogue that is epistemologically driven. We can deploy epistemic rationality by means of dialogues whose goals vary from arriving at true beliefs to avoiding any possible mistakes, conferring some plausibility to a hypothesis, making certain beliefs rational, rationally persuading a critic, etc. In each context of dialogue, each of these different epistemic goals will speak in favor of a different way of allocating the burden of proof, or of allocating no burden whatsoever. In any case, such allocation will amount to a practical requirement (i.e., a means to accomplish this or that epistemic goal, given the context), not to an epistemic obligation (i.e., an obligation that we must meet on pain of epistemic irrationality).

## Conclusion

If presumptions are a type of constative speech act in which a propositional content is put forward as something reasonable to assume, then a *correct* presumption is a speech act whose propositional content is something reasonable to assume indeed. Contrastingly, *burdens of proof* are procedural statuses that answer the question of how to develop an argumentative exchange: if you have the burden of proof, it is you who has to provide reasons for your claim instead of, for example, merely dismissing an opponent's refusal of it. However, this need will come as a practical requirement: if you fail to give reasons against the presumption, you will probably fail in persuading your addressees of your views. But there is no epistemic obligation of giving reasons for your views; in fact, as pointed out before, in some contexts, demanding reasons from our interlocutors in order to accept their claims may lead us astray from truth and knowledge.

At times, the expression "burden of proof" has been used to consider not only the question of *who* has to argue but also the question of *what* has to be argued for.[25] In this chapter, I have considered only the first use of the expression, although I think that much of what I have said here also applies to the other. In particular, I think that if you fail to give reasons for the actual claim under discussion, you do not really fail to meet any type of epistemic obligation but only fall short of showing that this claim is correct. Of course, if your addressees don't notice that you are not actually arguing for the claim under discussion but for some other claim, they may be deceptively persuaded of your view. But in that case, the epistemic flaw is on their side: they are taking for good an argument for $c_1$ which, in fact, is only a good argument for $c_2$.

## Notes

The work presented here has been financed by the Spanish Ministerio de Economía y Competitividad, FFI2014-54681-P. The author thanks Professor James Freeman for his revision of the original manuscript.

1. Fred Kauffeld, "Presumption and Shifting the Burden of Proof" (paper presented at the IPrA Conference, 2005), p. 2, http://www2.arnes.si/~ffljzagar/Kauffeld _paper.pdf.

2. Francis Wharton, *Disputed Questions of Evidence: Relevancy, Presumptions of Law, and Presumptions of Fact* (St. Louis, MO: G. I. Jones, 1877), 16.

3. Richard Whately, *Elements of Rhetoric: Comprising an Analysis of the Laws of Moral Evidence and of Persuasion, with Rules for Argumentative Composition and Elocution*, 7th ed., rev. (London: John W. Parker, 1846; repr., Carbondale, IL: Southern Illinois University Press, 1963).

4. Douglas Walton, *Burden of Proof, Presumption, and Argumentation* (Cambridge: Cambridge University Press, 2014), 2.

5. Charles T. McCormick, *McCormick on Evidence*, 7th ed., ed. K. S. Broun, G. E. Dix, E. J. Imwinkelried, D. H. Kaye, R. P. Mosteller, E. F. Roberts, and E. Swift (St. Paul, MN: Thomson Reuters/West Law, 2013), 342.

6. For example, Richard Gaskins, *Burdens of Proof in Modern Discourse* (New Haven, CT: Yale University Press, 1992); Fred Kauffeld, "Presumptions and the Distribution of Argumentative Burdens in Acts of Proposing and Accusing," *Argumentation* 12, no. 2 (1998): 245–66; Ulrike Hahn and Michael Oaksford, "The Burden of Proof and Its Role in Argumentation," *Argumentation* 21, no. 1 (2007): 39–61; Tim Dare and Justine Kingsbury, "Putting the Burden of Proof in Its Place: When Are Differential Allocations Legitimate?" *Southern Journal of Philosophy* 46, no. 4 (2008): 503–18; Raymundo Gama-Leyva, "The Nature and Place of Presumptions in Law and Legal Argumentation," *Argumentation* 31, no. 3 (2017): 555–72.

7. Gama-Leyva, "Nature and Place of Presumptions," 557.

8. David Kaiser, "Presumptions of Law and of Fact," *Marquette Law Review* 38, no. 4 (1955): 253.

9. Lilian Bermejo-Luque, "Being a Correct Presumption vs. Being Presumably the Case," *Informal Logic* 36, no. 1 (2016): 1–25.

10. Alfred Sidgwick, *Fallacies: A View of Logic from the Practical Side* (New York: D. Appleton, 1883).

11. Edna Ullmann-Margalit, "On Presumptions," *Journal of Philosophy* 80, no. 3 (1983): 143–63.

12. Hans V. Hansen, "Theories of Presumptions and Burdens of Proof," in *Informal Logic @ 25*, ed. by J. A. Blair, R. H. Johnson, H. V. Hansen, and C. W. Tindale (Windsor, ON: OSSA, 2003), available online in the OSSA 5 Conference Archive at http://scholar.uwindsor.ca/ossaarchive/.

13. Nicholas Rescher, *Dialectics: A Controversy-Oriented Approach to the Theory of Knowledge* (Albany: State University of New York Press, 1977); and Nicholas Rescher, *Presumption and the Practices of Tentative Cognition* (Cambridge: Cambridge University Press, 2006).

14. Douglas Walton, "Presumption, Burden of Proof, and Lack of Evidence," *L'Analisi linguistica e letteraria* 16, no 3. (2008): 143–63.

15. James Freeman, *Acceptable Premises: An Epistemic Approach to an Informal Logic Problem* (Cambridge: Cambridge University Press, 2005).

16. Such dialogues may be internal, but these authors' point is that a claim is a presumption only with respect to its status within a dialogue.

17. James Freeman, "Review of *Plausible Argument in Everyday Conversation*, by D. Walton," *Informal Logic* 18, nos. 2–3 (1996): 289.

18. Michael Rescorla, "Shifting the Burden of Proof?," *Philosophical Quarterly* 59, no. 234 (2009): 86–109; Conny Rhode, "The Burden of Proof in Philosophical Persuasion Dialogue," *Argumentation* 31, no. 3 (2017): 535–54.

19. Geoffrey Leech, *Principles of Pragmatics* (London: Longman Group, 1983). Kauffeld also mentions the presumption of veracity as one such type of nonadversarial communicative presumption. See Fred Kauffeld, "The Ordinary Practice of Presuming and Presumption with Special Attention to Veracity and the Burden of Proof," in *Anyone Who Has a View: Theoretical Contributions to the Study of Argumentation*, ed. F. H. van Eemeren, J. A. Blair, C. A. Willard, and A. F. Snoeck Henkemans (Dordrecht: Kluwer, 2003), 136.

20. By "obligation" I mean a command for action that does not depend on our goals. A prudential requirement, on the contrary, would be a command for action that makes sense to follow because we pursue such and such goals. Thus, if you don't meet a prudential requirement you can drop your goal and still be right, but if you don't meet an obligation, there is no way of making your behavior blameless in this respect.

21. As pointed out before, the disagreement about the correctness of the presumption itself may take place even if the woman is in fact the housekeeper and, as a consequence, takes what the stranger presumes to be correct.

22. Fred Kauffeld, "On the Difference between Presumptions and Assumptions," in *Argumentation and Values: Proceedings of the Ninth SCA/AFA Conference on Argumentation*, ed. S. Jackson (Alta, UT: Speech Communication Association, 1995), 509–15; Kauffeld, "Distribution of Argumentative Burdens," *Argumentation*, 12, no. 2 (1998): 245–66; and Kauffeld, "Presumption and Shifting."

23. Rescher distinguishes between *natural dialectics*, whose rules are a matter of epistemic rationality, and *conventional dialectics*, whose rules are "fettered by conventions" (*Dialectics*, 38).

24. Rescher, *Dialectics*, 38.

25. As, for example, in Timothy Williamson, "Philosophical Expertise and the Burden of Proof," *Metaphilosophy* 42, no. 3 (2011): 215–29.

# 20

# A Rhetorically Oriented Account of Presumption and Probative Obligations in Normative Pragmatic Terms

## Fred J. Kauffeld

## Introduction

This essay overviews and defends recent advances in our understanding of presumption and probative obligations developed by rhetorical/communications scholars. These scholars broadly share an orientation that Scott Jacobs and Jean Goodwin describe as "normative pragmatics."[1] In their view, key norms of argumentation (especially those having to do with the allocation of probative responsibility) arise out of commitments undertaken pragmatically in the execution of various speech acts.

## Speech Acts and Probative Obligations

Students of argumentation widely, though not universally, agree that practices corresponding to our notions of "presumption" and "burdens of proof" (or, as I prefer to call it, "probative obligations") are practically necessary components of reason-giving discourse both in highly institutionalized argumentation, for example, courts of law, and also in the looser discourse of ordinary day-to-day argumentation. The dialectically oriented philosopher Nicholas Rescher holds, "The workings of the conception of burden of proof represent a *procedural or regulative principle of rationality* in the conduct of argumentation, a ground rule, as it were, of the process of rational controversy—a fundamental condition of the whole enterprise."[2] This estimate is widely accepted among students of argumentation.

Accepting Rescher's assessment, scholars have sought to elucidate the structure and functions of presumptions and probative burdens. Two approaches can be discerned.[3] The first, associated with traditions of dialectical study, tends to work from the top down, starting from highly idealized models of argumentative exchanges and/or highly abstract classifications of argument types (schemes). The other, loosely associated with traditions of rhetorical/communications

study, tends to work from the bottom up, starting from the analysis and explication of specific kinds of communicative performances and particular cases of
argumentative exchange. Contemporary work promotes interaction between
these approaches, and recently steps have been taken to merge them. However,
they still proceed on tangential courses at some distance from each other.[4] In
order to more clearly apprehend the pragmatics of presumption and probative
obligation and, also, to better accommodate the great variety encountered in
day-to-day discourse, the present investigation will work primarily from the
bottom up.

Contemporary bottom-up normative pragmatic accounts have advanced our
understanding of presumption and probative burdens in the following ways:[5]

(1) They have clarified the nature of the relationship between presumptions and burdens of proof in persuasive discourse. Earlier accounts were
inclined to regard the "burden of proof" simply as a matter of the need
to provide skeptical addressees with reasons designed to persuade them.
While such views rightly focus on the practical nature of probative burdens, they oversimplify the relevant pragmatics and fail to recognize
something their dialectical counterparts have long understood, namely,
that many probative "burdens" of significance in persuasive discourse
are *obligations*.

(2) While dialectically oriented studies have long recognized that burdens of proof are *obligations*, they have typically adopted an unduly narrow construction of these obligations. They have, for the most part, held
that insofar as the burden of proof qualifies as an obligation, it simply
follows legalistic and dialogic rules mandating that "he who asserts must
prove."[6] This view, whatever its abstract merits, simply does not accord
with the great variety of ordinary day-to-day probative burdens.

(3) Addressing the variety among ordinary day-to-day probative burdens,
normative pragmatic studies have focused on the connections between
presumptions and probative obligations as constructed in various speech
acts. The idea that probative burdens are distributed in relation to presumptions is a longstanding notion arising from legal theories, formal
dialectics, and accounts influenced by Richard Whately. Previous work
in this area has been frustrated by fragmentary conceptions of presumption and by failure to recognize the ways in which presumptions and
corresponding probative burdens are engaged in the communicative acts
that generate and structure argumentative exchanges. Work in normative pragmatics has provided a more adequate analysis of ordinary presumptions and, drawing on work in the philosophy of language, a fuller

picture of how presumptions and corresponding obligations are generated in the performance of various communicative acts.

(4) These advances support an account of the unity within this domain and at the same time accommodate the great variety that obtains across particular cases. They also illuminate the genesis of the persuasive force in argumentation, that is, (a) the possibility of discharging a probative obligation, and (b) the consequence of realigning probative obligations (shifting the burden of proof).

In light of these advances we should be able to articulate a clear and adequate conception of ordinary day-to-day presumptions, identify how probative obligations are engaged in relationship to presumptions, and explicate the force of argumentation in terms of the consequences of discharging a probative burden. An adequate bottom-up account should satisfactorily discharge these tasks in terms that square with competent real-world practices and accommodate the variety these practices exhibit.

These advances afford correctives to inherited conceptions of the relation between presumptions and probative obligations. In rhetorical traditions, inherited conceptions of this relation, commonly traced to Archbishop Whately, hold that a proposition enjoying the status of a presumption is acceptable unless and until the presumption is overturned by advocates who accept and discharge the burden of proof, displacing it with reason and evidence. Presumptions, in this hoary view, are propositions (warranted inferences) with the peculiar force that they are to be accepted unless and until some party undertakes and discharges the burden of showing them to be false.[7] A party charged with criminal wrongdoing, for example, is to be presumed innocent, and the accuser has the burden of proof. Outside of the rule-bound procedures of the courts, this formulation is open to several interpretations. In traditions of rhetorical study, the more widely held interpretation has been that the burden of proof descends on advocates who want currently unconvinced others to accept propositions that run counter to their preconceptions. In this view the burden of proof is simply a matter of what one must do to persuade others in view of their cognitive and/or behavioral inertia. In dialectical traditions this view has been echoed by Sidgwick[8] and influential others, who hold that the only probative obligation that descends on advocates is imposed by the rule "he who asserts must prove." Alternative views hold that probative burdens are incurred in relationship to various presumptions and, in fact, are genuine obligations. This seems to have been Whately's view, though he has often been understood to have held the first.[9]

While parties intent on persuading others often need to provide reasons and evidence in order to achieve their objective, this "burden," if it can properly be so called, is not per se correlative to some presumption. In our ordinary understanding of these concepts and corresponding practices, presumptions and related burdens operate in the sphere of rights, duties, and obligations. That is not to say that they are entirely divorced from pragmatic considerations. A presumption is an inference to which a person is or purports to be entitled. Thus, a person might say, speaking presumptuously, "This is my home, you are to leave." Homeownership entitles an agent to issue this directive. Connections to normative considerations can be seen across a variety of ordinary presumptions. The presumption that a person is speaking the truth is related to our supposition that she is responsible for the truth of what she says. Likewise, when we presume that we are welcome at an event to which we have been invited, our supposition is related to obligations incurred when the invitation was tendered. When we presume something, we take it as something we are entitled to infer, and this entitlement comes with expectations regarding the responsibilities of others. Correspondingly, when someone behaves presumptuously, in the pejorative sense of the term, that person's actions lay claim to something to which he or she is not entitled.[10]

If we are to understand the genesis of probative obligations in ordinary argumentation, we must give clear-eyed attention to the nature and structure of this kind of inference, that is, to day-to-day presuming and its product, the presumption. This topic has been obscured by the widely held idea that the essential condition of presumption inferences is a feature of the force of their conclusions, namely, that they stand good unless and until a dissenting voice accepts and discharges the burden of showing otherwise.[11] While many presumptive conclusions do have this force, many do not; moreover, many inferences whose conclusions do have this force are not presumptions.

What, then, warrants the normative aspect of presumptive inferences? Sidgwick thought that they had little normative force beyond the maxim that he who asserts must prove.[12] Others have argued that they are warranted and governed by rules embedded in communicative practices and/or established by the inferential norms of discourse communities. Each of these views has some merit as regards appropriate fields of discourse and action, and each squares with some presumptions. However, careful reflection on presumption itself reveals a core structure to this kind of inference. A presumption is an inference based on the supposition that someone will have made it the case that $p$, rather than risk criticism, resentment, punishment, etc. for failing to do so. For example, where a person is speaking seriously with the manifest intention that we believe what she tells us (and in the absence of indications to the contrary), we presume that she will have made it the case that she is speaking truthfully, rather than risk criticism for mendacity should it turn out that she is not sincerely expressing beliefs whose rational foundation she has made a reasonable effort to ascertain.[13]

Presumptions comprise a large class of inferences that pervade our lives and merit more scholarly attention than they have received. Here we can only notice a few aspects of this complex phenomenon. First, we should recognize at least two broad types of presumptions: standing presumptions and special presumptions. Standing presumption are available by reason of the rules, conventions, and expectations of mutual regard that order our lives. Thus, without working the matter out consciously, we presume that our associates will manifest an appropriate regard for our interests, well-being, dignity etc., rather than risk the resentment incurred by failure to do so.[14]

Special presumptions arise from the possibility of strengthening and/or generating presumptions by deliberately and openly undertaking commitments that implicate the prospect of resentment, etc., for failure to fulfill those commitments. So, for example, should one need to borrow some significant object from a relative stranger; it would normally be presumed that one would return a borrowed object, but given the fact that one is dealing with a stranger who has no on-going relation to assure that one will take seriously the possibility of resentment for failure to return the borrowed item, one may leave a deposit to strengthen the presumption of its return.

Both standing and special presumptions are of interest in the genesis of probative obligations; however, special presumptions figure more prominently in our present inquiry because they often have a very direct connection to the distribution of probative obligations in reason-giving discourse. Special presumptions are commonly engaged to strengthen, focus, or otherwise enhance other presumptions, and sometimes in doing so they engage probative obligations. The use of special presumptions to augment the presumption of veracity nicely illustrates this potential.

The presumption of veracity engaged by (seriously) saying something is a potent but also, by itself, a remarkably vulnerable utility. In favorable circumstances, the fact that $S$ says that $p$ and thereby engages a presumption of veracity provides $A$ with adequate reason to believe that $p$. In such cases we say that $A$ trusts $S$. Notice here that $A$ has reason to trust $S$, $A$ presumes that $S$ would not risk resentment for failing to speak truthfully, that is, were $S$ not expressing beliefs $S$ sincerely holds on the basis of what $S$ supposes is a reasonable effort to determine their rational adequacy. However, this presumption of veracity is vague with respect to both its scope and depth. The presumption is that S is speaking on the basis of what $S$ takes or expects others to take as a responsible effort to secure an adequate basis for the truthfulness of what $S$ says. But this is a remarkably vague specification of the effort $S$ may be presumed to have exerted to ascertain the rational adequacy of what S says. Has S focused largely on her own concerns, giving relatively little attention to her addressee's concerns? Has $S$ hastily conceived her statement with little attention to her addressee's interests? Moreover, has her "sincere" expression plumbed the depth of her own beliefs, or is her statement merely an expression of superficial impressions which she might disavow upon deeper reflection?[15] In many circumstances the presumption of veracity needs to be supplemented by a larger pattern of commitments that focus, augment, elaborate, etc., the commitment $S$ incurs in seriously saying and meaning something.[16] So we have a large class of speech acts that effect such enrichment.

Consider, for example, the paradigmatic situation that typically calls forth a proposal and how the speech act of proposing is used strategically to provide an inducement needed to augment the presumption of veracity. Suppose that $S$ has a proposition that $S$ wants $A$ to consider, for example, that they should jointly invest in Northern Securities. $A$, on the other hand, is inclined initially to regard this proposition as not worth considering. It seems to $A$ that $S$ could not have carefully investigated the matter considering $A$'s interests. In this situation, were $S$ to simply say to $A$ that they should invest in Northern Securities, $A$ would engage a presumption that $S$ is speaking truthfully, that is, that $S$ is sincerely expressing beliefs that $S$ has tried to ascertain their rational grounds, but in these circumstances this presumption is too vague to provide $A$ with reason to suppose that this proposition might prove to be worth considering. By itself, the presumption of veracity does not convey much in regard to what $S$ has done to ascertain the soundness of $S$'s proposal in relation to $A$'s interests; that presumption does not provide $A$ with reason to suppose $S$ has carefully considered the matter taking $A$'s interests into account. In these circumstances, $S$ can augment the presumption of veracity by casting $S$'s proposition as a proposal, therein openly committing herself to answer $A$'s questions, doubts, objections, etc. regarding the proposition $S$ is advancing. In so doing $S$ strategically undertakes a probative obligation augmenting and strengthening the presumption that she is speaking truthfully with careful regard for $A$'s interests and for the rational adequacy of her proposition. This larger presumption may provide A with reason to presume that $S$'s proposition may at least merit tentative consideration and, thereupon to engage what $S$ has to say about the grounds for her proposal.[17]

A comparable strategy can be seen to underwrite the illocutionary act of accusing. Accusations are levelled in a variety of circumstances and with a variety of aims; however, it is possible to identify paradigm performances within which $S$ and $A$ undertake and fulfill commitments that provide a rational basis for adjudicating conflicting positions. In the typical situation, the instigating speaker, that is, the accuser $(AG)$, believes that the accused $(AR)$ has committed some act that has caused harm to $AG$ and/or $AG$'s fellows; moreover, $AG$

is strongly inclined to suppose that *AR* acted wrongfully. *AG* is disturbed by these beliefs and suppositions, but *AG* wants to treat *AR* fairly and to afford *AR* an opportunity to explain, justify, excuse, etc. *AR*'s seemingly wrongful act. *AG* reasonably supposes that *AR* owes *AG* an answer for what he is supposed to have done, but in these circumstances, it will often be the case that *AR* does not expect to be treated fairly by *AG* and so is willing to deny (perhaps falsely) that he performed the offending act. In these circumstances *AG* can level an accusation alleging that *AR* committed the offending act. This statement impugns *AR*'s conduct; should *AR* deny the allegation, his denial would simply raise a question about *AR*'s conduct. This condition of having his conduct impugned is harmful to *AR*, and in line with *AG*'s commitment to treat *AR* fairly, the latter can demand that *AG* substantiate her allegation, thereby putting *AR* in a position to defend himself. Here the primary speaker, the accuser, ultimately incurs a burden of proof as a consequence of commitments undertaken in making the accusation. In other circumstances, *AR* may accede to *AG*'s demand that *AR*'s answer *AG*'s charges with justification, excuse, confession, apology, etc. regarding *AG*'s allegation.[18]

Reflection on the illocutionary strategies that respond to the limitations and potentials of veracity illuminates core variations in the genesis of probative obligations. At the same time, recognition of the potentials of special presumptions for finer situational responsiveness also casts light on the variation in the genesis of probative responsibility. I want to illustrate this potential by reference to Dr. Martin Luther King Jr.'s "Letter from Birmingham Jail."[19]

Written in 1963 at the height of violent protest activities aimed at desegregating public spaces and services in Birmingham, Alabama, King's argument is highly regarded for its eloquence and persuasive power. The letter is ostensibly addressed to clergymen who had issued a public letter condemning protest activities sanctioned in part by King's leadership. The letter, as its title indicates, was written primarily while King was himself incarcerated. While not immediately influential, in due course this missive became widely recognized for the persuasive power of its argument. It nicely illustrates the capacity of our account to accommodate the rich variety of probative obligations engaged in day-to-day argumentation, and it also yields insight into how discharging a probative obligation may impact the alignment of argumentative burdens in a controversy. It holds special merit from the perspective of our consideration of presumption and probative obligations. First, it illustrates how sharply an advocate can tailor her probative commitments to the situation she is addressing, and, secondly, it illustrates how, by conspicuously discharging her self-imposed probative obligations, an advocate can modify the prevailing presumptions and discursive obligations regnant in the situation addressed (sometimes misleadingly called "shifting the burden of proof").

King's letter is divided into two major sections. The first attempts to fulfill his self-imposed obligation to answer his critics by exposing, in terms men of good will and sincerity can understand, the mistaken assumptions on which the clergymen's criticisms were based. In the second part King proceeds on the presumption that he has discharged his initial probative obligation and attempts to impose a corresponding obligation on his critics and their sympathizers. This section reproaches his fellow clergymen (and more broadly) white moderates for making the kinds of mistakes King diagnosed and refuted in the first part of his essay.

King opened the first section of his letter with a passage clearly identifying the (illocutionary) intentions with which he is speaking and the parameters of the probative obligations he is undertaking. Ostensibly addressing his "fellow clergymen," King wrote, "While confined here in the Birmingham city jail, I came across your recent statement calling my present activities 'unwise and untimely.' Seldom do I pause to answer criticism of my work and ideas. If I sought to answer all the criticisms that cross my desk, my secretaries would have little time for anything other than such correspondence in the course of the day, and I would have no time for constructive work. But since I feel that you are men of genuine good will and that your criticisms are sincerely set forth, I want to try to answer your statements in what I hope will be patient and reasonable terms."[20] Here King openly undertakes an obligation to respond to criticism from fellow clergymen, who charge that his recent actions (vigorously protesting segregation in Birmingham) were unwise and untimely. He carefully circumscribes the parameters of this obligation: a commitment made to men of genuine good will, who have "sincerely set forth" their criticisms. Insofar as the grounds for these criticisms can be seen to fail to exhibit sincerity and good will, they will fail to merit further consideration on King's part and, by extension, on the part of his larger readership. Moreover, King commits himself to answer in "patient and reasonable terms." Insofar as he can plausibly purport to have provided patient and reasonable answers, he can claim to have discharged his initially incurred probative burden.

By the midpoint of his address, King's posture changes. Whereas he had initially accepted the burden of proof and set out to answer his critics, here, having plausibly discharged that burden, King adopts a different posture and tone. He moves from defense to offense. He politely frames his "attacks" as confessions: "I must make two honest confessions to you, my Christian and Jewish brothers." These "confessions," however, are designed to reproach fellow clergy and moderate whites for their negative and/or indifferent responses to his activism on behalf of civil rights.[21] King professes to be disappointed by the shallow understanding reflected in the white moderates' failure to embrace civil rights activism. The argument King advances in connection with this expression of disappointment serves to establish basic conditions under which his critics have an obligation to repent of their mistaken, shallow understanding of the necessity of and urgency for activism on behalf of black civil rights—errors on which their lack of understanding and support has been based.

In the case of white moderates, King explains that he was expecting, indeed, relying on their support. This was, and continues to be, a reasonable expectation, given that they purport to be sincere persons of good faith, who profess commitment to the goals of King's movement. But his expectations have been disappointed, because the shallow understanding and mythic thinking of white moderates have kept them from fulfilling their commitments.[22] Given that his response to the criticisms leveled at him (presumably) has dispelled the errors under which he and his fellow black Americans continue to suffer, it follows that his critics and other white moderates have an *obligation* to redress these wrongs. At this point we may turn to analysis of *obligation* developed by the English philosopher Geoffrey Warnock. Professor Warnock argues convincingly that obligations are incurred where: (1) it is foreseeable that others will suffer or will continue to suffer harm in the event that the obligee does not act; (2) others are counting on his or her acting in order to avert, prevent, ameliorate, or rectify that harm; and (3) he or she must so act in order to avoid speaking or having spoken or even having acted *falsely*.[23] Notice that King's argument satisfies all three of these conditions. King has been expecting support from white moderates but they have failed to provide it; King and his fellows are suffering harm as a consequence of this failure; and in continued refusal to support his cause, white moderates are acting falsely.

King's second disappointment concerns specifically the white church and its leadership. "Let me take note of my other major disappointment. I have been so greatly disappointed with the white church and its leadership. [...] When I was suddenly catapulted into the leadership of the bus protest in Montgomery, Alabama, a few years ago, I felt we *would* be supported by the white church, felt that the white ministers, priests and rabbis of the South would be among our strongest allies. Instead, some have been outright opponents, refusing to understand the freedom movement and misrepresenting its leaders; all too many others have been more cautious than courageous and have remained silent behind the anesthetizing security of stained-glass windows."[24] Here, too, King's argument is designed to awaken his fellow clergy to their obligation to understand and support black civil rights activism. King had been expecting their support, he explains, for the Christian church has traditionally come to the aid of justice. But he has found that "white churchmen stand on the sideline and mouth pious irrelevancies and sanctimonious trivialities in the midst of a mighty struggle to rid our nation of racial and economic injustice."[25] In this failure to live up to King's expectations, he argues, the church is acting falsely; it has become timid; its traditional militancy has been preempted by its commitment to the status quo.[26] And as a result of this failure, King is suffering profound disappointment and his fellow black Americans continue to suffer the wrongs of segregation. In light of this, King would have his fellow clergy recognize their obligation to "meet the challenge of this decisive hour" and "come to the aid of justice."[27]

Thus, we see in King's address how a speaker can move into a position to awaken his audience to their obligations (indeed, to establish a presumption that they have such obligations) by discharging a corresponding probative obligation. Notice, however, that this realignment of obligations should not be simply described as a shift in the burden of proof. The obligation King would have white moderates recognize is not the burden of responding to his arguments as adversaries, rather, they are to take to heart the cause to which the protests are dedicated.

Our reflection on King's address shows, first, that an advocate can circumscribe his self-imposed probative obligation to fit the situation he is addressing, and second, that she can tailor those commitments such that the presentation of her discourse manifestly discharges the obligations she has undertaken.

From a bottom-up perspective we have seen (1) that a normative pragmatic account can explicate how, even in the absence of formalized rules and procedures, probative obligations can descend upon advocates in the performance of various speech acts; (2) that advocates can tailor their probative commitment to fit the situation addressed by their discourse; (3) that the burdens they accept can be articulated in terms that facilitate the speaker's manifestly discharging those burdens in the articulation of her discourse; and, (4) that manifestly discharging her self-imposed probative obligations can enable the advocate to demand that her addressee accept a corresponding burden of proof. These observations tend to clarify inherited conceptions of probative obligations in terms vindicating their congruence with our ordinary conception and practice of competent argumentation.

In addition, this normative pragmatic account supports the resolution of a problem that some have claimed bedevils such accounts of presumption and probative obligations. As Professor Rescher reminds us, it makes little sense to talk about parties incurring obligations which could not, at least in favorable circumstances (and at least in principle), be discharged.[28] Accordingly, in American criminal courts a prosecutorial party bringing a charge of wrongdoing has the burden of establishing the guilt of the offending party beyond a reasonable shadow of doubt. This standard is established by the code governing legal proceedings and related precedents. However, in argumentation outside the court and similarly regulated institutions, we cannot look to rules to establish the limits of an arguer's probative burden. Accordingly, we need to identify other sources that establish in a principled way the parameters of an arguer's probative commitments.

Students of argumentation have devoted a good deal of attention to identifying the limits and sources of the arguer's probative obligations. A variety of views have been advanced. Some hold that where the arguer has advanced a proposition and, consequently, has a probative obligation, she is bound to provide supporting reasons and evidence and, further, to answer *all standard* doubts and objections which might be raised regarding her proposition.[29] Others have thought that this view attributes an unduly large burden to the committed arguer. Perhaps she need only address the doubts and objections actually raised by parties to which her proposition is addressed. Alternatively, it has been suggested that she is bound to address whatever issues are deemed essential by the ideal community of arguers, but this raises the question of what constitutes membership in that community. Others have approached this question in terms of the requirement that the advocate's burden of proof commits her to providing a *prima facie case* in defense of her proposition, that is, a coherent body of good arguments addressing the issues inherent in her proposition. However, as Robert Scott long ago observed, this definition is all but vacuous, telling us only that a *prima facie* case consists in good arguments advanced in defense of some proposition(s).[30] These and other accounts contribute to our understanding of the parameters of the arguer's probative burdens, but they are more or less ad hoc and arbitrary.

The normative pragmatic account of presumption and probative burdens advanced above offers the foundation for a satisfying view of the parameters of the probative burdens arguers incur. According to this account, probative burdens are characteristically incurred in the performance of speech acts that typically initiate argumentation. We have seen that burdens undertaken in this way can be tailored to the interaction in which they are incurred and can be identified in terms enabling an arguer to make apparent how her arguments fit her probative obligations. Within this structure for the allocation of probative obligations, the parameters of the arguer's "burden of proof" are fixed by her self-imposed commitments. Moreover, as we have seen in our analysis of "Letter from Birmingham Jail," an arguer can, by discharging the probative obligation incurred with respect to a particular situation, realign the regnant probative obligations governing the interaction at hand, which in some cases shifts the burden of proof.[31]

## Concluding Response to Some Doubts and Objections

In the preceding discussion, I have tried to indicate how our normative account of presumptions and probative burden explicates the genius of probative obligations in the performance of various day-to-day communicative acts. We have addressed several problems that have bedeviled accounts of probative obligations in day-to-day discourse. We have seen how such obligations can arise in the absence of formal institutional rules and conventions. We have seen how the variety in the generation of such obligations can respond coherently to situational variation. We have seen how the parameters of such burdens can be fixed in their genesis, such that in favorable circumstances an advocate can reasonably make it apparent that her argumentation has discharged her probative commitments. This account speaks to difficulties argumentation theorists have raised in a long dialogue about probative burdens and probative obligations. The first, perhaps the most penetrating of these doubts, has questioned how and whether probative obligations can arise in ordinary discourse in the absence of regulatory institutional structure. We answer such doubts by recourse to widely accepted accounts of how obligations are incurred in the performances of various speech acts. Secondly, we have presented an account that coherently explicates the great variety exhibited by probative obligations as observed across plain discourse. Thirdly, we have seen how an arguer can develop an argument with the power to realign the probative obligations governing a discursive interaction.

Finally, we should notice that the story given above nestles nicely within a larger account of how obligations are engaged in the performance of a wide range of relatively well-understood communicative acts. Given that the present account starts from contemporary work in the philosophy of language and epistemology, rather than from views inherited in what may be regarded as the traditions of rhetorical and dialectical study, it has seemed to some that this account arises out of left field, divorced from the mainstream of scholarly inquiry into these topics. I submit that the preceding account speaks to inherited scholarly interest in these topics.

## Notes

1. Jean Goodwin, "One Question, Two Answers," in *Argumentation and Its Applications*, ed. by H. V. Hansen, R. C. Pinto, C. W. Tindale, J. A. Blair, and R. H. Johnson (Windsor, ON: OSSA, 2001), available online in the OSSA 4 Conference Archive at http://scholar.uwindsor.ca/ossaarchive/; Jean Goodwin, "Argument Has No Function," *Informal Logic* 27, no. 1 (2007): 69–90; Scott Jacobs, "Argumentation as Normative Pragmatics," in *Proceedings of the Fourth International Conference on the Study of Argumentation*, (Amsterdam: Sic Sat, 1999), 397–403.
2. Nicholas Rescher, *Dialectics: A Controversy-Oriented Approach to the Theory of Knowledge* (Albany: State University of New York Press, 1977), 29–30.
3. F. H. van Eemeren and Rob Grootendorst, *Argumentation, Communication, and Fallacies: A Pragma-Dialectical Perspective* (Hillsdale, NJ: Lawrence Erlbaum Associates, 1992).
4. F. H. van Eemeren, *Strategic Maneuvering in Argumentative Discourse: Ex-*

*tending the Pragma-Dialectical Theory of Argumentation* (Amsterdam: John Benjamin, 2010).

5. Work by Sally Jackson and Scott Jacobs pioneered understanding of the connections between speech acts and argumentation. See Sally Jackson, "Virtual Standpoints and the Pragmatics of Conversational Argument," in *Argumentation Illuminated*, ed. F. H. van Eemeren, R. Grootendorst, J. A. Blair, and C. A. Willard (Amsterdam: SicSat, 1992), 260–69; Scott Jacobs, "The Management of Disagreement in Conversation," in *Argumentation across the Lines of Disciplines*, ed. F. H. van Eemeren, R. Grootendorst, J. A. Blair, and C. A. Willard (Dordrecht: Foris, 1987), 229–39; Scott Jacobs, "Speech Acts and Argument," *Argumentation* 3, no. 4 (1989): 345–65; Scott Jacobs, "Rhetoric and Dialectic from the Standpoint of Normative Pragmatics," *Argumentation* 14, no. 3 (2000): 261–86; Sally Jackson and Scott Jacobs, "Structure of Conversational Argument: Pragmatic Bases for the Enthymeme," *Quarterly Journal of Speech* 66, no. 3 (1980): 251–65; Sally Jackson and Scott Jacobs, "Derailments of Argumentation: It Takes Two to Tango," in *Considering Pragma-Dialectics*, ed. P. Houtlosser and A. van Rees (Mahwah, NJ: Lawrence Erlbaum Associates, 2006), 121–34; Sally Jackson and Scott Jacobs, "Designing Countermoves to Questionable Argumentative Tactics," in *Contemporary Perspectives on Argumentation: Views from the Venice Argumentation Conference*, ed. F. H. van Eemeren, M. D. Hazen, P. Houtlosser, and D. C. Williams (Amsterdam: SicSat, 2006); and Sally Jackson and Scott Jacobs, "Speech Act Structure in Conversation: Rational Aspects of Pragmatic Coherence," in *Conversational Coherence: Form, Structure, and Strategy*, ed. R. T. Craig and K. Tracy (Beverly Hills, CA: Sage, 1983).

6. For a nuanced discussion, see van Eemeren, *Strategic Maneuvering*, 213–40. Also Alfred Sidgwick, *Fallacies: A View of Logic from the Practical Side* (New York: Appleton, 1884). See the selection reprinted in this volume, ch. 6.

7. A. C. Baird, *Argumentation, Discussion and Debate* (New York: McGraw-Hill, 1950); G. Cronkhite, "The Locus of Presumption," *Central States Speech Journal* 17, no. 4 (1966): 270–76; van Eemeren and Grootendorst, *Argumentation, Communication, and Fallacies*, 120–21; D. Ehninger, "Decision by Debate: A Re-examination" *Quarterly Journal of Speech* 45, no. 4 (1959): 282–87; R. H. Gaskins, *Burdens of Proof in Modern Discourse* (New Haven, CT: Yale University Press, 1992), 267–69; G. Thomas Goodnight, "The Liberal and the Conservative Presumption: On Political Philosophy and the Foundation of Public Argument," *Proceedings of the Summer Conference on Argumentation* (Falls Church, VA: Speech Communication Association, 1980), 312–14; B. Hill and R. W. Leeman, *The Art and Practice of Argumentation and Debate* (Mountain View, CA: Mayfield, 1997), 141–43; C. Perelman and L. Olbrechts-Tyteca, *The New Rhetoric: A Treatise on Argumentation*, trans. J. Wilkinson and P. Weaver (Notre Dame, IN: University of Notre Dame Press, 1969), 71; Rescher, *Dialectics*, 28–34; E. Ullmann-Margalit, "On Presumption," *Journal of Philosophy* 80, no. 3 (1983): 147–52; C. A. Willard, *Argumentation and the Social Grounds of Knowledge* (Tuscaloosa: University of Alabama Press, 1983), 131.

8. Sidgwick, *Fallacies* (see this volume, ch. 6).

9. F. J. Kauffeld, "What Light Does Gronbeck Shed on the Adequacy of Whately's

Account of Presumption and Probative Obligations in Everyday Argument?" (paper presented at the 17th Biennial NCA/AFA Conference on Argumentation, Alta, Utah, 2011); Jackson and Jacobs, "Designing Countermoves."

10. F. J. Kauffeld, "The Ordinary Practice of Presuming and Presumption with Special Attention to Veracity and the Burden of Proof," in *Anyone Who Has a View: Theoretical Contributions to the Study of Argumentation*, ed. F. H. van Eemeren, J. A. Blair, C. A. Willard, and A. F. Snoeck Henkemans (Dordrecht: Kluwer Academic, 2003), 133–47.

11. D. Ehninger and W. Brockriede, *Decision by Debate* (Toronto: Dodd, Mead, 1973); J. M. Sproule, "The Psychological Burden of Proof: On the Evolutionary Development of Richard Whately's Theory of Presumption," *Communications Monographs* 43, no. 2 (1976): 115–29.

12. Sidgwick, *Fallacies*.

13. G. J. Warnock, *The Object of Morality* (London: Methuen, 1971), 108.

14. P. F. Strawson, "Freedom and Resentment," in *Studies in the Philosophy of Thought and Action*, ed. P. F. Strawson (New York: Oxford University Press, 1968), 71–96.

15. R. Moran, "Problems of Sincerity," *Proceedings of the Aristotelian Society* 105, no. 1 (2005): 341–61.

16. Kauffeld, "The Ordinary of Practice of Presuming." 136–37.

17. F. J. Kauffeld, "Presumption and the Distribution of Argumentative Burdens in Acts of Proposing and Accusing," *Argumentation* 12, no. 2 (1998): 245–66.

18. Kauffeld, "Presumption and Distribution," 252–59.

19. M. L. King Jr., "Letter from Birmingham Jail," in *Reporting Civil Rights*, pt. 1, *American Journalism, 1941–1963* (New York: Library of America, 2003), 777–94.

20. King, "Letter," 777.

21. King, "Letter," 785.

22. King, "Letter," 785–86.

23. Warnock, *Object of Morality*, 94–117.

24. King, "Letter," 789.

25. King, "Letter," 790.

26. King, "Letter," 790–791.

27. King, "Letter," 792.

28. N. Rescher, *Presumption and the Practices of Tentative Cognition* (Cambridge: Cambridge University Press, 2006), 30.

29. R. Johnson, "Differences between Argumentative and Rhetorical Space," in *Argumentation and Rhetoric*, ed. H. V. Hansen, C. W. Tindale, and A. V. Colman (St. Catharines, ON: OSSA, 1998), available online in the OSSA 2 Conference Archive at http://scholar.uwindsor.ca/ossaarchive/.

30. R. Scott, "On the Meaning of the Term *Prima Facie* in Argumentation," *Central States Speech Journal* 12, no. 1 (1960): 33–37.

31. Commenting on my view that probative burdens are incurred in certain speech acts, Ulrike Hahn and Mike Oaksford suggest that if the performance of these speech acts give rise to no more than a commitment to saying *something*, then

no particular standards regarding the limits of associated burdens of proof are entailed. That might be so, but as we have seen, the performance of various illocutionary acts requires saying something with a rather specific propositional content and/or openly speaking with a specific addressee-regarding intention. Accordingly, they commonly commit a speaker to more than Hahn and Oaksford envision ("The Burden of Proof and Its Role in Argumentation," *Argumentation* 21, no. 1 [2007]: 39–61).

# A Bibliography for
# Argumentation Theorists

This bibliography is divided into two parts: (1) primary and secondary historical sources and (2) contemporary developments.

## Primary and Secondary Historical Sources

Anderson, Floyd Douglas, and Merwyn Hayes. "Presumption and Burden of Proof in Whately's Speech on the Jewish Civil Disabilities Bill." *Speech Monographs* 34, no. 2 (1967): 133–36.

Best, William M. *A Treatise on the Principles of Evidence and Practice as to Proofs in Courts of Common Law, with Elementary Rules for Conducting the Examination and Cross-Examination of Witnesses*. Philadelphia: T. and J. W. Johnson, 1849.

Bentham, Jeremy. "Of the Burthen of Proof: On Whom Shall It Lie?" Chap. 28 in *An Introductory View of the Rationale of Evidence for the Use of Non-Lawyers as Well as Lawyers*, vol. 6 of *The Works of Jeremy Bentham*, edited by John Bowring. New York: Russell and Russell, 1843.

———. *The Theory of Legislation*. Edited by C. K. Ogden. London: Kegan Paul, Trench, Trubner, 1931. Original work published 1802.

Blackstone, William. *Commentaries on the Laws of England*. 2nd ed. 2 vols. Boston: Bumsteads, 1799.

Chimovitz, David S. "The Play of Presumption: A Derridian Examination of Whately's Concept of Presumption." In *Proceedings of the Fifth Conference of the International Society for the Study of Argumentation*, edited by F. H. van Eemeren, Rob Grootendorst, J. A. Blair, and Charles Willard, 603–9. Amsterdam: Sic Sat, 2002.

Ehninger, Douglas. "Editor's Introduction." In Richard Whately, *Elements of Rhetoric*, 7th ed., ix–xxx. Carbondale: Southern Illinois University Press, 1963.

———. "Selected Theories of *Inventio* in English Rhetoric, 1759–1828." PhD diss., Ohio State University, 1949.

Franklin, James. *The Science of Conjecture: Evidence and Probability before Pascal*. Baltimore, MD: Johns Hopkins University Press, 2001. Contains a historical explanation about presumptions and burdens of proof in ancient law and medieval law.

Giuliani, Adolfo. "Civilian Treatises on Presumptions (1580–1620)." In *The Law of Presumptions: Essays in Comparative Legal History*, edited by R. H. Helmholz and W. D. H. Sellar, 21–71. Berlin: Duncker and Humblot, 2009.

Gronbeck, Bruce E. "Archbishop Richard Whately's Doctrine of 'Presumption' and 'Burden of Proof': An Historical-Critical Analysis." Master's thesis, University of Iowa, 1966.

———. "Theories of Presumption in Western Argumentation: Social Realism, Legal Axiology, and Psychological Uptake." In *Reasoned Argument and Social Change: Selected Papers of 17th Biennial Conference on Argumentation*, edited by R. C. Rowland, 284–92. Washington, DC: National Communication Association, 2011.

———. "Whately's Theory of Presumption and the Law." Presented at the Speech Communication Association Convention, Chicago, 1966.

Hill, Adam S. *The Principles of Rhetoric and Their Application*. New York: Harper and Brothers, 1878.

Hohmann, Hanns. "Presumptions in Legal Argumentation: From Antiquity to the Middle Ages." In *Argumentation at the Century's Turn*, edited by H. V. Hansen, C. W. Tindale, and E. Sveda. St. Catharines, ON: OSSA, 1999. Available online in the OSSA 3 Conference Archive at http://scholar.uwindsor.ca/ossaarchive/.

Ilbert, Courtenay Peregrine. "Evidence." In *Encyclopædia Britannica*, 11th ed., 10:11–21. New York: Encyclopædia Britannica, 1910.

Kauffeld, Fred. J. "What Light Does Gronbeck Shed on the Adequacy of Whately's Account of Presumption and Probative Obligations in Everyday Argument?" In *Reasoned Argument and Social Change*, edited by R. C. Rowland, 293–300. Washington, DC: National Communication Association, 2011.

Lawson, John Davison. *The Law of Presumptive Evidence: Including Presumptions Both of Law and of Fact, and the Burden of Proof Both in Civil and Criminal Cases, Reduced to Rules*. San Francisco: A. L. Bancroft, 1885.

Parrish, Wayland M. "Whately and His Rhetoric." *Quarterly Journal of Speech* 15, no. 1 (1929): 58–79. Reprinted in *Historical Studies of Rhetoric and Rhetoricians*, edited by R. F. Howes. Ithaca: Cornell University Press, 1961.

Richards, Ivor A. *The Philosophy of Rhetoric*. 1936. New York. Oxford University Press, 1965.

Schauer, Frederick. "Bentham on Presumed Offences." *Utilitas* 23, no. 4 (2011): 363–79.

Sidgwick, Alfred. *Fallacies: A View of Logic from the Practical Side*. New York: D. Appleton, 1884. See especially part 2, chap. 3, "The Burden of Proof."

Sproule, J. Michael. "The Psychological Burden of Proof: On the Evolutionary Development of Richard Whately's Theory of Presumption." *Communication Monographs* 43, no. 2 (1976): 115–29.

Stephen, James F. *A Digest of the Law of Evidence*. 4th ed. New York, 1887.

Thayer, James B. "The Burden of Proof." *Harvard Law Review* 4, no. 2 (1890): 45–70.

———. *A Preliminary Treatise on Evidence at the Common Law*. Boston: Little, Brown, 1898. See chaps. 8–9.

Whately, Richard. *Elements of Logic*. 9th ed. London: Longmans, Roberts, Green, 1875.

——. *Elements of Rhetoric: Comprising an Analysis of the Laws of Moral Evidence and of Persuasion, with Rules for Argumentative Composition and Elocution.* 7th ed. London: John W. Parker, 1846. Reprinted, and edited by Douglas Ehninger. Carbondale: Southern Illinois University Press, 1963.

Whedbee, Karen E. "Authority, Freedom and Liberal Judgment: The Presumptions and Presumptuousness of Whately, Mill, and Tocqueville." *Quarterly Journal of Speech* 84, no. 2 (1998): 171–89.

——. "Whately's Presumptions Revisited." In *Reasoned Argument and Social Change, Selected Papers of 17th Biennial Conference on Argumentation*, edited by R. C. Rowland, 309–16. Washington, DC: National Communication Association, 2011.

Wigmore, J. H. *A Treatise on the Anglo-American System of Evidence in Trials at Common Law, Including the Statutes and Judicial Decisions of All Jurisdictions of the United States and Canada.* 3rd ed. Boston: Little, Brown, 1937.

## Contemporary Developments

Aijaz, I., J. McKeown-Green, and A. Webster. "Burdens of Proof and the Case for Unevenness." *Argumentation* 27, no. 3 (2013): 259–82.

Allen, R. J. "Presumptions in Civil Actions Reconsidered." *Iowa Law Review* 66 (1981): 843–67.

Bermejo Luque, L. "Being a Correct Presumption vs. Being Presumably the Case." *Informal Logic* 36, no. 1 (2016): 1–25.

Bermejo Luque, L., and Cristina Corridor. "Introduction for a Special Volume on Presumptions, Presumptive Inferences, and Burdens of Proof." *Argumentation* 31, no. 3 (2017): 463–67.

Biddle, Phillips R. "Presumption and Burden of Proof in Selected Twentieth Century Textbooks on Argumentation." Master's thesis, University of Illinois, 1963.

Blair, J. Anthony. "Walton's Argumentation Schemes for Presumptive Reasoning: A Critique and Development." *Argumentation* 15, no. 4 (2001): 365–79.

Bodlović, Petar. "Dialogical Features of Presumptions: Difficulties for Walton's New Dialogical Theory." *Argumentation* 31, no. 3 (2017): 513–34.

Cleary, Edward W. "Presuming and Pleading: An Essay on Juristic Immaturity." *Stanford Law Review* 12, no. 1 (1959): 5–28.

Corredor, Cristina. "Presumptions in Speech Acts." *Argumentation* 31, no. 3 (2017): 573–89.

Cronkhite, Gary. "The Locus of Presumption." *Central States Speech Journal* 17, no. 4 (1966): 270–76.

Dare, T., and J. Kingsbury. "Putting the Burden of Proof in Its Place: When Are Differential Allocations Legitimate?" *Southern Journal of Philosophy* 46, no. 4 (2008): 503–18.

Epstein, Richard A. "Pleadings and Presumptions." *University of Chicago Law Review* 40, no. 4 (1973): 556–82.

Flew, Antony. "The Presumption of Atheism." *Canadian Journal of Philosophy* 2, no. 1 (1972): 29–46. Also in Flew's *God, Freedom and Immortality*, 13–20. Buffalo: Prometheus Books, 1984.

Freeman, James B. *Acceptable Premises: An Epistemic Approach to an Informal Logic Problem*. Cambridge: Cambridge University Press, 2005.

———. "The Appeal to Popularity and Presumption by Common Knowledge." In *Fallacies: Classical and Contemporary Readings*, edited by Hans V. Hansen and Robert C. Pinto, 265–73. University Park: Penn State Press, 1995.

———. "Comments on Fred Kauffeld's 'Presumption and the Distribution of Argumentative Burdens in Acts of Proposing and Accusing.'" In *Argumentation and Rhetoric*, edited by H. V. Hansen, C. W. Tindale, and A. V. Colman. St. Catharines, ON: OSSA, 1998. Available online in the OSSA 2 Conference Archive at http://scholar.uwindsor.ca/ossaarchive/.

———. "Review of Walton's Plausible Argument in Everyday Conversation." *Informal Logic* 18, nos. 2–3 (1996): 288–98.

Gama-Leyva, Raymundo. "The Nature and the Place of Presumptions in Law and Legal Argumentation." *Argumentation* 31, no. 3 (2017): 555–72.

Gaskins, Richard H. *Burdens of Proof in Modern Discourse*. New Haven, CT: Yale University Press, 1995.

Godden, David. "Presumption as a Modal Qualifier: Presumption, Inference, and Managing Epistemic Risk." *Argumentation* 31, no. 3 (2017): 485–511.

Godden, David, and Douglas N. Walton. "A Theory of Presumption for Everyday Argumentation." *Pragmatics and Cognition* 15, no. 2 (2007): 313–46.

Goodnight, G. Thomas. "The Liberal and the Conservative Presumptions: On Political Philosophy and the Foundations of Public Argument." In *Proceedings of the Summer Conference on Argumentation*, edited by Jack Rhodes and Sara Newell, 304–37. Falls Church, VA: Speech Communication Association, 1980.

Hahn, Ulrike, and Mike Oaksford. "The Burden of Proof and Its Role in Argumentation." *Argumentation* 21, no. 1 (2007): 39–61.

Kaiser, D. "Presumptions of Law and of Fact." *Marquette Law Review* 38, no. 4 (1955): 253–62.

Katzner, Louis. "Presumption of Reasons and Presumptions of Justice." *Journal of Philosophy* 70 (1973): 89–100.

———. "Presumptivist and Non-presumptivist Principles of Formal Justice." *Ethics* 81, no. 3 (1970): 253–58.

Kauffeld, Fred. "The Burden of Proof: A Macro or Micro Level Concept?" In *Reason Reclaimed*, edited by H. V. Hansen and R. C. Pinto, 65–74. Newport News, VA: Vale Press, 2007.

———. "On the Difference between Assumptions and Presumptions." In *Argumentation and Values: Proceedings of the Ninth SCA/AFA Conference on Argumentation*, edited by Sally Jackson, 509–14. Annandale, VA: Speech Communication Association, 1995.

———. "The Ordinary Practice of Presuming and Presumption with Special Attention to Veracity and the Burden of Proof." In van Eemeren et al., *Anyone Who Has a View*, 133–46.

———. "Pivotal Issues and Norms in Rhetorical Theories of Argumentation." In *Dialectic and Rhetoric: The Warp and Woof of Argumentation Analysis*, edited by F. H. van Eemeren and P. Houtlosser, 97–118. Dordrecht: Kluwer Academic Publishers, 2002.

———. "Presumption and the Distribution of Argumentative Burdens in Act of Proposing and Accusing." *Argumentation* 12, no. 2 (1998): 245–66.

———. "Ranking Considerations and Aligning Probative Obligations." In *Conductive Argument: An Overlooked Type of Defeasible Reasoning*, edited by J. A. Blair and R. H. Johnson, 158–66. London: College Publication, 2011.

———. "Strategies for Strengthening Presumptions and Generating Ethos by Manifestly Ensuring Accountability." In *Argumentation: Cognition and Community*, edited by F. Zenker. Windsor, ON: OSSA, 2011. Available online in the OSSA 9 Conference Archive at http://scholar.uwindsor.ca/ossaarchive/.

———. "What Are We Learning about the Pragmatics of the Arguers' Obligations?" In *Concerning Argument: Selected Papers from the 15th Biennial Conference on Argumentation*, edited by S. Jacobs, 1–33. Washington, DC: National Communication Association, 2007.

Knoll, P. X. "Presumption in the Introduction to the Argumentative Speech." *Quarterly Journal of Speech* 18, no. 4 (1932): 637–42.

Lewiński, Marcin. "Argumentation Theory without Presumptions." *Argumentation* 31, no. 3 (2017): 591–613.

Liu, Yameng. "Authority, Presumption, and Invention." *Philosophy and Rhetoric* 30, no. 4 (1997): 413–27.

Llewelyn, J. E. "Presuppositions, Assumptions, and Presumptions." *Theoria* 28, no. 2 (1962): 158–72.

Macagno, Fabrizio. "Dialectical and Heuristic Arguments: Presumptions and Burden of Proof." In *Dialectics, Dialogue and Argumentation: An Examination of Douglas Walton's Theories of Reasoning and Argument*, edited by Christopher Reed and Christopher Tindale, 45–57. London: College Publications, 2010.

———. "Presumptive Reasoning in Interpretation: Implicatures and Conflicts of Presumptions." *Argumentation* 26, no. 2 (2012): 233–65.

Macagno, Fabrizio, and Douglas Walton. "Presumptions in Legal Argumentation." *Ratio Juris* 25, no. 3 (2012): 271–300.

Marsh, Patrick O. "Is Debate Merely a Game for Conservative Players?" *Speaker and Gavel* 1, no. 2 (1964): 46–53.

McBaine, James P. "Burden of Proof: Presumptions." *UCLA Law Review* 2 (1954): 13–31.

McCahey, John P. "The Burdens of Persuasion and Production." *Proof: The Journal of the Trial Evidence Committee* 16, no. 3 (2008): 7–10.

McInerny, Ralph. "Why the Burden of Proof Is on the Atheist." *Truth: A Journal of Modern Thought* 1 (1985). http://www.leaderu.com/truth/1truth11.html.

Morgan, E. "Presumptions." *Washington State Law Review and State Bar Journal* 12 (1937): 255–81.

Morris W. "Knowledge as Justified Presumption." *Journal of Philosophy* 70, no. 6 (1973): 161–65.

Morton, J. C., and A. C. Hutchison. *The Presumption of Innocence.* Toronto: Carswell, 1987.

Nance, Dale. *The Burdens of Proof: Discriminatory Power, Weight of Evidence, and Tenacity of Belief.* Cambridge: Cambridge University Press, 2016.

———. "Civility and the Burden of proof." *Harvard Journal of Law & Public Policy* 17, no. 3 (1994): 647–90.

———. "Evidential Completeness and the Burden of Proof." *Hastings Law Journal* 49, no. 3 (1998): 621–62.

Parsons, Keith. *God and the Burden of Proof.* Buffalo, NY: Prometheus, 1989.

Petrosky, K. "The Public Face of Presumptions." *Episteme* 5, no. 3 (2008): 388–401.

Pigliucci, M., and M. Boudry. "Prove It! The Burden of Proof Game in Science vs. Pseudoscience Disputes." *Philosophia* 42, no. 2 (2014): 487–502.

Pinto, Robert C. "Dialectic and the Structure of Argument." In *Argument, Inference, and Dialectic.* Dordrecht: Kluwer, 2001.

———. "Burdens of Rejoinder." In *Reason Reclaimed,* edited by H. V. Hansen and Robert C. Pinto, 75–88. Newport News, VA: Vale Press, 2007.

Plumer, Gilbert. "Presumptions, Assumptions, and Presuppositions of Ordinary Arguments." *Argumentation* 31, no. 3 (2017): 469–84.

Räikkä, Juha. "Burden of Proof Rules in Social Criticism." *Argumentation* 11, no. 4 (1997): 463–77.

Rescher, Nicholas. *Dialectics: A Controversy-Oriented Approach to the Theory of Knowledge.* Albany: State University of New York Press, 1977.

———. *Methodological Pragmatism.* Oxford: Oxford University Press, 1976.

———. "Peirce and the Economy of Research." *Philosophy of Science* 43, no. 1 (1976): 71–98.

———. *Plausible Reasoning. An Introduction to the Theory and Practice of Plausible Inference.* Assen: Van Gorcum, 1976.

———. *Presumption and the Practices of Tentative Cognition.* Cambridge: Cambridge University Press, 2006.

———. *Rationality: A Philosophical Inquiry into the Nature and Rationale of Reason.* Oxford: Clarendon, 1988. See especially pp. 50–53.

———. "Response to Walton on Plausible Reasoning." *Informal Logic* 14, no. 1 (1992): 53–58.

Rescorla, M. "Shifting the Burden of Proof?" *Philosophical Quarterly* 59, no. 234 (2009): 86–109.

Rhode, Connie. "The Burden of Proof in Philosophical Persuasion Dialogue." *Argumentation* 31, no. 3 (2017): 535–54.

Scott, Robert L. "On the Meaning of the Term *Prima facie* in Argumentation." *Central States Speech Journal* 12, no. 1 (1960): 33–37.

Sillars, Malcolm O. "Audiences, Social Values, and the Analysis of Argument." *Speech Teacher* 22, no. 4 (1973): 291–303.

Ullmann-Margalit, Edna. "On Presumption." *Journal of Philosophy* 80, no. 3 (1983): 143–63.

———. "Some Presumptions." In *How Many Questions? Essays in Honor of Sydney Morgenbesser*, edited by L. S. Cauman, I. Levi, C. D. Parsons, and R. Schwartz, 451–73. Indianapolis, IN: Hackett, 1983.

Ullmann-Margalit, Edna, and Avishai Margalit. "Analyticity by Way of Presumption." *Canadian Journal of Philosophy* 12, no. 3 (1982): 435–52.

van Eemeren, Frans H. *Strategic Maneuvering in Argumentative Discourse.* Amsterdam: John Benjamins, 2010. See in particular chap. 8.

van Eemeren, Frans H., J. A. Blair, C. A. Willard, and A. F. Snoeck Henkmans, eds. *Anyone Who Has a View: Theoretical Contributions to the Study of Argumentation.* Dordrecht: Kluwer, 2003.

van Eemeren, Frans H., and Peter Houtlosser. "A Pragmatic View of the Burden of Proof." In van Eemeren et al., *Anyone Who Has a View*, 123–32.

———. "Strategic Maneuvering in Argumentative Discourse." *Discourse Studies* 1, no. 4 (1999): 479–97.

———. "Strategic Maneuvering with the Burden of Proof." In *Advances in Pragma-Dialectics*, edited by F. H. van Eemeren, 3–28. Amsterdam: Sic Sat, 2002.

Walton, Douglas N. "Burden of Proof." *Argumentation* 2, no. 2 (1988): 233–54.

———. *Burden of Proof, Presumption, and Argumentation.* Cambridge: Cambridge University Press, 2014.

———. "A Dialogical Theory of Presumption." *Artificial Intelligence and Law* 16, no. 2 (2008): 209–43.

———. *Plausible Argument in Everyday Conversation.* Albany: SUNY, 1992. Chap. 2 is about presumptions.

———. "Plausible Deniability and Evasion of Burden of Proof." *Argumentation* 10, no. 1 (1996): 47–58.

———. "Rules for Plausible Reasoning." *Informal Logic* 14, no. 1 (1992): 33–51.

———. "The Speech Act of Presumption." *Pragmatics and Cognition* 1, no. 1 (1993): 125–48.

Walton, Douglas N., and Erik C. W. Krabbe. *Commitment in Dialogue: Basic Concepts of Interpersonal Reasoning.* Albany: State University of New York Press, 1995.

Whedbee, Karen E. "Using Presumption as a Decision Rule in Value Debate." *Cross Examination Debate Association* 13 (1992): 25–36.

Williamson, T. "Philosophical Expertise and the Burden of Proof." *Metaphilosophy* 42, no. 3 (2011): 215–29.

# Works Cited

Adversi, Aldo. *Appunti biobibliografici sul giureconsulto Pillio da Medicina*. Florence: Sansoni, 1960.

Aijaz, I., J. McKeown-Green, and A. Webster. "Burdens of Proof and the Case for Unevenness." *Argumentation* 27, no. 3 (2013): 259–82.

Albert, H. *Traktat über kritische Vernunft*. 3rd ed. Tübingen: Mohr, 1975.

Allen, H. W., and J. Clubb. "Progressive Reform and the Political System." *Pacific Northwest Quarterly* 65, no. 3 (1974): 130–45.

Alston, William. "Concepts of Epistemic Justification." *Monist* 68, no. 1 (1985): 57–89.

Antiphon. *On the Murder of Herodes*. In *Antiphon. Andocides*, edited and translated by K. J. Maidment, vol. 1 of *Minor Attic Orators*, 147–231. Cambridge, MA: Harvard University Press, 1982.

Aristotle. *On Sophistical Refutations*. Translated by E. S. Forster. Cambridge, MA: Harvard University Press, Loeb Classical Library, 1958.

———. *Posterior Analytics*. In Barnes, *Complete Works of Aristotle*, 1:114–66.

———. *Rhetoric*. In *Basic Works of Aristotle*, translated by W. R. Roberts and edited by R. McKeon, 1318–1451. New York: Modern Library, 1941.

———. *Topics*. Translated by J. L. Ackrill. In Barnes, *Complete Works of Aristotle*, 1:167–277.

———. *Topics*. In vol. 1 of *The Works of Aristotle*, edited by W. D. Ross and translated by W. A. Pickard-Cambridge. London: Oxford University Press, 1928.

Asen, R. A., and D. C. Brouwer, eds. *Counterpublics and the State*. New York: State University of New York, 2001.

Bacon, Frances. *Novum Organum*. Edited by Lisa Jardine and M. Silverthorne. Cambridge: Cambridge University Press, 2000.

Baird, A. C. *Argumentation, Discussion, and Debate*. New York: McGraw-Hill, 1950.

Barnes, Jonathan, ed. *The Complete Works of Aristotle*. Vol. 1. Princeton, NJ: Princeton University Press, 1984.

Barth, E. M., and E. C. W. Krabbe. *From Axiom to Dialogue: A Philosophical Study of Logics and Argumentation*. Berlin: Walter de Gruyter, 1982.

Beanblossom, Ronald E., and Keith Lehrer, eds. *Thomas Reid's Inquiry and Essays*. Indianapolis, IN: Hackett, 1983.

Bentham, Jeremy. "Of the Burthen of Proof: On Whom Shall It Lie?" Chap. 28 in *An Introductory View of the Rationale of Evidence for the Use of Non-Lawyers as Well as Lawyers*, vol. 6 of *The Works of Jeremy Bentham*, edited by John Bowring. New York: Russell and Russell, 1843.

Bermejo-Luque, L. "Being a Correct Presumption vs. Being Presumably the Case." *Informal Logic* 36, no. 1 (2016): 1–25.

———. *Giving Reasons. A Linguistic-Pragmatic Approach to Argumentation Theory*. Dordrecht: Springer, 2011.

Best, William M. *A Treatise on the Principles of Evidence*. Philadelphia: T. & J. W. Johnson, 1949.

Biro, J., and H. Siegel. "Normativity, Argumentation, and an Epistemic Theory of Fallacies." In van Eemeren et al., *Argumentation Illuminated*, 85–103.

Bitzer, L. "Rhetoric and Public Knowledge." In *Rhetoric, Philosophy, and Literature: An Exploration*, edited by D. M. Burks. West Lafayette, IN: Purdue University Press, 1978.

Blair, J. Anthony. "Presumptive Reasoning/Argument: An Overlooked Class." *Protosociology* 13 (1999): 46–60.

Bodlović, P. "Dialogical Features of Presumptions: Difficulties for Walton's New Argumentation Theory." *Argumentation* 31, no. 3 (2017): 513–34.

Brock, B. L., J. W. Chesebro, J. F. Cragan, and J. Klumpp. *Public Policy Decision-Making: Systems Analysis and Comparative Advantage Debate*. New York: Harper Collins, 1973.

Brock, B. L., M. E. Huglen, J. F. Klumpp, and S. Howell. *Making Sense of Political Ideology: The Power of Language in a Democracy*. New York: Rowan and Littlefield, 2005.

Burke, Edmund. *Reflections on the French Revolution*. Vol. 24 of *The Harvard Classics*. New York: P. F. Collier and Son, 1909–14.

Cahn, Edmond. "Jurisprudence." *New York University Law Review* 30, no. 1 (1955): 150–69.

Cauman, L. S., I. Levi, C. D. Parsons, and R. Schwartz, eds. *How Many Questions: Essays in Honor of Sidney Morgenbesser*. Indianapolis, IN: Hackett, 1983.

Christenson, R. M., A. S. Engel, M. R. Jacobs, and H. Waltzer. *Ideologies and Modern Politics*. Nashville, TN: Thomas Nelson and Sons, 1972.

Cicero. *De inventione*.

Cicero. *Pro Caecina*.

Cicero. *Topica*.

Clarence-Smith, J. A. *Medieval Law Teachers and Writers, Civilian and Canonist*. Ottawa, ON: University of Ottawa Press, 1975.

Clarke, D. S., Jr. *Rational Acceptance and Purpose: An Outline of a Pragmatist Epistemology*. Totowa, NJ: Rowman and Littlefield, 1989.

Cleary, Edward W. "Presuming and Pleading: An Essay on Juristic Immaturity." *Stanford Law Review* 12, no. 1 (1959): 5–28.

Cohen, L. Jonathan. *An Essay on Belief and Acceptance*. Oxford: Oxford University Press, 1992.

Copi, Irving M., and Carl Cohen. *Introduction to Logic*. 12th ed. Upper Saddle River, NJ: Pearson/Prentice Hall, 2005.

*Corpus Iuris Civilis. Volumen Primum. Institutiones, Digesta*. 12th ed. Edited by T. Mommsen and Paul Krüger. Berlin: Weidmann, 1911.

Cronkhite, G. "The Locus of Presumption." *Central States Speech Journal* 17, no. 4 (1966): 270–76.

Crosswhite, J. "Universalities." *Philosophy and Rhetoric* 43, no. 44 (2010): 430–48.

Dare, Tim, and Justine Kingsbury. "Putting the Burden of Proof in Its Place: When Are Differential Allocations Legitimate?" *Southern Journal of Philosophy* 46, no. 4 (2008): 503–18.

De Morgan, Augustus. *Formal Logic; or, The Calculus of Inference, Necessary and Probable*. London: Taylor and Walton, 1847.

Dewey, J. *Democracy and Education: An Introduction to the Philosophy of Education*. New York: Macmillan, 1916.

———. *How We Think, a Restatement of the Relation of Reflective Thinking to the Educative Process*. Rev. ed. Boston: Heath, 1933.

———. *The Public and Its Problems*. Denver: Swallow, 1927.

Dickson, W. G. *A Treatise on the Law of Evidence in Scotland*. 2nd ed. Edinburgh: Bell and Bradfute, 1864.

Ehninger, Douglas. "Decision by Debate: A Re-examination." *Quarterly Journal of Speech* 45, no. 4 (1959): 282–87.

Ehninger, Douglas, and Wayne Brockriede. *Decision by Debate*. New York: Dodd, Mead, 1973.

Flew, Antony. "The Presumption of Atheism." *Canadian Journal of Philosophy* 2, no. 1 (1972): 29–46.

Fransen, Gérard. "Les Questions disputées dans les facultés de droit." In *Les Questions disputées et les questions quodlibétiques dans les facultés de théologie, de droit, et de médecine*, 223–77. Turnhout: Brepols, 1985.

Freeman, James B. *Acceptable Premises: An Epistemic Approach to an Informal Logic Problem*. Cambridge: Cambridge University Press, 2005.

———. "The Place of Informal Logic in Philosophy." *Informal Logic* 20, no. 2 (2000): 117–28.

———. "The Pragmatic Dimension of Premise Acceptability." In van Eemeren et al., *Anyone Who Has a View*, 17–26.

———. "Review of Plausible Argument in Everyday Conversation by D. Walton." *Informal Logic* 18, nos. 2–3 (1996): 288–98.

———. "Why Classical Foundationalism Cannot Provide a Proper Account of Premise Acceptability." *Inquiry: Critical Thinking across the Disciplines* 15, no. 4 (1996): 17–26.

Furberg, M. *Saying and Meaning: A Main Theme in J. L. Austin's Philosophy*. 1963. Oxford: Basil Blackwell, 1971.

Gadamer, Hans-Georg. *Truth and Method*. 2nd ed. Translated by J. Weinsheimer and D. G. Marshall. New York: Continuum, 1999.

Gama-Leyva, Raymundo. "The Nature and Place of Presumptions in Law and Legal Argumentation." *Argumentation* 31, no. 3 (2017): 555–72.

Gaskins, Richard H. *Burdens of Proof in Modern Discourse*. New Haven, CT: Yale University Press, 1992.

Genzmer, Erich. "Die Iustinianische Kodifikation und die Glossatoren." In *Atti del Congresso Internazionale di diritto romano (Bologna 1933)*, 1:345–430. Pavia: Successori Fratelli Fusi, 1934.

Givertz, H. K. *The Evolution of Liberalism*. Rev. ed. New York: Collier Books, 1963.

Godden, David. "The Importance of Belief in Argumentation: Belief, Commitment, and the Effective Resolution of a Difference of Opinion." *Synthese* 172, no. 2 (February 2010): 397–414.

———. "Presumption as a Modal Qualifier: Presumption, Inference, and Managing Epistemic Risk." *Argumentation* 31, no. 3 (2017): 485–511.

———. "Review of D. Walton, *Burden of Proof, Presumption, and Argumentation*." *Cogency* 7, no. 1 (Winter 2015): 91–107.

———. "Teaching Rational Entitlement and Responsibility: A Socratic Exercise." *Informal Logic (Teaching Supplement)* 34, no. 1 (2014): 124–51.

Godden David, and Douglas Walton. "A Theory of Presumption for Everyday Argumentation." *Pragmatics and Cognition* 15, no. 2 (2007): 313–46.

Goodnight, G. Thomas. "The Liberal and the Conservative Presumptions: On Political Philosophy and the Foundations of Public Argument." In *Proceedings of the Summer Conference on Argumentation*, edited by Jack Rhodes and Sara Newell, 304–37. Falls Church, VA: Speech Communication Association, 1980.

Goodwin, Jean. "Argument Has No Function." *Informal Logic* 27, no. 1 (2007): 69–90.

———. "One Question, Two Answers." In *Argumentation and Its Applications*, edited by H. V. Hansen, R. C. Pinto, C. W. Tindale, J. A. Blair, and R. H. Johnson. Windsor, ON: OSSA, 2001. Available online in the OSSA 4 Conference Archive at http://scholar.uwindsor.ca/ossaarchive/.

Govier, Trudy. "Arguing Forever? Or: Two Tiers of Argument Appraisal." In *Argumentation and Rhetoric*, edited by H. V. Hansen, C. W. Tindale, and A. V. Colman. St. Catharines, ON: OSSA, 1998. Available online in the OSSA 2 Conference Archive at http://scholar.uwindsor.ca/ossaarchive/.

———. *A Practical Study of Argument*. Belmont, CA: Wadsworth, 1985.

Grantham, D. W. *The Progressive Era and the Reform Tradition*. Indianapolis, IN: Bobbs-Merrill, 1964.

Grice, H. P. "Logic and Conversation." In *The Logic of Grammar*, edited by D. Davidson and G. Harman, 64–75. Berkeley: University of California Press, 1975. Originally lecture 2 of the 1968 Williams James Lectures, Harvard University.

Gronbeck, Bruce E. "Archbishop Richard Whately's Doctrine of 'Presumption' and 'Burden of Proof': An Historical-Critical Analysis." Master's thesis, University of Iowa, 1966.

Hahn, Ulrike, and Mike Oaksford. "The Burden of Proof and Its Role in Argumentation." *Argumentation* 21, no. 1 (March 2007): 39–61.

Hamblin, C. L. *Fallacies*. London: Methuen, 1970.

Hansen, Hans V. "Theories of Presumptions and Burdens of Proof." In *Informal Logic @ 25*, edited by J. A. Blair, R. H. Johnson, H. V. Hansen, and C. W. Tindale. Windsor, ON: OSSA, 2003. Available online in the OSSA 5 Conference Archive at http://scholar.uwindsor.ca/ossaarchive/.

Hawkins, Edward. *A Dissertation upon the Use and Importance of Unauthoritative Tradition*. Oxford: Baxter, 1819.

Hill, B., and R. W. Leeman. *The Art and Practice of Argumentation and Debate*. Mountain View, CA: Mayfield, 1997.

Hofstadter, R. *Anti-intellectualism in American Life*. New York: Knopf, 1962.

Hohmann, Hanns. "Rhetoric in Medieval Legal Education: Libellus Pylei Disputatorius." *Disputatio* 4 (1999): 59–73.

Horace. *Epistles*.

Horowitz, I. L. *Ideology and Utopia in the United States, 1956–1976*. New York: Oxford University Press, 1977.

Houtlosser, P. "Indicators of a Point of View." In van Eemeren, *Advances in Pragma-Dialectics*, 169–84.

Hungerland, Isabel. "Contextual Implication." *Inquiry* 3, nos. 1–4 (1960): 211–58.

Ilbert, Courtenay Peregrine. "Evidence." In *Encyclopædia Britannica*, 11th ed., 10:11–21. New York: Encyclopædia Britannica, 1910.

Jackson, Sally. "Fallacies and Heuristics." In *Analysis and Evaluation: Proceedings of the Third ISSA Conference on Argumentation*, edited by F. H. van Eemeren, R. Grootendorst, J. A. Blair, and C. A. Willard, 2:257–69. Amsterdam: Sic Sat, 1995.

———. "Virtual Standpoints and the Pragmatics of Conversational Argument." In van Eemeren et al., *Argumentation Illuminated*, 260–69.

Jackson, Sally, and Scott Jacobs. "Derailments of Argumentation: It Takes Two to Tango." In *Considering Pragma-Dialectics. A Festschrift for Frans H. Van Eemeren on the Occasion of His 60th Birthday*, edited by P. Houtlosser and A. van Rees, 121–33. Mahwah, NJ: Lawrence Erlbaum, 2006.

———. "Designing Countermoves to Questionable Argumentative Tactics." In *Contemporary Perspectives on Argumentation: Views from the Venice Argumentation Conference*, edited by F. H. van Eemeren, M. D. Hazen, P. Houtlosser, and D. C. Williams, 83–100. Amsterdam: Sic Sat, 2006.

———. "Speech Act Structure in Conversation: Rational Aspects of Pragmatic Coherence." In *Conversational Coherence: Form, Structure, and Strategy*, edited by R. T. Craig and K. Tracy, 47–66. Beverly Hills, CA: Sage, 1983.

———. "Structure of Conversational Argument: Pragmatic Bases for the Enthymeme." *Quarterly Journal of Speech* 66, no. 3 (1980): 251–65.

Jacobs, Scott. "Argumentation as Normative Pragmatics." In *Proceedings of the Fourth International Conference on the Study of Argumentation*, 397–403. Amsterdam: Sic Sat, 1999.

——. "The Management of Disagreement in Conversation." In *Argumentation across the Line of Disciplines*, edited by F. H. van Eemeren, R. Grootendorst, J. A. Blair, and C. A. Willard, 229–39. Dordrecht: Foris Publications, 1987.

——. "Rhetoric and Dialectic from the Standpoint of Normative Pragmatics." *Argumentation* 14, no. 3 (2000): 261–86.

——. "Speech Acts and Argument." *Argumentation* 3, no. 4 (1989): 345–65.

Johnson, Ralph. H. "Differences between Argumentative and Rhetorical Space." In *Argumentation and Rhetoric*, edited by H. V. Hansen, C. W. Tindale, and A. V. Colman. St. Catharines, ON: OSSA, 1998. Available online in the OSSA 2 Conference Archive at http://scholar.uwindsor.ca/ossaarchive/.

——. "More on Arguers and Dialectical Obligations." In *Argumentation at the Century's Turn*, edited by H. V. Hansen, C. W. Tindale, and E. Sveda. St. Catharines, ON: OSSA, 1999. Available online in the OSSA 3 Conference Archive at http://scholar.uwindsor.ca/ossaarchive/.

Johnson, Ralph H., and J. Anthony Blair. *Logical Self-Defense*. Toronto: McGraw-Hill Ryerson, 1977.

Johnstone, H. W., Jr. "Some Reflections on Argumentation." In *Philosophy, Rhetoric, and Argument*, edited by M. Natanson and H. W. Johnstone, 1–9. University Park: Penn State University Press, 1965.

Kaiser, David. "Presumptions of Law and of Fact." *Marquette Law Review* 37, no. 4 (1955): 253–62.

Kauffeld, Fred J. "On the Difference between Assumptions and Presumptions." In *Argumentation and Values: Proceedings of the Ninth SCA/AFA Conference on Argumentation*, edited by S. Jackson, 509–15. Alta, UT: Speech Communication Association, 1995.

——. "The Ordinary Practice of Presuming and Presumption with Special Attention to Veracity and the Burden of Proof." In van Eemeren et al., *Anyone Who Has a View*, 133–46.

——. "Pivotal Issues and Norms in Rhetorical Theories of Argumentation." In *Dialectic and Rhetoric: The Warp and Woof of Argumentation Analysis*, edited by F. H. van Eemeren and P. Houtlosser, 97–118. Dordrecht: Kluwer Academic, 2002.

——. "Presumption and Shifting the Burden of Proof." Paper presented at the IPrA Conference, 2005. Available online at http://www2.arnes.si/~ffljzagar/Kauffeld _paper.pdf.

——. "Presumption and the Distribution of Argumentative Burdens in Acts of Proposing and Accusing." *Argumentation* 12, no. 2 (1998): 245–66.

——. "Presumptions and the Distribution of Argumentative Burdens in Acts of Proposing and Accusing." *Argumentation* 12, no. 2 (1998): 245–66.

——. "What Light Does Gronbeck Shed on the Adequacy of Whately's Account of Presumption and Probative Obligations in Everyday Argument?" In *Reasoned Argument and Social Change*, edited by R. C. Rowland, 293–300. Alta, UT: Speech Communication Association, 2011.

King, Martin Luther, Jr. "Letter from Birmingham Jail." In *Reporting Civil Rights*, pt. 1, *American Journalism, 1941–1963*, 777–94. New York: Library of America, 2003.

Kirk, R. "Prospects for a Conservative Bent in the Human Sciences." *Social Research* 35, no. 4 (1968): 580–92.

Kunkel, Wolfgang. *An Introduction to Roman Legal and Constitutional History*. 2nd ed. Translated by J. M. Kelly. Oxford: Clarendon Press, 1973.

Kuttner, Stephan. "Réflexions sur les brocards des glossateurs." In *Mélanges Joseph de Ghellinck*, 2:767–92. Gembloux: Duculot, 1951.

Lamb, James. "Knowledge and Justified Presumption." *Journal of Philosophy* 69, no. 5 (1972): 123–27.

Lang, Albert. "Rhetorische Einflüsse auf die Behandlung des Prozesses in der Kanonistik des 12. Jahrhunderts." In *Festschrift für Eduard Eichmann zum 70. Geburtstag*, 69–97. Paderborn: Schöningh, 1940.

———. "Zur Entstehungsgeschichte der Brocardasammlungen." *Zeitschrift der Savigny-Stiftung für Rechtsgeschichte, Kanonistische Abteilung* 62 (1942): 106–41.

Langer, S. *Philosophy in a New Key: A Study in the Symbolism of Reason, Rite, and Art*. 3rd ed. Cambridge, MA: Harvard University Press, 1957.

Lee, M. J. *Postwar Words That Made an American Movement*. East Lansing: Michigan State University Press, 2014.

Leech, Geoffrey. *Principles of Pragmatics*. London: Longman, 1983.

Leff, Michael C. "Rhetoric and Dialectic in Martin Luther King's 'Letter from Birmingham Jail.'" In *Fifth Conference of the International Society for the Study of Argumentation*, edited by F. H. van Eemeren, A. Blair, C. A. Willard, and A. F. Snoeck Henkemans, 671–77. Amsterdam: Sic Sat, 2003.

———. "Rhetoric and Dialectic in the Twenty-First Century." *Argumentation* 14, no. 3 (2000): 241–54.

———. "The Topics of Argumentative Invention in Latin Rhetorical Theory from Cicero to Boethius." *Rhetorica* 1, no. 1 (1983): 23–44.

———. "Tradition and Agency in Humanistic Rhetoric." *Philosophy and Rhetoric* 36 (2003): 135–47.

Legal Information Institute. "Burden of Persuasion." Cornell Law School. Online at https://www.law.cornell.edu/cfr/text/12/108.10.

Lippmann, W. *Essays in the Public Philosophy: On the Decline and Revival of Western Society*. Boston: Little Brown, 1955.

Macagno, Fabrizio. "Presupposition as Argumentative Reasoning." In *Interdisciplinary Studies in Pragmatics, Culture and Society*, edited by A. Capone and J. L. Mey, 465–87. Cham, Switzerland: Springer, 2015.

Macagno, Fabrizio, and Douglas Walton. "Presumptions in Legal Argumentation." *Ratio Juris* 25, no. 3 (2012): 271–300.

MacKenzie, J., and P. Staines. "Hamblin's Case for Commitment: A Reply to Johnson." *Philosophy and Rhetoric* 32, no. 1 (1999): 14–39.

Manning, D. J. *Liberalism*. New York: St. Martin's, 1976.

McCahey, John P. "The Burdens of Persuasion and Production." *Proof: The Journal of the Trial Evidence Committee* 16, no. 3 (2008): 1, 8–9.

McCormick, C. T. *McCormick on Evidence*. 7th ed. Edited by K. S. Broun, G. E. Dix, E. J. Imwinkelried, D. H. Kaye, R. P. Mosteller, E. F. Roberts, and E. Swift. St. Paul, MN: Thomson Reuters/WestLaw, 2013.

———. *McCormick's Handbook of the Law of Evidence*. 2nd ed. Edited by E. W. Cleary. St. Paul, MN: West Publishing, 1972.

McKerrow, R. E. "Critical Rhetoric: Theory and Praxis." *Communication Monographs* 56, no. 2 (1989): 91–111.

Meyer-Nelthropp, Jürgen. *"Libellus Pylei Disputatorius Liber Primus."* PhD diss., Universität Hamburg, 1959.

Milton, John. *Paradise Lost*.

Minsky, M. "Frame-System Theory." In *Thinking: Readings in Cognitive Science*, edited by P. N. Johnson-Laird and P. C. Watson, 355–76. New York: Cambridge University Press, 1977.

Moran, R. "Problems of Sincerity." *Proceedings of the Aristotelian Society* 105, no. 1 (2005): 341–61.

Morley, J. *On Compromise*. New York: Macmillan, 1874 and 1891.

Morris, W. "Knowledge as Justified Presumption." *Journal of Philosophy* 70 (1973): 161–65.

Motzenbäcker, Rudolf. *Die Rechtsvermutung im Kanonischen Recht*. Munich: Kommissionsverlag Karl Zink, 1958.

O'Neill, James M., Craven Laycock, and Robert L. Scales. *Argumentation and Debate*. New York: Macmillan, 1917.

Park, Roger C., David P. Leonard, and Steven H. Goldberg. *Evidence Law*. St. Paul, MN: West Group, 1998.

Parrington, V. L. *Main Currents in American Thought, an Interpretation of American Literature from the Beginnings to 1920*. Vol. 1. New York: Harcourt, Brace, 1927.

Peake, Thomas. *A Compendium of the Law of Evidence*. London, 1801.

Peirce, Charles S. "Fraser's *The Works of George Berkeley*." In *The Essential Peirce: Selected Philosophical Writings*, edited by Nathan Houser and Christian Kloesel, 1:83–105. Bloomington: Indiana University Press, 1991.

Perelman, Chaïm. *Justice*. New York, Random House, 1967.

Perelman, Chaïm, and Lucie Olbrechts-Tyteca. *La nouvelle rhétorique: Traité de l'argumentation*. Paris: Presses Universitaires de France, 1958.

———. *The New Rhetoric: A Treatise on Argumentation*. Translated by John Wilkinson and Purcell Weaver. Notre Dame, IN: University of Notre Dame Press, 1969.

Pinto, R. C. *Argument, Inference, and Dialectic*. Dordrecht: Kluwer, 2001.

———. "Dialectic and the Structure of Argument." *Informal Logic* 6 (1984): 16–20.

Plano, J. C., and M. Greenberg. *The American Political Dictionary*. 4th ed. Hinsdale, IL: Dryden Press, 1976.

Plantinga, Alvin. *Warrant and Proper Function*. New York: Oxford University Press, 1993.

Plato. *The Republic*. Translated by Desmond Lee. London: Penguin, 1987.

Prakken, Henry, and Giovanni Sartor. "A Logical Analysis of Burdens of Proof." In

*Legal Evidence and Burden of Proof*, edited by Hendrik Kaptein, Henry Prakken, and Bart Verheij, 223–53. Farnham: Ashgate, 2009.

Quintilian. *Institutio Oratoria*. Translated by H. E. Butler. New York: G. P. Putnam's Sons; London: William Heinemann, 1922.

Randall, J. H. *Aristotle*. New York: Columbia University Press, 1960.

Rees, M. A. van. "Comments on 'Rhetoric and Dialectic in the Twenty-First Century.'" *Argumentation* 14, no. 3 (2000): 255–59.

Rescher, Nicholas. *Dialectics: A Controversy-Oriented Approach to the Theory of Knowledge*. Albany: State University of New York Press, 1977.

———. *Plausible Reasoning*. Assen: Van Gorcum, 1976.

———. *Presumption and the Practices of Tentative Cognition*. Cambridge: Cambridge University Press, 2006.

Rescorla, M. "Shifting the Burden of Proof?" *Philosophical Quarterly* 59, no. 234 (2009): 86–109.

Rhode, Conny. "The Burden of Proof in Philosophical Persuasion Dialogue." *Argumentation* 31, no. 3 (2017): 535–54.

Safire, W. *Political Dictionary*. New York: Random House, 1978.

Santini, Giovanni. *Università e società nel XII secolo: Pillio da Medicina e lo Studio di Modena. Tradizione e innovazione nella scuola dei glossatori*. Modena: S.T.E.M.-Mucchi, 1979.

Scott, R. L. "On the Meaning of the Term Prima Facie in Argumentation." *Central States Speech Journal* 12, no. 1 (1960): 33–37.

Searle, J. R. *Speech Acts. An Essay in the Philosophy of Language*. Cambridge: Cambridge University Press, 1969.

Shah, N. "Burden of Proof." *Political Geography* 51 (March 2016): 87–88.

Shakespeare, William. *Twelfth Night*.

Sibley, M. Q. *Political Ideas and Ideologies: A History of Political Thought*. New York: Harper and Row, 1970.

Sidgwick, Alfred. *Fallacies: A View of Logic from the Practical Side*. New York: D. Appleton, 1884.

Sperber, H., and T. Trittschuh. *American Political Terms: An Historical Dictionary*. Detroit, MI: Wayne State University Press, 1962.

Spitz, D. *Essays in the Liberal Idea of Freedom*. Tucson: University of Arizona Press, 1964.

Sproule, J. Michael. "The Psychological Burden of Proof: On the Evolutionary Development of Richard Whately's Theory of Presumption." *Communications Monographs* 43, no. 2 (1976): 115–29.

Stephen, James Fitzjames. *A Digest of the Law of Evidence*. 3rd ed. London: Macmillan, 1877.

———. *A Digest of the Law of Evidence*. 4th ed. London: Macmillan, 1887.

Strawson, P. F. "Freedom and Resentment." In *Studies in the Philosophy of Thought and Action*, edited by P. F. Strawson, 71–96. New York: Oxford University Press, 1968.

Taylor, J. *Modern Social Imaginaries*. Durham, NC: Duke University Press, 2004.

Thayer, J. "Burden of Proof." *Harvard Law Review*, 4, no. 2 (1890): 45–70.

Thucydides. *The History of the Peloponnesian War.* Translated by Benjamin Jowett. https://ebooks.adelaide.edu.au/t/thucydides/jowett/book2.html.

Toulmin, Stephen E. *The Return to Reason.* Cambridge, MA: Harvard University Press, 2001.

———. *The Uses of Argument.* 1958. Cambridge: Cambridge University Press, 2003.

Tyndall, John. *Essays on the Floating Matters of the Air.* New York: Appleton, 1884.

Ullmann-Margalit, Edna. "On Presumptions." *Journal of Philosophy* 80, no. 3 (1983): 143–63.

Ullmann-Margalit, Edna., and A. Margalit. "Analyticity by Way of Presumption." *Canadian Journal of Philosophy* 12, no. 3 (1982): 435–52.

van Eemeren, F. H., ed. *Advances in Pragma-Dialectics.* Amsterdam: Sic Sat, 2002.

———. "For Reason's Sake: Maximal Argumentative Analysis of Discourse." In *Argumentation: Across the Lines of Discipline. Proceedings of the Conference on Argumentation 1986,* edited by F. H. van Eemeren, R. Grootendorst, J. A. Blair, and C. A. Willard, 201–15. Dordrecht: Foris, 1987.

———. *Strategic Maneuvering in Argumentative Discourse. Extending the Pragma-Dialectical Theory of Argumentation.* Amsterdam: John Benjamins, 2010.

van Eemeren, F. H., J. A. Blair, C. A. Willard, and A. F. Snoeck Henkemans, eds. *Anyone Who Has a View: Theoretical Contributions to the Study of Argumentation.* Dordrecht: Kluwer Academic, 2003.

van Eemeren, F. H., B. Garssen, and B. Meuffels. "'I Don't Have Anything to Prove Here': The (Un)Reasonableness of Evading the Burden of Proof." In *Proceedings of the Fifth Conference of the International Society for the Study of Argumentation,* edited by F. H. van Eemeren, A. F. Snoeck Henkemans, J. A. Blair, and C. A. Willard, 281–84. Amsterdam: Sic Sat, 2003.

van Eemeren, F. H., and R. Grootendorst. *Argumentation, Communication, and Fallacies: A Pragma-Dialectical Perspective.* Hillsdale, NJ: Lawrence Erlbaum Associates, 1992.

———. *Speech Acts in Argumentative Discussions: A Theoretical Model for the Analysis of Discussions Directed towards Solving Conflicts of Opinion.* Dordrecht: Foris/Mouton de Gruyter, 1984.

———. "The Study of Argumentation from a Speech Act Perspective." In *Selected Papers of the International Pragmatics Conference,* edited by J. Verschueren, 1:151–70. Amsterdam: John Benjamins, 1991.

———. *A Systematic Theory of Argumentation: The Pragma-Dialectical Approach.* New York: Cambridge University Press, 2004.

van Eemeren, F. H., R. Grootendorst, J. A. Blair, and C. A. Willard, eds. *Argumentation Illuminated.* Amsterdam: Sic Sat, 1992.

van Eemeren, F. H., and P. Houtlosser. "Strategic Maneuvering with the Burden of Proof." In *Advances in Pragma-Dialectics,* 13–28.

van Eemeren, F. H., B. Meuffels, and M. Verburg. "The (Un)Reasonableness of the *Argumentum ad Hominem.*" *Journal of Language and Social Psychology* 19, no. 4 (December 2000): 416–35.

Venn, John. *The Logic of Chance.* London: MacMillan, 1866.

Viereck, P. *Conservatism Revisited: The Revolt against Ideology, 1815–1949*. New York: Scribner, 1949.

Walton, Douglas N. "Abductive, Presumptive, and Plausible Arguments." *Informal Logic* 21, no. 2 (2001): 141–69.

———. *Arguer's Position*. Westport, CT: Greenwood Press, 1985.

———. *Argumentation Schemes for Presumptive Reasoning*. Mahwah, NJ: Lawrence Erlbaum, 1996.

———. "Burden of Proof." *Argumentation* 2, no. 2 (1988): 233–54.

———. *Burden of Proof, Presumption, and Argumentation*. Cambridge: Cambridge University Press, 2014.

———. "A Dialogical Theory of Presumption." *Artificial Intelligence and Law* 16, no. 2 (2008): 209–43.

———. *Informal Logic: A Handbook for Critical Argumentation*. Cambridge: Cambridge University Press, 1989.

———. *The New Dialectic: Conversational Contexts of Argument*. Toronto: University of Toronto Press, 1998.

———. *The Place of Emotion in Argument*. University Park: Penn State University Press, 1992.

———. *Plausible Argument in Everyday Conversation*. Albany: State University of New York Press, 1992.

———. "Presumption, Burden of Proof, and Lack of Evidence." *L'Analisi linguistica e letteraria* 16, no. 3 (2008): 49–71.

———. "The Speech Act of Presumption." *Pragmatics and Cognition* 1, no. 3 (1993): 233–54.

Walton, Douglas, and E. C. W. Krabbe. *Commitment in Dialogue: Basic Concepts of Interpersonal Reasoning*. Albany: State University of New York Press, 1995.

Walton, Douglas, C. Reed, and F. Macagno. *Argumentation Schemes*. Cambridge: Cambridge University Press, 2008.

Warnock, G. J. *The Object of Morality*. London: Methuen, 1971.

Weimar, Peter. "Die legistische Literatur der Glossatorenzeit." In *Handbuch der Quellen und Literatur der neueren europäischen Privatrechtsgeschichte: Mittelalter (1100–1500)*, edited by Helmut Coing, 129–260. Munich: Beck, 1973.

Wenzel, Joseph W. "Jürgen Habermas and the Dialectical Perspective on Argumentation." *Journal of the American Forensic Association* 16, no. 2 (1979): 83–94.

Wharton, Francis. *Disputed Questions of Evidence: Relevancy, Presumptions of Law and Presumptions of Fact*. St. Louis, MO: G. I. Jones, 1877. Available at https://archive.org/details/disputedquestion00whar.

Whately, Richard. *Charges and Other Tracts*. London: B. Fellowes, 1836.

———. *Easy Lessons on Christian Evidences*. London: John W. Parker 1838.

———. *Elements of Logic*. 9th ed. London: Longmans, Green, 1875.

———. *Elements of Rhetoric Comprising an Analysis of the Laws of Moral Evidence and of Persuasion, with Rules for Argumentative Composition and Elocution*. 2nd ed. Oxford: W. Baxter for John Murray and J. Parker, 1828.

———. *Elements of Rhetoric: Comprising an Analysis of the Laws of Moral Evidence and of Persuasion, with Rules for Argumentative Composition and Elocution.* 7th ed. London: John W. Parker, 1846. Reprinted, and edited by Douglas Ehninger. Carbondale: Southern Illinois University Press, 1963.

———. *The Kingdom of Christ Delineated in Two Essays.* London: B. Fellowes, 1841.

Willard, C. A. *Argumentation and the Social Grounds of Knowledge.* Tuscaloosa: University of Alabama Press, 1983.

Williamson, Timothy. "Philosophical Expertise and the Burden of Proof." *Metaphilosophy* 42, no. 3 (2011): 215–29.

Wilson, R. J. *In Quest of Community: Social Philosophy in the United States, 1860–1920.* New York: John Wiley and Sons, 1968.

Wolfe, A. B. "Conservatism and Radicalism: Some Definitions and Distinctions." *Scientific Monthly* 17, no. 3 (1923): 229–37.

Zarefsky, D. H., and V. J. Gallagher. "From 'Conflict' to 'Constitutional Question': Transformations in Early American Public Discourse." *Quarterly Journal of Speech* 76, no. 3 (1990): 247–61.

# About the Authors

**Aristotle** (384–322 BC) was a student of Plato and is perhaps the world's most complete argumentation theorist. His original and perceptive work in logic (*Prior Analytics*), dialectics (*Topics*), and rhetoric (*Rhetoric*) richly repays study to this day.

**Jeremy Bentham** (1748–1832) was trained as a lawyer and was, as our selection indicates, especially interested in legal reform. He is thought of as the chief architect of modern utilitarianism and was a great influence on the young John Stuart Mill. Bentham's main work is the *Principles of Morals and Legislation* (1789).

**Lilian Bermejo-Luque** has written extensively on the central issues in argumentation. She is the author of *Giving Reasons: A Linguistic Pragmatic Approach to Argumentation Theory* (2011). Presently, she holds a research position in the department of philosophy at the University of Granada in Spain. Dr. Bermejo-Luque is one of the editors of this volume.

**Wayne Brockriede** (1922–1986) taught at a number of universities in the United States, including the University of Colorado. In addition to being coauthor of *Decision by Debate* (1963), he is remembered for his influential articles "Arguers as Lovers" (1972) and "Where Is Argument?" (1975).

**James Crosswhite** is a professor of English at the University of Oregon and Norman H. Brown Faculty Fellow in the Liberal Arts. He has directed writing programs at the University of California, San Diego, and at the University of Oregon. He is the author of *The Rhetoric of Reason: Writing and the Attractions of Argument* (1996) and *Deep Rhetoric: Philosophy, Reason, Violence, Justice, Wisdom* (2013).

**Douglas Ehninger** (1913–1979) taught for most of his career at the University of Iowa. In addition to being coauthor of *Decision by Debate* (1963), he was the author of a number of influential articles about arguments and argumentation.

**James B. Freeman** is a professor of philosophy at Hunter College of the City University of New York. His research includes logic (both formal and informal), argumentation theory, and epistemology, and currently concentrates on the problem of connection adequacy for defeasible arguments. His principal publications include *Dialectics and the Macrostructure of Arguments* (1991), *Acceptable Premises: An Epistemic Approach to an Informal Logic Problem* (2005), and *Argument Structure: Representation and Theory* (2011). He is one of the editors of the present volume.

**Richard Gaskins** is the Joseph M. Proskauer Professor of Law and Social Welfare at Brandeis University in Boston, where he directs the Legal Studies Program. He is the author of *Burdens of Proof in Modern Discourse* (1992). His most recent publication on argumentation is "The Legal Characterization of Facts at the International Criminal Court" (2016). He received his PhD (philosophy) and JD degrees from Yale University. In addition to teaching at universities in Philadelphia, Chicago, and New York, he has been a visiting professor in New Zealand, the Netherlands, and Iceland.

**David Godden** is an assistant professor of philosophy at Michigan State University. He is among the second generation of Canadian informal logicians, whose research addresses normative issues in the theory of reasoning and argument. His previous work on the topic of presumption includes the articles "A Theory of Presumption for Everyday Argumentation" (2005), coauthored with Douglas Walton, and "Presumption as a Modal Qualifier: Presumption, Inference, and Managing Epistemic Risk" (2017).

**G. Thomas Goodnight** is a professor at the Annenberg School of Communication. International studies of argumentation is his specialty; he served as a Fulbright Senior Scholar in Communication & Journalism. He has directed the Alta Conference on Argumentation and deliberated keynotes at the International Society for the Study of Argumentation and the Ontario Society for the Study of Argumentation. He has chaired over fifty dissertations in the area of rhetoric and argument. He directed doctoral programs at Northwestern University and at the University of Southern California. Presently, he works with Good Steward, an NGO.

**Hans V. Hansen** is a professor and head of the department of philosophy, and a fellow of the Centre for Research in Reasoning, Argumentation, and Rhetoric, at the University of Windsor. He is the author of the entry "Fallacies" in the *Stanford Encyclopedia of Philosophy*, editor of *Riel's Defence* (2014), and coeditor of *Fallacies: Contemporary and Classical Readings* (1995), as well as of the present volume.

**Hanns Hohmann** was born in Frankfurt am Main in Germany. He is now professor emeritus of communication at San Jose State University. His teaching, scholarship, and publications have focused on the history of rhetorical theory and the theory and history of legal argumentation, with special emphasis on the European Middle Ages and Antiquity, as well as the rhetorical criticism of contemporary public discourse.

**Peter Houtlosser** (1956–2008) was a lecturer in the Department of Speech Communication, Argumentation Theory, and Rhetoric of the University of Amsterdam. Dr. Houtlosser was a member of the research group Argumentation in Discourse. His pragma-dialectical research concerning argumentative discourse concentrated on argumentative indicators, the identification of standpoints, and strategic maneuvering. He coauthored the monograph *Argumentative Indicators in Discourse* (2007).

**C. P. Ilbert** (1841–1924) was a graduate of Oxford University and a distinguished British legal theorist and parliamentary draftsman. He was the author of several books, including *Legislative Methods and Forms* (1901) and *The Mechanics of Law-Making* (1914).

**Fred J. Kauffeld** (1942–2017) taught for nearly forty years at Edgewood College in Madison, Wisconsin. His research encompassed rhetorical theory and contemporary analytic work in the philosophy of language, eventually focusing on a Gricean/Austinian reformulation of inherited conceptions of presumption and probative obligations. The essay included in this volume attempts to synthesize work published over a period of years and scattered in various publications. Fred Kauffeld is one of the editors of this volume.

**Alfred Sidgwick** (1850–1943) was a British logician who published prolifically on logical theory. He was the cousin of the better-known Henry Sidgwick (author of *Methods of Ethics*).

**James B. Thayer** (1831–1902) was an American jurisprudent who taught at Harvard Law School. He had a special interest in the historical evolution of the law and was the author of *The Development of Trial by Jury* (1896) and *A Preliminary Treatise on Evidence at the Common Law* (1896).

**Edna Ullmann-Margalit** (1946–2010) was professor of philosophy at the Hebrew University of Jerusalem. She was the author of *The Emergence of Norms* (1978) and other influential articles in social philosophy.

**Frans H. van Eemeren** is cofounder of the pragma-dialectical theory of argumentation and editor of the journal *Argumentation*, the *Journal of Argumentation in Context*, and the accompanying book series. He is the author or coauthor of the following monographs: *Speech Acts in Argumentative Discussions* (1984), *Argumentation, Communication, and Fallacies* (1992), *Reconstructing Argumentative Discourse* (1993), *A Systematic Theory of Argumentation* (2004), *Argumentative Indicators in Discourse* (2007), *Fallacies and Judgments of Reasonableness* (2009), *Strategic Maneuvering in Argumentative Discourse* (2010), *Handbook of Argumentation Theory* (2014), and *Reasonableness and Effectiveness in Argumentative Discourse* (2015).

**Douglas Walton** is a Distinguished Research Fellow of the Centre for Research in Reasoning, Argumentation, and Rhetoric at the University of Windsor. He has been a visiting professor at Northwestern University, University of Arizona, and University of Lugano (Switzerland). He is the author of more than fifty books on argumentation. His latest book, with F. Macagno, is *Interpreting Straw Man Argumentation* (2017).

**Richard Whately** (1787–1863) studied at Oxford University and became a fellow there and eventually principal of one of the colleges. In 1832 Whately became Archbishop (Anglican) of Dublin. His *Elements of Logic* first appeared in 1826 and eventually ran to nine editions. The *Elements of Rhetoric* was first published in 1828 and ran to seven edtions.

# Index